Thomas Thornville Cooper

Travels of a Pioneer of Commerce in Pigtail and Petticoats

Or, an Overland Journey From China Towards India

Thomas Thornville Cooper

Travels of a Pioneer of Commerce in Pigtail and Petticoats
Or, an Overland Journey From China Towards India

ISBN/EAN: 9783744798440

Printed in Europe, USA, Canada, Australia, Japan

Cover: Foto ©Andreas Hilbeck / pixelio.de

More available books at **www.hansebooks.com**

HOGG'S GORGE ON THE LAN-TSAN-KIANG.

TRAVELS OF
A PIONEER OF COMMERCE

IN

PIGTAIL AND PETTICOATS:

OR,

AN OVERLAND JOURNEY FROM CHINA TOWARDS INDIA.

By T. T. COOPER,

LATE AGENT FOR THE CHAMBER OF COMMERCE AT CALCUTTA.

With Map and Illustrations.

LONDON:
JOHN MURRAY, ALBEMARLE STREET.
1871.

LONDON:
BRADBURY, EVANS, AND CO., PRINTERS, WHITEFRIARS.

TO

CHARLES A. WINCHESTER AND JAMES HOGG,

AND

THE OTHER MEMBERS OF THE FOREIGN COMMUNITY
OF SHANGHAI,

BY WHOSE AID I WAS ENABLED TO PROSECUTE MY TRAVELS,
THIS RECORD IS

Dedicated

BY THEIR SINCERE AND OBLIGED FRIEND,

T. T. C.

PREFACE.

By way of preface the Author desires to anticipate possible objections, from readers who may consider that he has said either too much or too little. The circumstances of the journey absolutely precluded scientific observation: the only instrument taken, viz., a thermometer, was broken at an early stage, and travelling by boat and chair is not favourable to minute investigation; but the Author can claim to have conscientiously recorded the facts which he was able to observe and learn, and the experiences undergone by him, and he trusts that these at least may enable some successor to learn more and accomplish far greater results than it was in his power to attain.

One other remark seems to be called for, with regard to the geographical nomenclature adopted. It has been his desire to represent as exactly as possible the Chinese names by English equivalents. The true names of Chinese provinces and cities, as well as in some cases the true limits, have been so disguised in their transmission through Portuguese and French media, that they are scarcely recognisable;—thus Pa-Chin is known as Pekin; and when the Author, misled by our maps, inquired for Chung-King, he with difficulty found the city of Chung-Ching. The adoption also of local dialects as representing the general pronunciation has tended to increase the confusion; and he has thought it the best method to obtain in each place the name by which it was known to the inhabitants, and express this in English letters as sounded by English tongues. With regard to the Map, it is not intended to show the correct geography of the countries, but merely to help the reader to follow the Author in his narrative; who in this, as in all other particulars, desires to be esteemed not a pretentious or scientific traveller, but a simple and truthful Pioneer of Commerce.

CONTENTS.

CHAPTER I.

INTRODUCTORY.

                                                                                                            PAGE

A Plea for the Chinese—The Overland Journey Suggested—A Way out of Difficulties—Mr. Wade's Advice—My Runaway Friends—An Infuriated French Consul—My Interpreter and Guide . . 1

CHAPTER II.

THE PLAINS OF HOOPEH.

Dispute with the Lowder—Salt Trade—Timber Rafts—Chen-pin Lake—Wild Geese—Offending the Wind God—Oil Mill—A Funeral Cortége—Arrival at Sha-sᵘ—Philip sees a Camel—A Chinese Hotel—A Family Dinner—Feminine Curiosity—Chinese Bedfellows—Small Feet—Disbanded Soldiers—Making a Night of it—Wau-chien Boat—Attempted Mandarin Squeeze—A Thunder Storm—Ichang City . 17

CHAPTER III.

ICHANG TO CHUNG CHING.

Ichang Gorge, Rapids of the Upper Yang-tsᵘ—Ascending a Rapid—A Portage—An ugly Tumble—A happy New Year—A Travelling Bookseller—Pelted by Gunboat-Men—the Boundary of Hoopeh—Philip's Indisposition—Taken for a Grandfather—Official Roguery—Wreck of a Junk—Dragon Procession—Chinese Christians—A Missionary Drowned—Sz-chuan Quarrymen—A Night in a Rapid—Spirit-rapping—Trade of the Yang-tsᵘ—Steamers on the Upper Yang-tsᵘ 61

CHAPTER IV.

CHUNG CHING.

The First Check—Reception of the Bishop—My Friend Fan—Taouist Rock Temples—Dinner with the Taou Jen—Decay of Chinese Art—A Royal Courier—The Sz-chuan Missions—Chinese Persecutions—Missionary Life—Respect paid to the Fathers—Boys' and Girls' Schools—Discouragement of Merchants—Chinese Theatre . . . 103

CHAPTER V.

CHUNG CHING TO CHEN-TU.

Novel Umbrella—The House-rag—Sz-chuan Fortifications—A Famous Kung-kwan—Do I look like a Devil?—A Great Soldier—Making way for a Mandarin—Marriage Customs—The Noseless Bride—Sale of Wives—An Awkward Predicament—Yamun Spies—The Paris of China—Rapacious Cooks—A promising Passport . . . 133

CHAPTER VI.

CHEN-TU TO HI-YAN-KY.

A Cooly Fight—Soldiers at free Quarters—Western Sz-chuan—Ya-tzow Brick Tea—Paddy Birds—A surly Pitman—The Foi-yue-ling—The Mountain Wind—Bishop Chauveau—Making a Gridiron—A Night on Ma-kia-shan—No Sport—The Soldiers are Coming—The Ruined Village 164

CHAPTER VII.

HI-YAN-KY TO TA-TSIAN-LOO.

Ceremonial of Atonement—Loo-din-chow Suspension Bridge—Don Quixote in Tse-tsang—Tea Carriers—Thibetan Hotel—The Border Town—Visit from a Lama—Prayer Cylinders—Lama Monks—Yunnan Lepers—Petticoats or Trousers—Mau-ts^u Ladies—Equipments for Thibet 193

CHAPTER VIII.

EASTERN THIBET.

The Chinese Frontier—A party of Tea Traders—The Hokow Ferry—Mountains and Valleys—The Zandi Tribes—the Town of Lithang—A thieving Interpreter—The Tsanba Range—The Taso Valley—A welcome Rest-house—A perilous Swim 221

CHAPTER IX.

BATHANG.

Making Friends with the Mandarins—A Morning's Trading—A Thibetan Turf-man—My Friend Tang—The Golden-roofed Lamasery—Small-pox in Thibet—More Frightened than Hurt—An Intrigue Discovered—Route to Assam—Tz Ta-Lowya—A Mandarin in Difficulties—Change for Yunnan 245

CHAPTER X.

BATHANG TO ATENZE.

I am Married unawares—Matrimonial Devotions—Robber Hill—Robbed of our Stores—A Song, but no Supper—Stopped on the Boundary—Refused Food at Tsung-tza—Banditti Repulsed—The Musk-hunter of Jessundee—A Terrible Woman—Tsali Shan—Passing a Snowdrift—First View of the Lan-tsan-kiang 271

CHAPTER XI.

THE TRIBES OF THE LAN-TSAN-KIANG.

Trade of Atenze—The Goneah Tribe—Hogg's Gorge—Sagacity of the Mules—Tz-coo Mission Station—The Lu-ts" Tribes—The Moso Tribe—The Ya-ts" Tribe—The Mooquor Chief—Deer-stalking at Compo—A Hunt Supper—Village of Kha-kha—Weisee-foo—The Tartar General—Soldier Robbers—A Yunnan Mahomedan . . . 299

CHAPTER XII.

AMONGST THE TZE-FANS.

Sz-se-to Village—The Lei-sus—Arrival at Tung-lan—My Politics Tested—Night Attack—The Tze-fan Village—The Mahomedan War—A Traitor Viceroy—Mahomedan Progress—The Scorpion Fly . . 333

CHAPTER XIII.

IMPRISONMENT AT WEISEE.

Tien Ta-lowya—In the Yamun—Rifle Practice—The Black-Nose—Tien Drunk—Lending a Mount—A Forced Loan Resisted—The Mandarins and the Revolver—Little Sen—Tien Dangerous—Playing with Edged Tools—Our Escape—Recaptured—Rescued by the Chiefs—Last Night in Weisee 355

CHAPTER XIV.

RETURN TO TA-TSIAN-LOO.

Departure from Weisee—A Ministering Angel—Return to Atenze—Thibetan Dairies—Bursting of a Rain-cloud—Renewed Hopes—Disappointment—Baffled Banditti—Tea-ferry on the Kin-cha-Kiang—Cold Reception at Bathang—An Act of Justice—Thibetan Necessity for Tea—Burmah and Yunnan Trade—Difficulty about the Despatches—A Wild Night 386

CHAPTER XV.

HOMEWARDS.

A Cooly Riot—Respect for Parents—The White Wax Country—Dogham—Gypsum Pits—Kia-ting-foo—Thibetan Trade Tricks—Salt Wells—Appointed an Arbitrator—The French Expedition—General Tin—Chinese Chess—The Hairy Tortoise—The Modern Army of Martyrs 424

LIST OF ILLUSTRATIONS.

	PAGE
HOGG'S GORGE ON THE LAN-TSAN-KIANG .	*Frontispiece*
WAN-CHIEN BOAT .	53
SZ-CHUAN QUARRYMEN .	92
THE DRAGON BRIDGE .	144
COOLIES CARRYING BRICK TEA .	201
PART OF MAN-TZŬ HOTEL IN TA-TSIAN-LOO	204
THIBETAN PRAYER: OM MANI PADME HUM .	208
TUNG-OLO VILLAGE .	224
THIBETAN SOLDIERS .	252
ROPE BRIDGE ON THE LAN-TSAN-KIANG .	309
THE SCORPION FLY .	353
DOUBLE HANDLED WHEELBARROW .	448
HAIRY TORTOISE . .	449

TRAVELS OF
A PIONEER OF COMMERCE.

CHAPTER I.

INTRODUCTORY.

A Plea for the Chinese—The Overland Journey Suggested—A Way out of Difficulties—Mr. Wade's Advice—My Runaway Friends—An Infuriated French Consul—My Interpreter and Guide.

THE great empires of Asia, almost up to our own time, presented an unknown field, which very few were able to enter upon and explore: religious prejudice and Oriental conservatism combined to exclude the intrusive Western strangers; and but recently have we begun to acquire anything like accurate knowledge, either geographically or historically, of the vast empires and peoples of the true East. An angry and jealous fear of the aggressive force of Western civilisation has succeeded to contemptuous prejudice, and, at the present time, renders the Oriental peoples yet more reluctant to admit the presence of the foreigner, whom still they feel themselves unable to exclude. Of this Oriental exclusiveness, the giant empire of China, slumbering in the conscious pride of its social and political system, which dates from the most distant ages, is the truest type. None of the adjacent kingdoms have equalled it in the perfection of its social and political organisation; none have surpassed it in a stubborn resistance to progress, and hostility to the intrusion of foreigners. It is true that, within the last thirty years, a vast trade has sprung up between Great Britain and China, not to speak of American and French intercourse; but this has only touched a few of the sea-ports, while the great provinces of the interior have been scarcely visited, and the life and condition of the majority of its millions but superficially observed. This statement may surprise those who know the number of books on China that have been published; but it will be acquiesced in by all who, as students, have sought to understand the Chinese. The jealous hostility of the educated and official classes to foreigners is the first great obstacle to increased and more intimate knowledge of the Chinese as they are. Next, the great difficulty of the language forbids its acquisition by those who might, from long residence at the open ports, possess fruitful opportunities of familiar intercourse. Men engaged in business cannot spare the time required for long and patient study; and, as they are thus compelled in their dealings to avail themselves of interpreters and go-betweens, they are really never brought in contact with the great middle-class, and are thus debarred from a thorough acquaintance with the more numerous and less prejudiced portion of the Chinese—an acquaintance which, if possible, would mutually lead to a better appreciation of each other, and do more to prevent outbreaks, and consequent wars, than treaties or gunboats. To the zealous and patient Protestant missionaries we owe several valuable works on China; but, as they mostly confine their residence and labours to the consular ports, they have but viewed the Chinese, as it were, from without, and at a distance. Of the more numerous Catholic missionaries, the early Jesuits have bequeathed to us almost all our stock of geographical knowledge. Their successors, the French missionaries, scattered through all China, are not permitted to impart to the world their accumulated knowledge, the results of years, or rather lives, spent amongst the Chinese. This is deeply to be regretted; for so many able men, carefully educated for their work, and living altogether as Chinese, must have acquired an accurate knowledge of the country, its language and literature, and the habits and modes of thought of the people, which, if communicated, would cause China to be no longer a *terra incognita*. It would be well for us if China and the Chinese were better known. Her great past, evidenced by the enormous mass of historical and philosophical literature, her memories of now almost extinct schools of art and science, and her imperial organisation, admirable in theory, though out of gear and sadly impaired in its practical effect, would command respect, and conciliate forbearance. And an Englishman, who has lived among them as one of themselves, may venture to tell his countrymen that to know the Chinese middle-classes and the peasantry is to like them. Kindly, courteous, yet impulsive, they are as easily moved to friendship as we now deem them readily excited to barbarous outrage. Their very faults excite pity rather than anger; and it has often occurred to me that the most barbarous Chinese treatment of strangers in the present day is no worse than the reception given to strangers and foreigners not so long ago in our own land. More unrestrained and extended commercial and political intercourse between China and the West will materially tend to remove ignorance, the source of prejudice; and foreign commerce, as it advances along her water highways, will be the herald of the superior Western civilisation, with its steamers, railways, and machinery, to be welcomed as the friend, not repelled as a foe. Such a movement of progress will, ere long, it is to be hoped, set in, to save the great empire from the internal decay and ruin which now more than threatens her. To aid in this, by making Englishmen better acquainted with a portion of China, and by pioneering a road for the advance of commerce, was the object of my travels; and to have done so will be a full reward.

Of the three great trade routes which in former days led from China westwards into Mongolia, and thence to India and Burmah, but one remains open at the present day, namely, the great highway from Sz-chuan to Lhássa, the capital of Central Thibet, *viâ* Ta-tsian-loo and Bathang. Various causes have combined to close the other routes. The difficult and dangerous road, traversed and described by Huc, from Pekin, through the province of Kan-soo to Lhássa, had long been increasingly embarrassed by the predatory attacks of the Mongol mountaineers, who, as the administrative power of the Government grew feebler, became more audacious. Still, however, in spite of the Mongol banditti, commerce continued to make its way along this route until within the last few years, when the Mahomedan rebellion in Kan-soo, which established their supremacy in that province, entirely closed it to trade. The other route, by which the south of China communicated with Burmah, *viâ* Talifoo in Yunnan, and Bhamo on the Irrawaddy River, was suddenly and effectually closed in the year 1854-5 by the Mahomedan rising in Yunnan; and thus the Empire of China has been left with but one route leading westwards—that from Sz-chuan to Lhássa; and by this she supplies Thibet annually with nearly six million pounds of brick tea, which finds its way west as far as the borders of Cashmere.

Causes political, religious, and economical combine to shut

Ch. I.] THE OVERLAND JOURNEY SUGGESTED. 5

out India from communication with China by this route; and it was with the view of discovering a shorter and more direct line of communication between the two countries that I started on the journey described in the following pages.

The project of an overland journey from India to China first suggested itself in the beginning of 1862, when, at Rangoon, I had the pleasure of meeting Dr. Clement Williams, who had just returned from an expedition up the Irrawaddy to Bhamo. From him I first heard the past history of the Bhamo and Talifoo route, and a prediction of its future importance to our British commerce, now verified by the growing interest taken in its probable re-opening. My purpose of attempting to reach China from Rangoon by following Dr. Williams's route had to yield to the force of circumstances, and all thoughts of travel were laid aside, and not revived until after a residence of several years at Shanghai, when, at the end of 1867, I found myself free to indulge in them. At this time, Dr. Williams's advocacy of the Bhamo and Tali route had attracted considerable attention; and, yielding to the desire of the merchants interested, the Government authorised an expedition, under the command of Major Sladen as political agent, to investigate the trade routes and difficulties, as well as the disposition of the Panthay or Mahomedan government installed at Talifoo. The knowledge of this then led me to abandon the idea of exploring a route between China and India, and turn my thoughts towards South America, as a promising field for travel. Happening, however, to mention this to my friend Mr. James Hogg, of the firm of Messrs. Hogg Brothers, Shanghai, I was by him induced to take up, in a new form, the long-cherished project of trying an overland journey from China to Calcutta. His long experience of China caused him to take considerable interest in the development of our commercial intercourse with that country. His personal knowledge of Captain Blakiston, and that officer's gallant attempt to reach India *viâ* the Yang-ts^u and Thibet in 1860, led him at once to propose to me that I should attempt to traverse the route suggested by Blakiston, leading from the farthest navigable point on the Yang-ts^u River, *viâ* Li-kiang-foo, in the north of Yunnan, to Sudiya, on the Bramapootra, in Northern Assam, and thence to Calcutta. A reference to a map of China by the eminent engineer, Sir Macdonald Stephenson, showing a projected railway from the Yang-ts^u to Bhamo, *viâ* Talifoo, showed the importance to Rangoon of commercial intercourse with China in that direction, while it needed but a glance to see that this line would not help to bring Calcutta into commercial relations with her, as the Irrawaddy would be the highway by which the trade would naturally descend between Yunnan and Rangoon, making that port, instead of Calcutta, the depôt of trade between our Indian possessions and Yunnan. Having arrived at this conclusion, little was needed to induce me to try for a more direct road to Calcutta, by which, if possible, that great Eastern capital might take part with Rangoon in the trade with China; and I decided, there and then, to attempt Blakiston's projected route.

Having determined to start on this journey, I felt that I had undertaken a very serious and arduous task. Fortunately, I had several months before me in which to think over and mature my plans. August, the hottest of all months in China, had just set in, and it would be unadvisable to start until the end of the year, for fear of encountering the winter on the snowy mountains forming the western boundaries of China, which would probably involve several months' detention there. Day by day for more than a month, all the difficulties and dangers likely to be met with were reviewed, and lost none of their magnitude on closer consideration. There was the jealous animosity of the officials, and, as I then believed, of the people, towards foreigners; wild tribes; barriers of terrific snow-clad mountains; the danger of carrying so large a sum of money as would suffice for a journey, which could not take less than a year to accomplish; and last, but greatest of all, I did not know a word of the Chinese language. The difficulty of passing through wild tribes and over mountains, subsided into insignificance, beside the danger of carrying a large sum of money about with me, and the apparent hopelessness of travelling through China without a knowledge of the language. In this state of perplexity, I had recourse to my esteemed friend M. Lamonier, Procureur des Missions Etrangères, residing at Shanghai. I knew that the posts of the French missionaries extended in an unbroken chain to beyond the western border of China; and I felt convinced that only by their help could I hope to pass through the empire. M. Lamonier, ever ready, as are all the Catholic missionaries, to forward all useful projects, soon dispelled my anxiety about the carriage of specie, for he arranged to give me a letter of credit for 600 taels (180*l.*, the sum he considered sufficient for travelling expenses), addressed to the mission stations in Yunnan, Sz-chuan, and Eastern Thibet; so that it would not be needful to carry a large sum in silver, until after passing beyond their posts. He also proposed a feasible plan for surmounting the difficulty of the language. A party of young missionaries were expected to arrive from France, towards the end of the year; if I accompanied them to Sz-chuan, I could hire a house in some village containing a mission station, and, under the protection of the missionaries, set to work and acquire a sufficient mastery of the language. This arrangement would prolong my journey by six months; but the delay was unimportant, so long as the difficulty of the language was got over. And thus, before leaving M. Lamonier, the two great obstacles which seemed for a time to render my journey impossible were disposed of.

Many friends who were interested in the project had looked upon my ignorance of the language, and the difficulty of carrying funds about with me, as fatal to the attempt. The promised assistance of French missionaries at once removed this impression; and some half-dozen of them, amongst whom were several professional men, proposed to share the expenses of the journey.

It might have been expected that the project would interest the mercantile community; but I was sorry to find a belief prevalent amongst them, that the opening of a route between Calcutta and China would in some way interfere with their own trade; and this for a time deprived me of the co-operation of those, to promote whose interests the journey had been planned. Still, among friends who did interest themselves in it were several of the most influential merchants of Shanghai; and their sympathy added much to the pleasure with which I set about preparing for a start.

As my intended *compagnons de voyage*, according to the invariable rule of the missions, would be to all outward appearance undistinguishable from veritable Chinese, I set to work to prepare myself for my own metamorphosis, and began to accustom myself to the tail and petticoats, walking in which required considerable practice before a proper and unembarrassed gait could be attained; and I daily rehearsed the part in còstume, that I hoped soon to have to play before the critical Chinese public.

A visit to Shanghai, paid by Mr. T. F. Wade, C.B., H.B.M. Secretary of Legation at Pekin, afforded an opportunity of obtaining the advice of one whose knowledge of the Chinese as a scholar and a diplomatist, combined with his thoughtful appreciation of their character, constitute him, in my humble opinion, an unrivalled authority; and I am glad to record my grateful sense of the cordial sympathy that he accorded to a project deemed by others presumptuous and Quixotic. He strongly advised me to follow the directions, and imitate the example, of the Fathers in all particulars, warning me at the same time to avoid shocking the prejudices of the natives, and to attract as little observation as possible, especially from the mandarins. Two other pieces of practical advice, given by him, proved of inestimable use; the first of which was, to take no instruments, as the use of them could not fail to be observed, and inevitably arouse the opposition of the people—a danger too often overlooked by those who seem to imagine it easy to make scientific observations in all countries; the second was to avoid procuring a consular passport at Shanghai, for fear of awakening the obstructive jealousy of the officials, but to obtain one at Kiu-Kiang, a port on the Yang-ts", describing me as an English Sz-foo, or scholar, desirous of travelling on the Great River, and through the countries beyond to India. The usual form of consular passports states that the bearer intends to travel by a certain route to a certain place, and from this the Chinese authorities will allow no deviation. How valuable, therefore, Mr. Wade's advice afterwards proved, by enabling me to change my route, after leaving the Yang-ts", will appear in due course. At last a letter from M. Lamonier announced the arrival of the missionaries, and I was speedily introduced to six young priests, fresh from the Parisian seminary, but wearing their Chinese garb, as if to the manner born. They were full of youthful zeal and enthusiasm, and I promised myself a most agreeable journey to Sz-chuan in their company; and it was arranged that we should start on the 13th of November for Hankow, the last open port, about 700 miles up the Yang-ts", where the final arrangements for our journey to Chung-Ching were to be completed.

A free passage had been offered to the Fathers and myself by the courtesy of Messrs. Russell and Co. and Messrs. Glover and Co., agents for the two lines of magnificent steamers which ply between Shanghai and Hankow. We accepted the offer of the latter firm, whose vessel happened to start at the time most convenient for us. I need not detain the reader with any particulars of the voyage; suffice it say, that on the third day we arrived at Kiu-Kiang, about eight hours' distance from Hankow; where according to previous arrangement, I landed for the purpose of procuring a passport, while the Fathers proceeded to Hankow, whither I followed them in due course, expecting to rejoin the party at the mission-house, situated in the native city. My astonishment may be conceived, on finding the mission-house untenanted, save by one or two native Christians, and being informed that the whole party had started that morning from Hankow! For some time I found it impossible to credit the fact that I had thus been left in the lurch by the young missionaries, with whom I had already become great friends, and who had expressed the greatest satisfaction at the prospect of our journeying together to Chung-Ching. The disappointment was, for the moment, overwhelming, and the apparently heartless conduct of the young Fathers was at first sight inexplicable; however, there was no use trying to speculate on the possible motives or mistake which had caused it, and I at once asked myself what was to be done. No time was to be lost, if I would overtake the missionaries, who could not possibly have got far away, as there had been no wind to help their boat against the current of the Yang-ts". Hurrying from the mission-house, I applied to the British consul, Mr. Medhurst, for the use of a small gunboat lying off the European settlement. Unfortunately, her engines were out of repair, and Mr. Medhurst gave me a letter to the French consul, M. Dabry, asking him to procure for me the French gunboat which had just arrived at Hankow. The French official received me with bare civility, and curtly declined my request for the use of the gunboat. In this extremity I called on Mr. Gower, representative of the firm of Jardine, Matheson and Co., and that gentleman at once placed his fast-sailing yacht at my disposal. Before we were well under weigh, a splendid fair breeze sprang up, to which we spread every stitch of canvas, and soon bowled along at the rate of seven knots in chase of my runaway friends. For six hours we kept on with an increasing breeze, which carried us past the Chinese junks bound in the same direction as though they were standing still. About six o'clock in the evening we arrived at a Chinese custom-house on the left bank of the Yang-ts", forty miles above Hankow, having hailed every passenger junk which we had passed. The officials at the customhouse told us that no foreigners had passed that day; for, as it turned out, their junk had taken the shorter route by the Han river and the lakes; so we put about, and commenced beating back for Kinkow, which we had passed ten miles below, on the right bank, and which we reached about 11 P.M.

It was just possible that the missionaries might have put in there for the night, but the custom-house people informed us that no junk with foreigners had put in that day. So, fairly beaten, Mr. Gower and myself returned the next day to Hankow, where during our absence, amidst the excitement caused amongst the community by the conduct of the missionaries, the fact had leaked out that M. Dabry, the French consul, had forbidden them to allow me to accompany them, and ordered them to leave Hankow before my arrival. Here was a difficulty with a vengeance. Deprived of the assistance of the missionaries, I foresaw the failure of my project!—this thought roused all my energy, and I forthwith called on M. Dabry, and found that gentleman still more uncivil than on my first visit. At once plunging into the subject of my visit, I begged him as a personal favour to remove his prohibition. Unfortunately, I was then ignorant of what had caused the irritable little Gaul to seize with avidity the opportunity of thwarting an Englishman. A short time previously, one of a party of French sportsmen, shooting in the neighbourhood of Hankow, had missed his hare, and wounded a countryman; whereupon some half-dozen of the villagers, naturally indignant, attacked the party, and drove them ignominiously to their boats. With a view to avenge the insult offered to the flag of France, M. Dabry, instead of patiently waiting for the action of the mandarins, ordered an armed party from a gunboat to make a raid upon the village, from which they returned bringing in triumph some half-dozen wretched villagers to Hankow. This high-handed conduct had been a few days previously severely commented upon by the Hankow *Times*, and M. Dabry let loose upon my unhappy head the wrath which was boiling in his bosom against the English editor for inserting, and the British consul for not punishing the publication of, an article reflecting on him, the representative of

France. As he spoke English very well, I cannot do better than describe his sentiments in his own words. In answer to my earnest representation that his interference with a private individual proposing to explore the West of China would entail on me a certain loss of time and money, and possibly prevent my proceeding, he replied, "Oh yes! you say you are a private traveller: you are a secret spy of your Government. I know all about you." Feeling rather amused, I disclaimed the honour; whereupon he burst out, "What, sir? I help you, an Englishman! Never! What have your English newspapers done? They have insulted me; they have insulted France; and your English consul has not had the politeness to make known his disapprobation of such conduct. I will throw every obstacle in your way: I will show you that I am not to be insulted with impunity."

Preserving my gravity with a struggle, I suggested that the criticisms of the English press were free, and that for myself I had not seen the article in question; but in vain. Swelling with fury, he vociferated, "You Englishmen think you can go everywhere, and do everything. Good! go to the West of China!" To this I quietly observed, for this purpose the help of the missionaries was required. "Ah, yes! you are obliged to come to the French missionaries. You see, without the assistance of the French, an Englishman cannot go through China." At last, finding it useless to reason with the irate consul, I took my leave and went to the mission-house, where I saw the procureur of the mission, Father de Carli. Having told him that the reason of the young missionaries' conduct was now no secret, I requested his advice as to the best mode of carrying out my original intention of residing in Sz-chuan. The father, however, told me that he could not act against the wishes of his consul; but if the prohibition were removed he himself would procure an interpreter to accompany me throughout, and a trustworthy Christian to act as guide so far as Chung-Ching, as the interference of M. Dabry would probably render my proposed residence not agreeable to the missionaries. Full of the renewed hope of reaching Sz-chuan, I returned to M. Dabry, and asked him as a personal favour not to visit the sins of my countrymen on me, but to allow the missionaries to give me their assistance.

Having thus humbled myself before the French official, he condescended to say, that if I would wait until the French expedition (then on its way from Saigon to Yunnan) arrived in Hankow, he would consent to the missionaries helping me.

This was out of the question, so I returned to Shanghai, and informed Mr. C. A. Winchester, her Majesty's consul, of the uncalled-for interference of the French official at Hankow, and then called on Vicomte Brenier de Montmorend, consul-general for France. His kindness was an agreeable contrast to the demeanour of M. Dabry, who, by his mediation, was induced to change his tone; and when I reached Hankow, a few days after, Father de Carli signified his readiness to supply me with two native Christians—one as interpreter, and the other as guide.

The expense of the delay, and the unlooked-for burden of followers, seemed after all likely to prove a new hindrance. Fortunately, however, the ungenerous conduct of M. Dabry had enlisted on my behalf the sympathy of the Shanghai mercantile community, and a movement (under the leadership of my kind friends, Messrs. Winchester and Hogg) was set on foot to lighten the expenses of my journey; so that the French consul's opposition resulted, after all, in securing the support of the Shanghai merchants.

A month's further delay in Hankow was unavoidable, as the interpreter and guide would not start until after the Christmas festival. I therefore spent several very pleasant weeks with my friend Mr. Cunningham, and enjoyed the festivities of Christmas, 1867, amidst the profuse hospitality of the Hankow community.

In the meanwhile M. Dabry, acting on the good advice of Viscount Breuier, his superior, gave me letters of introduction addressed to all the missions, requiring them to assist me as far as they could; and these were presented to Father de Carli to enable him to act openly in my behalf. Two Christians were at once engaged to fill the posts of interpreter and guide, the latter as far as Chung-Ching only: both were trustworthy men, and joined me rather for the sake of the missionaries than for any liking of the journey, while both were admirably fitted for their posts.

George Phillips, a native of Hankow, was the eldest son of a Christian Chinese, whose forefathers had been for several generations members of the Catholic Church; and he himself had been educated for the priesthood at the College in Macao; but, owing to his conviction that he was unfit to undertake the serious duties of a priest, he, much against the wish of his family, refused holy orders, and devoted himself to trade. His superior education rendered him, save in dress and manner, quite different to ordinary Chinamen, whose natural superstition and prejudice were replaced by intelligence, strengthened by the study of European philosophy and theology, while a knowledge of the Latin, English, and Chinese languages made the term of interpreter in his case no empty title. Such was my interpreter, who proved, as I expected, a useful servant and intelligent companion.

The guide, Timothy, or Lowlee, also a native of Hankow, was a devout Christian, and one of the staff of guides employed to conduct young missionaries to distant posts. He was very meek in disposition, and fully deserved the character for honesty and truth given him by Father de Carli. As an additional precaution, it was suggested by Mr. Medhurst that a Chinese passport should be procured from the Viceroy, resident at Woo-chang, the Chinese city situated on the right bank of the river, opposite to Hankow; and an application was accordingly made by the Consul for a pass addressed to the Viceroy of Sz-chuan at Chentu-foo, authorising the English scholar to travel on the Great River and through the countries beyond to India; and in due time an imposing Chinese document, some two feet square, arrived. By an unlucky oversight, not discovered till it was too late, the term "Sang-jen," tradesman, was substituted for "Sz-foo," or scholar, as the description of Tang Koopah, who, for the present, was happily unconscious of this, as it proved, unfortunate error.

On the 2nd of January, 1868, George Phillips, whom I called Philip for shortness, informed me that he had engaged a boat from Hankow to Sha-s^u, and proposed that we should start on the 4th. So I prepared by stowing away a European suit, and some flannel shirts, tooth-brushes, a patent manifold writer of 500 pp. for a journal, and some paper and envelopes, in a small box which could be easily shouldered. On the evening of the 3rd, Philip brought a barber, who shaved my head, and made, by judiciously interweaving false hair with the natural growth, a capital tail, transforming me at once into a fairly respectable-looking elderly Chinaman, and I spent my last night in Hankow in all the discomfort of pigtail and petticoats.

CHAPTER II.

THE PLAINS OF HOOPEH.

Dispute with the Lowder—Salt Trade—Timber Rafts—Chen-pin Lake—Wild Geese—Offending the Wind God—Oil Mill—A Funeral Cortége—Arrival at Sha-s⁰—Philip sees a Camel—A Chinese Hotel—A Family Dinner—Feminine Curiosity—Chinese Bedfellows—Small Feet—Disbanded Soldiers—Making a Night of it—Wan-chien Boat—Attempted Mandarin Squeeze—A Thunder Storm—Ichang City.

AT last all was ready, and on the 4th of January, 1868, I bade adieu to Mr. Cunningham and his hospitality. Several friends had assembled at his breakfast-table, intending to escort me to the boat; but wishing to depart with the least possible parade, I was obliged to ask them to forego their purpose. While getting into my sedan-chair, a crowd of Chinese collected in front of the Hong, pressed round to get a look at the foreigner dressed in their costume, while the compradore and house servants, who had assisted to some extent in my Chinese toilet, loudly complimented me on the effect, declaring "I was a very number one Chinaman," and as I left gave me a cheer. The chair coolies, evidently convinced that they were carrying a foreigner of distinction, hurried at a rapid trot through the British settlement, and, on entering the native city of Hankow, struck up their lively carrying song, elbowing their way through the crowded streets with loud jokes and Chinese chaff.

As I was thus carried along, an indescribable feeling of loneliness depressed me. I reflected that I was fairly started on a journey of several thousand miles, which might occupy months, and even years, in its accomplishment. My funds for the enterprise amounted to two hundred pounds. The people amongst whom I was about to sojourn, and whose manners and customs I had now adopted, had always been characterised in my judgment by a cruel hatred of foreigners. I seemed moreover to have lost my own nationality, and even identity, so powerful was the consciousness of the change produced by my shaven head and Chinese garb; and this I felt the more acutely as I passed unrecognised several friends of long standing; but if for a moment I shrank from the risks to be encountered, the next I felt a renewed energy and resolve to prosecute my purpose. I had given up a valuable appointment—I must go on, and not requite my friends for their support with disappointment; and remembering that a French official had said I should not proceed, I felt that death would be more tolerable than to give cause to have it said that a French consul could prevent an Englishman from travelling whither he would in China. But such reflections were speedily dispelled by our arrival at the south City Gate of Hankow. And at the bottom of a flight of stone-steps leading down to the river I found Philip and Lowlee waiting for me, and was led carefully to the boat.

I was glad to ensconce myself at once in the cabin, as a crowd of Chinese soon gathered round, attracted by the novel sight of a very tall foreigner, as he seemed to them, dressed in their costume. After a few minutes' delay, the Lowder, or boat captain, declared himself ready to start, and on receiving his orders, at once got under weigh. Leaving Hankow, we poled slowly along the bank of the river, threading our way amongst hundreds of salt junks, that lined the shore of the Yangts[u] for more than three miles above the British settlement. As we poled along, the crew accompanied their easy toil with a chorus of boat-songs, the performance of which surpassed in screaming and chattering anything I had ever heard. Having made our way for some three miles along the bank, the Lowder presented himself at the cabin door, his face wearing a cunning smile by way of apologetic preface to the impudent request he came to prefer. He addressed himself to Philip, who at once entered into a long and angry discussion, strongly objecting to the proposal. Upon this a dreadful hubbub arose, the Lowder's wife and crew joined in, and at last seemed only to leave off shouting for want of breath. Philip, who during this outcry had maintained a dignified silence, now condescended to take part again in the proceedings, and apparently succeeded in throwing oil on the troubled waters. He then informed me that the Lowder had demanded double fare and payment in advance, and had charged Philip with having cheated him in hiring the boat at the ordinary rate paid by Chinamen, when he knew that it was for a foreigner, who, according to custom, should pay double hire. Matters had, however, been arranged, in consideration of the Lowder receiving 6000 chen or cash* in advance— the full fare to Sha-s^u, to which town we had hired the boat, being 11,500 chen, equal to eleven dollars and a half. I cheerfully assented to this arrangement, and once more seated myself to continue on up-stream, wishing to get well away from Hankow before night-fall, but the Lowder stolidly refused to move, and informed me that he intended to remain here for the night; persuasion and an offer of 200 chen as a present were of no avail—move he would not, so I consoled myself with a pipe, and listened to Philip

* See Appendix, note 1.

while he related tales of the rascality of boatmen in general, declaring that our Lowder was an exception to the rule, inasmuch as he had consented to fulfil his original bargain.

Having made fast to the shore, the Lowder, his wife, and one of the crew left us to return to Hankow, with the assurance that they would join us early in the morning. They had not been long gone, when Lowlee informed me that he must also return to Hankow, as he had forgotten his clothes. I did not object, and he set to work to prepare my dinner. While waiting for it I had an opportunity of looking round the cabin; and a more uncomfortable place to be shut up in could scarcely be imagined. The boat was only thirty-five feet long, shaped like a small junk, and drawing when loaded two feet, with an absurdly disproportionate tall mast and small canvas square sail. About two-thirds of her length from the stern was taken up with cabins; in the fore part there was a clear space for the crew to row in. My cabin occupied about twelve feet amidships. Aft of it was an open hutch for the steersman to stand upright in, and in the stern compartment built over the rudder, the crew slept; in this also were the cooking stoves and utensils for all parties, while a species of stage projecting beyond the stern served as a lumber store for things in general. My cabin and home for the next twelve days was a rough wooden construction about six feet wide and five high; the mat-roof was perfectly water-tight; the windowless sides of rough boards admitted, through interstices some inches wide, both light and the keen frosty air in chilling plenty, and the draught soon extinguished our Chinese candles, and compelled Philip and myself to spend a couple of hours in closing up the apertures with mud and paper. By the time this operation was finished, Lowlee made his appearance with dinner, consisting of pieces of roast beef, fowl, fried vegetables, and rice, served after the Chinese fashion, and I made a hearty meal. Philip and Lowlee were greatly delighted at the dexterity with which I set to work with chop-sticks, and seemed greatly disappointed when, after a few minutes, the painful stiffness of my fingers caused by their use made me glad to drop them; however, after a few more trials, I became quite an expert in their use.

After dinner I walked along the bank of the river towards Hankow, and as it was night attracted no attention. Hundreds of junks, moored in tiers out from the shore, each heavily laden with salt, showed what an enormous trade exists between the coast and Hankow. I gathered from a custom-house watcher, whom we encountered in our walk, that upwards of fifteen thousand salt-laden junks arrive at Hankow every year; each carrying on an average 2300 piculs, equivalent to 166 tons, making up the enormous total of two and a half million tons. This I state on his authority, but I am inclined to believe that the real quantity is considerably less. The salt costs on the coast about eight chen per catty of $1\frac{1}{4}$ lbs., and sells in Hankow for 80 chen; but as the manufacture of salt is a government monopoly, the exorbitant duties leave a comparatively small margin of profit for the shippers at Hankow.

On returning to the boat, I desired Philip to ask the custom-house officer to drink a cup of Samshu. He gladly accepted it, and on taking his leave wished us a pleasant voyage to the "other side of the world," whither in his ignorance he fancied us bound, for I had told him that we were travelling to a country beyond Tsung-qua, or China, which, until that moment he had believed contained the whole of the habitable world. Feeling very tired I turned in, while Philip, in Lowlee's absence, busied himself in getting up from the hold our stock of provisions; dried ducks and fish, a side of bacon, and sausages, a leg of mutton, beef steaks and mutton chops, pheasants, wild fowl and cabbages were soon hanging from the roof and sides of the cabin, making a show that spoke well for his forethought. And now, having fairly started, my anxiety for the time was quieted; the thought of the greatness of my object, and the sense of having already overcome the difficulties so ill-naturedly thrown in my way by Monsieur Dabry, made my spirits rise and rejoice in the prospect of successfully contending against still greater ones, and with a cheery good night to Philip, I laid down and slept. Next morning, at daylight, Lowlee, the Lowder, and the other sailor turned up, and at 8·30, with a capital breeze in our favour, we set sail, and shortly after entered the Kuankow Creek at a village of that name.

This creek leads to the chain of lakes connected by natural and artificial canals, through which boats of a light draught navigate to the town of Sha-s^u, between which place and Hankow the river makes a bend to the south of 366 miles, while the distance by the lake route is only 100.

A strong six-knot current set down the entrance of the creek, and we were obliged to hire six coolies to track us up for two miles. The village of Kuankow is the first customs station above Hankow, and here my passports were demanded; on showing the one given me by Mr. Medhurst, we were allowed to pass on.

Towards the afternoon, the weather, which had set in very cold in the morning, became stormy, with drizzling rain, and by 4 P.M. we anchored for the night above a small hamlet; few boats were in sight, and it was a great relief to be clear of the river, which at this time of the year is full of timber rafts, brought from Honan. As we passed through them, some were being broken up, while others were in process of building, preparatory to their being sent down river to Chingkiang, and the ports nearer the sea. The rafts drift with the current, and take from six to eight months to accomplish a voyage of six hundred miles; when seen floating down river they resemble large islands, some having as many as twenty small cabins built on them, nearly every one with its piggery attached, while numerous children, dogs, and fowls running about, complete their village-like appearance.

Below our anchorage lay the village of Sheow-tza-wan, consisting of about forty brick-built houses, situated on a slightly rising ground, presenting the nearest approach to a hill in the neighbourhood. Philip informed me that these houses are used as granaries, where the produce of the surrounding low-lying plains is stored; like other little hills in the province of Hoopeh, this eminence is used by the inhabitants of the low country as a burying ground, and presents the appearance of being covered with gigantic molehills.

Next morning we got under weigh early, and for the following three days our journey was through a miserable country; we occasionally passed villages built on mounds of rough stone work, with fleets of small junks lying off them, laden with rice and firewood. The manner of advertising the cargoes was novel; a log or basket made fast to a rope, and hoisted half way up the mast, signified respectively firewood or rice for sale.

The weather had now become so raw and cold, that I was obliged to keep a charcoal fire burning in the cabin, and the wind was often so strong that we were compelled to bring up under the banks of the creek for hours together, which sadly impeded our progress; the country on either hand was covered with reeds, groups of reed-built houses being dotted along the banks of the creek, each surrounded by willow trees growing to a height of thirty feet, which act as breakwaters during the floods. But for the evidence of the drift stuff clinging round their trunks, on a level with the eaves of the houses, it would have been hard to believe that these hamlets, each with a population of 350 souls, are nearly submerged for four months of the year. A strange existence is that of the inhabitants of this reed-growing country; they alternately dwell in houses and boats, one moiety of the year tilling the ground and reed cutting, and the other fishing over their fields. The floods often overtake them before the harvest is secured, and that in successive years; but so fertile is the soil, that if one crop in four be safely harvested, it supplies their wants. Thus, at the time we passed, there had been no harvest gathered for three years, yet wheat and rice were selling in abundance at one tael five mace per picul, equivalent to ten shillings for one and a half bushels, while in harvest years the price falls to eight mace (rather less than five shillings) per picul. During the dry season their boats are carefully repaired and thatched over with reeds, ready for instant use; for so rapid is the often unexpected rise of the waters, that the River Han, a principal drainer of these plains, will (as I learned from a Protestant missionary residing at Hankow) rise 18 to 20 feet in three or four hours. Captain Blakiston has given an admirable description of the country, through a continuation of which we were travelling.

For three days we were wretched in the extreme; sleet and drizzling rain, with a raw, cold wind, obliged me to keep to the boat, but as we neared the Chen-pin lake, through a cutting from the creek, a magnificent scene opened before us.

The lake stretched away to the west, as far as the eye could reach, while the setting sun shed a flood of liquid gold on the glassy surface of the water, throwing on the wild waste a parting gleam of loveliness ere he sank below the western horizon. From the south, over a boundless sheet of water, unbroken save by patches of reeds, dead and blackened by the hand of winter, flew myriads of wild fowl, cleaving the air with a noise like the rush of some invisible cataract, while from afar and near their shrill note of calling was answered by thousands of their kind, already cradled for the night on the bosom of the surrounding waters. To the north, about three miles from the entrance of the lake, lay a little island, on which stood one or two houses surrounded by trees; we steered for it, and brought up under its lee for the night. On the following day, having passed through the Chen-pin lake, we entered another small one, a few miles to the west, called Yangchee, and about noon brought up at the village of Kwang-moo-sen, on its south bank. Here our boatmen went on shore to buy rice and vegetables, and we had not been at anchor long, before news of the foreigner's arrival spread through the village, and men, women, and children from every house flocked down to the boat. I would have gone out and let them have a good look at me, but Philip and Lowlee strongly urged me not to show myself. The good fathers in Hankow had cautioned me to trust entirely to the advice of Lowlee, while travelling in Hoopeh, as the people of this province are generally ill-disposed towards foreigners. I therefore kept quiet within the boat, but the crowd would not be satisfied without a view, and swarmed on board, getting on the roof, and peering through every chink in my cabin. So many at last got on board that Philip and Lowlee became nervous, and shoved the boat off from the shore, upsetting many of our visitors into the water. Upon this I fancied that a row was inevitable, but a Chinese crowd is a strange thing in its peculiarities; the people on shore roared with laughter at those who had fallen into the water, and the latter as they scrambled on shore made off to escape the bantering of the crowd. Our boatmen having heard the disturbance hurried on board, and it was with a considerable feeling of relief that I found myself once again out on the lake.

Towards evening we left this lake and entered a canal with a strong current, which obliged our boatmen to land and tow the boat by means of a rope from the mast-head. As Philip and myself were at dinner, the boat suddenly gave a lurch, sending our cups and chopsticks chasing each other about the cabin floor; the Lowder commenced yelling, and was loudly answered by the boatmen from the shore; I was not long in getting on deck, when I found the boat drifting sideways down the canal. The Lowder told us that in attempting to stem the current rushing from the canal into the lake, the boat had touched the ground and become unmanageable.—After some little difficulty, we managed to get her head up-stream, and the coolies towed us up to the rush of water, when just as we were well up, crack went the towing line, and away we drifted down-stream again. The whole scene was very absurd; the Lowder screamed at the boatmen, one of whom was quite deaf, and the other, after repeated vain efforts to make him understand something commenced a series of pantomimic gestures that sent the Lowder nearly mad. As we were getting into a state of utter confusion, and drifting down-stream at the rate of four miles an hour, I thought it was time to interfere; so Philip and myself set to work with poles, and succeeded in fetching the boat up alongside the bank, when a new tow-rope was fastened to the mast, and away we went, this time getting up the rush of water all right. We anchored for the night at a point some distance above; and for the first time since leaving Hankow, I went on shore. About a quarter of a mile from our anchorage, on the banks of a large pool, we saw numbers of wild geese; so I sent to the boat for my rifle, and while waiting within three hundred yards of the birds, watched them at their evening toilet. Their numbers were astonishing even to one who has shot among the lagoons of East and West Australia, and the jheels of India, where wild fowl are considered numerous, but they are nothing to be compared to the numbers to be seen on the lakes in the neighbourhood of the Lower Yang-ts^u river. I have often heard, while in the centre of one lake, the noise of a flock of geese rising from another more than three miles off, so wonderfully numerous are they. The Chinese never seem to trouble themselves about catching wild fowl, except in the vicinity of large towns, consequently the birds visit the lakes undisturbed during the winter months, and leave in the spring for their breeding grounds, but where these may be, I could never ascertain; the Chinese all assured me that they are far away to the north—how far it is impossible to say, only it is certain that they do not breed in the lakes in the central or southern part of China.

Philip having brought my rifle, I stalked the flock to within 200 yards, when a few began to rise. Wishing to see them on the wing in a body, I discharged a barrel in the air, when up rose a perfect cloud of birds all round me, and the noise of their wings was deafening. In the confusion of their rising I fired, bringing down a single bird, and having secured this, returned to my boat; but during the whole night we were disturbed by the flock returning in detachments to their resting place.

The Chinese tell a very pretty story of the matrimonial affection of wild geese. They say that on the death of the male bird the female never mates again, but lives for the rest of her days a widow, mourning the loss of her first love; and the male bird is equally constant, never supplying the place of a lost consort.

Next day we passed the villages of Fang-kow and She-wan-sha-kow, each containing about 2000 inhabitants. At the latter, Lowlee informed me that a native Catholic missionary resided, in charge of a congregation of over 300 converts; but we did not land, and passed on to the village of Nu-kwan, where the Customs officials demanded our passport. I sent Philip with it, and he returned accompanied by a mandarin of inferior rank, who seated himself in the cabin, and proved very inquisitive. My knives, combs, brushes, watch, and looking-glass, were closely examined. He wished to buy everything, evidently in the hope that I would gratify him with a present of some article; in this, however, I disappointed him, and he turned his attention to my clothes. My flannel hunting-shirts were objects of great interest, and he could not resist asking for one; and on my declining, he appeared very much astonished at my refusal, but turned the conversation, and complimented me on my appearance, saying that I was not like a foreigner, but more resembled a Chinaman. Having at his request lighted my meerschaum, charged with good Cavendish tobacco, I handed it to him, whereupon he puffed away with great gusto; but, alas! it was very strong; he soon complained of feeling unwell, and hastily left the boat with his satellites, scarcely able to bid me good night. During the day I took a walk on the banks of the canal. Before going ashore I had tied a crimson silk scarf round my waist; but when Philip saw it, he asked me to take it off, as it was a rebel sign, and would alarm the people. Of this I soon had confirmation, for as I was taking it off an old Chinaman passed us, and on seeing the scarf, shook his head at me. I also made another unlucky mistake during the day. While standing smoking on the deck in front of my cabin, I happened to expectorate over the bow, when one of the boatmen pulled me violently on to my back, amidst the howling of himself and mate. For a moment I felt inclined to throw the fellow overboard, but Philip explained to me that I had, according to Chinese superstition, offended the wind god, so I told him to tell the boatmen that the god would excuse me, as I had done it in ignorance. They were, however, very much put out, and said that we should know to-morrow whether the god was angry or not; if he was, we should have a foul wind, and his wrath would have to be appeased with fire crackers, to purchase which they demanded some chen, and on the recommendation of Philip I gave them 250, with which they purchased crackers at a village, and in the evening duly discharged them in a propitiatory fusillade.

The natural creeks had now been replaced by cuttings between the lakes, and as I walked along the banks I saw away inland vast alluvial plains, intersected by dykes, which I have no doubt in former times were carefully maintained, and served as a barrier against the floods; but the decay universal in China has overtaken them in many places, and they now serve only as causeways and partial barriers against inundations. In some places about the plains the water still formed large shallow lagoons, and in others young crops of wheat, barley, and rice looked luxuriantly green. The dykes forming the banks of the canal rose thirty feet in height, and were of great thickness; numerous houses were built on the summits, while on their slopes peas, beans, tobacco, and cabbages were growing in abundance. Near every house were stacks of wheat and rice straw, used as provender for the bullocks and buffaloes, and cotton and bean stalks, which are used in this neighbourhood for fuel. Along the foot of the dykes, and near the water's edge, willow trees of great height were growing, and in the reaches lent quite a Dutch appearance to the canal. Crows and a species of white-breasted jackdaw formed colonies on their branches, and kept up a constant noisy chorus. In these dyke lands much care is bestowed upon the planting and pruning of the willows, which here also serve as a breakwater in the summer floods, while their roots bind the soil of the dykes together.

In the construction of the canals there is a great peculiarity; their course is serpentine, having from three to four large curves to the mile, which again contain smaller ones. This method of construction appears at first sight ill adapted to the requirements of traffic or drainage, besides involving much additional dyking; but the people assured me that this system of canal making in such a plain as that of the south and east of Hoopeh, which for four months of the year is one great lake intersected by innumerable dykes, is of great importance, for should the canals be cut straight from lake to lake, the water in the autumnal fall would gain such velocity as it rushed to its parent, the Yang-tsü, as to entirely prevent navigation, and cause great damage to the dykes.

During my walk I came to a large village built along the dyke-top, at this point some 200 yards wide. Near every house numbers of pigs were tethered to pegs in the ground by ropes passing through holes in their ears; they had no kind of shelter over them, and I did not see a single pig running loose. The result of this rough treatment was visible in their stunted growth.

Passing along the main street of the village I noticed a great number of oil mills, where oil was being pressed from cotton seed, and entered one of them to examine the process, which was apparently simple. The seed was ground into meal by means of a large mill-stone about five feet in diameter, travelling in a circular trough, and revolving on a pole leading from a post fixed in the centre of the circle made by the trough; to the end of the pole projecting outside the stone a bullock was harnessed, and supplied the motive power. The seed, when ground, was put into rough hempen bags, and steamed over a large boiling cauldron, and then transferred into round moulds for the pressing machine, and the oil expressed. The people were very civil, and were proceeding to show me the press, when in walked a Hankow boatman, who, immediately recognising me, called out, "Iyaw! Yang-jen!" (foreigner). This produced an instant commotion; the mill people left work, and crowded round me, for they had evidently up to this moment taken me for a mandarin from Canton, my fair complexion resembling that of the Cantonese. Outside, people were shouting "Yang-kwai-ts^u!" "Foreign devil," and soon the whole village collected in front of the mill. I felt very nervous when I heard the war cry of "Foreign devil," and Philip anxiously urged me to make for the boat; but that was some distance ahead, and we were therefore obliged to face the crowd. The moment I got into the street I was greeted with groans and loud angry shouts of "Yang-kwai-ts^u."

Feeling that it would be useless to run, I filled my long Chinese pipe, and seeing a respectable old man who stood by smoking, with apparent indifference I asked him politely for a light. He gave me one, and Philip at once engaged him in conversation. This distracted the attention of the crowd —just exactly what I wanted; he became very inquisitive, and was greatly entertained by Philip's account of me. During all this time we had been quietly walking towards the boat, which we could see waiting at the far end of the village. Whenever any one pressed too close upon us, our new friend rebuked them, and the crowd, seeing that he treated me politely, seemed at once to regain their good nature, but they followed us to the boat. Having regained it I asked the old man into the cabin, and invited him to drink a cup of Samshu with me. He was a kind old fellow, and turned out to be the proprietor of the mill I had entered. He asked me to excuse the rudeness of the villagers, who he said did not understand manners, and were very much afraid of foreigners.

After drinking a cup of Samshu he asked permission to go, and I escorted him to the cabin-door, where we took a ceremonious leave of each other. The crowd had nearly all dispersed while we were inside, and the few people remaining retired with the old man, anxious to hear from him all about "the foreign devil."

As soon as we were clear of the village I began to breathe freely again. This was my first collision with a hostile Chinese crowd; I had got well out of it, but only by assuming a coolness that I was very far from feeling. Philip was greatly delighted, and he and Lowlee talked our adventure over with apparently great pleasure, repeatedly telling me that I had had a narrow escape, and but for my "savee,"—*i.e.*, coolness —might have been badly treated. Philip's quickness in perceiving my object in asking the old man for a light, and at once entering into conversation with him, did much to show me that I had in my interpreter a man to be depended on in case of difficulty, and I confess that I felt easier and elated rather than otherwise by the adventure.

A few miles above this village we passed under the first bridge since leaving Hankow. It was a wooden structure, with supports some ten yards apart; and about thirty feet from the right bank of the creek a sort of trap-door arrangement, which permitted the boat's mast to pass. A road leading from the south to the city of Main-yang, about twenty miles distant to the north, crossed the bridge, which was only wide enough to allow two horses to pass each other.

From this point the country gradually became more elevated, and I noticed in the fields the dried stalks of cotton, and young crops of wheat, barley, Chinese cabbages, and winter broad beans in great plenty. Our progress was still slow, for a light breeze from the north-east blew in our teeth, compelling us to make our way with oars, and occasionally by tracking.

The dykes hereabouts are frequently used as burial places, the nearest hill being nearly forty miles off. As we were often obliged to make fast to the bank in order to let funeral processions pass, I had an opportunity of seeing that of a man of fortune. The *cortége* was very grand; mourners, bands of musicians, and banners were numerous. The body, in one of the large coffins peculiar to China, was placed on a catafalque elevated on planks lashed across three boats, and decorated with flags on poles six feet high. The widow and mother of the deceased sat on the coffin, wailing most piteously, while numbers of hired female mourners dressed in white, the garb of mourning in China, filled another of the six boats following the coffin. Each boat was slowly propelled by oarsmen, keeping stroke to the solemn beating of a gong, while bands of reed and brass instruments occasionally struck up mournful tunes, and drowned the wailing of the female mourners.

The interment was to take place a long way from the point where we met the procession, which would probably occupy a week in reaching the burial ground.

We were now nearing Sha-s^u; a fair wind would have taken us there in six hours, but having both wind and stream against us, we made very slow progress.

On the morning of the 13th of January, nine days after leaving Hankow, we entered the Tsang-hoo lake, and anchored in the middle for the night. We had poled all day, there being but little water in the lake, the greatest depth found being four to five feet.

Numbers of large boats were engaged in trawling, their huge sails appearing three times too large for their hulls. Their trawls were very large, and the weedy bottom of the lake greatly impeded them, rendering the large sails necessary. The immense numbers of large and small fish taken by this method are almost incredible, and fishing gives occupation to the crews of a large fleet of boats, besides numbers of men engaged in fishing with cormorants. Near to where we anchored two men in their canoes were fishing with a flock of some forty birds, and I sat for some time greatly interested in their proceedings. Along the sides of their canoes were lashed bamboo poles, forming perches for the birds, which, as they rose to the surface near the boat, were dexterously lifted on to them by the men, who each carried a long bamboo with a blunt hook at the end; this they put under the bird as it sat in the water, and by a sudden jerk landed it on the perch. Sometimes a cormorant would come up with a fish as big as itself, and weighing from seven to eight pounds; then a great commotion would take place; all the cormorants near would hurry to its assistance with hoarse cries, and the men would cheer them on by shouts of "Haw-haw, yup!" until they could get near enough to whip up the fish in a landing-net, after which they would perch their birds, and removing the rings round their necks, feed them with pieces of fish.

On the following day, after leaving the lake, we passed several small villages, the people of which seemed principally engaged in the sale of spars for boat masts. These spars are brought down from Honan during the summer floods.

The banks of the canal leading from the Tsang-hoo lake were in many places faced with stone, and as we neared Sha-s^u, the pagodas of which were visible, the bed of the canal widened, but the water became shallower, causing great obstruction to traffic. Hundreds of boats laden with cotton and cotton piece goods for shipment to Sz-chuan, and others laden with vegetables and oil for Hankow, almost blocked up the channel, which within a mile of Sha-s^u became unnavigable; so we came to an anchor in an immense crowd of boats, just above the Customs station, at the village of Chow-see, where our passports were demanded, and the mandarin immediately passed us, sending me a message to the effect that he was very busy, or he would have visited me.

Our first stage was accomplished, and it was necessary that we should here change our boat for one of a different class, used in ascending the Yang-ts^u rapids. Our first task, however, was to procure quarters in the city; I therefore sent Philip ashore to hire rooms in an hotel.

Seen from where we lay, the town of Sha-s^u was not very imposing, a few joss houses and wood yards, with their stacks of spars, forming the principal features; while round the suburbs I noticed a few fir trees, the first trees, except willows, we had seen since leaving Hankow. Sha-s^u is situated on the left bank of the Yang-ts^u, and derives its principal importance from the transit trade through it from Sz-chuan to Hankow. A great many of the junks from Chung Ching discharge their cargoes here, instead of taking the long river journey to Hankow, and reload piece goods brought to Sha-s^u by the route we had followed.

From the nature of the country travelled through up to this point, there are few spots suited for the sites of large towns, and there are consequently but few of any importance. The city of Main-yang, situated about fifty miles N.W. of Hankow, is the seat of government, and the country lying between the Han river and Sha-s^u is under its jurisdiction. On the journey I collected some interesting facts, as to the relations of the people living in the dyke lands, as well as those living in the reed-growing country, with the government. The only officials with whom they are brought in contact, are the few petty mandarins at the Customs' stations, who at stated seasons travel through their districts collecting ground rent, and beyond paying this tax, the people see little of the mandarins, and trouble them less. There are no soldiers to be seen, each village and hamlet maintaining its own watchman by public contribution. The isolated position of the people struck me so forcibly, that I was led to make inquiries at many of the villages passed through, as to the administration of the law amongst them, and from what I gathered it may be said that they literally govern themselves.

All civil disputes are settled by the two oldest men of the families of the disputants, who act as arbitrators, their award being practically final, subject, however, to an appeal to the civil mandarin at Main-yang; but such an appeal is rarely ever made, and then only in cases where the parties are wealthy, and one or the other seeks the utter ruin of his opponent. Lesser criminal cases are likewise disposed of by the elders of villages; but criminals charged with capital crimes, must be sent to Main-yang to be tried by the mandarins. This mode of partial self-government seems to be successful, if one may judge from the industrious and peaceful appearance of the people, who also look well-to-do, and are well and warmly clad in winter. Contrary to what might be expected from the nature of the country, they seem subject to few diseases, those of an ophthalmic and asthmatic nature being most common. As a rule they are a healthy looking race, of fair stature, with strongly marked Tartar features.

Philip, on his return to the boat, informed me that he had hired a room in an hotel, and that we would have to take up our quarters there in the morning. He was full of the strange sights that he had seen, one of which was a camel; some Pekinese drug merchant having brought the animal with him, its rarity in this part of China serving as a capital advertisement.

In the evening our boatmen had a feast, and towards bed-time asked leave to present themselves, that they might take leave of me; the fellows had really behaved well during the journey, so I gave permission for them to enter, and had to drink Samshu with each of them, receiving from the old Lowder a long address, in which he conveyed to me the good wishes of himself and crew, for my safety in the wonderful journey before me, after which I gave them each a present and sent them off quite happy. The occasion of my having inadvertently spat over the bow of the boat, was the only time that I had reason to complain of rudeness on the part of these men, and it is worthy of remark, as showing what a superstitious class they are.

Next morning about ten o'clock, the people of the hotel, where our rooms had been engaged, sent a chair for me, and baggage coolies; on our way from the boat to the hotel we passed through about a mile and a half of suburbs, where every available clear space was covered with mats, on which was spread orange peel to dry in the sun; this, when dried and pulverised, is highly esteemed by the Chinese as a stomachic. Along the main street we met string after string of donkeys, ponies, and mules, laden with country produce for the market. The shops were generally of a good class, and from the number of those in the pipe trade, one might suppose that the inhabitants did little else but smoke. Provisions of all kinds, and in great plenty, were exposed for sale, and amongst them I noticed mutton, pheasants, and potatoes.

After more than an hour's jolting, I was set down before the hotel door. A descent of three or four steps led to the first, or entrance hall; facing us, over an inner door, were large pictures of Omee and To-foo, princes who, as Chinese legends say, were sent to the west from China, to search for the man who, according to visions seen by the Emperor in his dreams, would by his great wisdom diffuse universal peace throughout the Empire,* then distracted by rebellion. On each side of the pictures, in niches in the wall, were the small gilt Josses or household gods, with a lamp burning in front of them. In the outer hall many guests were assembled to get a look at the foreigner on his arrival; when they saw me, however, dressed like one of themselves, with a shaved head, and a respectable tail, they appeared disappointed, and I passed through them without causing any excitement.

* Appendix, note 2.

The landlord on ushering me into my room, requested three hundred chen per diem, instead of one hundred and fifty, the usual price, as agreed to by Philip, who on hearing the demand was very angry, and it was not until after I had threatened to seek quarters elsewhere, that we settled for the usual charge, which included two cups of rice and a plate of salt cabbage twice a day, and a saucer of cotton oil with rush wick, to light our room.

We ordered breakfast to be served in the inner hall, into which our room opened, and sat down in the presence of more than a dozen people, lodgers in the house; they had assembled for the purpose of seeing the foreigner eat, expecting a treat, but were again disappointed by seeing that I fed like one of themselves, and all, with the exception of three women, went about their business before I had finished. Although they seemed anxious to hear and see all about me, they were quiet, and did not offer the least insult. Curiosity is a characteristic of the Chinese, and its gratification possesses an irresistible charm for them. I remember with shame now, that before I went amongst them, and understood their ways, I had often treated as impertinence a harmless curiosity, and in doing so, offended the sensitive disposition of a really good-natured people.

After breakfast, I paid a visit to the Catholic Mission Agent, Chee-sien-sen by name, a wealthy merchant engaged in an extensive trade with Sz-chuan, with whom I had to arrange about funds for our journey to Chung Ching. We were shown into a little room next the counting-house, where we found several Christians, merchants from Chung Ching, smoking their pipes, each with his cup of tea on a small table before him. As soon as I seated myself, a little boy placed a tea cup before me, and throwing in a pinch of fragrant tea, poured in boiling water from a large kettle, which he took from a little stand over a charcoal fire burning in an iron brasier in the centre of the room; having thus helped me to tea, he took my long Chinese pipe, and filling it with tobacco, handed it to me with a light, and then took up his place behind my chair. Nothing could exceed the quiet politeness and quickness, with which this little fellow served me; to every one in the room I was a perfect stranger and a foreigner, yet being in a house of business no distinction was made between me and any of the Chinese present. Several other little waiters shewed the Sz-chuan merchants the same attention as had been paid to me; my presence caused no interruption to the conversation, which was being carried on when I entered, and while I waited for the merchant, I smoked and drank tea at my leisure.

After waiting about half an hour, the merchant came from the counting-house, and saluting me very courteously, apologised for having kept me waiting, and after a few remarks on the crops and weather, enquired my business.

On learning the object of my visit he appeared quite pleased, and expressed himself delighted to be able to do anything for a friend of the Fathers, and leading me into his office, he paid me over the sum I required, merely taking from me a receipt for the amount. We then went back to the waiting-room, where he introduced me to several of the Chung Ching merchants, and explained to his guests that I was a foreign merchant undertaking a great journey to open up commerce, and complimented me on my courage in starting alone on so great an enterprise.

We all sat smoking and drinking tea for nearly two hours, when I rose to go; but my host said that dinner was just ready, and he would be glad if I would join himself and guests, apologising at the same time for his homely fare, saying that if he had known I was coming, I should have had a proper dinner.

I was so charmed with the manner of this Chinese gentleman—for such in bearing he really was—that I accepted his invitation, and sat down again; and in a few minutes all the other merchants, except two young men, who were permanent guests, left, and a serving-man then laid out the table, placing a pair of ivory chop-sticks, tipped with silver, for each of us, and brought in the dinner, consisting of fish soup, boiled and fried fish, stewed ducks, mutton and fowl. We took our seats—the host last—and were then handed cups (about the size of a large breakfast-cup) of rice, and in the interval before the soup and fish were brought in, baked melon seeds were placed before us on small plates; these we nibbled at for a few minutes, until our host, taking his chop-sticks up, put their points into a plate of fish, and looking round the table, bowed to us, whereupon we simultaneously helped ourselves, and commenced our meal. I kept up a lively conversation on the subject of foreigners and their wonderful inventions during the dinner, which I thoroughly enjoyed. When we had finished we all stood up, holding our chop-sticks by the tips with both hands horizontally in front of our foreheads as a sign of thankfulness, and also respect to our host. We then sat down again, and little kettles of hot Samshu were brought in, and we commenced to drink wine with each other.

The two young merchants soon became very loud in my praise, saying that I was quite different to the foreigners in Hankow, I was more like a Chinaman; but were very anxious to know if I was of the same religion as themselves, and when told that I was a Christian, repeatedly embraced me, calling me a brother. We sat over our Samshu and smoked for a long time, the absence of anything like constraint amongst us, and the genuine hospitality of our host, making the hours pass quickly. I felt that I was seeing Chinese life from a stand-point hitherto unknown to most Europeans, especially Englishmen; and I felt much gratified with this my first admission into the private life of the people whose manners and customs I had adopted. During the time I was in the house I saw no females, with the exception of a servant, nor did I ever in the house of any respectable Chinaman meet the womankind during the greater part of a year spent amongst this people.

It was past six before I rose to go. I could have stayed longer, but the potent Samshu was gradually shortening my memory of passing time, and at last after a pressing invitation to visit my host again, he led me to the outer court of his house, where his sedan-chair, coolies and lantern-bearers were in waiting for me.

One of the young Sz-chuan merchants embraced me several times at parting, pressing me to call on his father at Chung Ching. At last I got into my chair, and bade a good night to Chee-sien-sen.

As I was going towards the hotel I could not help reflecting on the scene I had just left, so different in all respects from any previous idea I had formed of the Chinese character, of which, though I had dwelt for years in their country, I confess with shame, I had until now known nothing. I could not help contrasting the reception my host had given me, a total stranger and a foreigner, with that which he would probably have received at my hands had he visited me in Shanghai, when, as is usual with us Englishmen, he would very likely have had to come into my office without the least polite encouragement from me, and have transacted his business standing, after which I should probably have dismissed him with a gesture of impatience. It seems a great pity that we Englishmen, being such a great commercial people, do not associate ourselves more with the people amongst whom we trade. In China we would do wisely to remember the old adage which tells us to "do in Rome as the Romans do," and to meet the Chinese more on a footing of equality; in fact, adopt as much as possible their ways of business, and by this means do away with the system of go-betweens which is so detrimental to us in all our dealings with the people, of whom we really know nothing. By being brought more in contact with them we should pick up their language, and instead of being at the mercy of that villanous thing known under the name of Compradore, we should at once preserve our dignity, and enter into more pleasant and profitable relations with a people whose closer acquaintance is better worth cultivating than we in our national insularity are prone to believe.

On reaching the hotel I was glad to get to my room, and had just taken off my jacket and outer long coat, when some one knocked at the door, and a Chinaman, accompanied by three ladies, who were lodging in the hotel, presented himself, asking if they might come in and see the foreigner. Not thinking it wise to attempt seclusiveness, I invited the party in, and giving the visitors our only two chairs, Philip ordered in our teapot and kettle, and old Lowlee acted as waiter.

We all freely entered into conversation, and the ladies soon made known the real purport of their visit, namely, to inspect the curious things which foreigners are supposed generally to carry about with them. My pipe, brushes, and comb, looking-glass, rifle, and pistol, were all examined most minutely. One of the ladies, whose husband was a Hankow trader, said I was not like the foreigners she had seen there, but looked more like a Canton mandarin, which she laughingly said she believed me to be. On taking off my green spectacles which I had put on previous to admitting them, to disguise my eyes, the three ladies visibly started, and confessed that I must be a foreigner, from the look of my eyes. When pressed to tell me what peculiarity they saw in them, after a good deal of hesitation the lady who had first spoken said they looked "like devil's eyes." I did not feel much flattered at hearing this, and put on my spectacles again. This seemed to remove their timidity, and we continued talking until a late hour. During their visit I succeeded in making a friend of one of the ladies, whose baby, about eight months' old, I nursed and eventually put to sleep in my lap. On taking it from my arms she told Philip that if I had any washing or sewing to be done, she would do it for his kind "old" master.

My visitors left about 11 P.M., and I then prepared for bed. Shortly after turning in, I suddenly began to feel an uncomfortable crawling sensation in several parts of my body, accompanied by great irritation. I mentioned this to Philip, who thereupon advised me to get up, and he would see what it was. We looked, and discovered insects innumerable. This was my first experience of Chinese beds. The first shock was painful, and I hesitated to turn in again; but Philip, and Lowlee, who had come in to help in the search, assured me that every hotel in China was the same, and if these small matters prevented me sleeping, I should have a bad time of it. I suppressed my horror as much as possible, and turned in again, but not before I had the straw mattrass, which is always provided at hotels, thrown into the court-yard. In a very short time my torments began again, sleep I could not, and I lay tossing about on the hard boards in perfect agony. At last I groaned aloud, and attracted the attention of one of my neighbours and visitors of the evening in an adjoining room, who inquired what was the matter, and on Philip informing her, she and her companions screamed with laughter. Finding sleep impossible, I got up and dressed, and sought solace in my pipe, while I sat for hours thinking over the day, and making a survey of the room. It was blackened by the tobacco smoke of ages, and smelt like a ferret cage. Dirt formed a coating several inches thick on the floor, and would have rendered living in such a place impossible, but for the ventilation admitted through a large hole in the wall which did duty as a window. Two of the four walls were mat-partitions separating our room from two other dens, in one of which an aged Celestial coughed throughout the night with asthmatic energy, while in the other were my lady visitors and their children, which little cherubs occasionally joined in a duet of screams. Towards morning I fell asleep, and slept undisturbed in my chair until Lowlee brought me a cup of tea and my pipe.

On leaving my room about ten o'clock, I found many of the lodgers were out in the court-yard, performing their toilet; men were cleaning their teeth, and the women combing each other's hair. The house barber waited on me to know if I wanted shaving, and as my hair and beard had begun to grow again, I ordered him to come in the afternoon. The cook then informed me that my morning rice was ready, and I sat down to a breakfast of rice, salt fish, and stewed duck, Lowlee having procured the latter at a cookshop next door. We had also very good fried potatoes, and little wheaten cakes, and I made a capital meal in the presence of a number of people, who, however, paid little or no attention. Several children were running about, and on giving them some oranges they crawled about me without the least fear; nor were their mothers afraid, the general impression being that I was not a Yang-kwai-ts^u such as are seen in Hankow. This confidence of the people gave me great pleasure, especially as I remembered how, when travelling in the neighbourhood of Hankow, children on seeing the Yang-kwai-ts^u would run screaming to their mothers, who, folding them in their arms, would hurry away as from an evil spirit.

After breakfast, many women came to the hotel on pretended visits to the female lodgers, only, however, to gratify their curiosity about the male foreign devil, and as I sat smoking they with their children gradually drew round me, and, some sitting on the ground, and others on benches, plied their needles at various articles of dress and silk-embroidered shoes. In the course of the morning I chatted freely with them, asking through Philip many questions as to their manners and customs. Many of their children were great fat things, their faces and hands covered with sores. On asking the cause of the latter, the women told me that, as a rule, mothers do not allow their children to taste any other food but milk until they are two years old, at which age they are weaned, and the sudden change of diet from milk to rice, salt vegetables, and pork caused the sores I had noticed.

Seeing a number of little girls toddling about with their feet tightly bandaged, I could not help asking their mothers why they tortured their children in such a manner. My question appeared to cause some amusement, and they replied it was China custom, and no female of any respectability could possibly have large feet. It is very strange that Queen Fashion should, even amongst the practical Chinese, reign supreme, in defiance of comfort. The Chinese, however, claim a show of reason for the deformity, which, they say, prevents the women gadding about, and jeopardising the honour of their husbands, while it adds to that helpless dependence on man which, even to our European ideas, adds so much to the natural charms of woman. Chinese poets liken the helpless, tottering gait of the small-footed woman to the graceful waving to and fro of the lily.

Some writers have said that the small foot is not common throughout China, and have probably arrived at this conclusion from observations made at Canton and Hong-kong, where the lower classes do not practise the deformity so much as in other parts. It is, however, a fashion that exists everywhere as a mark of respectability, and in no city more so, perhaps, than in Canton, though amongst the Tartar women the deformity is never seen. It is an old custom in China, and was in vogue before the time of Confucius. The common version of its origin is that it first originated in the seraglio of one of the emperors, whose favourite wife eloped with a water-carrier. This is doubtless a popular legend, founded on the probable fact that the custom first originated amongst the ladies of the imperial seraglio, before the Tartar dynasty reigned, not as a punishment, but growing out of the desire to make their feet look small by bandaging, instead of wearing tight shoes with heels in the centre of the foot, which they found, probably, caused them as much pain in the wearing as the bandage, without half its effect.

Whatever influence this deformity may have had on the virtue of the inmates of the palace, it is certain that China, like all other civilised countries, has as yet failed to put down prostitution, in the ranks of which the small foot attains its greatest perfection; and I am inclined to think with Doolittle, the ablest of our English writers on the social life of the Chinese, that the custom originated rather in the caprice of fashion than in the desire of the Chinese by this means to guard the chastity of their women; and this appears still more likely from the absence of any legislative enactment on the subject.

Differing from other writers on the subject, I am disposed to believe that the compression does not inflict the pain it is supposed to cause, for I have noticed in children in all stages of bandaging that they crawl and toddle about without much apparent difficulty or pain. The bandage is first applied when the child is three or four years old, and operates so gradually that I am certain the pain is much less than is generally supposed. All the females that I have spoken to on the subject assured me that the most painful time is when they are about ten years of age, and growing very fast. I have never been able to get a look at the deformed naked foot, but, as may be supposed from the extremity being so small, and from what I have been told, the foot is reduced to a shapeless mass, and is offensive to look at, for it is generally covered with ulcerated sores from the breaking of the skin.

About mid-day a party of disbanded soldiers on their way to Sz-chuan arrived, and took up their quarters at the hotel. They were a set of lawless rascals, and as soon as they entered took possession of the house, driving all the respectable lodgers to their rooms. Several of the fellows came to my table, and helped themselves to tea and tobacco, and asked Lowlee some questions about me. When informed that I was a foreigner, they told me they had been fighting against the rebels in company with some Europeans, and seemed very proud of the fact. I learned, however, afterwards, that they had been disbanded by an Imperial order, made at the petition of the people whose country they had pillaged on the march to meet the rebels.

After they had dined, they came and sat down close to me, and commenced to gamble for chen with dice and dominoes. They asked me to join them, so I sat down, and was soon deep in the game of chance. They were a true type of the Chinese soldier—braggarts, thieves, opium smokers, and inveterate gamblers. We smoked and drank Samshu the whole afternoon, each of us ordering liquor in turn; the landlord supplied them because he was afraid to refuse, well knowing that if he did they would take it; as to payment, he never imagined for a moment that they would be guilty of such a thing. However, to me they were very civil, and vied with each other in showing me attention.

As soon as the barber made his appearance he was taken possession of, and the ragamuffins went in for a shave, each in his turn. As soon as the last one was operated on, and the grumbling barber had been rewarded with ten chen, about a twentieth part of what he was entitled to, I took my station on his stool and submitted to the operation, not without a slight feeling of discomfort at the idea of being operated on by the same fingers and instruments as my disreputable companions, some of them being very scabby and covered with sores. However, an effort at self-control helped me, and I went through the ordeal while they continued to play.

The Chinese use no soap in shaving, but the head and face are bathed in very hot water until the hair is soft, and then the razor passes over one's scalp as smoothly as possible, without causing the least discomfort. It is surprising how little smarting accompanies the process. Every part of the face, head, and neck is shaved, and afterwards one feels a sensation of pleasure similar to that after a good bath. It is certainly the great luxury of the Chinese toilet.

After our evening meal I received several presents of oranges from the soldiers and lodgers. The former all went out for the night, and I received several new visitors, amongst them Captain Murking-kow, who took Captain Blakiston and his party up the Yang-ts^u in 1860. It was amusing to be told by him what strange individuals the foreigners were—fierce and hairy, but great men, and capital paymasters. He thought I must be quite a different kind of foreigner to those he had taken up the river, and while he sat in my room told me wonderful stories about them. It will be gratifying to Captain Blakiston to know that the "devil" who looked at the sun so much was quite a favourite with this junk skipper, who appeared to think him a very great scholar, with much "fire"—*i.e.*, bravery—in his heart. A dog belonging to some of the party held an important place in the superstitious memory of the old man, who assured me very confidentially that it was a devil-dog.

In the evening Philip informed me that he had hired a boat to take us to Chung Ching, and we decided to leave Sha-s^u next morning. He had made a very good bargain, the Lowder having agreed to take 48,000 chen for the voyage, 28,000 to be paid at starting, and the balance on arriving at the City of Quifoo, half way between Sha-s^u and Chung Ching. This did not include the customary weekly present of 20 chen to each of the boatmen; this weekly payment is so much a recognised custom, that on hiring a boat it must always be taken into consideration, as it makes all the difference whether the passenger or the

Lowder pays it; in the latter case it must be specified in the agreement, or charter-party, without the signing of which document by both parties, no boat can safely be hired.

In the night, after I had been some time in bed, I was roused by a dreadful disturbance in the house; our soldier friends had returned in a very noisy mood, and bent on mischief, had entered several rooms occupied by females, in spite of the loud remonstrance of the terrified landlord, who followed them about half undressed. The females whose room adjoined mine, broke into my room screaming, and were followed by several soldiers, who when they came against me as I blocked up the doorway, winked in a familiar and anything but pleasant manner; they did not, however, attempt to enter, but turned away with some jocular remark to Philip on the good fortune of his master. Shortly after this, the landlord came to me with a request that I would join them, as they were going to make a night of it. I refused at first, but on second thoughts, thinking that they might be troublesome if I refused, joined them; they were very noisy, but appeared satisfied and even pleased at my having accepted their invitation. I was obliged to submit to their drunken embraces, while they declared repeatedly that I was a "how jen," *i.e.* capital fellow. After Philip and myself had sat with them some time, I complained of being tired, and asked them to go to bed; they were almost incapable of shewing resistance, and went off quietly. On returning to my room, I found the women who had sought refuge in it asleep on my bed, so I turned in alongside of Philip, and was soon asleep.

At a very early hour next morning the soldiers went away, having first come to take leave of me, when I thought I was fairly rid of them; but they soon returned with the landlord, who complained that they wished to cheat him, having only paid half their liquor bill, which, they all speaking at once, assured me was most liberal on their part, considering that they were soldiers. Not wishing to be bothered with them, I told the hotel-keeper, that I would pay for the other half, amounting to 2,800 chen, and the fellows took themselves off in high good humour, not, however, without a suspicion on my part, that I had been looked upon in the light of a pigeon by them; but I felt thankful that I was not subjected to further inconvenience.

As we did not intend to embark until midday, I ordered breakfast, and during the meal received visits from numerous sick people, who came to ask for medicines to cure their various complaints; some were asthmatic, others almost blind from ophthalmia, and not a few were inveterate opium smokers, who asked for medicines to cure their appetite for opium. To attempt prescribing for them all would have been vain, so I was obliged to say that my medicines were on board my boat. As I was getting into my chair, two lepers stretched out their fingerless hands, entreating me to cure them; they were a shocking sight, and I was much grieved at not being able to help them.

By noon our boat was properly stowed, and though less than the one we had travelled in from Hankow to Sha-su, was comfortable and, above all, safe. It was thirty feet long, with four feet beam, the bow and the stern turned up canoe-fashion; a space of twelve feet in the centre part was covered over with water-tight reed matting, forming a capital protection against wind and rain. In the fore-part of this little cabin, which was divided by a cross-rail, we kept our small earthenware stove, cooking utensils, and baggage. Philip and

Lowlee also made up their beds there; the other division I occupied, which was long enough for me to lie down at full length, but I was obliged to crawl in and out on my hands and knees. A space of ten feet from the bow was occupied by the three boatmen, who at night covered it over with mats, making themselves very snug, and an equal space aft, served as a shelter for the Lowder. This description of boat is admirably adapted for the navigation of rapids, for they draw very little water, and are built of an exceedingly tough wood, which

WAN-CHIEN BOAT.

grows in the district of Wan-chien, a small town on the left bank of the Yang-ts\u, in the province of Sz-chuan, whence they are known along the line of river as Wan-chien boats; they are propelled by oars, and a square sail set on a pair of shears by way of mast, which can be easily lowered or hoisted. A tow-rope is attached to the mast-head, by means of which the boatmen haul the boat up rapids, and also track when the nature of the river banks permits them to walk.

Having made all snug, we were about to cast off from the

shore, when Captain Blakiston's old Lowder came running towards us, evidently in a great state of excitement. He informed us that he had just been told by another Lowder, newly arrived from up river, that one of the six young Fathers, who had left me behind at Hankow, had been drowned in ascending one of the rapids. This was not at all cheering, and had a disheartening effect on Philip and Low-lee; they shook their heads, and foretold all sorts of mishaps for ourselves. Seeing that they were so much affected, I pretended not to believe the story, and said that he had only made it up to frighten us; both, however, begged me not to start until next day, by which time we could ascertain the truth. I refused to delay, feeling quite sure that if the man's tale should turn out correct, it would only tend to dishearten them more. So I made Philip give our Lowder his sailing orders, and we started on our toilsome ascent of the great river, passing along the stone dyke, by which the town of Sha-s^u is protected against inroads of the Yang-ts^u. It is a massive work, more than a mile long, and of great thickness, rising some forty feet above the winter level of the river, and faced with dressed granite. A Mandarin stationed at the city Kin-kow, some seven miles from Sha-s^u, is specially deputed from Woo-chang to look after this dyke, which is kept in repair by contributions from the inhabitants of Sha-s^u, whose safety, during the summer floods, depends on its efficiency, as the whole of their town, with the exception of that part which is built along the dyke, is some twenty feet below the summer level of the Yang-ts^u. It happened to be a lucky day, according to Chinese ideas, for starting on a journey, consequently we had nearly a dozen boats in company, bound like ourselves to the fertile province of Sz-chuan. When we anchored for the night, after tracking along the left bank all the afternoon, several boatmen paid our fellows a visit, and took their evening rice with them. Just before turning in, I was informed that our Lowder and crew wished me to drink to the prosperity of the voyage, and on signifying that I would comply with their request, they crawled into the fore compartment of my cabin, and the Lowder presenting me with a small cup of Samshu, made an obeisance, as did also each of the crew, while I drank it, and wished us all a prosperous voyage.

A tedious journey of two days brought us to the village of Tung-tzee on the left bank, and my passports were demanded by the customs' officials, so I sent Philip on shore with the one given me by Mr. Medhurst. He soon returned, saying that the mandarin had demanded 350 chen. As this was a "squeeze," I refused to pay it, and this had the effect of bringing the official to the boat. The fellow crawled into my cabin, upsetting everything in his way, and shaking his fist at me in a menacing manner, demanded instant payment. When I represented that I was a foreigner, and disinclined to submit to a "squeeze," he consigned all yang-kwai-ts^u to the care of the father of devils, and insisted on payment. I called his attention to my passport, which he snatched out of my hand, saying, "I don't care for that piece of paper, and know nothing about it." Having thus delivered himself, he threw it on the floor and spat on it. Seeing this I knew that the fellow was a reckless scoundrel, for no moderately decent Chinaman would treat any written Chinese characters with disrespect, such an act being considered disgraceful. I, therefore, picked up the document, and folding it with apparent respect, put it in the bosom of my coat, from which I took out the Viceroy's passport, and handed it to him; and as soon as he had read it, he asked for the consul's pass, which he wiped with his coat-sleeve, and refolding it, handed it back to me with a respectful bow, begging me at the same time to excuse his violent conduct, remarking that he had not thought such an insignificant looking document as the British consul's passport could have been of any importance. He then took himself off quietly without his 350 chen, and we shoved off from the shore. It seems a mistake that we do not in some measure try, by noticing the Chinese official manner of doing things, to command more respect in China. It is well known that all Chinese passports are documents of great size. Those given by officials corresponding to the rank of our consuls, are scarcely ever less than eighteen inches square, printed in large type, and look very imposing, while the British passport is about as large as small sized letter paper, printed in small type — a saving of paper doubtless; but if they were printed on Chinese paper six times as large, they would perhaps not cost one quarter as much as on English paper, and would appear in the eyes of the Chinese respectable documents. But then we are much more powerful than the Chinese, and it is perhaps not worth while to notice their prejudices; an appeal to the British gun-boat soon puts these little matters straight, especially if the peaceful Protestant missionary be concerned in any little misunderstanding with the literary or official class of the population of China.

On the evening of the fourth day from Sha-s^u we sighted the Pah-yang hills near Ichang. Inland, on either bank, the country was strewn with quartz and granite boulders like those embedded in the tufa rock of the river bed. Numbers of speckled kingfishers, resembling in plumage those seen along the river Ganges, plied their busy avocation; these were the first large kingfishers I had seen in China, though,

I believe, in the southern provinces they are common enough. As we approached the Pah-yang village through a fine river scene, our boatmen seemed suddenly to wake up and assume a different character. On the left bank high sandstone cliffs, rising perpendicularly from the river, threw back the echoes of their joyous boat-songs. In place of the dull, sleepy, and spiritless fellows who had toiled along from Sha-s^u, they became full of fun and frolic, working with an irresistible will against the increased current of the river, and seeming to recognise in the hills which we were entering, old and familiar friends. At night we anchored a few miles above the Pah-yang village, and towards midnight were roused by a terrific thunder-storm, which raged with great violence for several hours, causing great consternation amongst the crews of the boats in our company. Our men crawled into the quarters of Philip and Lowlee, and smoked during the storm, which they deemed a foreboding of war and fearful calamity to the country, occurring as it did in the winter season. The serious and prophetic air with which the men talked, while ever and anon vivid flashes of lightning lighted up our cabin, added not a little to the enjoyment with which I listened to the loud peals and roaring of the thunder. As Philip interpreted to me the forebodings of our Lowder, I could not but think what a true type he was of the mass of Chinamen. Underneath their practical and sensible exterior there lurks a sleeping demon of the blindest superstition, which requires only the slightest touch to change them into insensible madmen, reckless of life, and savage as wild beasts; and this dreadful curse is not only common amongst the uneducated, but amongst the literati and governing classes also. It was daylight before the storm died away, and as the cold was intense we pushed on for the city of Ichang, and by ten o'clock sighted its large octagonal pagoda, distant about seven miles. Some two miles below Ichang a turn in the river shut out the view of the plains of Hoopeh behind, and we were fairly amongst the hills. Before arriving at Ichang we passed the village of Coolow-pai, above which the hill scenery (in contrast with the plains we had been sailing through) was magnificent; huge masses of coarse conglomerate rocks rose towering from the water on our right, and compelled the boatmen to use their oars instead of tracking along shore, and as we glided on they commenced a boat-song, which the overhanging walls re-echoed in wild plaintive strains. On our left, mountain on mountain towered up until their sharp peaks were lost in low misty clouds, while on their lower slopes the fresh verdure of young wheat and barley crops lent a softening tint to what would otherwise have been savagely grand. Passing through such scenery as this we neared Ichang, and threaded our way through an immense fleet of junks bound up-river, and waiting at this point for the last day of the last month of the Chinese year, on which, according to ancient custom, they can pass the customs' station without paying duty.

About 2 P.M. we came to an anchor off the city, and for the rest of the day our crew busied themselves in laying in a store of provisions, bamboo ropes for tracking up the rapids and other necessaries, making a thorough preparation for the rough work before us.

Ichang, though a city of the first grade and of considerable size, derives its importance principally from its position as a border town of the plains, and the first customs' station at the entrance of Hoopeh from Sz-chuan. Here also the heavy Chung Ching junks on their down voyage to Sha-s[u] and Hankow re-ship fresh crews accustomed to the navigation of the lower Yang-ts⁰, and on their return voyage again ship crews accustomed to the rapids of the upper Yang-tsᵘ. These Sz-chuan junks, many of them carrying 120 tons of cargo, require from forty to sixty men to navigate them in ascending, and about fifteen in descending, the upper Yang-tsᵘ, while below Ichang a crew of six to eight men are sufficient, as sails alone are used to propel them.

We bought fowls in the market here at the rate of 120 chen each, rather dear, owing to the near approach of the Chinese new year, which raised the price of everything. Charcoal was 750 chen per picul. Vegetables, such as cabbages, potatoes, and leeks, were twenty chen per catty; beef, 48; pork 100; and beef and pork suet 160 chen per catty.

By sundown we had completed all arrangements necessary to continue the voyage, and in the evening I took a walk with Philip amongst the houses that line the river bank outside the city wall. Most of them were of a temporary nature, and the river being very low, they were built down to the water's edge, and consisted principally of cook-shops, samshu and tea-houses, seemingly doing a thriving business, and well filled by boatmen. There were also a great many barbers' shops, which attract numerous customers, as the discharged crews, after being paid off, never do anything until they have indulged in the luxury of a clean shave.

Late at night I had a visit from a customs' mandarin accompanied by half a dozen of his satellites; he was most polite, and took a cup of tea with me. After smoking nearly an hour, during which time he asked many questions about the "Ta-Ing-qua Tefang," "Great Country of England," he took his leave, and I was glad to turn in.

The prospect of entering the famous Ichang Gorge (about

the grandeur and terrible appearance of which our Lowder had fairly exhausted his imaginative powers of conversation) served to enliven my spirits. I was eager for the excitement of ascending the rapids, and for the prospect of the garden-like province of Sz-chuan. A total change of scenery was before me, and behind me lay the dreary plains of Hoopeh.

CHAPTER III.

ICHANG TO CHUNG-CHING.

Ichang Gorge, Rapids of the Upper Yang-tsᵉ—Ascending a Rapid—A Portage—
An ugly Tumble—A happy New Year—A Travelling Bookseller—Pelted
by Gunboat-men—The Boundary of Hoopeh—Philip's Indisposition—
Taken for a Grandfather—Official Roguery—Wreck of a Junk—Dragon
Procession—Chinese Christians—A Missionary Drowned—Sz-chuan Quarrymen—A Night in a Rapid—Spirit-rapping—Trade of the Yang-tsᵘ—
Steamers on the Upper Yang-tsᵘ.

THE morning broke with thick rainy weather, which compelled us to remain at Ichang until nearly mid-day, when it cleared up, and we, in company with several other boats, got under weigh. A couple of hours' rowing brought us to Blakiston's Mussulman point, rounding which we entered the mouth of the Ichang Gorge; the scene was magnificent, the mighty river, up which we had been toiling for several days past, had narrowed to a channel about three hundred yards wide, in which it glided, a black, sluggish-looking body of water, its surface unbroken save by the wake of a few Sz-chuan junks bound to Ichang, or the sudden splash of a school of porpoises as they sported round the mouth of the gorge, apparently afraid to enter its confined waters, for beyond this point I did not see any more. Rising perpendicularly on each bank were huge walls of rock, throwing their sombre shadow over the river, and resembling, in their peculiar castellated formation, the turreted strongholds of giants. In contrast with the dreary sameness of the plains of Hoopeh the sudden effect of the solemn grandeur of this gorge was overpowering. As we proceeded, an occasional ravine interrupted the wall-like sides of the gorge, opening to us views of distant mountain peaks tipped with snow.

I had expected to find the current in the gorge much stronger than we had experienced below, but such was not the case. The river had worn a deep channel through the hills, and I found from soundings at the mouth of the gorge eighteen fathoms, and some three miles further I could not fetch bottom at twenty fathoms.

At 4·30 we passed the locality of the first rapid mentioned by Captain Blakiston, but we found the water unbroken even by increased current. Above this point we passed an island of boulders in mid-stream, and the banks on either hand were piled up in confused masses of granite boulders; we made fast to the right bank for the night, and while my evening meal was being prepared, I landed, and clambered with difficulty up the rugged sides of the gorge; the sun had just set behind a range of hills to the west, and the twilight threw a gathering gloom over the scene before me. No house, tree, or vestige of cultivation spoke of man—all was bare, silent, and awful.

The steep sides of the gorge seemed to be composed of the *débris* of shattered hills; huge masses of rock were everywhere piled in formless and chaotic disorder, some projecting hundreds of feet above us, as if poised, ready to roll from their resting place and crush the intruder. In mid river similar masses, as though hurled from the cliffs, reared themselves from the water in fantastic confusion. The whole formed one of the wildest scenes I had ever witnessed, and as I gazed I felt overpoweringly impressed with a sense of the littleness of man and the mightiness of his Creator.

After dinner I sat down in the stern of the boat to examine

more leisurely the chasm which seemed to hem us in. Close below us lay the island of huge boulders, immediately beyond which the wall-like sides of the gorge seemed to close in; about a mile ahead, another projecting point at a sharp turn of the river closed the view, and as I looked I could hardly realise the fact that we were on the great water highway, so much did the scene resemble some black, silent lake, secluded amidst inaccessible mountains.

Some eighty feet above us the water-mark on the cliffs showed the height of the summer flood. I could easily see that the boulder island in mid-stream must in the first spring floods occasion a formidable rapid; but as the plains of the lower Yang-ts^u become flooded in summer by the inundation caused by the local rains and the overflow of the Han river and the Tung-ting and Poyang lakes, the waters of the upper Yang-ts^u are kept back, and rise to their highest level by the middle of August. At this time this island and many other obstructions are deeply submerged, and offer no obstacle to navigation.

I had to-day another opportunity of witnessing the effect of superstition on our boatmen. While passing along a very narrow part of the gorge, where its sides were perpendicular, and rising 800 or 900 feet high, I gave the Australian cry of coohee, and after repeating it once or twice, answered each time by a thousand echoes, a large piece of rock, several tons in weight, fell within ten yards of our boat, deluging us with the spray from its plunge into the river. The first notice I had of the falling mass was a crash like thunder as it struck a projecting crag 200 or 300 feet above us, and as I caught a momentary glance of the huge rock disappearing beneath the water, I shuddered at the danger we had so narrowly escaped. When I turned to see the effect on the boatmen, they were kneeling in the bottom of the boat, nor did they stir until every echo awakened by the report of the falling mass striking the water had died away amongst the distant hills; then they rose cautiously, as though still afraid of impending danger, and rowed us swiftly to the other bank, along which they kept for more than an hour, without a single word spoken by any of us. Meanwhile, I fell asleep in my cabin, but was roused by Philip, who, laughing, informed me that the Lowder and crew were anxious to speak to me. On going out to them I was made quite uncomfortable by the dreadfully serious expression on each of their faces, and inquiring what was the matter, the Lowder informed me that I had made the god of the hills very angry, and he had tried to kill us by hurling a rock at us; under these circumstances, if I had no objection, they would anchor for the night, and burn a few sacred tapers to appease his anger. To this, however, by the advice of Philip and Lowlee, I objected, but told them that I would have no objection to their making it all right with the offended spirit in the evening, after our day's work was over. So we continued on our way, but the fellows were evidently ill at ease, and immediately after their evening meal commenced burning tapers and letting off crackers to such an extent that I found it difficult to sleep.

Next morning, having started at daylight, we arrived about 9 A.M. at the Ta-tung rapid, called by Blakiston Kwadung. It is a dangerous rapid, caused by a rocky island in mid-channel, dividing the river, which on either side rushes in a foaming torrent for more than 300 yards, until it becomes calm round a point below.

It was an ugly place to look at, and the wrecks of two junks on the banks showed that we had now reached the Yang-tsʉ rapids in earnest. By the advice of our Lowder, I landed and walked along the rugged banks to the head of the rapid.

Our boat, small as she looked, ascended the rapid with little difficulty. Some half-dozen villagers (many of whom are always on the look out to earn a few chen by helping to haul up junks or boats) laid hold of our towing line, and soon dragged her up; it was, however, an anxious time for me, as I had left everything I possessed in her, and in ascending she appeared almost buried in the foam; the water curled off the bows two or three feet above the gunwale, and looked every moment as if it would swamp her, but she got up without shipping a drop.

A large junk, which was lying at the foot of the rapid, waiting for trackers, next made the ascent; but as she was a craft carrying about eighty tons of cargo, and drawing over five feet, the task was not so easy for her. Upwards of 100 men, who had been collected from many of the adjacent villages, laid hold of the long plaited bamboo rope attached to her mast-head, and dragged her up, moving her inch by inch, while a few hands on board worked steadily at the bow sweep, by which she was steered clear of rocks and the river bank. It was often necessary for the trackers to slacken the tow line or make a sudden stop, and in order to convey the orders from those on board, a man sat on the deck beating a monotonous tune on a tom-tom, using certain variations of the tune as signals to those on shore.

In the crew of these large junks there are always several men called water-men, whose duty it is to clear the towing line from projecting and sunken rocks. This, as may be imagined, is a very arduous and dangerous occupation, for it often happens that the line gets foul of a sunken rock in the middle of the rapid, and then these water-men have to clear it. They are, however, very expert in swimming and diving, and appear quite at home in the midst of the fiercest rapid; but it occasionally happens that they get jammed among the rocks by the tow-line and lose their lives.

I think, without exception, the Sz-chuan junk-men are the most hard-working beings I have ever seen; they are at it from early morn till sundown. Their pay is from 100 to 150 chen and six cups of boiled rice per diem, yet the fellows are always cheerful, and as harnessed to the tow-rope they drag the junks along the banks of the Yang-tz^u, they sing unceasingly, swinging their arms from right to left in time to the cadences. They are fond of fun, too, and every large junk carries one or more jesters. These fellows, whenever a hard piece of tracking is to be done, jump out from the rest, armed with a long piece of rope, with which they belabour their companions, and cut the most absurd capers, yelling, shouting, and urging them to pull with the most frantic gestures; and woe be to the unlucky wight that is caught shirking; he is covered with ridicule by these jesters, who shout out his name, calling him a lazy rascal or some such epithet, and the whole line joins in with groans and yells at the defaulter. These jesters are invariably gang-masters—that is to say, in a crew of fifty men, there will be perhaps five of them, who are paid by the junk captains to find ten men each at so much per head for the voyage, and they make a good thing out of it, for at the end of the voyage the crews, being so badly paid, are invariably in debt to the gang-master, and must accept his terms for another trip.

We ascended the rapid on the right bank, that on the left being used exclusively for junks descending, and some three hours' pulling brought us to the Tungnin Rapid, formed also by rocks in mid-river. Having ascended it without difficulty, we came in sight of the Lukan Gorge.* The view from this spot was very fine; the mouth of the gorge resembled a cleft in the face of a huge mountain, the peaks of which were covered with snow. In an hour we reached the gorge; it seemed as though we were about to enter some subterranean passage, so great was the gloom. The river, scarcely 100 yards wide, flowed between walls of rock rising perpendicularly several hundred feet, and then sloping at an angle of perhaps 80° till they terminated in peaks at least 2000 feet high. This is the most striking of the Yang-tz^u gorges in its solemn grandeur, and is well worth travelling a thousand miles to see.

We passed through the gorge, and reached the villages of Ta and Show Tsing-tung, or Great and Little Tsing-tung, picturesquely perched on the right and left banks of the river, just below the series of rapids of the same name. This is one of the most dangerous rapids, and as it was necessary for us to discharge everything from the boat before attempting the ascent, we made Ta-tsing-tung our halting-place for the night, and I took a run on shore.

A great many junks were discharging their cargoes of cotton bales, which were being carried up to the head of the rapid by mules and coolies. The mules were harnessed between two long poles, the ends fitting into wooden saddles, forming a kind of stretcher, and the bales and packages were slung on the poles. Whole strings of mules thus laden, together with hundreds of coolies, each carrying a bale of cotton, were busy until a late hour, working by moonlight.

The little village also presented a busy scene; its single street was crowded with boatmen engaged in purchasing supplies of vegetables and rice, while the number of fowls and

* See Blakiston's Yang-ts^u Sketches by Dr. Barton.

crackers exposed for sale denoted the Chinese festival of the New Year.

As the night closed in it became very cold. On the opposite bank to us, mountains 2,000 feet high, rose almost immediately from the river, their summits covered with snow, from which a cold piercing wind descended in gusts that almost froze us. The country around was very wild, though a few patches of cultivation in the neighbourhood of the villages nestling at their base spoke of the industry of the inhabitants. These villages are famous for peaches, which grow plentifully in the sheltered nooks of the surrounding hills.

I was roused early in the morning by our fellows, who commenced unloading the boat, and I walked on to the head of the rapid, from which spot I had a capital view of the Mitan Gorge and the rapids, three of which follow each other in close succession, the last and most dangerous one occurring some 200 or 300 yards below the mouth of the gorge, from which the river rushes in an unbroken volume, until interrupted by a bar of rock, over which it pours itself in a fall of some five feet, during the winter months. At this season, all boats and junks are, by order of the mandarins, obliged to discharge half their cargo before attempting this rapid, so that few accidents occur.

The velocity of the stream is so great that the junks always descend partly sideways, to prevent their going bows under. Several that descended, while I stood waiting for our boat, seemed for a second or so to have gone under, but they soon reappeared, hurried down the rapid at a tremendous pace.

Our boat came up in its turn, but it was not until nearly three o'clock that we had reloaded and entered the Mitan Gorge. After rowing some two miles up the gorge, we anchored at the mouth of a small mountain stream, which falls into the Yang-tsᵘ from the left bank. As soon as we had made fast, the Lowder and boatmen waited upon me with the request, that I would allow them to remain here to-morrow, as it was their New Year's Day. I was not at all sorry to comply with their request, for the close confinement of my cabin was beginning to tell upon me. I could not stand upright in it, and had only the alternative of lying down; writing, sketching, or any other occupation, while under weigh, was impossible, and want of change of position caused my body to ache most painfully, and I realised the misery of the unhappy captives confined in cages by Louis XI.

Had I at any time called a halt in our voyage, I should have had to pay 500 chen per diem for the boat, besides the daily wages of the crew and Lowder, so that I was lucky now to have the luxury of a run on shore without paying for it.

As the evening was very fine, Philip and myself went on shore, and by way of exercise, ascended a hill, about 600 feet high; it was very steep, and almost bare of vegetation, and we found it very difficult to keep our footing. Philip, half way up, complained of giddiness, and lay down on his back, while I managed with considerable difficulty to reach the top, from which I had a fine view of the mountains, which rose peak after peak, as far as the eye could reach. I found it almost impossible to keep my feet on the steep declivities, covered with a loose hard gravel. I had, therefore to squat, and literally slide down in a very undignified manner, and very soon gathered such way that I could not stop, and gradually going faster and faster, at last went head over heels in a vain endeavour to put on the drag, and rolled down at a tremendous pace, cutting and bruising myself terribly, bringing up at last a little below the spot where Philip was lying on his back. Having ascertained that my damages were not serious, I tried to induce Philip to follow me down, but he was afraid to move, being very giddy, and seemingly quite overpowered; however we got down to the boat, and during our after-dinner smoke had a good laugh over our adventure of the afternoon, and I turned in, feeling all the better for the walk, and in light spirits, anticipating another ramble in the morning. Two other boats had anchored near us, and during the evening, the crews kept up an incessant beating of tom-toms, and our fellows joined them in a feast, prolonging the harmony until one o'clock in the morning, when they returned, bearing unmistakeable marks of their having spent a jolly evening.

Shortly after I had dressed next morning, my Lowder and crew presented themselves with a tray of boiled fowl, rice, samshu, and sweetmeats, which they placed before me, with many good wishes for a happy new year. I drank a cup of spirit with them, and returned the compliments of the season, accompanied by a present of 500 chen, to buy crackers; and then started with Philip for a ramble in the hills.

At the landing-place, the Lowders of the other boats came and wished me a happy new year. Clasping their hands in front of them, they made a low obeisance, after the common mode of salutation amongst the Chinese, which I returned in like manner, with many good wishes.

Leaving the river, we struck up the bank of the little stream, which soon led us amongst the hills—and followed the path several hundred feet up the side of a high mountain, from whence we looked down on the cascades of the stream, winding down in the glen below, the far roar of which, now and then reached us, as a faint murmur. Above and around us towered huge black mountains, their snow-capped peaks wreathed with clouds—here and there, close to, and in the distance, little white houses peeped from patches of cultivation on the mountain sides, looking like gems of civilisation in a setting of the wildest natural surroundings.

I strolled along enjoying the freedom and fresh air, occasionally passing some little cottage, surrounded by fields of beans in flower, loading the air with delightful perfume, and towards midday entered a small village. The people were intent on holiday-making, men, women, and children, were dressed in their best, and groups of old and young men were standing about talking over the prospect of the new year. My appearance at first was scarcely noticed beyond a passing salutation, with the compliments of the day. But as soon as it was known that I was a foreigner, a number of the elders of the village joined me, and in the name of the community, invited me to partake of tea and a smoke. Feeling somewhat fatigued with my walk, I was glad to take a seat on a bench, in front of the head man's house, while his wife, and some other female members of his family, brought out a table, and laid before me sweet cakes, walnuts, and honey, and handed round tea and tobacco. I was soon engaged in conversation with the old man; the whole village gathered round us, and I found enough to do in answering all their questions about the Se-yang-jen (men from the west). Such was the term applied to foreigners, and I did not once hear the opprobrious term yang-kwai-ts" used. I was treated with great kindness, and in return delighted them by sketching a few portraits of the children; which were handed round and immensely admired. Several females, at the command of their lords, brought me small presents of tobacco and walnuts, and when, after spending more than two hours with these kindly-disposed villagers, I rose to go, I did so amidst the generally expressed good wishes of them all. The head man and the patriarchs of the village, escorted me nearly a mile on the road back, where I bade them a final adieu, and went through a formal leave-taking with the head man, each of us bending the left knee, and raising our clasped hands to our foreheads. And his parting words were, that the visit of a foreign scholar on the first day of the year, was an omen of good for their village.

I learned from the people, that the harvests of wheat, barley, peas, and beans, are generally good in these mountains, while fruit, such as oranges, pomeloes, and walnuts, also grow abundantly. On this bank of the river, little silk is grown; but on the south bank, some distance inland, it is largely cultivated, and of a very fair quality. Some cocoons which I procured, and forwarded to Mr. James Hogg, of the firm of Messrs. Hogg Brothers, Shanghai, were pronounced a fair sample, but the web was not considered so good as that produced in Sz-chuan. In my walk, I observed on the mountain sides, numerous bushes of wild roses, and what I took to be myrtles, and a luxuriant growth of various ferns.

Several kinds of pheasants, foxes, wild goats, and boars, were described to me as denizens of the mountains, and snakes from 20 to 30 feet long are sometimes killed, but I heard of none that were poisonous. We met, about two miles from the boat, the Lowder and crew who, dreading some mishap, had come in search of us; they had evidently been keeping up the new year, for on seeing us, each in turn embraced me, swearing that their hearts had been sore on account of Ta-jen's absence. As I was really very tired, I was not at all sorry to get back to our boat, where Lowlee was waiting anxiously; and the good old fellow evinced great delight at my return, as he also had feared some accident. He had studied my taste, in preparing a roast fowl for dinner, to which I did ample justice; and so I ended my Chinese New Year's Day, as a Chinaman.

At Ichang we had taken in a passenger, but as he kept very quiet, and lived behind with the Lowder, I had not noticed him, until he wished me the compliments of the season in the morning before starting on my ramble. So, after dinner, I called him into the cabin to have a talk; he turned out to be a travelling bookseller, from the province of Kiang-see, on his way to Sz-chuan. He had travelled much in his native country, and I learned from him that the province of Kiang-see produces paper and wooden type cheaper than that of any other province in the Empire. The publishing trade confine themselves to the issue of dictionaries and collections of legends; our bookseller had several cases of such works, and wooden types on board, for which he informed me he would find a ready market in Chung Ching and Chen-tu, the capital of Sz-chuan. He would at the latter place lay in a return stock of novels and historical works, which he would dispose of at a large profit in Hoopeh, Kiang-see and the neighbouring provinces. On asking him why novels and historical works were cheaper in Sz-chuan than in his own province, he said, that as this province had for years been undisturbed by wars (except a few insignificant outbreaks) the people were rich and prosperous, and generally well-educated and fond of reading—novels especially. Chen-tu, the capital, boasts a celebrated college, which turns out more literary graduates than even that of Canton; and thus there is a constant demand for the reproduction of the standard historical works, which constitute the subject of examination.

The book and type trade throughout China, is a safe one, returning small but sure profits, and is one of the very few exempt from duty.

I showed him a copy of Blakiston's work, to his great delight; the illustrations appeared to astonish him, and he much admired the neatness and style of Mr. Murray's binding, and when quitting my cabin, begged leave to take it with him to examine the workmanship more closely.

Leaving our anchorage next morning at daylight, we tracked a considerable distance along the left bank, against a strong current, and about noon passed, without stopping, the fortified, but unimportant, town of Kwei-Chow. The country was more open, the mountains receding from the river, their sides clothed in many places with a kind of low scrub, resembling boxwood.

Above Kwei-Chow, we came to a long reach of the river, somewhat difficult to navigate; for the banks of sandstone, which rose perpendicularly from the water, presented a perfectly smooth face, without affording the least hold for boat-hooks, though above the higher water-mark, there were hundreds of holes drilled by sand martins.

A small path was cut out of the face of the rock for the trackers, and at projecting angles, large wooden rollers were let into the rock for the towing lines to slide on.

Towards the afternoon we reached the Tintan Rapid, which in winter is of considerable strength, but does not exist in summer, and near to the foot of the rapid I landed, and walked up to the head of it, where I sat down to smoke until my boat came up; and here for the first time I suffered rudeness from the people. Just above me a Chinese gunboat which had come from Hankow was lying at anchor; the mandarin, seeing me sitting on the bank, sent some of his men to inquire who I was. The fellows, on learning that I was a foreigner, went back with the information, and shortly returned with several others. They commenced throwing stones at me, and soon collected a crowd of junk-men, who, seeing the soldiers treating me in this manner under the eyes of a mandarin, fancied, I suppose, that I was lawful game, and commenced pelting me also. Seeing me thus beset, Philip and Lowlee rushed up in a great state of alarm, and the former, having the Hoopeh Viceroy's passport with him, hurried me off, amidst a shower of stones, to the gunboat, which we boarded. Walking up to the mandarin, who was lying in the stern, apparently enjoying the sight of my discomfiture, I sat down beside him and drew my revolver, which I quietly placed on my knee; Philip then asked him how he dared to see a foreigner carrying a Viceroy's pass molested by his crew. He read the passport, and immediately became very civil. He called his crew on board, rated them severely, evidently much to their astonishment, and ordered the crowd to disperse; he then begged me to excuse his men, and assured me that had they known who I was nothing would have happened. I, however, said that I would report him to the Viceroy at Chen-tu, to whom my passport was addressed, and insisted on his crew escorting me to the boat. He at once gave the order, and half a dozen fellows waited on me, and my boat having by this time ascended the rapid, they made way for me through the wondering crowd on shore, and did not leave me until I was on board, when they retired, very crest-fallen, before the crowd.

These gunboats are employed on preventive service, one

being stationed above or below every Customs station on the Yang-tsu, ready to give chase to any junk that may attempt to run past without having paid the legal and illegal duties imposed. This class of Customs boat is to be met with on all navigable rivers and creeks in China; they carry two guns, stern and bow chasers, and are manned by crews of from thirty to forty men, commanded by a mandarin of low rank. Like the soldiery on land, these fellows are most unscrupulous ruffians, the terror of all peaceable traders and travellers by water, levying black mail, or rather robbing defenceless junks whenever they can do so with impunity. I remember a party from one of these boats boarding my boat when on a shooting excursion in the Ta-hoo Lake, and one of them, thinking the foreigner was on shore, forced his way into the cabin to plunder, but unexpectedly encountered the yang-kwai-tsu, from whom he met with such a warm reception, that he retreated without delay over the bow into the water.

I felt much relieved when we were once more under way, while Philip and Lowlee commenced praying and telling their beads. The poor fellows were some time before they recovered their fright, and for the rest of the day were much depressed. I have no doubt that but for Philip's presence of mind in bringing the passport to my relief, I might have fared very roughly at the hands of these ruffianly gunboat sailors and excited junk-men, who, it appeared, belonged to a junk bound to Chung Ching from Hankow.

Just before dark we ascended the somewhat dangerous rapid of Nieu-kow, and anchored for the night just above it. We passed a great deal of the peculiar glazed sandstone mentioned by Blakiston, looking like large blocks of black lead, which when broken is a common dark sandstone. I have noticed sandstone wearing the same appearance on the banks of the Bramapootra, in the Mishmeë country.

The next day we passed Pah-tung, the last town of importance in the province of Hoopeh. It is a small town, built at the foot of a hill on the right bank, existing principally on its trade in coal, which is extensively worked in the neighbouring hills, and potatoes, which find a ready market in Hankow. From this point until we entered the Wu-shan Gorge the country was open, and the hills on each bank gradually receded in gentle slopes, which were carefully cultivated with peas, beans, wheat, Indian corn, and potatoes.

At noon we passed the village of Kwan-du-kow, situated at the mouth of the Wu-shan Gorge. For nearly a mile below the village we had to contend against a very strong rush of water, forming along each bank a continued rapid. The entrance of the Wu-shan Gorge is scarcely so remarkable for scenic effect as the Lukan Gorge, although at its mouth lofty perpendicular walls of blackish limestone present a very imposing aspect. This stone is exceedingly hard, and it was with great difficulty that I succeeded in knocking off a piece of it; the people in the neighbourhood call it iron-stone on account of its hardness. We happened to have a good breeze to enter the gorge, which enabled us to sail up a few miles to the village of Lam-min-yuen, where we anchored for the night.

We continued our voyage next day with a fair wind, and passed the boundary of Hoopeh, marked by a deep fissure in the mountains on the left bank, and on the right bank by a small mountain torrent, which runs into the river a few hundred yards above. From this point we gradually lost the breeze which we had carried with us all the morning, and in its place got a strong head wind, which compelled us to anchor at 2 P.M.

Just below our anchorage we passed under the wreck of a very large Sz-chuan junk, which from its position, ten feet above the level of the river, had apparently struck on a projecting rock and sunk stern foremost, during the summer flood.

Towards evening Philip, who had been all day complaining of indigestion, brought on by a surfeit of unripe pears and raw salted turnips, was seized with a violent attack of colic. He refused all medicine until, as he screamed with pain, I forced some chlorodyne down his throat. Lowlee protested against "foreign medicine," and, like a true Chinaman, sat with his face buried in his hands, moaning, and utterly useless. I stirred him up, and pointing to the kettle with a menacing gesture, made him at last comprehend that he must boil it. In the mean time Philip kept crying out that he was dying, and calling now upon the Virgin and saints to spare him, and now on dear Mr. "Copper" to save him.

By the use of actual force I got him to submit to the application of flannel steeped in boiling water, and the pain abating, he fell asleep, having first kissed my hand and blessed master's care of him. This was my first great anxiety; as I watched him till midnight, I had ample time to reflect on my possible situation should anything deprive me of his services. I realised forcibly how hitherto his attention had prevented my experiencing the slightest inconvenience from my ignorance of the language, and how disabled I should be without him. He at last awoke, and asked for more of the black medicine; I gave him thirty drops of chlorodyne, and he fell asleep again. Lowlee, whom Philip's partial recovery seemed to have restored to his senses, now signified his willingness to watch, and I thankfully availed myself of it.

Next morning I found Philip better in body, but desponding in mind. He said his brother-in-law had warned him that this journey would be his death. I wished him to take quinine as he was very feverish, but he objected, and Lowlee supported him, saying foreign medicines would "kill him." It suddenly struck me that fear of the enterprise had a good deal to do with Philip's illness, so I peremptorily forbade Lowlee to meddle further, and made Philip reluctantly swallow the dose, and he sulked all day, though apparently better. I was loath to believe that he was inclined to shirk the journey, but I now remembered that for the last two days he had messed with Lowlee instead of with myself, as he had previously been wont to do.

I felt convinced that the two were concocting some plan, and I anxiously mused over the chance of my interpreter's desertion; in which case I could not proceed, nor could I hope to reside with the missionaries in Chung Ching long enough to acquire such a colloquial mastery of the language as would render me independent of his aid.

About noon we reached Wu-shan-chien, a walled city on the left bank, just above the western entrance of the Wu-shan Gorge. As the Lowder's family lived here, he of course asked leave to remain for the rest of the day. Philip, accompanied by Lowlee, went on shore to the barber's, and returned in an hour or so, the former decidedly better; but I could see, now that my attention was aroused, that he was ill at ease, and seemed anxious to talk to me. So I proposed a walk on the river bank. We landed and strolled out of the city, and about a quarter of a mile beyond the wall sat down to smoke. The poor little fellow was very serious, and after one or two attempts to speak, blurted out that master was very kind, but he feared our undertaking was very dangerous. Every one spoke of the danger of passing through Yunnan, where the Mahomedans would be sure to catch us, and as certainly cut off our heads. And, besides, to the west of Sz-chuan there were numerous tribes of wild men, who killed every Chinaman that fell into their hands. I let him run on until he had exhausted his stock of information, and then simply replied that we could not depend on the tales of ignorant boatmen, but would satisfy ourselves as to the danger of proceeding when we had heard what the bishop at Chung Ching had to say. Reassured by this, he seemed suddenly to brighten up.

As we were returning towards the city we met a very pretty girl walking out with her brother, and as we passed her, my little dog Zeila, a tiny but accomplished black and tan terrier, ran up to her and stood on its hind legs, performing various antics for the purpose of attracting attention. The girl, on seeing it, exclaimed to her brother that it was a yang-gow, "foreign dog," and stooping down took Zeila in her arms. I stopped and sat down on the side of the road near her, and through Philip asked her many questions; to which she replied without the least embarrassment, but with a pleasing air of modesty. My little dog greatly interested her, and on its leaving her and coming to me, she caressed it while it lay in my lap. She had been on a visit to the city with her brother, and was returning up the mountain to her home. I was much struck with the confidence she displayed towards me; even on learning that I was a foreigner, she did not appear the least afraid, and I could not resist asking her how it was that she did not fear the Yang-jen, when she replied, "Old men like you are too old for girls to fear;" but added, that had I been a young man, the custom of her country would have prevented her, an unmarried woman, from speaking to me. On taking leave of her, I told Philip to wish her a good husband for me, and she in return wished me a pleasant journey. Here again I had been taken for an old man—for a grandfather, 'as Philip said. So much had shaving my head and beard altered me, that youth had disappeared, and spectacles had completed the change, by giving me a venerable appearance. My lady visitors in Sha-s^u had spoken of me to Philip as his kind *old* master, and several times during my walks on shore I had been asked by men if I had any sons in Sz-chuan. From this time, as long as I travelled in China, I assumed the character of an elderly man. It was an unexpected incident of travel, thus suddenly to step from youth to age; but I maintained the latter character throughout my journey in China Proper without the least apparent effort.

We did not leave Wu-shan until 10 A.M. next day, and at 1 P.M. ascended the Tung-kan-tz^u Rapid, at this time of the year a dangerous place for navigation, but presenting no obstacle in summer. We continued our course through a succession of small rapids until 6 P.M., when we moored to the left bank for the night, about twenty miles below the city Qui-foo. The country on either side was open and undulating, and covered with growing crops of wheat, barley, peas, beans, and poppy, the latter now about two inches above ground. The river banks in many places consisted of large boulders of hard clay-stone, broken with difficulty, but when broken splintering into pieces about half an inch square; others, of the same formation, were quite brittle, crumbling under pressure of the fingers.

Our boat had rough work all day, very often she was pulled bodily over rocks, thumping and grinding in an alarming manner, so much so, that I remonstrated with the Lowder, who, however, only laughed, and informed me that the wood of the Wan-chien boat could stand a great deal of this kind of work without damage, and I must say, in spite of the rough usage, she appeared quite uninjured.

Philip was decidedly better this evening, and discussed cheerfully our prospects of reaching Calcutta. While we sipped our tea, he grew quite communicative, and told me a wonderful story of five tea-trees, which grow on the Chusan island, in the Tung-ting Lake, and produce tea of an extraordinary description, with a leaf of great size, one being sufficient to brew ten cups of strong tea. All the tea manufactured from these trees is sent to Pekin for the Emperor, whose personal property the island is considered to be, and as such is guarded by imperial soldiers.

The trees, which grow near a small fountain of water, annually give an immense yield of leaf, and it is supposed that the waters of the fountain influence the growth of the trees, as slips or roots transplanted to other soils always die.

Next morning we entered Fungsiang, or Wind-box Gorge, remarkable for the spacious caverns scooped out beneath the overhanging cliffs, in which the fishermen snugly lie-to, and ply the universal scoop-net. On issuing from the gorge, we sighted Qui-foo on the left bank, and passed a temporary village built on the now dry shingly margin of the river. This place presented a very busy scene; hundreds of men and women were engaged in boiling salt, there being several brine springs existing near the low water-line, which are worked only in the winter months, from November to March, and are covered during the summer rise.

The wells were sunk about twelve feet and boarded, forming a kind of shaft, from the bottom of which four naked fellows handed up the salt water to others standing on a stage half-way up, who in turn handed it to others on the bank, from whence it was carried to small mud reservoirs near pans placed over mud-built fire-places; the fuel used being very fine bright coal, brought in abundance from the surrounding neighbourhood. These salt-works belong to government, and are a source of considerable revenue to the chief mandarin at the city of Qui-foo, who, by means of the "squeeze" system common amongst his class, pockets enormous sums. The pans yield on an average 1000 piculs per diem, which is sold at 32 chen per catty. I landed and spent more than half an hour looking over the works and then started for my boat, which had gone ahead, and before I caught her up, had anchored off the custom-house at Qui-foo. Here I found Philip in a towering rage, surrounded by some half-dozen custom-house officials, who were demanding the sum of 750 chen before giving the permit necessary to pass the gunboat stationed above the city. They had seen the British consul's passport, which they however treated with the greatest contempt. On my arrival they retired, saying, they would return in half an hour for the chen. I, therefore, dispatched Lowlee with the Viceroy's pass to the mandarin, who, doubtless being a party to the squeeze, referred him to the officials who had already visited us, and they returned with him, demanding to be paid at once on pain of having my boxes broken open. On this I ordered Philip to count out the chen, and placed them on a box in front of me, and desired the mandarin to produce a receipt stamped with the seal of the custom-house. This he refused to give, and triumphantly placed his hand on the chen; but he had reckoned without his host, for I removed his hand, saying, it was not my custom to pay money without getting a receipt. The fellow became very angry, and ordered us to open our boxes. I said that my boxes were ready, and having unlocked them myself, I told him to begin. At the same time producing my note-book, I asked his name, and declined further conversation. He commenced to pull one of my boxes about, but soon desisted, and laughing, said it was all fun; but it was customary for passengers to make the customs' officials a present, and if I would give him 360 chen it would be all right. I simply replied by a request that he would proceed with the search; but the whole lot took themselves off, and returned in a few minutes with another mandarin of higher grade. He having first requested permission to enter my boat, asked for the Viceroy's pass. On reading it, he said I must excuse what had happened, but that a present was customary, and if I would give something it would be all right. So I paid a person calling himself a broker 160 chen, saying, that had I been asked civilly for a present at first I would have given it. The mandarin then called another officer, who accompanied us to the gunboat, and having passed us, took his leave. I have mentioned this little adventure with the customs' official only as an illustration of the difficulty a traveller would experience in travelling in the interior of China without any other document than a passport given him by a consul, and I firmly believe, that in the absence of the Viceroy's pass, I should have run a great risk of being often maltreated, if not altogether prevented from prosecuting my journey.

Qui-foo is a city of the first grade, and the first customs' station on the Yang-ts", after entering the province of Sz-chuan. It is pleasantly situated on the left bank of the river, and contains many fine joss-houses and temples. The country surrounding it is very fertile, producing opium and sugar in large quantities; the best coal in the province is also found in the district of which Qui-foo is the chief city.

I was glad to get clear of Qui-foo, and we did not anchor for the night, until we had reached a point some miles above the city.

Next day we ascended the Tung-yan Rapid, which is considered by Chinamen, at this season, one of the most dangerous, so much so that here also a mandarin is stationed to see that boats partly unload their cargo, and that all passengers disembark before shooting the rapid. Just before we arrived, a large junk, laden with cotton, in trying to ascend had struck on a sunken rock and gone down, within ten yards of the spot; she had been buoyed up by four large boats, and her crew were busy baling out the water. She was very much damaged, and even while her crew were busy at work about her, numbers of wreckers were deliberately pillaging her spars and cargo, while her owner, a Sz-chuan merchant, sat by utterly helpless. I believe, however, that there is some custom on the upper Yang-ts^u, by virtue of which, the people of the neighbourhood claim part of all wrecks that come to shore.

There were extensive works in course of progress for improving this rapid; large embankments were in process of construction on the left bank, and masses of rocks, appearing above the surface of the water, were being blasted by way of deepening the bed of the river. The expense of the work, which had been in progress for several years, was defrayed by contributions levied on the owners of junks and cargoes passing up and down, and this contribution will be levied until the work is finished; when that will be it is difficult to say, as the several mandarins, under whose supervision it is carried on, reap a grand harvest of wealth from it, as I was informed that fully two-thirds of the annual amount raised for the work goes into their pockets.

We had a capital breeze with us after ascending this rapid, and by the time we moored for the night had made a run of more than forty miles since the morning. Between the Tung-Yan Rapid and the town of Yung-yan-chien, the river banks for more than a mile, rose in a regular line of pyramidal hills, about 300 feet high, with bases of equal dimensions, each in succession presenting a uniformly scarped face, while the sides sloped, at exact and uniform angles, down to the intervening ravines; the whole formation, in its apparently artificial regularity, being one of the most remarkable scenes so far met with on the Yang-ts", which here narrows to fifty yards in width, and is very deep. I felt strongly inclined to christen this Pyramid Gorge, but for my intense objection to substitute English names for the Chinese designations; every part of the river already having its native significant name in use amongst the boatmen.

Two days' journey through a fine country, with well tilled fields of peas, beans, and poppy, brought us to Wan-chien. This city is conspicuous from the river for its picturesque appearance; two very fine joss-houses adorn its eastern and western suburbs, which occupy a considerable extent of the river bank.

Wan-chien chiefly derives its importance from being an opium market, to which large quantities of the drug are brought for shipment to Chung Ching. We happened to arrive just as the great annual new-year procession was moving along the river banks, attended by hundreds of people dressed in their holiday clothes. An old law or custom obliges all the chief officials to take part in this procession in full state costume, and so strong is the public feeling on the matter, that ill-health, or the death of a parent, could alone be sufficient to excuse the absence of any officer, no matter how high his rank.

One of the chief objects in the procession, was an immense figure of a dragon, some fifty feet long, carried on poles by a number of grotesquely dressed men, who by moving their bamboo poles, caused the figure to imitate the undulating motion of a serpent. Numerous bands of musicians accompanied the procession, whose music combined with the shouts of the crowd to produce a deafening noise.

As a procession of this sort naturally excites the people, I gave orders to proceed, much against the wish of our boatmen, but a present of 200 chen overcame their objections; and we proceeded up-stream, after having laid in a few provisions, and hired another boatman in the place of one who left us.

Towards sun-down we reached the little Hu Rapid. Though there would have been little danger in ascending it by daylight, our task was not so easy, as it was nearly dark, and the wind blew a perfect hurricane up-stream; we dared not approach the shore, the river was a perfect boiling cauldron, and our men were obliged to jump from the boat on to the rocks, and so doing fell into the water, without any damage, however, beyond a wetting, and being knocked about by the waves. As soon as the men had landed, and commenced tracking us up the rapid, I perceived that our position was becoming dangerous; it was quite dark, and the wind howled so loudly, that the boatmen on shore could not hear the bowman, and before I had time to finish taking off my heavy garments, we struck heavily on a sunken rock, and broached broadside to the stream; how we got clear of the rock, I don't know, for we were free by the time I had succeeded in getting off my long coat; but our boat was half full of water, and still out in the centre of the rapid. With the increased weight in her, our coolies could not make way against the current, and we had to wait for nearly a quarter of an hour, until half-a-dozen villagers came to our assistance; the darkness was increasing, and every moment seemed an age, until we were clear of the rapid, and in still water. Fortunately for us our boat was strong; had she been stove, we should have gone, and nothing could have saved us. The Lowder had underestimated the strength of the current, and fancied that our men could haul the boat up without assistance, in which he was deceived; but he, and also the bowman, proved themselves staunch fellows, for they were cool and quiet throughout the whole accident.

As my bed and everything were wet, I was not sorry to get on shore, and take my dinner in a little tea-house on the river bank, frequented by boatmen, and by midnight my blankets were dry enough to turn into.

Starting early next morning, we passed several villages, their little white houses looking very clean and nice, with many detached dwellings embosomed in gardens and orchards of orange trees; in fact, this style of single homesteads and cultivation seemed to have superseded the small clusters of houses, and formed a peculiar feature of the country. The river bed, wherever exposed in long shingly beaches, was, in many places, converted into gold washings; a great many men were busy in gold seeking, which, as far as I could learn, seemed to return but scanty profit, and those employed in washing appeared, as a rule, very old and poor.

Towards evening we passed the village of Shi-pow-chai, with its famous seven-storied pagoda, built like a staircase against a huge square rock, the upper story communicating with other temple buildings on the summit, while the village nestles round the base of the terrace on which it stands.

Nothing could be more charming than the successive views of the fertile country from Shi-pow-chai to our halting-place for the night. The hill-sides running up from the river were literally covered with groves of orange and pumiloe trees, while peach and pear-trees were white with blossom near every little white house, many of which peeped out from the foliage, recalling to mind scenes that I remember seeing in Wales when a boy. The river above Shi-pow-chai opens out considerably, and must in the summer-rise average for several miles more than half a mile in width. On leaving our anchorage next morning we entered a very wide reach of the river, which was divided into numerous channels by ledges of flat rocks, about six feet out of water. This part of the river is exceedingly dangerous in summer on account of these then submerged reefs.

In the afternoon we arrived at the small town of Chung, one of the prettiest towns on the Yang-ts^u. It contains numbers of pagodas, temples, three-storied houses, and ya-muns, which, seen from the river, peeping out of the luxuriant foliage in and about the town, compose a very pleasing picture.

We had not anchored more than half an hour before several Chinese Christians entered our boat, and among them a student of the Mission school. This young man politely invited me to come with him to see the Chinese priest, who resided in the town.

Having accompanied the student to the Mission-house, I was most kindly received by the Father, who was a fine specimen of an educated Chinaman. He was an elderly man, with a long white beard, stately and venerable in appearance, with grave and courteous manners.

After conversing with me awhile, during which I learnt that he had been educated in Rome, he ordered me some port wine and cake. The wine was a great treat, and my evident enjoyment of it caused him to smile. While we were conversing, several merchants came on a visit. Having heard of the arrival of a foreigner, they had concluded that I must be a Father, and on entering the room each of them came up, and, bending his knee, asked for my blessing. When told that I was not a Father they appeared surprised, but did not in any way alter their respectful behaviour. After an hour or two spent at the Mission, I bade good-bye to the Father, and strolled through the city with the young student and Philip. The cleanliness of the town was remarkable. The temples were very fine buildings, gorgeously decorated with carved work, and resplendent with gilding and colour. Our young guide led us to the Ya-mun, and would have taken me in to see the mandarin, whom he described as a very great friend of the missionaries, but I refrained from troubling him, as such visits are generally costly, owing to the custom of giving presents.

In many shops I noticed abundance of cotton piece-goods for sale, and much opium. I observed for the first time in Chung a custom which, though I believe it to be common in China, I had never heard of or noticed before. At the corners of streets, in niches at the ends of houses, were long white deal boxes, which I learned were coffins; and on asking why they were so placed there, I was told that they were provided by the various city wards for the purpose of burying paupers, of whom, I was glad to learn, few were to be found in Chung. The town was well built, and the wall surrounding it in thorough repair. Altogether, I was struck with the general well-to-do air of the place, which on a closer view does not disappoint the expectations raised by its imposing appearance as seen from the river.

Its superiority in this respect, as contrasted with the general dirt and neglect of Chinese towns, can only be attributed to the influence of the Christians, who comprise nearly one-third of the population, and chiefly belong to the wealthier classes, which, I may say, have furnished most of the converts through Sz-chuan.

I learnt with great regret that the tale which Blakiston's Lowder had told us about the drowning of the young Father was too true. It appeared that in ascending one of the rapids he was holding on to the tow-rope, by which the junk was being dragged up, when it broke, and the recoil threw him overboard into the middle of the rapid, when he sank, and was never seen again. One of his companions jumped over after him, and was nearly drowned in his efforts to save him. This piece of news seemed to affect Philip and Lowlee considerably, and the former, when turning in, again complained of being ill. Just before I retired for the night, the Chinese father sent me two fowls and a basket of delicious little sponge cakes as a present, and I sent him in return a bar of common brown soap and half a dozen wax candles, articles of rare value in the eyes of native Christians. Foreign soap is a luxury highly prized by all Chinese, and I was asked for it whenever I went on shore. The common soap of China is a very coarse article, made of tallow mixed with ashes, and sometimes from the soap nut, and very expensive; the soap nut is principally used by the poorer classes in Sz-chuan for washing clothes, for which purpose only soap in any form is used, as the people never employ it to wash their persons.

We left Chung next morning, continuing through a well-cultivated country. The fragrance of the bean flowers was delightful. The last few days' travel had brought us into

SZ-CHUAN QUARRYMEN.

quite another climate. In place of the cold, piercing winds from snow-capped mountains, we had now delightful balmy breezes laden with delicious perfume, while the hills were smiling with luxuriance, cultivated to their very summits.

The day after leaving Chung we passed without stopping, the city of Fung-chien. Near the river were numerous quarries, where numbers of quarrymen were hard at work, some dressing the blocks, and others splitting large masses of sandstone into squares by means of iron wedges and huge iron hammers, weighing from twenty to thirty pounds. I watched the stone-splitters at their work, in which they displayed great dexterity, each man selecting a huge piece of sandstone free from cracks, bored small holes about three inches deep and eighteen apart, marking the outline of the square block required; he then inserted a wedge-shaped piece of iron into each hole, and struck them in rotation until the stone split, leaving a large square block fit for dressing with mallet and chisel. The use of the hammers requires great expertness, as the handles are made of flexible cane, about the thickness of one's finger, and four feet in length. The hammer is allowed to hang between the workman's legs, his body is then moved to and fro till the hammer swings over his head, and is then by a sudden jerk brought down with tremendous force on the wedge, each blow being accompanied by a loud "ugh."

In the evening we anchored at the walled city of Fu-chow above the mouth of the Kung-tan-ho, a small river which flows into the Yang-ts^u on the right bank. This river is navigable all the year round for several days' journey, and is the highway of a considerable trade, judging from the numbers of large junks lying at its mouth. There is a peculiarity of build in these vessels by which they are known from others. At a certain point of the river Kung-tan-ho there is a narrow passage, in which a rock projects over the stream; and, to enable the junks to pass, they are built with a twist in the stern that gives them a curving, one-sided appearance. As we were leaving Fu-chow, after making a few purchases in the way of provisions, a fire broke out amongst the wooden houses built along the river bank outside the city wall. It burned with such rapidity that, before we were fairly out of sight of the town, it had made a clean sweep of every house along the bank for more than 200 yards.

Next day we intended anchoring for the night at the city of Chung Chow; but, in bringing-to, we ran into another boat, and did her considerable damage. Of course, there was a dreadful row between the two crews; and the Lowder of the damaged boat demanded 100 taels' compensation; but after a long talk, consented to take twenty, five of which our Lowder paid down and promised the balance in the morning; and this arrangement having been made, the other Lowder retired to his boat, and all was again quiet. Just, however, as I was about to turn in, I heard our men moving quietly about the boat, and shortly after I felt we were under weigh. Rousing Philip, I strongly objected to travelling in the dark; but the Lowder had made up his mind to evade the promised payment in the morning, and on we went, feeling our way in the dark. After pulling about two miles, we came to a small rapid, and our fellows jumped on shore with the tow-rope, and commenced hauling; but we stuck half way. The Lowder begged Philip and Lowlee to help the crew, and I turned out with them; but all our efforts proved unavailing. The current was too strong, and the bank was so precipitous that we could not get fair foot-hold in the dark. We could not venture to descend the rapid again for fear of the numerous rocks; and there was nothing for it but to make fast where we were, and we had the pleasure of trying all night to sleep while the water boiled and roared about us. We were lying in a strong eddy inside the rush of water, and every few minutes our boat was swung round like a top, and was only saved from being completely smashed by two of the men keeping a sharp look-out at the bow and stern. Our position, at last, became so dangerous that I landed, and sat on the rocks smoking till daylight, and on its first appearance we all set to work manfully, and succeeded in getting up the rapid. The river here made a sharp curve; and while the boat was rounding the bend, wishing to enjoy the beautiful morning, I walked across the country to meet her. A little path led us through very beautiful country: sometimes we walked through patches of sugar-cane, eight and nine feet high; then through fields of beans all in flower, affording a rich repast to myriads of honey bees; while the wheat and barley, all dibble-sown, according to the immemorial practice of Chinese agriculturists, were a foot high, and very luxuriant. In fact, the whole country now—in the month of February—wore the appearance of spring as seen in the month of May about the neighbourhood of Shanghai. Large patches of poppy, more than half a foot high, were distinguished by their lovely green appearance; while numbers of the little white farm-houses lent an additional charm to the landscape.

Entering some of these cottages in quest of a drink of tea and a light, I could not help contrasting their extremely dirty interior with their pleasingly clean exterior. Inside, pigs were lying under tables and in corners of the rooms; while children, dogs, fowls, and ducks indiscriminately occupied the dirty mud floors. This Irish style of interior is common everywhere in China amongst the agricultural population, but is certainly more remarkable amongst the people of Sz-chuan, who are exceedingly well off, and pay so much attention to outside appearances. By noon we passed the large village of Lo-shih, on the left bank; and on the neighbouring hills I observed a great many iron-smelting furnaces, the country being exceedingly rich in this metal.

About 6 P.M., we anchored for the night at the village of Hutung, surrounded by beautifully fertile country, and less than a day's walk from Chung Ching. After dinner Philip and myself indulged in one of our usual nightly conversations, which generally followed my lesson in the colloquial Chinese. He was particularly communicative : the prospect of reaching Chung Ching on the morrow having temporarily dispelled his illness and low spirits. Our conversation turned on Chinese conjurors—a class of strolling blackguards, both clever and numerous. From this subject we came to the supernatural; and he then related to me how certain people in China communicate with spirits. A mode common amongst women is as follows: on the thirteenth day of the first moon the female spiritualists shut themselves up in a room; a bamboo basket, something like our clothes' basket, is placed upside down on a table, with a chopstick laid on the bottom; two women grasp the lower rim with their right hands, while a third, (the medium, I suppose!) bowing her face to the ground, continues crying out, "Have you come yet? have you come yet?" After some time spent thus the spirit's presence is announced by the rapping of the chopstick on the basket; he is then interrogated as to the age of those present, which he tells correctly by a rap for every year. Other questions are then put, generally relative to the prospect of a husband or of children. When I heard this story it struck me so much as like the reproduction of our own spiritualists' séances, that I fancied Philip might be exercising his powers of sarcasm; but, after questioning him very closely, I could not doubt that he was relating to me what he considered a fact, while he assured me that he had never heard of foreigners indulging in this amusement. He informed me that the practice was considered low amongst the Chinese, and that few people indulged in it, as they were afraid, and many Chinese, whom I have spoken to on the subject, appeared to be well aware of the practice, and to believe in the communication with spirits; but they invariably spoke of such doings as bad and disreputable.

Many men also gain the reputation of demoniacal possession; the presence of the demon in them is manifested by a display of preternatural powers, the energumene breaking thick bars of iron, handling red-hot masses of metal, eating crockery, and writing on paper without touching it, simply by describing the characters in the air, after which the paper is held to the fire and the writing appears. These tricks, however, are evidently mere legerdemain; but the basket-rapping struck me as worthy of description, as it so much resembles our table-rapping at home.

Next morning we started at daylight, and, passing through a hilly country, by noon entered Blakiston's "Iron Gorge," where numerous columns of smoke marked the place of iron-smelting furnaces; and by 2 P.M., we sighted the tops of pagodas and junk-masts at Chung Ching, where we arrived at 3·15, and anchored in the Chung Ching river, which enters the Yang-ts^u from the left bank, and divides the town of Li-min from the city of Chung Ching.

Immediately on arrival I dispatched Philip and Lowlee with my letters of introduction to the Catholic bishop residing here. After an absence of two hours, Philip returned with a message from Monseigneur Desfleches, to the effect that his house was at my disposal; but as I should have to receive many visitors, if I would wait until the morning he would procure me a mandarin's house for myself. Philip further informed me that his lordship had received a letter from Monsieur Dabry, in which I was described as a government confidential agent on my way to open a trade route through Burmah. From this the good bishop thought I was a man of great consequence, who would require a very grand residence in Chung Ching, and expressed his intention of visiting me on the morrow. Fortunately, however, for me Lowlee remained at the palace over-night, and having no doubt had his instructions from the good father, G. de Carli, fully explained my position to the bishop. Early next morning he returned to the boat, bringing with him the bishop's chair and bearers, and a message to the effect that rooms were ready for me at an hotel in the city. Proceeding thither I took up my quarters, glad at last to escape from the boat. Our journey from Sha-s" to Chung Ching had occupied twenty-five days, making a total of twenty-nine from Hankow, an average passage for a small boat at that time of the year. Before proceeding further with my narrative, I must trouble the reader with a few remarks on the great river and its navigation, which I leave at this point to continue my journey by land.

The Yang-ts", from its great length, depth, and enormous trade, may be assigned a prominent place amongst the great rivers of the world. Taking its rise in Thibet north of the latitude of Lhássa, it follows an east course for some distance under the name of Kincha-kiang, or Gold Sand River, and then turning sharp, it flows for more than 300 miles due south, until, reaching the Province of Yunnan, it again flows eastward, augmented by the Ya-long-kiang, by a somewhat tortuous course of more than 1800 miles to the sea, under the names of Yang-ts"-kiang and Ta-kiang, or Great River, the latter being applied to it after its junction with the Ya-long.

As Swi-foo may be practically regarded as the terminus of river-borne trade, very few boats ascending further, and none being able to proceed beyond Pei-cha, we may consider that the river from this to the sea, following the broadly-marked divisions of the hilly and champaign countries traversed by it, is divided into the Upper and Lower Yang-ts^u, the first name being given to the stream as it forces its way amongst the hills of Sz-chuan through a succession of rapids and gorges, terminating at Ichang, 600 miles from Swi-foo.

From the entrance of the Ichang Gorge it broadens into the majestic stream which rolls its waters for 1000 miles through the plains of Hoopeh, Ngnan-hoei and Kiang-see to the sea.

The Upper Yang-ts^u receives several navigable tributaries, the Kung-tan-ho on the right bank, and on the left the Hotow, sometimes called Limin or Chung Ching river, at the city of that name, and the Min at the city of Swi-foo.

The Kung-tan-ho and Limin are navigable during the whole year for junks drawing five feet water, the first for nearly sixty miles into the interior of Kwei-chew Province; and the second as far as the city of Chong Ching. During the summer months the ordinary Sz-chuan junks ascend the Min to Chen-tu, the capital of Sz-chuan, and all the year round to the city of Kia-ting-foo, about two-thirds of the distance between Chen-tu and Chung Ching, which last is the emporium of all the trade in Western China. To this centre all the large traders from the principal marts of Yunnan, Kwei-chew, and Sz-chuan are obliged to bring their merchandize before they can obtain the Sycee silver to buy foreign goods, the trade in which is held by the Chung Ching merchants as a monopoly; thus the richest products of

Sz-chuan, such as silk, the so-called vegetable wax, sugar, and opium find their way to Chung Ching.

The means of navigation on the Upper Yang-tsu, as already described, is the common flat-bottomed square-bowed junk, propelled sometimes by oars, but generally by tracking. The task of ascending the dangerous rapids requires considerable skill and fortitude, beyond which few difficulties occur to interfere with the constant traffic passing up and down.

Over the worst of the eight principal rapids there were six feet of water when I ascended in February during a remarkably dry season. Want of water, therefore, can never interfere with an improved mode of navigation, and I think that, with a little expenditure of capital and engineering skill, the Upper Yang-tsu might be made perfectly safe for properly constructed steamers, and indeed, in its present condition, I can see no obstacle that would prevent such a steamer reaching Chung Ching. I venture to express this opinion, though contrary to that given by Mr. Dawson,* on the simple ground that where a loaded junk of 120 tons burden can ascend, a boat with the aid of steam could perform the same feat, though she might require the additional assistance of towing in some rapids. There are several hundred miles comparatively free from rapids, where the junks are propelled by oars, or slowly tugged along by trackers, at a snail's pace, whereas a powerful steamer could easily make six miles an hour. Stress has been laid on the fact that the descent would present the most serious difficulty in the way of steam navigation; but without pretending to any practical knowledge of the navigation of vessels amongst rapids, I would hazard the remark that steamers adapted to such navigation could shoot a rapid as safely as a junk of the same size, and

* *Vide* Consul Swinhoe's Report, 1870.

I fully believe with Captain Blakiston, that an attempt, such as has not yet been made, to ascend the Upper Yang-ts^u in a "high-power light-draught steamer, with double engines and disconnected paddle-wheels, especially constructed for river navigation," would prove successful, and open a new channel for British commercial enterprise.

For the purpose of developing the trade of Sz-chuan and securing it to the British merchants at Hankow and Shanghai, steam navigation is of great importance. Exports from Chung Ching will naturally find their way to the Hankow market, by descending the Yang-ts^u in from eight to ten days, in preference to seeking a market in Burmah viâ Tali-foo and Bhamo, by an overland journey of several hundred miles. As to the produce, therefore, of the Sz-chuan and Kwei-chew provinces, our Chinese merchants need never fear the competition of the British merchant in Burmah, save in the event of a maritime war; nor after the introduction of steam on the Upper Yang-ts^u, need they be at all uneasy as to their trade in piece-goods with Sz-chuan. The province of Yunnan will probably give her trade in imports (and exports if she has any that will find a market) to Rangoon by some direct route, such as that advocated by Captain R. Sprye, to Burmah; but beyond that province it seems difficult to conceive what further advantage Burmah will reap from communication with Western China.

At present there remains but one great step to be taken by our China merchants to secure to themselves the whole trade of Eastern, Central, and Western China (exclusive of Yunnan), and that is the introduction of steamers on the Upper Yang-ts^u. The abundance of coal, worked and unworked, in Sz-chuan secures the necessary supply of fuel on the spot; and the city of Qui-foo, situated about midway between Ichang and Chung Ching, would be admirably suited for a coaling depôt. Before quitting this subject, on which I do not wish to be thought to speak as a nautical authority, I would refer my readers to the able paper read by Consul Swinhoe before the Royal Geographical Society, and published in extenso in their Journal, giving the results of the most recent expedition on the Upper Yang-tsu. They will there find much more accurate and scientific observations on the navigability of the river than it was in my power to make as a simple *Chinese* traveller.

CHAPTER IV.

CHUNG CHING.

The First Check—Reception of the Bishop—My Friend Fan—Taouist Rock Temples—Dinner with the Taou Jen—Decay of Chinese Art—A Royal Courier—The Sz-chuan Missions—Chinese Persecutions—Missionary Life—Respect paid to the Fathers—Boys' and Girls' Schools—Discouragement of Merchants—Chinese Theatre.

THE city of Chung Ching, at which I had now arrived, may be aptly described as the Liverpool of Western China. It is a walled city of the first rank, containing with its extensive suburbs, a population of about two hundred and fifty thousand inhabitants, whose dwellings cover the slope of a hill, forming a point at the junction of the Hotow river, with the Yang-ts^u. On the opposite bank of the Hotow, stands the smaller city of Li-min, from which the river often takes its name. Altbough the city of Chen-tu, as the residence of the Shai-tai or Viceroy, and head-quarters of the Provincial Government, holds the first rank, yet politically Chung Ching is of great importance, as it contains the imperial treasury, where all the revenue of the province is received and stored, and the office of the paymaster of the Western Frontier Army, under the administration of an official appointed direct from Pekin, independently of the Viceroy.

Numerous roads from all parts lead to this great Emporium, which also has water-communication with all the principal cities of Yunnan, Kwei-cheu, and Sz-chuan. Twice a year, that is just after the Chinese New Year, and again after the subsidence of the summer floods, the port is crowded with hundreds of junks, lying in tiers off the river banks. This scene on our arrival presented an appearance of bustling activity, which at once impressed me with an idea of the enormous trade carried on in this great inland mart. About a day's sail below the port, we had encountered more than a hundred junks, the first instalment of the downward bound fleet, which annually leaves just after the New Year. This is considered a lucky period, and the junks starting at this time with their cargoes of produce, are able to accomplish their return voyage from Hankow, before the navigation is impeded by the summer floods. Very little traffic takes place at that season, owing as well to the want of freight, as to the increased labour and danger of the voyage. After the floods, the junks start on their second downward voyage, returning by the New Year, thus accomplishing the journey to Hankow and back twice in the twelve months.

 The Chung Ching merchants have the reputation of being the richest in China, and their credit is established in the remotest part of the empire, while the Sycee silver bearing the local marks of this city, on account of its purity unalloyed by copper, is gladly taken at a considerable premium; in every other province, the Chung Ching "shoes," as the ingots of silver (which from their shape appear to have been moulded in a diminutive pie dish) are commonly called, are easily distinguishable by their smallness of size from the larger and more alloyed Sycee of other towns. The landlord of the hotel, having received advice of my coming from the bishop's messengers, was ready to give me a civil reception, and a comfortable breakfast was speedily served by the chef-de-cuisine of the establishment. My new quarters were a great improvement on my first experience of Chinese hotels at Sha-s"; the apartments were roomy and clean, the house being reserved for the exclusive use of mandarins, one or two of which class, with their families, were staying there at the time.

Having settled myself in my new quarters, I had leisure to calculate the chances for and against the successful prosecution of my enterprise. Philip was evidently wavering, if not altogether disinclined to proceed; but his decision would be, I knew, mainly influenced by the wish of Monseigneur Desfleches; Lowlee had already said he would not proceed beyond Chung Ching, at which point, his engagement to act as guide terminated.

The consistent reports, current everywhere of the successes of the Mahomedan rebels in Yunnan, had made it too probable, that the route to Likiang-foo was impracticable; this would entail the abandonment of my original project of taking the comparatively straight line from Likiang to Sudiya, on the Bramapootra. The only other chance of reaching India, seemed to be by striking northwards to Chen-tu, to which point my route was rendered secure, by the passport addressed to the Viceroy there resident, and thence through Thibet to Nepaul. Had I possessed anything like an ample supply of funds, this change in my route would have caused me little concern, for I had but a slight idea of other obstacles which were destined to prove insurmountable. Time and distance were nothing to me. As it was, this change of route, involving an unknown amount of expense, was a subject of serious and somewhat anxious contemplation. However, the thought of retreat did not enter my mind, and the flattering vision of success gradually dispelled all forebodings; and when in the afternoon, Father Deschamps arrived with an invitation to the palace, I met him cheerfully, and spoke with such apparent certainty of proceeding, that the good missionary clapped me on the shoulder, saying, "You Englishmen are brave men, and make light of difficulties, but there are many before you."

I was soon following the Father through the city, in the bishop's close chair. As the palace was at some distance, there was a good opportunity of noticing the aspect of the streets thronged with people, intent on business. Many streets appeared to consist entirely of shops devoted to one particular branch of trade, and but for the Chinese lettering on the advertising boards hanging outside, and the Chinamen inside, there was little to distinguish them from the ordinary London shops. In several streets, nothing but foreign piece-goods were exposed for sale; others were full of watchmakers' shops, the windows stocked with cheap foreign watches and American clocks. In fact, we seemed to pass from Goldsmiths' Square along Toy Shop Lane, through Draper Street into Butchers' Lane, and then along Bird Street, where live pheasants, wild ducks and geese, and song-birds were kept in bamboo cages, and then into Bootmakers' Square, up Bakers' Hill, down Greengrocers' Hill, along Mandarins' Gardens to the Bishops' Palace. This was a fine building, purely Chinese in architecture, and richly ornamented with carving and gilding. Having entered through the grand porch, we proceeded through two large outer halls, and were set down at the inner folding-doors. Here Monseigneur Desfleches, habited as a high-class mandarin, received me with kindly courtesy, scrupulously observing, however, the punctilious ceremonial prescribed by Chinese etiquette; I might have imagined myself in the presence of a Christian Shai-tai, especially as his costume was of the green colour, which none below that rank presume to wear.

Refreshments were served in an inner room, and we at once entered on a discussion of my plans. Having first clearly explained to him, that the British Government was not in any way interested in my project, I requested his advice as to the best route for reaching India. He replied, that if I was resolved to attempt the Likiang route, he would gladly give me a letter to the Bishop at Swi-foo, but cautioned me at the same time, that in his opinion the Mahomedan rebellion rendered such an attempt hopeless. He then described three other routes : 1, direct to Talifoo in Yunnan, and thence to Bhamo on the Irrawady, which however, was closed for the same reason ; 2, through Chen-tu viâ Ta-tsian-loo, Lithang and Bathang in Eastern Thibet, to Sudiya on the Bramapootra * ; and 3, the same route to Bathang, thence diverging in a north-westerly direction, through Central Thibet, into the Indian frontier district of Darjeeling. He promised me the help of all the missionaries as far as Bathang, but distinctly declined the responsibility of recommending any particular route. He further said, that a passport from the Viceroy of Sz-chuan to the Chinese Minister at Lhássa, would be requisite to enable me to proceed beyond Bathang. To a question, whether Monsieur Dabry had represented me as a Government agent, he replied, that Monsieur Dabry was a good gentleman, and had probably been misled. He invited me to dinner the next day, with an apology for not having given me quarters in the Mission-house, and expressed his intention of paying all my expenses in Chung Ching, and providing me with trustworthy servants.

I took leave of the good bishop, much impressed with his kindness, and, having reached the hotel, I found Philip com-

---

* About this route the Bishop was uncertain, but it will be seen that a Chinese trader afterwards removed all doubt on the subject, at Bathang.

plaining of illness, so I tried the effect of three Cockle's pills ground up and mixed with water. Next morning the bare suggestion of a repetition of the dose proved most salutary, for, on the arrival of the bishop's chair, he was well enough to accompany me. During dinner, Monseigneur Desfleches told me that the Chen-tu Viceroy had sent repeatedly to him to inquire whether I had arrived. We talked over the route through Eastern Thibet, which I had decided on following, and he promised to communicate with Bishop Chauveau at Tat-sian-loo. He also talked to Philip, who confessed to him his fears as to our journey; and on our return to the hotel I was glad to hear that he would proceed to Tat-sian-loo, as Fan Ta-jen (the bishop's Chinese name) had desired him to do so.

On the day following, a merchant under whose care the bishop had placed me, came to take me for a walk round the city. He was very particular about my appearance—nothing less than my best suit would please him; and my spectacles which were somewhat dilapidated, were at once replaced by a pair which he produced from his pocket with an air of proud satisfaction, and adjusted *à la Chinoise*. If there is a vanity the Chinese youth indulge in, it is the wearing spectacles, made of pebbles, and set in horn or silver. Thus a young graduate affects the learned man by aid of his goggles and long finger-nails. As soon as I was dressed to his satisfaction, we sallied forth, myself somewhat oppressed by his multiplied cautions as to the necessity of not betraying the fact that I was a foreigner, while he assumed an air of importance that was intensely amusing. As I walked in front of him through the outer court-yard of the hotel, he suddenly stopped me, and gave me to understand that I did not walk with sufficient dignity. He then proceeded to give me a lesson, strutting up and down the yard, nodding at me at every step, saying, in Chinese, "Like this! like this!" and then I, in turn, went through my drill, strutting up and down before him, till, having acquitted myself to his entire satisfaction, we sallied forth. As soon as we were in the street, Fan began to talk as though we had some subject of interest under discussion. On looking at him inquiringly, he gave me a most expressive wink; and as I, taking up the cue, occasionally gave utterance to a very correct "Aw!" he looked at me with an approving smile. We walked, unmolested, through many of the principal streets, and called upon one or two wealthy merchants, personal friends of Fan's, with whom we smoked and drank tea. I was greatly surprised to notice the number of shops stocked with foreign manufactures only. Glass and crockery ware, wax matches, scented soap, cheap engravings, obscene French photographs, watches and clocks, brass buttons, pocket-knives, and foreign piece-goods, were everywhere exposed for sale.

After having taken a survey of the town, we made for the river bank, and, taking boat, crossed the river to the hill opposite the city, where landing, we hired chairs, and ascended a series of long flights of stone steps leading up the river bank. After proceeding a couple of miles, we alighted at a tea-house, Fan's importance vastly increasing as my dignified presence attracted the attention of a number of respectable men. He gave them to understand that I was a great scholar from Kwangtung (Canton), and produced my pocket-book, containing a few rough sketches, for their edification, evidently greatly impressing them with the importance of the stranger who, he condescended to inform them, was his "Low pungyew" (old friend). We adjourned from the tea-house to visit a celebrated pagoda, called "Powngan Ta" (great pagoda), of nine stories. The approach to this building was extremely pretty. Following the bank of a little stream, we passed through a large ornamental stone gateway into a series of gardens picturesquely laid out with evergreens, beds of camellias, dwarf trees, and ponds. We ascended the pagoda, and from the top story commanded a magnificent view over the surrounding country. This edifice, and all the lesser buildings attached to it as residences for the Buddhist priests, were in unusually good repair; though most of the public buildings within the city of Chung Ching were suffering more or less from neglect and decay.

The priests had hung outside many of their dormitories large barrel-shaped beehives, made of wicker-work, plastered with mud, in and out of which swarmed myriads of bees. At one of the large ponds the priest whom Fan had secured as a guide, ordered a boy to beat a piece of hollow wood to attract the fishes, and soon numbers of large fellows rose lazily from the bottom. The boy proceeded to feed his finny flock with boiled rice, which they devoured greedily. These Buddhist priests consider the preservation of all animal life as a most meritorious action, and feed numbers of goats, dogs, and cattle.

As we were leaving the pagoda, Fan asked me to make a sketch of it, and brought out a chair from a little house close by. A few people stopped to look on at my work, and gradually others, attracted by curiosity, joined them, until, in a few minutes, a considerable crowd had assembled, and so great was the excitement amongst them that those outside pushed those inside, until I was knocked over, and in a fair way of being trampled upon. Poor Fan was dreadfully alarmed, and dragged me into the house, through which we made our exit, and procuring chairs, started for the country.

We jogged along for several miles through an undulating country, the low hills richly cultivated to their summits; small but carefully-tilled fields, or rather patches, of wheat, barley, beans, peas, sugar-cane, and poppy in succession diversified the terraced hill-sides, while every here and there the slopes were gay with the yellow flowers of the Hunggowhar, a species of madder. I noticed in several places indications of surface coal on the hills. The valleys were devoted to the cultivation of rice, the rice-grounds being now flooded, in preparation for sowing the crop. Here and there were little homesteads surrounded by fruit-trees, and, in the distance, one or two large villages. I was struck by the numbers of small birds of very gay plumage, which were, apparently, fearless of molestation. At length we reached a hill covered with pine-trees, and ascended one of the usual flights of steps which form hill-roads in China, and having descended a little distance on the other side of the brow, entered a gate in an enclosure. We soon reached a terrace, one of a succession of terraces occupying a great portion of the side of the hill. The whole formed a Taouist temple enclosure, containing numerous edifices; some were literal rock-temples, excavated in large masses of sandstone which jutted out of the hill at different heights; others were built against the face of the rock. Flights of stone steps, some carved in the rock, led up and down, and the terraces and intervening slopes were picturesquely laid out with beds of camellias, and plantations of shrubs, interspersed with ponds full of the flowering lotus, and every here and there small stone grotto-like summer-houses; the whole forming a beautiful pleasaunce, laid out and kept with the greatest care. Our chairs were halted on the terrace in front of one of the rock-temples; a portal, some ten feet high, with pillars and architrave adorned with a Chinese inscription, gave admission to the cavernous interior; the façade on either side was ornamented with the various fantastic forms of the Chinese Pantheon beautifully carved like the portal, in *alto relievo*, out of the sandstone, and overlaid with gilding; every here and there was to be seen the mystic symbol, "Tai-ke," which denotes the union of the Yan and the Yin, the two principles of growth and decay, and signifies the finite being.

The richly painted and gilded door stood invitingly open, and entering, we found ourselves in a hall, about forty feet square, and twenty feet high, dimly lighted by small oil-lamps; facing us at the end, sat three gigantic figures, fifteen feet high, representing the Taouist Trinity, or Three Pure Ones, before which was a gilt railing. On either side stood a row of figures, ten feet high, representing the various elemental deities and tutelary genii. These figures, many of which were splendid with gilding, were carved out of a greyish stone, different from the sandstone of the temple itself; some were unfinished, and two sculptors were busily engaged chiselling the lower extremities. There were no worshippers, or offerings to be seen, but the whole interior was spotlessly clean. A narrow passage to the left, also lighted by oil-lamps, led into a smaller chamber, in the centre of which stood a stone table, and three large stone chairs, and at the end of the room a stone couch, all hewn out of the living rock; from this room we emerged into the daylight, through another carved and ornamental doorway, and proceeded to stroll through the gardens, passing every now and then, through one of the grotto-like buildings, each of which was fitted up with chairs and tables. Numerous visitors, all apparently like ourselves, simply actuated by curiosity, were walking about the grounds; but I noticed that some, whom by the way Fan pointed out with a contemptuous gesture, as they passed before the deities represented on the façades of the temples, devoutly chin-chinned them. These temples were all of recent construction, the expense having been defrayed by the voluntary subscriptions of the wealthier classes of Chung Ching and the neighbourhood, while the poorer people had assisted by giving their labour gratuitously.

As we were resting ourselves in one of the temples which was built against the face of the rock, we were joined by a Taouist priest, who politely saluting me, asked if I would take some refreshment. Fan accepting, on my behalf, his proffered hospitality, he retired, and soon returned with a tray containing dishes of preserves, sugared fruits, crystallized sugar, and tea. During his absence, Fan pointed to my mouth, and placed his hand over his own, telling me not to speak; so when the priest, having done the honours, commenced making inquiries about me, my protector confidentially whispered in his ear, with a knowing wink at me; the priest opened wide his eyes, and making me a profound bow, commenced a long confab., evidently fully intent on being mystified by Fan, who, enjoying his important position of confidential companion to a swell mandarin, highly entertained the priest, and saved me from committing myself in conversation. We sat for some time enjoying our tea and sweetmeats. Our host then proposed that we should dine with him, and we adjourned to a grotto where a priest, evidently of lower rank, brought in several plain but good dishes, of stewed fish, fowl, and pork, and then handed round the rice. Fan and myself made a hearty meal, washed down with very good samshu, something particular, which the priest informed me was Kwang-tung Chu, wine made in the province of that name. He himself eat sparingly of rice and fish, and begged to be excused joining us in the wine; nothing could exceed the dignified politeness of his behaviour, and I confess that I was much struck by it, for I had looked upon priests in China as a set of scoundrels holding a very low position in the social scale; and so far from expecting such hospitality as I had met with, had naturally concluded that we would have to pay for the privilege of visiting the temple; our host, however, declined a present of several hundred chen which Fan deposited without remark on a small side table, but was greatly delighted with a small plain gold ring which I took from my finger and presented to him.

From the peculiarity of his dress, which consisted of a black flowing gown, similar to the yellow ones worn by the Buddhist priests, and a small round cap made of black silk, through the crown of which protruded a knot of hair, I had concluded that he was either a priest of peculiar rank amongst the Buddhists, or of another religion; and it was not until after leaving the temple and inquiring of Fan, that I discovered he was a Taou-jen, or Taou-man, *i. e.*, a priest of another religion, differing widely from Buddhism, and which may be said to represent the ancient polytheism of the country, as reformed and engrafted with a peculiar theosophy by Laotse, the great rival of Confucius. At last we took our leave, and descending to the river which ran through the valley, returned along its bank. I much regretted that I could not make a sketch of these Taouist temples and their picturesque surroundings; never until I visited them had I seen anything in the Celestial Empire which at all realised my expectations; from my boyhood I had formed, what experience proved to be, very exaggerated ideas of the beauty of Chinese scenery. Many a wistful look at the familiar willow plate, and the scenes depicted on japanned tea caddies, had filled my imagination with pictures of luxuriant gardens and rich if fantastic architecture; while, more recently, the study of porcelain vases, jade carvings, and the works of Chinese artists, had impressed me with the hope that in the interior of the country many a scene of beauty which wealth and taste had combined to adorn would reward the traveller. I must say that such in my experience have been very few and far between; China's age of art and decorative taste seems to have passed away; the cruel rapacity of the rebels and of the unrestrained imperial soldiery has laid waste her most famous Eastern cities. When I visited Soo-chow-foo, the city of beauty, the theme of many a Chinese poet, whose fair-complexioned maids are now only remembered in the proverb, "As beautiful as a Soo-chow woman," rank beds of weeds overgrowing the ruins of the once splendid villas, alone marked the sites of her renowned gardens. Pekin itself is a city of ruins and decay, though there, to some extent, and at Chen-tu, Chung Ching, and Canton, but scarcely anywhere else besides, is encouragement still given to the works of art, and even in those cities the secrets of the manufacture of the finest porcelain and most precious enamels are said to be lost. The workmen of Kiang-see now only turn out articles of ordinary quality, and specimens of the ancient craft of her ceramic artists are growing daily rarer; the taste and luxury which once everywhere embellished the retreats of the officials and nobles, seemed to me to have taken refuge in this Sz-chuan sanctuary.

Late in the afternoon we reached the hotel, much to my relief, for on our return journey my friend Fan was in rather a captious temper, having taken either too much or too little of the famous Kwang-tung Chu. I was too tired to preserve the swaggering gait befitting a Mandarin of my assumed dignity; my hat too, which had been knocked off in the boat and replaced too much after the English fashion of wearing hats, square on the head, was to him a source of great irritation. Several rather sharp digs in my side from his elbow, accompanied by contortions of his rubicund countenance and frowning looks at my head, intimated that it was out of order, and I twice endeavoured to place it on the back of my head with the proper Chinese jauntiness, but I could not please him; at last he took a stealthy look round to see that he was unobserved, and making a grab at my hat adjusted it according to his idea of correctness, and continued his walk with an air of having accomplished an act of stern justice.

I had barely time to change my swell attire before my protector walked me off to his house, some few doors distant from the hotel; there I met a number of respectable Christian merchants. Philip having accompanied me, I was asked a number of questions relative to myself and my country. Their inquiries about Insurance Companies showed that such schemes were not unknown to them, but the prevailing idea, expressed without the least reserve, was that with regard to fire and life insurance no insured person's life would be safe, and junks would certainly never reach their destination, while houses would be burnt most advantageously to the owners—but to the utter ruin of Insurance Companies; and they unanimously agreed that under Chinese management such schemes would never pay. As to steamers plying on the Upper Yang-tsu, they seemed to think the foreigner's steam ship was all-powerful, and expressed the strongest wish for its arrival.

On the following day as I was engaged with a Father, who

called on me by order of the bishop, to arrange as to the amount I would require to draw here, our hotel was suddenly thrown into great confusion by the arrival of a royal courier bearing despatches from the Viceroy of Sz-chuan to Pekin, relative to the Nepaulese Embassy, which rumour stated had been detained in Chen-tu and ordered to return to Khatmandoo.

The courier dismounting from his jaded pony, called out for food and fresh horses, and depositing his saddle-bags containing the despatches on a chair, sat down on them and proceeded to abuse everybody, and the landlord in particular, for not using sufficient alacrity in attending to the wants of a royal courier. The fellow was dressed in scarlet trousers and jacket, with the Mandarin hat and long thigh boots, a long clumsy sword hung from a leather waistbelt, and a light gingall or matchlock was slung across his shoulders. He was evidently tired, and apparently suffering from want of opium; this latter want, however, was soon supplied, as one of his attendants quickly prepared his pipe in a room opposite to mine, to which he retired, carefully taking with him the despatch bags which he converted into a pillow. Out of the two hours that he remained in the hotel he smoked opium for at least an hour and a half, the rest of the time he spent in eating and being shaved; and when at length fresh ponies were brought, the one reserved for him, as soon as it was saddled, was further weighted with the despatches and a huge mattrass, on top of which the bold courier threw himself, and, preceded by a subordinate to clear the way through the crowded streets, he departed on his journey towards the capital, which he had condescendingly informed me would occupy him twenty days, travelling day and night.

During the day I had many visitors from amongst the

wealthy merchants of the city, and was up to a late hour engaged in answering their numerous questions, principally directed to find out the object of my travels in their country. I however succeeded in getting rid of them at last, and gladly retired to bed, from which I was unceremoniously roused at daylight next morning, Sunday, by my friend Fan-sien-sen, who gave me to understand that he was going to mass, and Tang Ta-jen must accompany him. The good fellow was too thoroughly kind to be refused, so I resigned myself to his direction and quietly submitted to be dressed in my Sunday suit. When properly attired to his satisfaction, expressed by jerking out his fist with the thumb pointing upwards, I followed him to the residence of a Christian merchant, where in a large inner court I found an altar raised, and a number of benches filled with a silent and devoutly attentive congregation, the men and boys occupying several of the front rows divided by a temporary sort of railing from those behind occupied by the women and girls.

On the altar, covered with a red velvet cloth, stood the usual Romish ornaments, &c. Shortly after our entrance a Chinese father accompanied by two Chinese youths as acolytes entered from a side door, and the service commenced; mass, of course, was said in Latin, but the congregation sang twice in Chinese what appeared to be hymns; and the priest delivered in an impressive manner a Chinese sermon.

Throughout the whole service there was visible the greatest reverence and attention to what was going on, and as I looked round me and saw this little band of Christians worshipping the God of my fathers with a devout decorum unsurpassed in any European church, I could not help feeling influenced by their example, and offered up a silent prayer for the success of the Catholic Missions in China.

After service I remained behind with my conductor, and was introduced to several Christians and the priest, who all thanked me with unfeigned sincerity for condescending to attend their little chapel. One and all, on learning that I was not a member of the Church, expressed a hope that I would become a Catholic.

The impressions left on my mind of its marvellous success caused me to acquaint myself, as far as possible, with the history and machinery of the Western China Mission, whose agents, moreover, rendered so much assistance in my journey, and at the head-quarters of which my first observations of a Chinese Catholic congregation ministered to by a Chinese priest, were made. The results of my inquiries will not, I hope, be deemed irrelevant; if so, the reader can skip them. The present power of the Catholic Missions in China is a most striking instance of the inutility of coercion directed to restrain freedom of mind in religion. The fearful persecutions that assailed the missionaries and their converts during the eighteenth century failed altogether to arrest the spread of Catholic Christianity, which now, but a hundred years later, numbers its adherents by hundreds of thousands, to be found in all the provinces of the empire.

The history of the Sz-chuan Mission, from its commencement to the present time, differs widely from that of the Jesuits. From the day that the two brave followers of Xavier, Fathers Ricci and Ruggieri, baptised their first convert in Chao-King, the missionaries of the Society of Jesus seem, with trifling checks, to have achieved the most astonishing and rapid successes. Huc has vividly described the impression made by the scientific attainments, combined with the most fervent zeal for conversion, of Schall, Verbiest, Gerbillon, &c. The grand design of winning over the emperor and grandees, and, in their train, the whole nation, to the Catholic faith, seemed almost accomplished when the magnificent church reared itself in Pekin, adorned with inscriptions, presented by the first Mantchoo Emperor, the representative of Confucius, and the President of the Board of Rites. It seemed, then, without doubt, that this would prove the mother church whose daughters would speedily cover the length and breadth of the Flowery Land. The first blow to these sanguine hopes was given by the death of the young Emperor Chun-che. I will not enter further into the vicissitudes of the Pekin Missions, which ended in their virtual suppression. The disputes as to conformity with the custom of veneration of ancestors, and the well-known decree of Clement XI. not only alienated the Emperor Khang-hi, but also made the class of literati understand that this new religion of the Lord of Heaven was absolutely intolerant, and that their fixed principles of government and religion must give place to the new law. From that time they were resolute in their opposition to the religion whose teachers would not be content with a contemptuous or complimentary toleration, but required unconditional submission. This class has ever since been the promoters of all persecutions of the converts, who are still in danger whenever the annual examinations at once assemble and excite the animosity of the candidates for literary honours. The Jesuits soon exchanged their prosperity for persecution; and, instead of counting among their hearers princes and magistrates, were obliged, like other missionaries, as the "Lettres Edifiantes" tell us, "to find their converts among the poor and in the country." The Sz-chuan Missions, from their first actual commencement by Appiani, in 1704, had to encounter a series of persecutions unrelieved by imperial favour. The Jesuit Fathers Buglio and Magalhaens had essayed to propagate the faith with slight success. At the time that the blood-thirsty Tchang-hien tyrannised over this province they had, however, barely escaped with their lives; and the utter desolation of this fertile country, which Tchang-hien had declared " should remain for ever a desert," prevented the resumption of their abortive mission.

The vacant field was occupied by the Lazarists. Their work was speedily interrupted by an edict of banishment, Appiani being imprisoned till his death. Twenty years after the intrepid Bishop Mullener succeeded in returning and labouring undetected until 1743. Another violent persecution broke out in 1745, during which all the missionaries were detected and sent away; while in other provinces several suffered death. The success of the Sz-chuan Mission dates from the arrival of Monseigneur Pottier, in 1755, at which time the converts numbered 4000. Notwithstanding the persecution in 1767, two years after, at the date of the consecration of Bishop Pottier as Apostolic Vicar of Sz-chuan, with charge of the Missions of Yunnan and Kwei-chew, the Christians amounted to 7000, and, in a few years more, their numbers were doubled.

Under the superintendence of Monseigneur Pottier and his successor Didier, the mission held its ground, though repeatedly assailed by the Chinese authorities. During the troublous times of the French Revolution the missionaries were sustained by little help from home, and were oftentimes expelled from the country, or obliged to lurk as fugitives from their persecutors. The converts, however, steadily increasing, numbered 40,000 at the beginning of this century. However much one must regret that the devoted men who laboured in the arduous and dangerous work of these missions were not the apostles of a simpler and purer faith, it is impossible to withhold a tribute of unqualified admiration for their self-denying and heroic perseverance.

The Sz-chuan mission can boast of one martyr bishop, Monseigneur Dufresse, whose successful labours as Vicar Apostolic were closed in 1814 by his decapitation in Chen-tu, while ten of the native priests perished under the hands either of the torturer or executioner during the four following years.

A more peaceful period commenced in 1822, and in the year 1839 the Christians in Sz-chuan were computed at 52,000, under the charge of two bishops, nine French and thirty native priests. Huc states that at the time of his visit this province counted nearly "100,000 Christians, whose numbers were obviously on the increase from year to year." I do not, however, think that at present the number amounts to 100,000; as to the annual increase, I am not able to give any precise statements.

They are recruited principally from the well-to-do middle class, although in the villages there are many little Christian communities whose members belong to the industrious peasant class. They at present enjoy complete toleration, and, indeed, command respect, while in Chung Ching the numbers and wealth of the converts give them, as a society, considerable weight. The account of the precautions which Monseigneur Desfleches, then in hiding for fear of the persecutors, was obliged to take in communicating with Messrs. Huc and Gabet, was strikingly contrasted with the circumstances under which I made my acquaintance with this good bishop. But this apparent prosperity and tranquillity might at any moment be exchanged for all the perils of persecution; I myself observed the marked dislike of the Christians displayed by the literati and officials at Chen-tu. During the annual examination, held just before my visit, the bishop had been obliged to absent himself for fear of violence; further west, this contempt and hatred of the Christians were continually manifested. Truly these missionaries carry their lives in their hands. But it is time to give some account of the system by means of which they carry on their work among a population at one time indifferent, and at another capable of being roused to fierce anger against all religious innovators.

The Société des Missions Etrangères, which from its headquarters in Paris direct the affairs of this mission, is most careful in the selection and training of the candidates for missionary life. As their work lies much among the wealthy and educated, though the poor and ignorant are by no means neglected, every missionary sent to Sz-chuan is specially educated for the purpose of meeting the Chinese literati on equal terms. They land in China generally as young and newly-ordained priests, under vows by which the rest of their life is dedicated to the Sz-chuan Mission. Once having entered upon their work, they never abandon it, nor return to their native country; indeed, it is impossible for them to do so, for I have good reasons for stating that any recreant who may seek, in violation of his engagements, to quit the country, is certain to be apprehended by the Mandarins and sent back to the jurisdiction of the mission. This has an apparent connection with the edict of Khang-hi, which accorded toleration to those missionaries only who would swear never to return to Europe. The young missionary on entering China strips himself of his nationality; he shaves his head, and adopts the Chinese costume, and conforms in all respects to the Chinese mode of life. His first two years are spent either at one of the principal mission stations or at some out station, in close attendance on an old and experienced Father, under whose care he systematically studies the language and manners of the people to whose service he has devoted his life. He is also trained in the working of the mission, and as soon as he is a proficient in the language, is appointed to a permanent post, under general orders from the bishop of the district to which he has been sent from Paris.

It can easily be imagined that a mission numbering its converts by tens of thousands, and carrying its labours over such a vast extent of country as Western China and Eastern Thibet, must be a well-organised institution, systematically administered.

Taking advantage of the division of all the provinces into districts, each district is worked by the mission with more or less activity, as the disposition of the people will allow. The Apostolic Bishop resident at Chung Ching exercises a metropolitan authority over four other bishops, who reside at Chen-tu and Swi-foo, in Sz-chuan, Yunnan-foo in Yunnan, and in Kwei-chew, and Bishop Chauveau at Ta-tsian-loo. The latter has charge of the mission stations of Eastern Thibet established at Bathang, Yengin, and Tz-coo, on the western banks of the Lantsan-kiang. I was informed that there were in 1868, 300 French missionaries, besides native priests and catechists, engaged in the missions working in the above provinces. The pay of a missionary varies from 100 taels per mensem—the salary of a bishop—to 20 taels, the scanty stipend of the simple Fathers. Out of this they provide themselves with everything. At small out-stations, of course, the people give many presents of food, but even then the pay is so trifling, compared with the salaries drawn by Protestant missionaries, that one can only wonder how these French missionaries manage to exist, and it is only when their self-denying and abstemious mode of life is witnessed that an adequate idea can be formed of real mission work.

By a strict system of reports, coming from every missionary in charge of a district through his bishop to the metropolitan bishop at Chung Ching, the affairs of the mission are administered with the regularity of a well organised government. Every station maintains its own courier, and thus a strict system of communication is kept up. Closely observing the Chinese customs, the bishops assume the title of Ta-jen, "Excellency," and the Fathers, according to their precedence in the mission, Ta-low-ya, "Great Elder," and Low-ya, "Elder."

Every convert coming into the presence of a Father is obliged to bend the knee, a custom which a recent able French writer declares he has himself heard the Christians complain of as unbecoming. In exacting this apparently slavish mark of homage from their flock the Fathers imitate the magistrates, and by this means, as well as by the influence they naturally acquire in the direction of civil affairs among their converts, they very probably excite the jealousy and hatred of the governing classes. As an illustration of this, I may quote the words of an old and experienced Father: "We are not persecuted on religious grounds, but on political, because they fear our influence over the people." From my own experience of the Chinese, I must say that (however repugnant to our Western ideas) the exaction of the utmost respect from their converts is absolutely necessary to the maintenance of the religious authority of the clergy, for the Chinese, as yet, know no intermediate step between servile submission and insolent independence; and when compared with that of any Protestant mission in the world, their success is so wonderfully great, that I feel inclined to give them the full credit of knowing from experience what is best for the interest of their mission. As it is, the peculiarities of the Chinese character cause occasional difficulties. The number of natives who are deemed fit for the priesthood is very small in proportion to that of the converts, and those selected are not always disposed to be subordinate. While I was at Chen-tu a grievous scandal disturbed the minds of the Christian community. A native priest had been for some time ministering at an out-station with complete satisfaction to his congregation; a French Father was sent by the Bishop to assume the charge, but his Chinese reverence, backed by the leading converts, resisted the intrusion, and maintained his ground *vi et armis*, refusing to let the new-comer into the mission premises. In this difficulty the Bishop appealed to the Mandarin, who, however, Gallio like, declined to interfere, as he held it to be a religious quarrel between two members of the Christian community; and when I left the dispute was still unsettled. I am not aware that since the time of the learned Lopez any Chinese priest has been advanced to the episcopate, and the present rule is decidedly to hold out no expectation of such advancement. The reason assigned is that the ineradicable propensity of every Chinaman to sell any appointment in his gift would certainly lead to the simoniacal bestowal of the priesthood. In connection with this, I remember an amusing instance of another Chinese characteristic, viz., overweening self-conceit. A young catechist remarked to his bishop, in a serious and reflective manner, "Father, I see many French bishops and priests, and a few Chinese priests; why are there not Chinese bishops?" The Bishop, in reply, reminded him of the failing of his countrymen, and ended by asking him if he knew any Chinese whom he could point out as fit for the episcopate, whereupon the youth replied, with a gesture of complete self-confidence, "Father,

I am fit to be a bishop." His conceit was punished by the bishop calling in all the Christians in the house, and presenting him to them as the self-designated bishop.

The education of the young is a special object of care; at all the principal mission stations there are separate schools for boys and girls. The boys are taught to read and write Chinese and Latin, besides geography and other useful information, which tends to dispel their Chinese prejudices. Promising candidates for the priesthood are usually sent to Macao and Hong-kong, and occasionally to Rome, to receive their professional education. The girls are taught to read and write Chinese, and are instructed in sewing, &c.

At Chung Ching and Chen-tu there are boarding-schools, where young girls are educated till they are marriageable. These pupils are eagerly sought for by the converts in marriage, and are reputed to make excellent wives. The native Christians, as a rule, are remarkable for their good character; their houses are distinguished by their superior cleanliness and order. The habit of opium smoking is only tolerated in those who, having been accustomed to the drug before conversion, are considered unable to discontinue it without prejudice to their health: such persons obtain a special dispensation, but any convert who is discovered to have newly adopted this pernicious custom is excommunicated.

I cannot but record how forcibly I was impressed by their devout attention to the offices of their religion, and this is not merely superficial, they are staunch adherents of their faith, but few being ever found to apostatise even under the pressure of persecution; and having myself witnessed the beneficial effects of their labours, I conclude with wishing the utmost success to the pious and laborious agents, whose self-denial has been rewarded by such extraordinary results.

On the Sunday evening about eight o'clock, Philip, who had asked leave to spend the day with his convert friends, returned accompanied by several of the merchants who had visited me the day before; as soon as they had comfortably settled down to their pipes, the subject of Insurance Companies was again introduced, and after I had explained as well as I could the system on which they were worked in Europe, I was somewhat startled by one of my visitors becoming quite enthusiastic; he entered into a long conversation with his companions, which ended by their offering to provide 30,000 taels* to start a company in Chung Ching, if I would only undertake it in my own name, in order to secure it from the depredations of the Mandarins, who they said would not dare to squeeze a foreigner. As a proof of the treatment that the native promoters of such an undertaking would be likely to experience, they related a most flagrant instance of bad faith and rapacity on the part of their local Mandarins, which was now causing great indignation. Two years ago 128 Christian merchants negotiated with the local authorities a concession of the right to manufacture and export salt, and an enormous sum was agreed upon as the price to be paid by instalments within two years. The last instalment having been paid, the Mandarins simply revoked the concession, retaining the monopoly which they had sold and been paid for! My visitors urged my acceptance of their proposal, but of course to no purpose. They then departed somewhat chagrined, leaving me to reflect on the anomaly of the existence amongst the Chinese, so eminently mercantile in their pursuits, of such an obstacle to trade, as the inter-

* £10,000.

ference of the officials. But such is the fact; the energy of the Chinese merchant, upon which the very life of the empire depends, is crushed by the extortion practised by those who should encourage it; and capital, instead of circulating, is buried; banks are eminently unsafe, from the fact that they are preyed upon under the most impudent pretexts by the thoroughly corrupt mandarins, and a name for wealth acquired by any individual, converts him into a miserable wretch, from whom the leech-like officials extort money, till in the end, by the most abominable persecution, they kill the goose that lays the golden eggs. It must not be supposed that I have here drawn an exaggerated picture of one of the numerous evils which are retarding the progress of the Chinese empire. No one can live long in this country without observing that for the want of good government her vast resources remain undeveloped, and a great aptitude for advancement is neutralised by a misrule so complete as to be utterly beyond the control of the Pekin government, and it needs only a slight acquaintance with the Chinese who are immediately concerned in trading with foreign merchants at the open ports, to convince the impartial observer that they are not only keen and successful speculators, but just and liberal minded in their dealings with those who by a similar line of conduct gain their confidence and respect.

The misrule so prevalent throughout the country, cannot fail to alienate from the government all the sympathy of the people, and especially the mercantile classes, who are ever ready to evade the taxes, the bulk of which goes, not towards benefiting the empire, but into the pockets of the governing class. This is the cause of all the rebellions that shake the empire to its very foundation, and will continue to do so until the country is opened to closer intercourse with the free and enlightened countries of the west; and the force of commerce demands quicker means of communication throughout the empire. Such communications by land and water, and the free expression of public opinion, must be secured, before the theoretically perfect system of Chinese government can be properly administered. And as other countries have risen from a state of barbarism to hold their place amongst the great nations of the earth, so will China in her turn assume the station amongst them for which she is eminently fitted by her wonderful internal wealth and resources.

I had now been five days in Chung Ching, and felt anxious to proceed westwards, so that when Father Deschamps again visited me next day, by request of the Bishop, I signified my intention of leaving Chung Ching on the following Wednesday.

In course of conversation, the good Father informed me that he had been upwards of thirty years in Sz-chuan, long enough to see the growth of opium introduced—for when as a young priest he first entered the province, its cultivation was scarcely known. This statement of Father Deschamps will fairly account for the comparative silence of Huc on the cultivation of the drug in that province.

After the Father had taken his leave, Fan-sien-sen made his appearance, and informed me that I must come and see the Chinese theatre. I proceeded to dress myself without his assistance, as he had evidently been walking fast, and was out of breath; but he watched my toilet with a very critical eye; having tied my silken scarf somewhat carelessly, he shook his head and made a guttural noise, like an animated death-rattle, just by way of caution; and on my readjusting the scarf, signified his approval with a sharp shake of his head, and a prolonged cough.

We visited several very fine Buddhist temples, conspicuous for their carving, gilding, and painted Josses; connected with one of which was a theatre, kept up by voluntary subscription. The stage, which was decorated with a proscenium gorgeous with carving and gilding, was built at one end of a spacious courtyard, about fifty yards square, round which were wooden galleries, also very handsomely decorated; in these galleries were arranged chairs and tables, at which the audience, men and women, sat and sipped tea, which was supplied gratis.

A large band of brass and reed instruments was stationed in one corner of the stage, and kept up a continual noise, that was almost deafening.

The actors, amongst whom were the first females that I have ever seen on the stage in China, were gorgeously dressed in silk and satin embroidered vestments of great beauty and costliness, and although I watched the performance for more than two hours, I did not notice any indecent gestures, such as, as a rule, disgrace theatrical representations in China. Numbers of Buddhist priests strolled round the building, acting as hosts; and they too were superior in their appearance to the general run of their brethren. In the large courtyard, forming the centre of the building, rows of chairs and tables were arranged, at which in the summer evenings, the audience sit and enjoy their tea.

Having spent a somewhat tiring day I was glad to get back to my hotel, and enjoy a little quiet, but this was denied me, for numerous visitors again took possession of my room, and I was obliged to entertain them until nearly midnight, when I got to bed, fairly knocked up, and feeling the effects of a severe cold.

In the morning I was quite ill, but by the aid of chlorodyne managed to take a farewell dinner with Monseigneur

Desfleches. He had received a letter from the bishop at Chen-tu, saying that the Nepaulese Embassy had been ordered back, and advised me to hold as little intercourse as possible with the Ambassador on my arrival at the capital, as the officials were sorely incensed against him; but to obtain my passports and push on for Thibet. After bidding a hearty farewell to this accomplished gentleman, I returned, and commenced packing for a start in the morning, glad at last to escape from the constant labour of answering the numerous questions of my Chinese visitors.

Just before I turned in, Lowlee presented himself, to take leave of me; the old fellow shook his head, and looked very sorrowful, telling me to pray to the Virgin for protection, as I was going into a fearful country, where in all probability I should lose my head; a present of 2000 chen seemed to cheer him, and confiding my letters, a box of specimens, and my little dog Zeila, to his care for Hankow, I took leave of him. My tiny pet and companion, Zeila, created so much attention and excitement on our arrival at Chung Ching, that I feared to take her any further, thus depriving myself of a great source of amusement in her affectionate little ways. So ended my first visit to Chung Ching. And my next stage will lead me through the most fertile province of China, the description of which I must reserve for the next chapter.

CHAPTER V.

CHUNG CHING TO CHEN-TU.

Novel Umbrella—The House-rag—Sz-chuan Fortifications—A Famous Kung-kwan—Do I look like a Devil?—A Great Soldier—Making Way for a Mandarin—Marriage Customs—The Noseless Bride—Sale of Wives—An Awkward Predicament—Yamun Spies—The Paris of China—Rapacious Cooks—A promising Passport.

EARLY in the morning of February 19th, we were roused by the arrival of two chairs, for Philip and myself, with eight coolies as carriers. These at once commenced a noisy wrangle over the adjustment of their respective loads. Though feeling much indisposed, and inclined to postpone my departure, I managed, with the help of a strong dose of chlorodyne, to dress and inspect the vehicles provided for our land journey. They were simply constructed of bamboo wicker-work, covered with oil-cloth, resembling nothing so much as a milliner's basket of Brobdingnagian dimensions, and just large enough to contain the passenger in a sitting posture, without an inch to spare. Each chair was carried by three men. Two poles, fastened on either side, terminated in a cross-piece; to this, in front, a smaller pole was attached, the projecting ends of which were grasped by two bearers, while one supported the weight behind. We were still delayed by the non-arrival of a money-changer, who was to bring 10,000 chen for our expenses on the road,—a necessary provision against loss on the exchange of silver. When he did come, a new dispute broke out, the baggage coolies objecting to carry the copper coin; and a wordy warfare at last ended in half the chen being stowed in my chair, an arrangement which seriously curtailed the already scanty room, and obliged me to sit with my knees and chin in uncomfortable proximity. Just as we were starting, Father Deschamps arrived, intent on seeing me off, bringing kindly messages from the bishop. Our mutual farewells were cut short by the coolies, who hoisted my chair, and, followed by the rest of the little *cortége*, hurried me through the city at a good six-mile-an-hour trot.

We passed out by the western gate, and after making our way through the crowded suburbs, got into the open country. We travelled for some twenty-five miles along a road about six feet wide, well paved with granite, and in good repair. At different intervals, especially near the villages, we passed under lofty stone arches, handsomely ornamented with the usual carving and gilding. These apparently useless constructions resemble in their purpose our own triumphal arches, and are memorials of departed worthies. An affectionate widow will often perpetuate the virtues of a deceased husband, or a village community honour the memory of a benefactor, or head-man, by building one of these arches, which set forth, in large gilt letters, the names and merits of the deceased. All along the road I was surprised by the spectacle of innumerable beggars, principally women and children: they seemed out of keeping with the otherwise prosperous appearance of the adjacent country on all sides. The hills and valleys alike presented a succession of lovely landscapes; everywhere the pretty whitewashed farm-houses peeped out from their surrounding fruit-trees, now white with blossom, and the eye roved over an endless succession of fields of growing corn, sugar-cane, poppy, and other crops, the forwardness of which, together with the delicious softness of the atmosphere, made one feel as if it were May instead of February. Many of the low-lying fields were flooded, preparatory to sowing rice; and the miniature lakes thus formed glistened in the sunlight.

We passed many villages and road-side houses. At the entrance of some of the villages the road was roofed over with a rough straw shed, under the shelter of which hucksters of every kind exposed their wares for sale, while groups of idlers lounged about, with no apparent occupation but that of examining every traveller as he passed.

In the open streets and market-places were many *al fresco* shops, the owners of which protected themselves and their wares from the sun and rain by huge umbrellas of the dimensions of small tents, made of oiled paper stretched on bamboo frames, and gaudily coloured and lettered with the advertisement of the shopkeeper: these were often as much as fifteen feet in diameter. They formed a picturesque feature in the busy scene, and were, as far as my Chinese experience enabled me to judge, peculiar to Sz-chuan.

The endurance of our porters was remarkable. They trudged along, accompanying their work with a cheerful cry, and rested but six times during the day, halting twice for food at one of the many rest-houses scattered along the road. At these, rice, vegetables, pork, and samshu were procurable. At one of the rest-houses I took a meal, consisting of some fowl which Philip had brought from the hotel, supplemented by rice and cold salt cabbage. I did not alight from my chair, but had my rice, &c., handed to me as I sat inside, Chinese dignity not allowing a great man to alight at such places. The coolies gorged themselves so much that I felt some anxiety about their power to proceed;

but after their meal, and a smoke, I was again taken up, and carried along at the usual pace, while a number of wretched-looking coolies, in the last stage of seediness from excessive opium-smoking, followed us, begging our bearers to allow them to carry the chair. Our fellows kept up a running haggle with these poor wretches, which ended in a bargain on the part of three of them to carry my chair for three miles at the rate of three chen per mile per man. The eagerness with which the poor creatures changed places with the bearers showed how terrible was their poverty.

I had imagined that the Sz-chuan boatmen were the worst paid of any class in China, but, compared to them, the chair coolies are mere slaves. We had arranged with a chair proprietor in Chung Ching to provide chairs and coolies to Chen-tu, at the rate of four taels per man, including the chairs, and he, according to custom, engaged the coolies at about two and a half taels per head (tael = 6s. 8d.), or at the rate of 250 chen each man per diem (about 1s. 8d. English). For this small sum these poor fellows carried me nearly six hours every day, and found themselves. This cost them 180 chen, and their daily opium cost them 50 chen more. They are a wretched class of men, poorly clad, and wearing an emaciated look, that speaks very strongly of the effects of hard work and opium. From constantly carrying the chair, the muscles of their backs and shoulders are so much developed as to resemble a deformity, while the skin in texture is like the hide of a pachydermatous animal. It seems that they are rarely long-lived, hard work and opium generally breaking down their constitutions before they reach thirty years of age.

About 6 P.M. we reached the end of the first day's stage from Chung Ching, and stopped for the night at an hotel in a small village. My baggage was stowed in a very dirty room, the sole furniture of which consisted of two bedsteads, supplied with straw mattresses. This room, like all the other guest-rooms, opened directly from the centre common hall. When all had been safely carried in, a house cooly brought me a little wooden basin of hot water, with a piece of rag in it, to serve as a sponge. While passing through the hall, I had seen a very dirty-looking cooly washing himself with the same rag, and using the same basin, so I desired that fresh water might be brought. This, however, the waiter informed me could not be done, as the supply of hot water was nearly exhausted. I was therefore, notwithstanding the uncomfortable thought of my dirty predecessor, obliged to content myself with using the water in my own basin; and I took my wash, and felt considerably refreshed. We then had our dinner, and a smoke. Though feeling better for the fresh air of the country, my bones ached fearfully from my cramped position during the day's ride, and I was glad to throw myself on one of the beds, having first had the more than suspicious-looking mattress replaced by my own blankets and pillow.

About eight o'clock the cook, or man-of-all-work of the hotel, jumped on a table in the hall, and made an oration to the coolies :—" Lodgers, if any of you have not had enough to eat, speak at once; if any of you wish to take a hot bath, speak; if any of you want tea, speak now, for in half-an-hour the fires will be out, and you will not be able to get anything." Having delivered himself thus, he took his stand behind a sort of counter in one corner, and all the lodgers in turn received from him a large cotton-lined counterpane, equipped with which they retired into their rooms to smoke opium, the fumes of which soon filled every part of the house·

About an hour after, just as we were turning in, the proprietor presented himself, according to the universal custom at these stage houses, with his bill for food and lodging for the night. For the room we paid 400 chen, and for rice 200 chen each; this included a cup of tea and two poached eggs, which, he promised, should be brought to us early next morning. After the proprietor had departed, the cook, or man-of-all-work, presented himself for his customary fee, which, he informed us, was, "whatever I chose." I presented him with 100 chen, which was really much more than he expected. The fellow, however, looked at it as a cabman might at a shilling, and asked for more. Philip flew in a passion, and asked him what he meant; when he very coolly replied, "Oh, it's only the custom. We always ask for more than we get. Don't be angry; I'm quite satisfied, for, as a rule, I never get more than twenty chen from any gentleman or mandarin who occupies this room,—the coolies never pay anything, so I get as much as I can from the passengers." Having thus enlightened us somewhat as to the customs of Sz-chuan hotels, he bade us a very civil good-night.

Exactly at four o'clock next morning the cook entered my room with a basin of hot water, and *the rag* in it. I insisted on having fresh water, which, after a deal of fuss, he brought me, saying that I seemed to be very particular. He had been many years in an hotel, but had never known even a mandarin of the highest rank refuse to wash with *the house rag*. As soon as I was dressed the poached eggs and tea were brought in and soon discussed. My chair was brought up to the door of the bedroom; and, having again doubled myself up in it, we started on our day's journey before daylight. Save a few early travellers, like ourselves, there was no one astir in the village street; but lights and the sound of hammers in many of the houses bore evidence to the industry of the inhabitants. From the top of a hill, some distance along the road, we had a fine view of the sun rising from behind a range of lofty hills to the east. As the day wore on we overtook numerous droves of buffaloes, shod with straw shoes, on their way to the market at the little town of Winchin-chien. Towards the afternoon we ascended a high and regular range of hills, running north-east and south-west; their counter-slope was very precipitous, and cut up by deep, narrow defiles, across which were erected strong fortifications or walls of masonry, with massive arched gateways over the road. These fortified hills are celebrated in Sz-chuan, and would, no doubt, present a capital line of defence against an army of rebels marching from the west against Chung Ching and the surrounding country. I saw no soldiers in charge of the gates in these fortifications, which were all more or less dilapidated,—the normal condition of most public works in China.

We were now fairly into the heart of the province of Sz-chuan, and I already began to notice a slight difference in the appearance of the people. The countrymen were of middle stature, healthy-looking, and robust; but not so much so as I had been led to expect. They were well clad, with white turbans of cotton in place of the skull cap, or wide-awake, common in the eastern provinces. The women were fair and good-looking, wearing pieces of cotton cloth on their heads in the shape of hoods, very becoming to the young women. Most of the women had feet of the natural size, about one in ten only having the deformed small feet so universal elsewhere. I suffered much all day from thirst, the tea supplied at the rest-houses being mouldy, and the water muddy and strongly impregnated with decomposed vegetable matter, so I refreshed myself with sugar-cane and oranges, which, as well as toffy, were sold in all the villages.

In the surrounding hills coal was very plentiful; and we overtook numbers of coolies carrying it in the direction of Win-chin-chien, where we arrived at 5·30 P.M., and put up for the night in an hotel in some degree better than our last night's resting-place.

Small brasiers, containing charcoal fires, are much used by the people in China. Nearly every house in winter has its little fire in the centre of the room; and many persons carry about with them little brass pans with perforated lids, resembling the scaldini, so dear to the Tuscans, in which live charcoal is kept. These warming-pans are even sometimes worn suspended round the waist, under their garments. Charcoal is, therefore, a very necessary article everywhere, and in thinly-wooded districts is very expensive. In the district of Win-chin-chien it is manufactured in large quantities from a kind of thorn, which is planted everywhere as hedging.

Continuing our journey next day, we passed through a very rich country, thickly cultivated with opium, madder, and sugar. Herds of very large black swine, straw-shod for the journey, were being driven to and from Win-chin-chien market, and large flocks of tame ducks were to be seen feeding in the flooded paddy fields, tended by old men or boys, whose cheery voices were often heard calling back stragglers from their flocks. The birds seemed to be well trained, following their keepers like sheep.

In the evening we halted at Win-tsang-chien, a small, walled city, and put up at the Kung-kwan for the night. In travelling from Chung Ching to Chen-tu there is a marked improvement in the appearance of the towns nearer to the latter capital. The streets are much wider, and the walls and public buildings seem to be maintained in slightly better condition. Leaving Win-tsang-chien, we crossed a fine stone bridge, with a roadway some thirty feet wide, spanning, with one arch, the river Tho-king, a lesser tributary of the Yang-ts", about sixty yards wide at this point. Numbers of small boats, laden with coal, were plying up and down the river, some bound for Chung Ching, and others to the capital.

In the evening we arrived at the famous Kung-kwan, or Public Guest Hall, in the town of Loung-chang. This building was originally built for the residence of a Mandarin, but had been purchased by the government, and converted to its present use. It is quite famous in Sz-chuan, conferring celebrity on the small town of Loung-chang. It contains upwards of fifty rooms, in two stories, surrounding an immense hall, nearly 100 yards square, covered by a highly ornamented roof; from the centre of which hangs a large brass chandelier, with sockets for 100 candles. These, however, are only lighted on the arrival of high officials. The custodian of the establishment at first refused us admittance, on the plea that I was not a Mandarin, and accompanied his refusal with an angry address to the inmates on the presumption of a person in my station of life daring to seek admission to his Kung-kwan. His eloquence had so much influence on the crowd of idlers that they began to hoot me; but, at this juncture, Philip came up, and, alighting from his chair, forced himself through the crowd—already closely packed round me; swelling with dignity, and in a loud tone of voice, he called out for the master, who, evidently impressed by little Philip's lofty demeanour, stepped forward with a bow, and, in return received the Viceroy's passport, with an order to "read that." Mine host, having cast his eye over it, hurried to my chair, and, opening the door, begged me to alight; and as I stepped out he knelt before me on one knee; then, rising, called out in a loud voice, "A room for Tang Ta-jen," Tang being my Chinese name. The discomfited mob collapsed and disappeared; while the master escorted me to a room, where, again bending his knee, he refused to rise until my pardon for his rudeness was granted. So I graciously assured him I would overlook his first behaviour, and dismissed him by a wave of the hand.

In less than an hour he ushered in a capital dinner, and insisted on serving me himself; indeed, his attentions were so overpowering that it was quite a relief when bed-time came and he left us.

Next morning he again waited on me at early breakfast, reiterating his entreaties for forgiveness, so I gave him a present, which reassured and comforted him, and with voluble good wishes for our safe journey, we started before the stars had disappeared. About mid-day we halted at a small rest-house; on entering it I saw hanging up on the wall of the room a sketch of a foreign steam-boat, which the landlord informed me he had purchased of a travelling Chinese artist a few weeks before. There was no mistaking the picture for anything but a Chinese production, it was all hull and wheels, with an enormous chimney pouring forth a huge cloud of smoke. On asking the owner what the picture represented, he replied, "A fire-boat used by the people in the Hankow country." Being further asked whether this was not the kind of boat used by foreigners, he said, "He didn't know anything about the Hankow people, he had never been there. The Hankow people used fire-boats, and that was all he knew about it."

Quite a crowd gathered round me while questioning our surly host about his picture, and several of them asked me about the Se Yang-jen, *i. e.*, Western foreigners, if I had ever seen any of them, and if it was true that they were yellow-haired men, looking like devils?

Seeing that the crowd was composed of good-natured fellows, I took off my spectacles and making a polite bow, asked "if I looked like a devil?" For a moment or two they laughed immoderately at what they thought was a capital joke, but I very soon heard one or two saying "Look at his eyes!" and there was a sudden silence, of which I took advantage to ask the proprietor for wine to enable his guests to drink my health. This at once took with my audience, and more than a dozen of the older men saluted me and drank my health. The little hotel soon filled, and every table was taken up by knots of men all intent on watching the Yang-jen. As soon as breakfast was over my chair was brought up, and as I rose from my seat and bowed they all got up and simultaneously returned my bow, testifying the greatest respect.

During the day we passed a grotesque but pretty stone bridge, built in the shape of a dragon, the legs composing the arch thirty feet in diameter, and the roadway carried along his back, while the wings rose as parapets on either side. In the evening we stopped at the walled city Nincheang-foo, on the right bank of the Liu Kiang. There was an appearance of busy traffic about this city, numbers of large Chung Ching junks were lying in the river loading sugar and salt, the latter article being made in large quantities from salt wells on either bank of the river. This city abounded in large and handsome shops, and coal yards were very numerous. It is also a great market for ginger and glue, which is exported to every part of the empire. I observed large quantities made up in strips three or four feet long, and several inches wide, exposed for sale in nearly

THE DRAGON BRIDGE.

every shop. At Nin-cheang-foo we experienced great difficulty in passing the chen brought from Chung Ching, indeed the people absolutely refused to take them except at a discount of twenty-five per cent., at which we were obliged to exchange all our cash, as beyond this point the Chung Ching chen would not pass.*

I made a great effort this evening to get a bath; the landlord of the hotel, however, expressed an opinion on the request which rather startled me. On being informed that I wished to wash my body, he laughed at what he fancied was a joke; but as I insisted on having water, he replied that it really could not be done in my room, and as for going

* See Appendix I.

outside where the coolies were washing, of course a man of my position could not do that; and, moreover, a gentleman like myself who never did any hard work ought not to require washing, but if I was determined, why then I must do it the best way I could. So there was nothing for it but the universal bribe, which procured the bath at last, much however to the surprise of mine host. One soon gets accustomed to Chinese want of cleanliness, but to the traveller putting up at hotels, vermin are an absolute torture; the false alarms and real attacks of the Chinaman's pet render waking life a perfect misery, yet, strange to say, the more respectable Chinese pretend to have a great horror of vermin, and would not for the world admit that they are infested by them; but it is universally admitted that both high and low suffer equally, the only difference being that the cooly will take off his jacket by the road side and search for the common enemy in the face of all men, while the Chinese gentleman goes through the same performance in the privacy of his chamber as regularly as a Christian is supposed to say his prayers.

The next morning we followed the Liu Kiang for several miles through a very fine country. The sugar-cane was all harvested, while the luxuriant crops of barley and wheat were in full ear. Along the roadsides the dandelion and primrose bloomed as in England. In one or two villages that we passed through I was surprised to see large flocks of Muscovy ducks, which were very tame. Towards evening we neared the city of Tz^u-chow, the last under the jurisdiction of the Chung Ching Mandarin, surrounded by a very fine country, composed of undulating hills of sandstone covered with a surface soil of light clay cultivated to the highest pitch.

About a mile from the city I alighted for a walk, and just before entering the gates happened to take off my spectacles to wipe them, when a little girl exclaimed, "Yang-jen! Yang-jen!" This immediately attracted the attention of a number of soldiers and youthful candidates for military honours, who were returning from the annual competition in archery. They at once surrounded me, hooting loudly; one fellow, evidently the worse for samshu, caught hold of my skirts and nearly pulled me backwards; the usual crowd speedily assembled, and things began to look awkward. A happy thought occurred to me, viz., to chance an appeal to the sense of the ridiculous, which is strongly developed in John Chinaman; so I made my persecutor a reverential bow, and, striking an attitude, exclaimed, with a wink to the bystanders, "Surely this is a great soldier!"

Now, he was hump-backed, and very ugly, and by no means heroical, and the crowd yelled with derisive laughter. The hero, much abashed, let go my dress at once, and in retreating tumbled down, whereupon I jumped over him and got away. My coolies arrived on the instant, and took me in to my chair, congratulating me with boisterous laughter on my escape from "the great soldier."

Nothing is easier than to influence a Chinese crowd, if collected by curiosity only. They are fond of a joke, and are always readier to laugh than to come to blows.

I had now practised self-restraint among the Celestials for so long, that I did not on this occasion betray the slightest symptom of anger. Had I done so, the crowd would have caught the infection, and vented their wrath on me. As it was, I took it all as a joke, and made them laugh in spite of themselves, and so escaped further molestation. On such trifles may the life of a traveller in China hang, for this crowd, easily moved to laughter, would have been as easily led on to bloodshed.

While at dinner, soon after our arrival at the hotel, a great number of the townspeople came to see " the foreigner ; " so I sent out word that I would show myself immediately after I had dined. The landlord was rather nervous, and once or twice came in, begging me to hurry, as his house was full of people, who were sadly in the way ; so, carefully adjusting my spectacles, and lighting my long pipe, I leisurely sauntered into the public hall, and taking a seat vacant at a table partly occupied by three respectable elderly men, called for wine and tobacco. Philip then joined us, and I entered freely into conversation with my neighbours, asking many questions about the crops, &c. I found the old men very talkative, and our evident friendliness seemed to impress the crowd, which gradually melted away after having been gratified, or rather disappointed, by a close view of the Yang-jen, for I was so much like one of themselves, that my new friends laughingly told me my appearance made the people look foolish. I heard several say as they departed, " Tung, eyangde, Tsung-qua-de-jen ! " (He is the same as a Chinaman.)

Three days' journey from Tz^u-chow brought us to Kienchow, a fine walled city on the Liu Kiang; the principal incident *en route* was of a disagreeable character. A short distance from Tz^u-chow we met the advance escort of a military Mandarin of high rank, consisting of two mounted soldiers carrying the banners of the Mandarin, on which were painted in large letters his name and rank, followed by coolies carrying his baggage. There was plenty of room to allow of both parties passing, and my chair coolies gave them the inside, keeping themselves as close as possible to the edge of the road, which was bordered by a ploughed paddy field, newly flooded. The soldiers ordered my fellows off the road into the field; and on their naturally objecting, one of the soldiers, without more ado, rode at my chair, knocking chair and coolies head over heels into the field. Fortunately, no great harm was done beyond a wetting, and bespattering with the soft mud, about two feet deep, and in which I left my satin boots, while struggling to regain the road. But when we had picked ourselves up, one of the soldiers added insult to the injury, uttering a volley of foul abuse. I was so infuriated, that I made a spring at him to drag him from his pony, but before I reached him blood gushed from my nose; this sobered me, and ordering the coolies to get me some water, I walked on, pursued by the laughter of the soldiers. It was fortunate that I was stopped in time from inflicting a richly-deserved thrashing on the ruffian, for some two hours afterwards we met the Mandarin himself, with a numerous escort; we halted, and as he passed he scowled at me fiercely, and ordered one of his ragged followers to inquire who I was. The fellow executed the order by dragging me most unceremoniously from my chair, and delivering his message, garnished with a good sprinkling of oaths. After reading my passport, he merely remarked, "Aw! yang kwai-ts^u," and walked after his superior.

Shortly after our encounter with this Mandarin we met another procession, which turned out to be that of a bride going to the house of her husband. First came a band of music, immediately followed by two coolies carrying a huge chest of drawers, and others laden with four boxes of clothes; then came two little boys, bearing a silk-embroidered tablecloth over a bamboo, from which streamed twelve handkerchiefs; next in order came a washing tub and wooden buckets, then a pet dog, a cat, a duck, and a fowl, each carried by a coolie; then, preceded by a second band of music, came the bride's two youngest brothers in chairs, escorting her chair, which was very gorgeous with gilding and silk curtains. Behind the bride's chair marched eight coolies, each carrying a beautifully embroidered silk pillow; and the rear of the procession was brought up by the "go-between" by whose intervention, according to custom, the marriage had been arranged.

The bigoted adherence of the Chinese to "custom" prevents them from altering many of the social laws, which they themselves admit to be productive of much misery. This applies in the greatest degree to the social regulations concerning marriages and burials. Both are celebrated with the most extravagant outlay, which, in case of the latter, often reduces the family of the deceased to utter beggary. The marriage ceremonial, though ruinously costly, does not, of course, produce so much mischief, but the principle of matrimonial contracts maintained by custom destroys the happiness of hundreds of thousands. Except among the labouring classes, husband and wife, save perhaps by stealth in some cases, never see each other until the day of marriage; all is arranged by the go-between, or match-maker, who is usually a mutual friend, but employed by the family from the heads of which the first overtures proceed. Thus the parents of a marriageable daughter will settle upon a young bachelor, perhaps not among their acquaintance, as a suitable husband for her; they then apply to a mutual friend of respectable standing to give his services in the business. After all particulars as to dowry, &c., have been explained to him, he is introduced to the damsel; having taken a mental inventory of her charms and accomplishments, he visits the parents of the desired husband. He tells them that So-and-so has a daughter with so much fortune, just suitable as a wife for their son; he extols her beauty and excellences, according to the amount of reward he expects to obtain if successful. If the first proposals are entertained, he carries further messages between the families until matters are fully arranged, the wedding-day settled, and the bridegroom's cadeau delivered to the bride, with her birthday, age, and the time at which the marriage is to take place, engraved on it. In the meanwhile the go-between is sumptuously entertained by both families.

When the wedding-day arrives, which is often some years after the betrothal, the bride goes in grand procession to the house of her husband, at the door of which she is met by the mother-in-law, and other females of the house, who escort her to an inner room, where the bride, still closely veiled with a red silk kerchief, kneels while the bridegroom advances and welcomes her. He then performs his devotions to the household gods; after which they retire to drink tea together, and then generally for the first time do the future man and wife behold each other's face. If the bride is good-looking, and without deformity, the go-between is rewarded handsomely by the husband; if not, he escapes as quickly as possible, after delivering over the bride to her husband. It often happens that the go-betweens are bribed to give a false description of the lady, which naturally causes much misery; for after the bride has once unveiled herself before her husband, he cannot refuse to take her, even though she be deformed.

I was once dining with an old military Mandarin, who told me a capital story illustrative of the rascality sometimes practised by go-betweens.

"In the city of Pekin there lived a wealthy merchant,

who had an only son, to whom he purposed making over his business, in order that he himself might enjoy his ease during the remainder of his life. As may be supposed, the son of such a wealthy father was regarded as a prize by all fathers of marriageable daughters, and many were the go-betweens that were sent to open negotiations; but for a long time none were successful. There resided in a distant part of the city a Mandarin, who had retired from the service, having been allowed to retain the rank of his office, as an especial mark of the Emperor's favour; he was necessarily obliged to keep up great state; so much so, that he found it difficult to make both ends meet. The old gentleman heard one day of the rich merchant's son, and having an only daughter, he bethought himself of marrying her to the young heir, and thus replenishing his almost exhausted coffers. There were, however, two great difficulties in the way. First, his pride rebelled against the idea of allying himself to a base-born merchant; this impediment, however, vanished before the increasing pressure of impatient creditors; but the second was not to be so easily got rid of; his daughter, though a highly accomplished needlewoman, had *no nose;* and it was not likely that the young merchant prince would take to wife a woman so terribly disfigured. However, the old Mandarin took into his counsels a neighbour, one of the literati class, but out of office, who was accordingly poor, and ready for any intrigue by which money could be made, without his appearing to work for it. No sooner had this worthy been placed in possession of the old man's confidence, than he declared himself ready to undertake the post of go-between, and assured his principal that the young merchant should soon become his son-in-law.

"The old merchant was becoming anxious that his son

should be married before assuming the responsible position of head of such a large business, and had very nearly listened to the proposals of a go-between from another wealthy merchant, when he was favoured by a visit from the Mandarin's literary friend, who condescendingly informed the old gentleman that an illustrious Mandarin desired a marriage between his only daughter and the merchant's son.

"The old merchant could not refuse such an honour, and his son was in raptures, especially when he heard that the young lady was highly accomplished. He timidly asked if she was beautiful? to which the go-between unhesitatingly replied in the affirmative. Her feet were the smallest of the small, her hands were delicate, and her finger-nails unusually long. Her hair was abundant, and as black as the crow's wing; her eyes were glorious as the stars, and her gait as graceful as the waving of the lilies. Her father, though of illustrious descent, was not rich, and she would bring no dowry—and indeed, she would come to him wanting many things usually deemed essential to the outfit of a bride; she had but few silk dresses, and she had not got a *needle-stone*. These deficiences, however, were regarded as unimportant, as the wealth of the young merchant could easily more than supply them.

"The youth and his father were delighted at the prospect of a marriage with the daughter of a Mandarin. So matters were soon arranged, and an early day fixed for the marriage, the go-between having been very handsomely feëd by both parties. The happy day arrived, and the eager bridegroom uncovered the face of his bride, when—horrible sight!—he beheld a face without a nose! Pushing the trembling girl away from him, he rushed from the room and proclaimed the horrible news to the assembled guests, who joined him in loudly abusing the go-between for his fraud. He calmly replied: 'Did I not tell you that the daughter of my friend had not a needle-stone. Why, then, do you accuse me of deceit?' The poor bridegroom remembered that he had been told his bride had 'no needle-stone;' and retired to grieve over the blight which had been cast upon his domestic happiness."

To understand the equivoque of the go-between, it must be explained, that Chinese women are very expert with the needle; and those who are rich enough generally possess a needle-stone, a little article somewhat like a razor-strop. On one side they sharpen their needle, and on the other there is a piece of oiled cloth, on which they grease their needle, to keep it from rusting, and make it work smoothly. This little article is considered a necessary possession by all ladies. The poor women, however, who do not possess them, rub their needles on their noses, instead of the strop; hence the term "needle-stone," as applied to a woman's nose.

When once the preliminaries of a marriage have been settled by the go-betweens, neither party is expected to cry off. If, however, the man chooses to do so, he may, but forfeits the betrothal presents. When the woman's family breaks off the match, the man can bring an action and recover heavy damages.

When a widow signifies her intention to marry again, her deceased husband's relations generally dispose of her to the lover who bids the most. This is often the cause of great mischief, for the widow may prefer a husband of her own selection, and this leads to an elopement, which somehow always results in a fight, and the favoured suitor has both her relatives and those of the highest bidder to contend against. A widow has, however, one privilege; she cannot be forced to marry against her will.

Women in China have no legal status; they cannot give evidence in a court, and are the absolute slaves of the men. The father may sell his daughter, and the husband his wife, which latter transfer is executed in a somewhat curious manner. The deed, after reciting the circumstances under which she is sold, and the amount to be paid for her, is signed by the purchaser and the husband, and, by way of adding a seal, the husband smears the palm of his right hand and the sole of his right foot with ink, and then makes an impression of both on the deed, and the transfer is complete. In justice to the Chinese, however, I must say that the practice of wife-selling is not considered respectable, and it rarely happens but amongst the lower orders. Concubines are permitted, and live in the house with the wife proper. The sons of the latter take precedence over those of the former, but generally all inherit in equal proportions. Concubines are sold without any formalities, and are often the first sacrifice made by a Chinaman who has to "reduce his establishment."

One day's journey south of Chen-tu-foo we passed through the walled city of Kien-chow, built on the right bank of the Liu Kiang, the market-place of a large district nearly in the centre of which lies the capital of the province.

Some distance beyond this city we met four prisoners under sentence of transportation to Tartary. They wore bright red coats, with a small chain wound round the waist. Their heads were unshaven, and their hair, instead of being plaited into the queue common in China, was simply twisted with black cord, and rolled round the head in the shape of a turban. In company with these political offenders was an old man under sentence of death for being concerned in a murder at a small village near to Kien-chow. He was dressed in a complete suit of scarlet, with a heavy chain round his waist, and escorted by two soldiers. The Viceroy had passed sentence on him, and he was being taken for execution to the village where he had committed the crime.

A short stage from Kien-chow brought us to the capital, which we entered by the east gate after passing through an immense extent of suburbs, and proceeded down the leading thoroughfare of the city. I was much struck with the spaciousness of the streets, and the handsome appearance of the shops, with their large and massively-gilded signboards.

We happened to arrive during the annual examination of candidates for literary and military honours, and the city was crowded with excited students. This alarmed both Philip and myself. Our chair-coolies, too, not knowing where to find the Mission-house, were afraid to ask any one lest the very name of Christian should rouse the passions of the populace; so, after we had completely lost ourselves in the city, Philip suggested that I should remain at the corner of a street closely concealed in my chair, while he went alone on foot in search of the Mission-house.

We had tried several hotels, but all were full of students. There was nothing for it, therefore, but to send off Philip, and patiently await his return.

For two long, weary hours I sat in my chair trembling, as every now and then bands of riotous students passed up and down the street. I was quite alone; for the moment that Philip left, all the coolies betook themselves to the nearest wine-shop, leaving me, like a bale of goods, in the street. A more helpless condition than that in which I now found myself, it would be impossible to conceive. If I should be discovered, my ignorance of the language would be sure to subject me to the jests of the crowd, if not to violence; and my fears were shortly much increased by the coolies turning up all much the worse for their visit to the wine-shop. They talked loudly among themselves, and grumbled at being kept so long waiting; and as they frequently used the term "Yang-jen," an inquisitive crowd soon gathered round, and a serious disturbance seemed inevitable. Luckily, however, Philip turned up just as one or two of the crowd, more inquisitive than the rest, were lifting up the curtain of my chair, and, with his usual tact, gave the coolies directions to proceed towards the Mission-house, and off we started, followed for some distance by the crowd, which gradually dispersed.

After threading our way through numerous streets, we again halted at a quiet corner. Philip now informed me that the bishop and priests had all left Chen-tu on account of the examination, and the native Christian in charge of the Mission-house declined to receive me or in any way to identify himself with us, as he feared to attract attention by harbouring a strange foreigner who was not a missionary. Philip, who had tried in vain to find a room at an hotel, was dreadfully alarmed, and asked me what we should do, so I at once gave orders to go to the Mission-house. On our arrival, the native Christian, named Peter, came out, begging that I would go away. I replied by getting out of my chair and walking into the house with him. The poor man was evidently alarmed, but civilly ordered tea and cakes, which were most acceptable, for I was faint with hunger and anxiety. Somewhat refreshed by my cup of tea, I informed the good Peter that I wanted a room at an hotel, or, in default of it, would have to remain in the palace, whereupon he sent off a messenger, who, in less than half-an-hour, returned with the welcome news that he had found a room for me at a large hotel. On our arrival we found the landlord waiting to receive us. He was very civil; and after showing me the room, asked for my passport, to send to the Yamun.

Having paid off the chair-coolies, I dined, and then feeling quite tired out, turned in. Next morning, Mr. Peter paid me a visit, and in course of conversation, informed me that the Nepaulese ambassador was about to leave Chen-tu for Nepaul, and that I had better accompany him, otherwise the Mandarins would not let me proceed. He then told me that last year the bishop's palace at Chung Ching had been wrecked by an excited mob of candidates; and hence his fear of admitting me yesterday. While he was with me a soldier arrived from the Yamun with my passport, and a message, to the effect that it would be unsafe to show myself in the streets, owing to the number of candidates at present in the city.

My chief anxiety now was to have my passport changed for one authorising me to proceed through Thibet to India. I therefore sent Philip with my old passport to the Yamun, and wrote a note to the Nepaulese ambassador to the effect that I had just arrived, and begged to be allowed to pay my respects to him.

Philip soon returned from the Yamun with a message from the Mandarin that I could have a passport to go through Yunnan, but that the Viceroy declined to give me one for Thibet. I had expected to meet with hindrances from the Mandarins, and therefore troubled myself little about their message, well knowing that it was simply a dodge, as an Imperial pass would be quite useless in the Mahomedan part of Yuunan. In the afternoon two understrappers or spies from the Yamun, introduced themselves, pretending that they were merchants, and asked a great many questions. Among others, they asked how I intended to get through Yunnan? as they had heard that I was to have a passport for that country. I replied that I did not intend to go to Yunnan at all, as I could not go through rebel country, and if the Mandarins would not give me a passport for Tse-tsang (Thibet), I would go on without one, and they would be responsible for my safety. The fellows took their leave; and just before dusk, a message came from the Yamun through Peter, to the effect that I must write a letter to the authorities, upon receipt of which they would consider my request.

I also received a note from the ambassador, saying that he would come and see me in the morning; an honour that caused Mr. Peter to treat me with great respect. And I learnt, for the first time, from him, that in the passport procured for me by Mr. Medhurst, the consul at Hankow, I was described as a "tradesman," and that this was the reason that no Mandarin would come near me.

On the following day, His Excellency Juggut Share, the Nepaulese ambassador, arrived. He was a young man of very courteous bearing, but seemed ill, and his conversation soon showed me that he was not only ill in body, but greatly depressed in spirits. His position was anything but pleasant, and he confided to me the history of his embassy on its way so far towards Pekin. He had left Khatmandoo nearly two years before, and after a long journey through Thibet, had arrived without encountering any serious difficulties at Ta-tsianloo, the border town of China. Here he met his first repulse; a messenger from Pekin brought him an Imperial order to deliver the presents sent by Jung Bahadoor to the Emperor at that place, and return to Nepaul, as the road to Pekin was rendered unsafe by the Nien-fei rebels. This the young ambassador refused to do, pleading his instructions from Jung Bahadoor, which compelled him to deliver the presents in person. The authorities were determined to enforce the Emperor's orders, and Juggut Share was equally determined to proceed to Pekin; another application accordingly had to be made to the Emperor, for a reply to which he waited several months. When it came, it was in the form of a permission to him to proceed as far as Chen-tu, in order to dispose of several hundred chests of opium, brought for sale in China, and then to return home. He soon reached Chen-tu, and hoped to proceed further; but the authorities made this impossible. He could hire neither coolies nor boats, and what was worse, no one would buy his opium; it was too strong, and the people preferred the native drug.

At the time of my arrival, he had spent several months at Chen-tu, vainly pressing his request for leave to proceed to Pekin. The officials treated him with great discourtesy, hoping by this means to force him to return, and had lodged him in a dirty hovel outside the city, which, as he said, was so filthy, that he was ashamed to ask me to visit him in it.

The visit of Juggut Share, who spent a couple of hours with me, caused me to rise in the estimation of the Mandarins; and I had during the next two or three days several visits from understrappers of the Yamun. I was informed that the Viceroy would grant me a passport for Thibet, but that I must wait a few days. I therefore, having leisure time, started to take a walk round the city, first carefully disguising myself with large spectacles.

Philip and I soon found our way into one of the main streets, in which there were a great number of drug shops, and an all-pervading odour of musk, immense quantities of which, and hartshorn, are brought by traders from Thibet to Chen-tu, and are thence exported to Chung Ching. Chen-tu-foo deserves to be called the Paris of China. Its shops contain the richest collections of works of art, which find a ready sale amongst the numerous Mandarins who constantly reside in the city, and give it an aristocratic air that I have not noticed anywhere else in China. The number of silk mercers, clothiers, and book shops is prodigious; and from the number of well-dressed and spectacled individuals constantly walking in and out of the latter, it is plain that literature is greatly patronised. The city, built in the centre of a large fertile plain, is surrounded by very extensive suburbs, and fortified by a wall nearly twenty feet in thickness. The main street, leading from the east to the west gate, is probably one mile and a half in length. All the streets and buildings have a modern look, greatly in contrast with other large cities that I have visited. This is probably due to its having been rebuilt after the great fire which, during the last century, almost destroyed the old city. Its public buildings, such as Yamuus, temples and massive gateways, are in an excellent state of preservation, and conspicuous for their architecture and massive decorations. In the course of my walk, I entered a temple erected to Confudzu.* Passing through a handsome stone gateway, we found ourselves in a large open court, nearly 150 feet square, paved with granite, which was covered with a rank growth of slippery moss, showing how little it is visited by the followers of Confudzu. At the opposite end, a flight of stone steps, occupying the entire

* Confucius.

width of the court, led into a hall open in front, and built of massive granite, beautifully ornamented with carved scroll-work.

The hall was completely empty, save for a low pulpit, standing against the wall at the upper end; on each side of which hung two tablets, commemorating the great sage. The building wore a look of simple grandeur, more imposing than the gaudy magnificence of the Buddhist temples we afterwards visited. We passed through a door into extensive gardens, tastefully laid out with numerous fishponds and grottoes.

A solitary watchman, whom we found smoking his opium in one of the out-buildings, informed me that this temple was quite modern, having been erected by order of the present Emperor's father; but that, except at the annual ceremony of sacrificing to the memory of Confudzu, the temple was never visited.

On returning from my ramble through the city, the hotel cook informed me that, according to the custom prevailing in all first-class hotels, he had prepared a dinner for me at his own expense, simply, as he said, that the distinguished foreigner might speak well of him in distant countries; but in reality to "squeeze" the stranger. We had roast pigeons, stewed fowls, boiled beef, fish, and tender bamboo shoots. The dinner was very good; but I had to pay very dearly for it. Before we left I handed him five taels, enough to pay for his dinner three times over, and leave a very handsome tip; but the rascal pocketed the money, and very coolly asked me for another three taels for the dinner presented by him. It was no use growling. "Custom," universal tyrant, was appealed to, and I was obliged to pay.

These hotel cooks were the greatest pest that I met with in

China; they are leeches never to be satisfied; they receive no wages, but, on the contrary, pay large sums, like our waiters at home, for the privilege of preying upon unfortunate travellers, for whom they do nothing but boil rice. Yet, whatever fee is given to them, they demand more, and almost invariably abuse you.

On the sixth day after my arrival at Chen-tu, the Bishop returned to his palace; but it was not until the day after that I heard of his lordship's arrival, and the next day received from him an invitation to dinner for the morrow. I answered the invitation in person, and learned from him that my passport would be sent to me next day; so I at once returned to the hotel, and sent for a cooly contractor, who agreed to furnish two chairs and nine coolies to go to Ta-tsian-loo, on the frontiers of Thibet, for 68,000 chen. Highly elated at the prospect of an early start, in the evening I sent for a band of native musicians, and invited my next door neighbour, who was a military Mandarin, with a wife and seven children, on his way from Yunnan to Pekin, to spend the evening with me.

Our musicians were supposed to be the first artists in Chen-tu; and for six long hours they kept my guests and Philip in raptures. One of the performers was blind, and played a stringed instrument which gave forth really very sweet music. It was a species of dulcimer, shaped like a toy harmonicon, but, in the place of glass, there were sets of wire strings, like those of a piano, upon which the performer played with two small wooden hammers, covered with leather. Another played on a three-stringed fiddle; and a third on the bones; while they sang in turn in different voices, —one singing bass, another tenor, and the third soprano.

They carried with them a case of small books, each containing the words of an opera, which, before commencing, they handed to us, and my military friend selected several favourite pieces, which were played during the evening. The Chinese play entirely by ear; and although, according to European ideas, they know nothing of music, yet, after their own fashion, they are no mean performers. I had to pay each performer two taels for the evening and give them a supper. They were in the service of the Viceroy, and came to me as a great favour.

On the day appointed I dined with the Bishop, and had the honour of meeting a Roman Catholic Mandarin of high rank, and two French priests. We had an excellent dinner, consisting principally of fish, as it was Friday, and, what to one who for two months had been living à la Chinoise, was a great treat, a bottle of raisin wine.

At the hotel I found my passport waiting for me, and a message from the chief civil Mandarin, wishing me a pleasant journey.

Nothing now remained for me to do but pursue my route as quickly as possible. The Sz-chuan Viceroy's passport was addressed to the Chinese minister resident at Lhássa, the capital of Thibet, and ordered all Thibetan and Chinese officers to aid me. It further stated that on my arrival at Lhássa, I was to present it to the minister, who would change it for one authorising me to proceed into Nepaul or Darjeeling.

Armed with such credentials, for an hour or so I indulged in a dream of successfully reaching India; then I completed my packing ready for the morrow's start, glad of the prospect of once more being on the move.

CHAPTER VI.

CHEN-TU TO HI-YAN-KY.

A Cooly Fight—Soldiers at Free Quarters—Western Sz-chuan—Ya-tzow Brick Tea—Paddy Birds—A surly Pitman—The Fei-yue-ling—The Mountain Wind—Bishop Chauveau—Making a Gridiron—A Night on Ma-kia-shan—No Sport—The Soldiers are Coming—The ruined Village.

OUR departure from the hotel at Chen-tu on the morning of the 7th March was preceded by the usual wrangling and shouting on the part of the chair coolies. Threading our way along numerous small streets, we left the city by the west gate. Here a delay of ten minutes occurred while a Customhouse officer, having examined my passport, registered my name, destination, date of departure, and number of attendants, with the name of the contractor who had furnished the coolies, and the number of packages comprising my baggage. Then having passed through the extensive but dirty and straggling suburbs, the road led through the fertile plain of Chen-tu.

During our first halt at a rest-house a number of the usual half-starved idlers eagerly offered to relieve my bearers; the latter having agreed to hire four, at three chen per mile, the chair poles were at once seized by four eager pairs of hands. The poor wretches were at once displaced by others as eager, and in less than no time some fifty coolies were struggling for the coveted job, and dragging the chair about the road; my coolies thereupon came to the rescue, and used their bamboos freely on the heads of the rivals. A general fight ensued, sticks and stones flew about, and at last the chair was capsized, the top pulled off, and the occupant rolled out on the road. I jumped up, and began to lay about me John Bull fashion ; the sight, however, of my tall figure produced an immediate effect on the mob. "Ta-jen" was whispered about, and so great was the terror produced by the discovery that they had, as they thought, molested a Mandarin travelling *incog.*, that all fell on their knees begging for pardon.

The rest-house people came forward with profuse apologies, and some of the more respectable villagers caught the ringleaders and tied them as captives to my chair. Within ten minutes hardly a soul was to be seen ; all had fled from the wrath of Ta-jen. When all was over the head man of the place appeared, and by his orders the village blacksmith repaired the chair, which had suffered considerably.

The coolies, also, who had received a full share of cuts and bruises, had to be doctored, and we were delayed for two or three hours repairing damages ; but my feeling, on the whole, was one of amusement at the effect produced by my sudden and undignified appearance on the scene, while it was a great relief to have escaped a too probable detention and examination by the authorities.

At last we continued our journey. The plain presented a succession of most luxuriant spring crops of wheat, barley, sugar-cane, and opium. The country was thickly dotted with small farm-houses surrounded by plantations of bamboos and white pine trees, the whole enclosed by low whitewashed mud walls, which contrasted picturesquely with the verdure of surrounding crops.

It happened to be market day in Chen-tu, consequently the road was crowded with country people. We met women astride of ponies, smoking their long brass pipes and driving strings of oxen and mules laden with vegetables, grain, coal, charcoal, and coke; and pedestrians, both men and women, carrying newly-made chairs, tables, buckets, and stools, made of deal, all for the Chen-tu market.

Towards evening we crossed a ferry on the Kin-ma or Golden Horse river, a tributary of the Min, which in winter is about forty yards wide, and navigable for small boats drawing not more than eighteen inches from the Yang-tsŭ river as far as Kin-chin-chien, a walled city on its right bank, where we halted for the night.

The large gateways of this city, as of others in this district, were walled up, with the exception of a doorway just large enough for one man to pass through. They had been thus blocked up in 1860, when a body of rebels, organised in the city of Swi-foo, ascended the river Min as far as Kiating-foo, and threatened even the viceregal city of Chen-tu. The country people of Kiating-foo, however, rose, and defended their country for several months against the lawless bands, eventually dispersing them without any aid from Imperial troops, which, as usual, existed only on paper. In all the large towns on the main road from Chen-tu, as far as the city of Ya-tzow, on the western branch of the Min river, the people, in order to secure themselves in the absence of troops, built up their city gates.

Fifteen miles to the west of Kin-chin-chien we passed through the city of Chung-chow, famous for its paper manufactories. The rice-straw paper manufactured here is unrivalled in quality as writing paper; it is also extensively used to make spills, as it possesses all the properties of a slow match; when lighted it smoulders, and is easily blown into a flame. These spills are sold in bundles of fifty or more all over China.

The whole country so far was well irrigated by numerous natural and artificial water-courses, which turned the wheels of numbers of corn and sugar mills.

We halted at Chung-chow for the night, and put up at an hotel occupied by several military Mandarins and a detachment of 150 soldiers, the sole representatives of an army of 40,000 men, which, according to Imperial orders, was supposed to have marched from Chen-tu-foo six months previous to suppress the Mahomedan rebellion in Yunnan.

The general commanding this mythical army had never left Chen-tu, but had resided there, and, in collusion with the Viceroy of Sz-chuan and other high officials, had drawn pay from the Imperial treasury for 40,000 men at the rate of four taels four mace per man per mensem.

This mighty army, the muster-roll of which had never exceeded 250 men, had occupied nearly six months in marching a distance of thirty miles, and had been without pay up to the time of my arrival in Chung-chow, the result of which was that they had fairly gutted the town, and the greatest distress and confusion prevailed everywhere. Nearly every shop was closed, and the city more than half empty. Ruffianly and unshaven men, only recognisable as soldiers by the discoloured shreds of what had once been a red coat, roamed everywhere about the city like so many wolves, some dragging helpless, screaming women along the streets by their hair, others loaded with broken doors and window shutters, which they were carrying off to the hotel for firewood. Altogether, the city more resembled a place that was being sacked by the enemy than a peaceful and industrious town, as it were under the shadow of a viceregal court, and occupied by an Imperial army.

It was with no slight anxiety that I found myself located

in the same house with such a band of ruffians; and as soon as we were settled in a room I sent Philip with my passport to the Mandarins, requesting protection from the soldiers, who had entered my room and commenced pulling my baggage about very inquisitively. Philip soon returned, accompanied by an officer of inferior rank, who ordered the soldiers to leave my room, and posted up a notice on the door, to the effect that any person found in the room of Ta Ingqua Tang Koopaa (the English merchant Tang Cooper) would receive 100 strokes of the bamboo. I scarcely hoped that this would have any influence, but it proved most effectual. The soldiers were completely under the control of their officers, who, like themselves, were without pay, and held authority over their men by protecting them against the complaints of the inhabitants and sharing the plunder.

Beyond stealing the best part of my dinner on its way to my room from the cook-house, my military neighbours did not molest me in any way, letting me off, as the landlord said, very cheaply.

Some of my readers, unacquainted with Chinese manners and customs, may suppose that the picture I have drawn of the state of Chung-chow is an exceptional case, but it is not. The march of troops through any part of the Empire is invariably characterised by such scenes as I witnessed on this occasion, and is a calamity from which the unfortunate people of China are constantly suffering, varying in magnitude according to the forces of the marching army, so that they are scarcely less dreaded than a foreign enemy. Properly administered, the military system of China would be far from bad, but the prevalent corruption in this, as in every branch of the service, weakens the Empire and ruins its prosperity.

I was glad next morning to leave the unfortunate city of Chung-chow, acting on the advice of the landlord, who hinted that it would be as well to put as much distance as possible between us and the soldiers before daylight.

Outside the city we crossed a stone bridge of fifteen arches, spanning the Tung-nan river. This bridge was a fine specimen of Chinese skill; the roadway was at least forty feet in width, and each arch was over thirty feet in span. We had now commenced ascending the line of hills which bound the plain of Chen-tu on the west, and the increasing cold made it necessary to use charcoal-pans in our chairs. The scenery was lovely; hill-sides clothed with woods, alternated with fertile and cultivated valleys, forming one of those landscapes which make all visitors to Sz-chuan enthusiastic in their praise of its scenery.

To the west of us loomed a high range of mountains, their sides rendered black by distance, contrasting with the white wreaths of clouds which hung round some of their loftier peaks. Though scarcely fifty miles from Chen-tu and its environs, clothed with the luxuriant verdure of spring, the country hereabouts seemed scarcely to have shaken off the grasp of winter. The wheat and barley were hardly two inches above ground, and beyond this point westward but little opium was cultivated.

The peasantry of this district were conspicuous for their fine physique, being much more robust than those of eastern Sz-chuan; the women especially were fine creatures, and were, like those met with *en route* to Chen-tu, free from the fashionable deformity of small feet. We met many women carrying apples, pears, and walnuts to market; and numbers of men staggering along under heavy loads of pig-iron and iron ware. All, however, appeared well dressed and happy;

men, women, and even the children, smoking their long pipes.

That the men of this district did not belie their appearance, we soon experienced. A party heavily laden with iron ware, lead, coal, and slabs of a kind of cedar wood used for making coffins, stopped just in front of us, and threw down their loads to rest. My coolies peremptorily ordered them out of the way, but they took no notice, whereupon my fellows commenced to hurl all kinds of abuse at them, and soon both sides were yelling at each other at the very top of their voices. My coolies attempted to force a passage, and in doing so gave one of the countrymen a push, who returned it with a shove, and this was the signal for a regular set-to. Sticks, stones, bamboos, and splinters flew about, and at it went both sides like perfect devils. My chair-poles were pulled out and broken, and in the *mêlée* I was again upset, and obliged to get out of the chair, receiving in doing so a severe blow on the leg. My august presence seemed to throw a wet blanket on the fun, and both sides drew off, my coolies having had decidedly the worst of it, much to the delight of the countrymen, who shouldered their goods, and passed on, leaving our discomfited party to bind up their wounds and repair damages.

At the end of two days' journey from Chung-chow, we crossed the Ya-ho river by means of a floating bridge of bamboos. The river was some fifty yards wide, running through a broad and fertile valley, in which lies the city of Ya-tzow, famous for the manufacture of the brick tea used in Thibet.

At the gates of the city the customs' officials, a number of whom kept the strictest watch, ordered us to stop and open our baggage for inspection. On production of my passport, however, an officer stepped forward, and making a profound bow, informed me that my arrival had been long expected, as the Viceroy had sent orders that the English merchant was not to be subjected to the Custom-house regulations. The officials were most polite, and sent a soldier to conduct me to an hotel, where a room was ready for my reception.

The city of Ya-tzow is the last large city of importance in the west of China. Besides the celebrity of its tea manufactories, it is also famous as a great military stronghold, being well fortified, and containing, for a Chinese city, a large garrison of regular troops.

During the wars which ended in the annexation of the eastern kingdom of Thibet to the province of Sz-chuan, Ya-tzow was the head-quarters and basis of all military operations, and has ever since been the great military depôt of Western China.

The district of Ya-tzow is extremely rich in minerals. Coal, iron, lead, and copper are very abundant; and it is principally from this district that Sz-chuan is supplied with metals, especially steel and copper.

But the greatest source of wealth to the city and surrounding district is the brick tea, which gives employment to thousands engaged in the manufacture and portage of tea from Ya-tzow to Ta-tsian-loo. The tree from which this peculiar kind of tea is manufactured grows chiefly along the banks of the Ya-ho, and, unlike that which produces the tea exported to Europe, is a tall tree, often fifteen feet high, with a large and coarse leaf. Little care is bestowed on the cultivation. It is often planted along the borders of fields and homesteads, each farmer gathering his small crop of tea, and finding a ready sale for it in Ya-tzow to merchants who pay the government enormous sums for the monopoly.

I never had an opportunity of witnessing the process by which the tea is made into the exceedingly hard bricks which find their way to Thibet; and so great is the jealousy with which the monopoly is guarded, that even bribes failed to procure permission to enter the warehouses where the tea is packed for exportation. I am indebted to the landlord of the hotel where I lodged during both my visits, for the following imperfect description. The first quality is gathered in June and July, or shortly after the commencement of the summer rains in the end of May, when the leaf is about an inch long. When gathered, it is spread in the sun till slightly withered, and then rolled with the hand until moist from the exudation of the sap. In this state it is rolled into balls about the size of a large tea-cup, and laid up till it ferments. It is then ready for the wooden brick-moulds, which are made with the ends movable, and fastened by pegs. The moulds, when filled, are dried over charcoal fires until the tea is baked into a tough solid mass. When taken from the moulds, the bricks are ready for delivery to the merchants of Ya-tzow. By them the bricks are enveloped in peculiar yellow paper covers, bearing a government stamp and the trade-mark of the exporter, and are packed in baskets four feet long, made of thin strips of bamboo. The bricks thus packed form what is called a basket of tea, weighing about twenty pounds. These baskets are carried by coolies to Ta-tsian-loo, a distance of two hundred miles, where they are carefully covered with green hide, as a protection against wet, and are then ready for exportation to Lhássa, and the countries to the west of it, where this particular kind of brick tea is principally consumed, selling for about fifteen taels per basket, or four shillings and eightpence per pound.

The second quality, which consists of the older and yellower leaves, is manufactured in the same manner, and exported principally to Lithang and Bathang, where it is sold at five taels per basket, or about one shilling and sixpence per pound.

A third quality is made entirely of clippings, without the leaf, and resembles bricks of chopped twigs. The manufacture of this kind differs from the others, rice-water being used to make the twigs adhere and retain the brick form. This quality is only used in Ta-tsian-loo and its immediate neighbourhood, selling for ninepence per pound.

The quantity of brick tea annually exported from Ya-tzow to Thibet has been roughly estimated at over six million pounds.

We remained only one night at Ya-tzow, continuing our journey next day through a mountainous country. The road in places was very bad, being little more than a path about two feet wide, cut along the sides of almost perpendicular hills three or four hundred feet high, rising from the bank of the Ya-ho river. The country was exceedingly wild, and covered with a rank vegetation, while parasitic plants, and ferns growing in the forks of trees, betokened a damp climate. Where practicable, the hill-sides were cultivated in terraces, and in the valleys extensive tracts of rice-stubble were flooded two or three inches deep, preparatory to being ploughed for another crop. Numbers of the white-crested paddy birds were busily engaged in feeding on the numerous small fry which find their way into the fields from the streams which feed the artificial water-courses. It was amusing to watch the methodical dexterity with which these graceful little birds secured their prey. They would first run rapidly up the field between the rows of stubble, into which the frightened fish were thus driven; then, slowly retracing their steps, they struck with their feet each tuft of stubble, and, as the fish darted out from their hiding-places, they were picked up with marvellous quickness.

As we approached the end of our day's stage, I left my chair, the continual jolting of which, owing to the constant slipping of the coolies as they toiled up and down the greasy paths along the hill-sides, had become almost unbearable.

At a turn of the road I met three men in charge of a pack of thirty-two dogs all coupled together, and attached to a long leading-string held by a man walking in front of them. They were a peculiar breed, so remarkably uniform in colour (tan, with a black shade along the back, and black pointed muzzle), that they attracted my attention. The owner informed me that he had purchased them at Ta-tsian-loo, from the Man-ts[u] (as the Chinese call the Thibetan people). They are highly prized as watch-dogs in Sz-chuan, and realise high prices. They are handsome hound-like dogs, standing about eighteen inches, clean-limbed, and deep-chested, with shapely quarters; their ears hang, but are small. The Mau-ts[u] use them principally as retrievers in the chase of wild boar and deer. They hunt by scent, with a musical cry, and rarely fail to bring the wounded quarry to bay. I gave the pack a "Yoicks!" which echoed through the mountains, and roused the dogs to frenzy. They answered with a burst of melody that made my very heart tingle. There was the true, clear, musical note of the hound, which sounded in the mountains like fairy music; and as I again and again hallooed to them, they grew so excited that the men in charge became alarmed, and begged me to pass on. When I left them, their struggles grew fierce; and as I turned a corner of the road, the men were laying about them with their whips.

Every day's journey westward now took us into wilder country, where for miles neither houses nor cultivation were to be seen, the hills gradually assumed the size of mountains, and the road was dreadful; some parts were so steep that I was obliged to walk, getting however many severe falls on the large slippery stones with which the path was paved. The coolies secured their foothold by the use of crampons or iron plates studded with spikes, and fastened, when required, to the heels and toes of their hempen sandals. Besides the blue cotton jacket and drawers, the coolies plying between Chen-tu and Ta-tsian-loo wear a turban of thick coarse blanketing, and bandage their legs from the swell of the calf to the ankle with strips of the same, leaving the knees bare; this serves as a protection from cuts and bruises, and as a preservative from severe pains in the legs, with which the traveller if unprotected in a similar manner is sure to be attacked; both Philip and myself suffered severely, until by the advice of the coolies we adopted their method of bandaging, and felt no further inconvenience. Just before reaching the village of Quan-yin-foo, where we were to sleep, we passed some coal mines. A number of shafts or adits, about three feet square, were driven horizontally into the face of the almost perpendicular hill side; I entered one, and crept along it for forty or fifty yards through a seam of fine bright coal, resting on a soft slaty stratum. At the end crouched a solitary miner hewing the coal with his pick by the light of a candle,—he was as black, and proved to be as bearish, as a pitman of our own "black country," resenting my intrusion with a volley of growls, winding up with an intelligible demand for chen. Having gratified him, I tried to ask a few questions; but he resumed his pick, and beyond muttered growlings vouchsafed no further notice.

Starting at daylight from Quan-yin-foo, we at once began to climb the Yang-Nin mountains, running N.E. and S.W., the first of the series of great ranges to the west of Chen-tu. We were obliged to walk to the summit, getting thoroughly wetted as soon as we entered the clouds, which clung half way down the mountain. The summit was reached at noon, and we breakfasted at a solitary rest-house. The western slope was perfectly dry and free from cloud, and a bright sun soon dried our saturated garments. Near the foot of the mountain we overtook a party of travellers; these proved to be Man-ts^u women,—a lady and two attendants, wearing their remarkable costume, viz., a voluminous turban of blue cloth, and a coat-like dress of the same reaching to the ankles, and confined by a yellow girdle. They were fair and good-looking, and devoid of that shyness which marks the Chinese women, owing to their seclusion. The mistress who, with her young infant, travelled in a chair, was the wife of a Chinese merchant of Ta-tsian-loo, whither she was returning, from a pilgrimage undertaken to offer thanks for the birth of her first-born son, at the celebrated Buddhist shrines of the Holy Mountain, Omee Shan, near Kiating-foo. We travelled almost in company during the rest of the day. In the afternoon we met two other pilgrims, Chinamen, proceeding in accomplishment of a vow to a temple some twenty-five miles distant. They wore white coats and drawers, and travelled barefoot, stopping every three steps to bend their heads to the ground. They were bound thus to perform the journey day and night, wet or fine, only halting thrice a day to eat rice. Win-che-chien, our next halt, is famous for its manufactures of iron and brass, the adjacent country containing numerous iron and copper mines worked by monopolists, the government drawing a large revenue from mining grants.

THE FEI-YUE-LING.

Having tried one hotel in Win-che-chien, we were obliged by its unusual wretchedness to go to another, where we found the Man-ts^u party who had passed us near the town, and by them we were warmly greeted. After dinner the lady sent to ask for some opium, which however it was not in our power to supply; but, notwithstanding, we smoked our pipes together, and by means of one of the attendants who spoke Chinese, had a long and pleasant conversation. She declared that I must be a Man-ts^u, though at first she had taken me for a missionary.

We were now among the eastern spurs of the great snow-clad Fei-yue-ling range, and made our way slowly up the paths that the Chinese describe as only fit for birds; the road led up a ravine, down which a mountain torrent fell in a succession of noisy cascades on its way to the Ya-ho. The sides of the glen were gay with the white flowers of the large-leaved tea-tree, from which rang out the clear loud notes of a Bell bird, carrying my thoughts back far away to the bush of Australia. At a turn of the glen we came to an iron suspension bridge, constructed of double chains stretching thirty yards from rock to rock, about 120 feet above the torrent. The roadway was formed of planks laid on the chains without side-rails or support of any kind, and as we crossed over, the structure vibrated and swung beneath us so as to make the passage somewhat perilous. We afterwards passed two other similar bridges, and halted for the night at a little village called Show-quan, nestled just below the snow line, so as to commence at daylight the difficult and dreaded crossing of the Fei-yue-ling. At day dawn we left the little cabin, from the roof of which hung icicles two feet long, and commenced the ascent. The snow lay several feet deep on the steep sides of the mountain peaks which towered above us, while down the ravines avalanches of thawing snow shot with thundering reports into the lower valleys.

The track was often blocked up by these fallen masses of snow, obliging us to dig our way through it. In other places the snow had been trodden down, and the previous night's frost had converted it into sheets of ice. In such places we were obliged to tie ourselves together with long ropes, and scramble along, often on hands and feet. At other times we crept along the edge of fearful precipices, overhanging terrible chasms of unknown depth.

As we were cautiously making our way over the frozen surface of a snow bank, which some days before had slipped from above and lodged half way down a small ravine, two of the coolies carrying my chair, trusting too much to their spiked sandals, slipped, pulling the other two after them,— chair and coolies made a glissade down the ravine for about twenty yards; fortunately one of the chair poles stuck in the snow and brought the party to a stand still, not ten yards from the brink of a precipice 400 feet deep. We, who were up above, were obliged to crawl along on our hands and knees, and after getting safely over the dangerous part, let down a rope to the terrified bearers, who dared not stir lest a movement should dislodge the chair pole, which alone saved them from destruction, and nearly an hour passed before they were all rescued from their perilous position. At rare intervals we came upon sheltered nooks free from snow, where moss and stunted ferns and brambles grew in profusion, and tiny yellow primroses peeped even through the snow where it lay in thin patches. After seven hours' severe toil, rendered more difficult by the dense mist which hung over the mountain and whitened our clothes and faces with rime, we surmounted the summit, which to my surprise was free from snow, and arrived at a little rest-house just below it, and more than 12,000 feet above the level of the sea. On nearing the house we heard a loud roar which I imagined to be caused by an avalanche, but which the people at the rest-house informed me was the sound of a violent wind, which, during ten months of the year while the snow lies on the eastern slope, blows on the western side, invariably commencing as soon as the sun reaches the meridian, and continuing till sun-down.

As there was not a particle of snow on the western side, the descent offered no difficulties, save those caused by the steepness of the declivity. Like most of the great ranges which lie between Chen-tu and Bathang, the Fei-yue-ling mountains rise by very gradual ascent from their eastern base; while the counter-slope falls so abruptly, as to seem almost perpendicular.

For 2000 feet a thick mist, hiding every object more than ten yards distant, enveloped us as we made our way down a zig-zag path, cut in the bare limestone, not a sign of vegetation being visible. Suddenly we came out of the mist into brilliant sunlight, and the whole appearance of the mountain seemed changed, as if by magic; instead of the bare and rugged limestone the mountain-side, though steep, appeared perfectly smooth, and was clothed with a dense growth of dwarf male bamboo, presenting the appearance of high grass. We looked down upon the walled town of Chin-chi-chien, lying as it were at our feet in a basin-like plain, surrounded by hills covered with bamboo. In that clear atmosphere the roofs of the houses appeared quite close to us, yet we occupied four hours in traversing the road which we saw, like a white line, winding down the mountain and through the verdant plain.

After leaving the line of mist we were overtaken by a violent wind which swept down the mountain with the sound and force of a hundred avalanches, rendering it difficult for us to keep our feet; indeed, during occasional gusts of unusual violence, we were obliged to crouch down until its fury was somewhat abated. This was the wind which had been described to us by the keepers of the rest-house. It continued to blow till sun-set, and we heard it roaring outside after we were safely housed in an hotel at Chin-chi-chien. In the evening two Christians, residing in the town, paid us a visit; and from them I learned that Monseigneur Chauveau, the Vicar Apostolic of Thibet, was very ill, and residing at a mission station called Ta-lin-pin, on the banks of the Ta-tow-ho, a day's journey to the south of Chin-chi-chien. Next morning, therefore, we struck off from the high road to Ta-tsian-loo, and proceeded southwards to a village named Hi-yan-ky, about a mile and a half from the Bishop's residence. Leaving my baggage and coolies at an hotel, I proceeded with Philip to Ta-lin-pin, along a broad bed of sand and shingle about a quarter of a mile wide, and more than two miles long, enclosed on either hand by a wall of steep mountains. A small stream meandered through this glen, which, in the summer rains, is completely occupied by the swollen waters pouring themselves into the Ta-tow-ho, about two miles west of Hi-yan-ky. A zig-zag path led up to the village of Ta-lin-pin, consisting of two farm-houses, and the mission station, perched 500 or 600 feet up the mountain. Our approach was descried, and, half way, we were met by a young priest, Father Careau, the Bishop's secretary. Immediately on our entrance dinner was served by order of the Bishop, who sent a kind message that he would rise and receive me after dinner. On our journey from Chen-tu, save at one or two small towns, nothing but rice and salt vegetables had been procurable in the way of food; so that the unexpected feast of roast kid, potatoes, bread and butter from Ta-tsian-loo, with an abundance of excellent rice-wine, was done justice to in a manner which elicited many expressions of sympathy from Father Careau, who knew by experience the hardships of our route.

After dinner, and a social chat over our pipes, the Bishop signified his readiness to receive me. On entering his room I perceived a venerable old man, dressed in Chinese costume, with a long, snow-white beard. I shall never forget him as long as I live. He was sixty years of age, forty of which he had spent in China as a missionary. But long illness made him look even older. His countenance was very beautiful in its benignity; his eye, undimmed by age and suffering, lighted on me with a kindly expression; and he bade me welcome in English, which he had learned from his mother, an English lady, with a tremulous but musical voice.

My arrival was unexpected. The more so, as he had written a letter which I should have received in Chen-tu saying that he was confined to his bed, and advising me to continue on to Ta-tsian-loo and wait his arrival there. However, Providence, as he said, had directed me to him at Ta-lin-pin; for, since writing, he had lost the use of his legs, which would have prevented his joining me in Ta-tsian-loo for some weeks. At his request I explained the object of my journey, namely to reach India either by Lhássa or Assam; and, further, that I was only a private individual travelling for my own pleasure, and in no way connected with the British Government. To this he merely replied that he had been misinformed on the subject of my journey; and explained that I could not proceed beyond Ta-tsian-loo for several weeks, as the road was still closed by the snow. This interval he advised me to spend at Hi-yan-ky, where his people would assist me in procuring food. This would, also, be more convenient for him, as I would not require to draw upon him for funds until we reached Ta-tsian-loo, where he kept the treasure belonging to the mission.

After an hour spent in conversation, I took my leave of the Bishop, promising to remain at Hi-yan-ky for a few weeks, until he should be ready to accompany me to Ta-tsian-loo, and returned to the hotel not sorry at the prospect of a rest, as I was feeling rather the worse for the last ten days' journey on short allowance of food.

Still, my prospects now were anything but cheering. Besides the certainty of an unexpected detention of at least a month, it was evident that the chance of my reaching India seemed very doubtful to the Bishop, who, from his long residence on the borders of Thibet, and his thorough knowledge of the Chinese and Thibetan officials, knew, too well, the difficulties. However, nothing but the prospect of my funds not holding out till I could reach British territory, caused me any anxiety; and I set about making myself as comfortable as my circumstances would admit of. Having returned to Hi-yan-ky I discharged the coolies, who claimed their full fare to Ta-tsian-loo, a demand which, though it involved a clear loss of twenty taels, it was impossible to dispute. My first day was devoted to securing myself against a scarcity of food, and, by the evening, we rejoiced in a larder well stocked with pheasants, of the Lady Amherst species, and half a pig, purchased from a countryman, besides a present from the Bishop of remarkably fine kidney potatoes, and some loaves of bread, made by his own cook under the superintendence of Father Careau.

My next move was to devise a culinary means of deliverance from the everlasting round of greasy Chinese stews. At a blacksmith's, next door to the hotel, I succeeded in partly making a gridiron; while the smith sat looking at me in good-natured astonishment, apparently quite content for me to usurp his place at the anvil, so long as I gave him tobacco and paid him for his iron. By noon the gridiron was finished to my entire satisfaction.

I had no difficulty in rigging up a suitable fire-place, for charcoal, brought from Chin-chi-chien, was easily attainable; and a large iron cauldron, set on four stones just outside my door, answered all the purposes of a cooking-range, so that in the evening my exertions were rewarded by the appearance of grilled pheasant, pork chops, and boiled potatoes, which I washed down with rice wine; and forgot, for a time, that I was alone in the West of China, far away from friends, surrounded by a people buried in the darkest superstition, and liable at any time to fall a victim to their passions or prejudices.

Thus I spent several days in recruiting my strength. Father Careau paid me a visit nearly every day, which I returned at Ta-lin-pin. During one of my visits to the Bishop, he proposed that I should accompany Father Careau on an excursion into the Ma-kia-shan mountains, which were said to abound in wild boars, deer, and pheasants. I had had no sport since leaving Shanghai, and was highly pleased at the prospect of some deer stalking, or a chance shot at a boar. So arrangements were soon made for a start on the next morning. Leaving Philip in charge of my baggage, I set out alone for the Mission-house, and arrived in time for breakfast; and then, in company with the young priest, and a number of mountaineers carrying bedding and provisions, started for the mountains.

Our road led up the side of the mountain above the mission station. The ascent was very steep and dangerous, and the sun shone with oppressive heat; but three hours' toil landed us on the summit, from which we obtained a view of the Ma-kia-shan snow-capped mountains, frowning down upon us from an enormous height, and dwarfing to a mere hill the mountain on which we stood.

Seeing that it would be impossible for us to reach our intended resting-place for the night (in the hut of a mountaineer, perched on the steep declivity of Ma-kia-shan, just below the line of snow), I proposed to halt for the night at a nearer hut, visible some distance above us. This proposition, however, seemed to inspire the young priest with a spirit of emulation; for he good-naturedly laughed at my fears, and challenged me to a race up the mountain, and with the light-heartedness of his countrymen started off with a merry ringing laugh, and soon hailed me from a great height above.

It was plain that we could not hope to reach the snow-line of Ma-kia-shan until long after dark, even if our endurance held out; for myself, I had little fear, I was in capital walking condition, and so far had taken it very coolly; but I had noticed that my companion, on reaching the summit of the first range, looked flushed and exhausted; so much so, that I had persuaded him to join me in a reviving pull at the flask. However, I answered his hail with a cheer, and settled down to my work. In less than two hours I overtook him, sitting down, evidently much distressed, but still full of pluck, and we jogged on together for a few hundred yards;

when he again pulled up, looking so ill that I became alarmed, and quickly administered another dose of alcohol.

It was already late, and our destination was fully five miles off, so I begged of my companion to return to the nearest hut we had passed, a mile below; but he continued obstinate, and we again pushed onwards. We had scarcely travelled another mile, when the poor fellow, utterly exhausted, and perceiving too late that we could not reach our journey's end, threw himself down and fainted.

Our coolies were far ahead, and night closed on us; while a fierce cold wind, which grew in force towards sunset, almost froze us to death. I could not let my companion lie where he was, though I doubted being able to find the hut below us in the dark. However, I soon decided on the course to pursue. I hailed the coolies, and after making the mountains echo with repeated "coo-ees," succeeded in attracting their attention.

They understood that something was wrong, and turned back. In the meantime my unfortunate companion lay insensible, and was only restored to partial consciousness by a large dose of rice-wine poured down his throat. He was quite unable to stand, and as the severe cold made it dangerous to wait for the coolies, I hoisted him on to my shoulders, and commenced a downward march, and with much difficulty, and not without help from a cooly, we at last arrived safe at the hut. This was only a shanty with a flat roof of boards, covered with mud, resting on low stone walls built against the mountain, which formed the back wall. The interior was divided into three stall-like compartments, tenanted by three mountaineers and their families.

Round a coal fire, kindled on an open hearth, were huddled men, women, and children, several mangy dogs, and three lean pigs, besides numerous fowls. The poor people, who were Christians, gave us a kindly welcome, and hastened to place the young priest in one of their bed places, which were bunks scooped out of the mountain rock.

I soon had the satisfaction of seeing my companion fall into a sound sleep; and then joined the family round the fire. They were busy at their evening meal of potatoes roasted in the ashes, and timidly asked me to take a share; and I added some rice-wine from my flask, which was a great treat to my poor hosts—with whom I sat smoking for a long time.

Next morning, long before daylight, I was roused by the crowing of cocks, and general stir among the live stock, impatient to commence the day; so I turned out again, and joined the family in a pipe until daylight, when the young priest, quite recovered from his exhaustion, joined us. Unfortunately, our provision cooly had not been amongst those who had returned with us to the hut; so we were glad to share our host's breakfast of roasted potatoes and salt. The people of the house were delighted when they knew that our object in visiting their mountains was to kill wild boars, which they pronounced to be their greatest enemies, destroying their only crops—potatoes* and Indian corn. Herds of these animals descend from the almost inaccessible heights, and, if undisturbed, destroy in one night acres of potatoes. The unfortunate people are therefore obliged to keep a constant watch over their cultivation; and the boars are so cunning and bold, that the people consider themselves fortunate if one half of their crops are saved.

---

* The Chinese name for the potato is Yang-yu, or "foreign root," and in Sz-chuan I was informed that it had been introduced long ago, by the foreign teachers, i.e., the early French missionaries.

We soon faced the mountain again, and by 8 A.M. reached the hut to which we were bound. The owners of it were Christians, and delighted at our visit. With a kindly thoughtfulness they had prepared breakfast, and expressed great sympathy for our troubles on the previous night. After a hasty meal, we sallied forth in quest of sport, accompanied by several mountaineers.

From the summit of Ma-kia-shan, we looked down on the Ta-tow river, and could see the Jeddo snowy range, lying to the west of Ta-tsian-loo; everywhere around us, huge peaks towered into the clouds, their bare and rugged sides utterly destitute of vegetation, except here and there in sequestered valleys, where patches of coarse grass and stunted trees furnished the coverts for herds of wild boars.

To one of these valleys we bent our steps; from where we stood it appeared quite close, but it took nearly three hours to reach it, and then, much to our disappointment, the beaters failed to start even a pheasant, and we returned to the hut quite tired with our morning's work, took dinner, and turned in long before nightfall; such was our day's sport among the heights of Ma-kia-shan. In high disgust, we decided on returning to Ta-lin-piu on the morrow.

The inhabitants of these mountains, though quite Chinese in habits, language, and costume, are not of pure Chinese race; in fact, nearly the whole population, west of the Fei-yue-ling range of mountains, are of mixed breed, between Chinese, Thibetans, and Lo-Los; which latter are a very powerful tribe, inhabiting a considerable tract of country, lying to the west of the Ta-tow river. Though nominally tributary to China, they have never yet been thoroughly subjugated, and are constantly engaged in predatory forays into the country lying between the Fei-yue-ling mountains, and the Ta-tow river.

During times of peace many Lo-Los emigrate to the settled districts bordering the left bank of the river, and intermarry with the people, whom they closely resemble, even to costume, language, and habits. Their houses are precisely similar, and Buddhism is their professed religion.

It happened that during our visit to Ma-kia-shan a party of Lo-Los were out on a foraging expedition, and had visited the hut of our Christian friends, and, strange to say, had left them unmolested on learning that they were followers of the new Law, which even these tribes had heard preached from the lips of the brave and persevering French missionaries.

We descended Ma-kia-shan next day, and reached Ta-lin-pin, considerably disgusted with our trip, in which we had undergone so much toil without seeing so much as a feather. Philip, however, rejoiced at my early and unexpected return, for during my absence he said he had thought too much of home. Indeed, our sojourn at this place was dull enough—a daily lesson in Chinese, cooking, skinning and preserving ornithological specimens brought in by the natives, with an occasional visit to Ta-lin-pin, made up the routine of our life, and so the time passed gradually.

We managed to extract some amusement from an almost daily review of mules brought for sale. As beyond Ta-tsian-loo the baggage would have to be carried by mules instead of porters, the Bishop had advised me to procure them here; placards, accordingly, had been posted, advertising that a number of suitable beasts were required, for which good prices would be given. In consequence, all the mule-owners for miles round brought their vicious and broken-down animals for inspection, each vaunting his miserably blemished or intractable brute as the most perfect and gentlest in the world. A crowd always gathered to enjoy the fun, as on the arrival of an unusually vicious mule the owner was always compelled to mount and show his animal's paces, a proceeding which invariably ended in his discomfiture, to the great delight of the lookers-on.

Out of more than fifty I only bought one, a little grey mare, standing about twelve hands. As her owner said, she was of the "iron breed," a term commonly applied to the mules of Yunnan, which, though small, perform prodigies in the way of weight-carrying and travel, 400 pounds weight being an ordinary load. The "Iron Duchess," as I named my purchase, did credit to her breed, for she was the only animal out of six that held out during several months' journey.

I had been living for nearly three weeks at the hotel quite contentedly; the people were very friendly-disposed, and never attempted to molest me in the least; I rambled about the country alone, and often went visiting at the houses of many of the more respectable people. Suddenly one morning I was aroused out of a deep sleep by the landlord, who, knocking furiously at my door, shouted in a voice of great alarm, " The soldiers are coming." Outside, there was heard loud crying and wailing of women, and a great uproar.

Dressing hurriedly, I armed myself with revolver and tomahawk, thinking that the house was attacked. Philip soon gathered all our baggage together and placed it under my bed, and nailed up the doors leading from our room to the two adjoining ones. Somewhat amused by his notions of security, I laughed, and told him to arm himself with my long hunting-knife; it was now his turn to laugh, for he replied, "Oh, the soldiers are not coming to fight; they are only those fellows we saw at Chung-chow, on the march."

On going out into the main street of the village the confusion was dreadful; people were leaving for the country, carrying with them all their portable valuables, and every shop was closed. An advance guard of some half-dozen red-coated ruffians were going round, fixing arrows with small three-cornered flags to all the hotel and wine-shop door-posts. The flags were numbered, and as the main body, some 200 strong, marched, or rather straggled, into the village, each company took up its quarters at the house marked with its number; 100 were billeted on our hotel, which was the largest house.

Some of the soldiers made straight for my room and burst open the door. On asking the foremost fellow what he wanted, he answered by telling me to go to a certain place, and ordered Philip to bring tea and tobacco; then putting down his baggage, he threw himself full length on my bed, and asked where his pipe was. I quietly informed him that he could not smoke in my room, and must leave it; he only replied by snatching up my pipe, and shouting at me to bring a light on pain of instant punishment. As I was in the act of crossing the room to throw him out another wretch knocked open the door, which swung back, striking me on the temple; this roused me, and as the fellow put his face in I knocked him down; it was now his comrade's turn, so taking him by the throat, I dragged him to the door, where I held him in one hand and felled him with the other. This brought the rest of his companions upon me like a pack of howling wolves, but as I drew my revolver and covered them, they recognised me as a foreigner, and checked their advance. Just then the mandarin in command rode up on a small white pony. When he learnt what I had done he was furious, and rushed at me in a frantic manner, nearly bringing his face in contact with the revolver; the moment he perceived it he calmed down, and requested me to speak to him inside. I ushered him in and presented him with a pipe and tea, and desired him to read the Chen-tu Viceroy's passport. This was quite sufficient; he called up the soldiers to my door, showing them the passport, and pointing to the seal, on seeing which they all kowtowed, *i.e.*, bent the knee.

This mandarin turned out a very good fellow; he dined with me in the evening, was very amusing, affected the languid swell to admiration, and, as Philip said, was a great poet. He got very drunk, however, and I was very glad when, long after midnight, two soldiers carried him off to bed.

Next morning, getting up rather late, I received a very polite note from him, wishing me in poetry farewell and a pleasant journey, and begging my acceptance of a packet of rare tea, which, as he poetically wrote, his sons of tigers had borrowed from the baggage of an illustrious traveller. This packet of tea had positively been stolen from my baggage by the scoundrel who had lain on my bed. I laughed heartily over the joke, and then went out to console with my landlord, whose house was fairly gutted. He and his family were praying in the midst of their ruin to the little household joss, and upbraiding him for having permitted such a calamity to fall upon them. Doors and window-frames had been broken up for firewood; even the partitions of many of his rooms had been torn down for the same purpose. Broken chairs, tables, and crockery were scattered about all over the place; a large kitchen garden, which the day before was full of vegetables, was bare, and the paling surrounding it had been burnt.

Throughout the village the same devastation prevailed,

while the wretched people sat in the streets bewailing their misfortune. Only yesterday the place had been a thriving little village, and the people happy and contented; to-day all was ruin and misery.

The Bishop wrote word to say that he intended to start for Ta-tsian-loo the next morning; I therefore packed up, and at 9 A.M. on the 3rd of April the Bishop and his party arrived. We breakfasted together, and then I once more turned my steps westwards, and left behind me the ruined village of Hi-yan-ky.

CHAPTER VII.

HI-YAN-KY TO TA-TSIAN-LOO.

Ceremonial of Atonement—Loo-din-chow Suspension Bridge—Don Quixote in Tse-tsang—Tea Carriers—Thibetan Hotel—The Border Town—Visit from a Lama—Prayer Cyliuders—Lama Monks—Yunnan Lepers—Petticoats or Trousers—Man-tsʉ Ladies—Equipments for Thibet.

WE left the village of Hi-yan-ky in great state. The Bishop's attendants, including coolies and mounted followers, numbered nearly forty men, and, added to my party, made up quite an imposing procession. His flag-bearer led the way, carrying a small triangular yellow silk flag, on which were painted, in red letters, the Bishop's Chinese name ("Ting") and title. Immediately following, came the Bishop in his large green chair, carried by four coolies, and eight were pulling in front by means of long ropes attached to each pole of the chair. Close behind came the baggage-coolies, each carrying, besides his load, a small flag resembling that in front, and after them three mounted servants and Philip. My chair and baggage brought up the rear of the cavalcade. This order we preserved nearly all throughout our journey to Ta-tsian-loo.

A little difficulty occurred at starting, which was characteristic of the greed of the cooly contractor; for the journey, so far, nine coolies had sufficed; and as Philip had now exchanged his chair for the saddle—riding the Iron Duchess—it had been agreed that seven only would be required to take myself and baggage to Ta-tsian-loo. These the contractor had agreed to furnish for a sum of two taels each, though he only paid them one tael, thus clearing a hundred per cent. by the transaction. Not satisfied, however, he informed me that I must engage two extra hands, and on receiving a refusal, insolently threw the seven taels paid him in advance, on the ground, telling me to find a chair and coolies for myself. He was, however, brought to his senses by entreaties on the part of the Bishop's Chinese secretary, forcibly supported by Philip with his whip. During the day he continued to complain that he had been forced against his will to accompany us, and at the hotel, in the evening, was overheard volubly discoursing on the bad treatment he had received from the "foreign devil." Now, I was aware that, according to custom, the bearers had, on receiving a portion of their pay, returned to him a certain sum as commission, which entitled them to the possession of the chair, so, next morning, in presence of all the people to whom he had complained, I informed him that I could not think of forcing him to accompany me against his will, and therefore absolved him from his engagement; telling him, at the same time, to return me the amount advanced to him, and that I would settle with the coolies for their day's work.

The fellow had not a word to say, and, amidst the laughter of all, with a very bad grace handed back the money; thereupon I engaged the coolies, for a tael and a half each, to Ta-tsian-loo. Both they and myself benefited by the new arrangement, and all parties were satisfied except the contractor, who, besides losing his profit, was ridiculed on all sides.

For the first two or three days after leaving Hi-yan-ky we traversed a wretchedly barren mountainous country, resting occasionally at small villages, and putting up at the Kungkwans. The small cultivated fields were enclosed with rough stone walls, to protect the crops from donkeys, droves of which were from time to time met with, laden with coal for Chin-chi-chien. One little town, named Ngee-too, lay in a happy valley, the fertility of which was evident in the flourishing vegetable gardens surrounding the place, the houses of which were of a superior description. Ngee-too, from the salubrity of its climate, and the fame of its vegetables and wine, attracts all the rich people of the surrounding country, who resort to it as if it were a fashionable watering-place. At the time of our visit it presented a very gay appearance. A great religious ceremony had just taken place, namely, praying for forgiveness of sins and deliverance from an epidemic which had been for some time prevalent. The ceremonial, which was neither Buddhist nor Taouist, but belonged to the true popular polytheistic religion of China, consisted in processions and litanies, while fowls had been sacrificed, and their blood sprinkled on the door-posts. All the houses, both inside and out, were decorated with green boughs and garlands of wild flowers, in token that atonement had been made, and the scourge of sickness removed. Bands of music were playing in the main streets, and the people, chiefly Chinese, all dressed in their holiday clothes, hurried about, intent on paying mutual congratulatory visits. This ceremony is very common in the western provinces of China, but I have never, on occasions of epidemic sickness or other general calamity, witnessed it in the eastern.

At the end of three days' march we put up for the night at the military station of Owha-lin-pin, lying at the western foot of a very high range of snowy mountains, at the pass over which our passports were demanded by a guard stationed at a kind of tower, with a gateway through which the road passed. The guard, however, recognising the Bishop, were very respectful, and caused us no delay.

The station of Owha-lin-pin is built on a spur of the great range, and commands a strong position. Four rows of wooden houses, numbering about fifty in a row, constitute the barracks for four hundred soldiers, a detachment of the Western Frontier Army, supposed to number several hundred thousand, distributed along the borders from Yunnan up to the Great Wall. Nearly every man has a family, and carries on some trade or calling; most of them, in addition, cultivating little farms of Indian corn and potatoes. None but soldiers and officials are allowed to reside in the station, the few shops to be seen being all kept by the red coats. We found quarters in the Kung-kwan, and I was amused to see, on my arrival, that Philip, who was determined not to be behind-hand in doing things properly, had made me a flag, black and white, with my name, "Tang Koopah," painted on it. This flag he had stuck in the door-post, opposite to the Bishop's flag. Flags similar to these are always carried by Chinese men of rank, and are regarded very much as a livery or coat-of-arms in England. At some hotels in the more populous parts of Sz-chuan I have seen as many as a dozen different flags stuck in the door-posts, announcing the presence of the owners.

From Owha-lin-pin a day's march brought us to the city of Loo-din-chow, famous for its chain bridge, which spans the Ta-tow river. This city is the last in Sz-chuan *proper*, as distinguished from the border territory, within which the authority of the Man-ts" King is acknowledged, and to which the local name Manchia is given. Amongst its inhabitants (numbering, probably, eight thousand souls) there are

CH. VII.] LOO-DIN-CHOW SUSPENSION BRIDGE.

a great number of Thibetan and Chinese half-breeds, the females generally wearing a modified Thibetan costume, and greatly surpassing the Chinese women in their personal appearance. The dialect spoken, a mixture of Chinese and Thibetan, proved a difficulty for Philip, whose pure Pekinese was in its turn almost unintelligible to the natives. The famous bridge happened, luckily, to be out of repair, and our whole cavalcade had to cross the river by the safer means of a large ferry-boat. While crossing, the head ferryman, who was very communicative, told us the history of the chain bridge of Loo-din-chow.

Shortly before the annexation of Eastern Thibet by the Chinese the Pekin Government offered a reward of 30,000 taels to any one who could succeed in building a bridge over the Ta-tow river, which, from its sudden floods and great depth, was a serious obstacle to regular communication between China and Thibet. The swiftness of the current, flowing between very high banks, rendered all efforts to span the river by means of stone arches unsuccessful. At last, however, a blacksmith of the town hit upon the idea of a chain bridge. The officers appointed to receive proposals approved of his plan; and, according to Abbé Huc, in 1701 the bridge was completed. Its construction is very faulty Nine large chains, not quite so thick as a ship's cable, with a space of four feet between each, are stretched over large square buttresses built against each bank, and securely built into masses of masonry; the roadway is simply a flooring of boards, unsecured by any ballast or handrail; and the vibration is so great, that at times it is almost impossible to keep one's feet. At noon every day the gates leading to the bridge are closed until 4 P.M., and no person is allowed to cross, as the terrific winds sweeping along the gorge between the mountains which rise on either bank render the passage excessively dangerous. For a year or two after its construction it is said to have answered its purpose very well; but of late years most shocking accidents, causing great loss of life, have occurred through the chains breaking.

Having safely crossed the Ta-tow, we continued our journey for a few miles along its right bank, and put up for the night at the small Man-ts^u village of Ta-lee, the first under the jurisdiction of the old Man-ts^u King, whose rule, under that of the Viceroy of Sz-chuan, extends from Ho-kow, on the Ya-long river, west of Ta-tsian-loo, to the right bank of the Ta-tow river.

Our landlord, a half-breed, was a man of great literary and artistic taste. His house was full of Chinese works of art, such as paintings, bronzes, and old porcelain; while the garden, adjoining the house, was a perfect little Chinese Eden : orange, lemon, shaddock, and pear trees grew most luxuriantly; and the water of a pond, tastefully surrounded with rockwork, glittered again with gold-fish. After I had been shown over his house and grounds, and praised them to his heart's content, he ushered me into what he called his guest chamber, furnished according to the Chinese ideal of luxury. The small tables and chairs were all of highly-polished ebony, and the walls were covered with choice specimens of Chinese pictorial art. Two tables, in the centre of the room, were loaded with beautiful bronzes and china vases ; but the great treasure of all was a steel engraving of " Don Quixote received by the Duchess' Women," which a missionary had given him several years before. The care bestowed on the picture by its dilettante owner was most amusing: it was encased in a yellow silk cover, bound with black, and having above it a scroll of scarlet paper, on which in golden Chinese characters were inscribed the name of the donor and date of presentation. Mine host was very anxious to obtain a description of the scene represented; so, after dinner, I gave him a sketch of the history of Don Quixote and Sancho, which greatly delighted him; and long after the good Bishop had retired for the night my host ordered a hot supper, and produced some very delicious wine, which, he informed me, was a present from the Chinese minister at Lhássa, who had been his guest on his way to Thibet.

Next morning, when starting, I was surprised to find a basket in my chair, containing wine, lemons, and a cold roast fowl, provided by the kindly host, who, in taking leave, embraced me, begging me to remember him always, and when I returned to my own country to think of Leantalowya and his little house in the mountains of Tse-tsang.

Our road from the village of Ta-lee led for several miles along the right bank of the Ta-tow-ho, which flowed directly at the base of the precipitous cliffs some hundreds of feet below. Just before entering the gorge of Ta-tsiau-loo, a narrow path about three feet wide, cut in the perpendicular side of the precipice, led upwards to a shoulder of the mountain, from the angle of which we looked sheer down on the river 600 feet below. One of my front chair-coolies became giddy, and fell; the chair-pole nearest the edge snapped, and the chair, with the weight of my body, hung suspended over the precipice. For a second or two I sat looking down into the frightful depth at my feet, paralysed and unable to move. The bearers, though as much terror-stricken as myself, held on to the chair until some of our baggage-coolies came up and dragged the chair on to the ledge again. When I got out, I nearly fainted; in fact, but for the coolies commencing to cry and make a great noise, I believe that I should have become insensible. The agonising feeling of suspense, in every sense of the word, while hanging over the frightful precipice was terrible ; and it was a day or two before my nerves recovered the shock.

No sooner had we recovered ourselves sufficiently to proceed, than we were obliged to run for our very lives, for the noise of the mid-day hurricane was heard coming up the valley of the Ta-tow, and we only just succeeded in getting into the Ta-tsian-loo gorge as the furious whirlwind passed up the river with a fearful roar. Nothing can exceed the terrific force of these whirlwinds, and woe to the unfortunate traveller caught by them when on the verge of the precipice, for he would be swept away like a feather. Many dreadful stories are told of the fate of unfortunate people who have been hurled into the Ta-tow river from this dangerous height.

At the entrance of the gorge we overtook a string of nearly two hundred coolies carrying tea from Ya-tzow to Ta-tsian-loo. We had already passed hundreds along the road, who excited our sympathy as they toiled along with their heavy burthens ; the party now met with, however, particularly arrested my attention. They were carrying a large consignment of tea, sent as a present by the Chinese Government to the Grand Lama at Lhássa, and had been impressed for the service by the Mandarins, who, out of their daily wages of two hundred chen, pocketed one hundred and fifty, leaving the poor wretches barely sufficient to purchase half a ration of Indian corn-meal. Their aspect was pitiable in the extreme ; each man carried on an average eight baskets of tea, equal to 160 lbs., and many of them carried twelve baskets or 240 lbs. weight. The baskets were packed one above the other in a wooden frame, slung on the shoulders by means of broad leather straps; the frame was so constructed as to curve over the head, causing fully half the load to rest above the

COOLIES CARRYING BRICK TEA.

shoulders, and compelling the bearer to march with his head bent forward; thus equipped and half starved they had to perform their laborious journey of one hundred and fifty miles, the legitimate profit of their toil not coming to them, but going into the pockets of the Mandarins.

We had now fairly entered the terrible and gloomy gorge of Ta-tsian-loo, at the head of which lies the border town of that name. This defile strikes at right angles the west or right bank of the Ta-tow-ho, where it receives the waters of the Ta-tsian-loo river, or rather torrent, which foams down a succession of falls through the gorge.

For twenty miles on either hand cliffs one thousand to twelve hundred feet high, and approaching each other sometimes within twenty or thirty yards, rise perpendicularly, their summits capped with snow, while a cloud of mist overhangs the lower depths, producing even at mid-day an obscure twilight. The torrent, as it leaps on its headlong course to the Ta-tow-ho, washes in many places the narrow path running along its right bank with spray from numerous waterfalls; while huge boulders, forced from their resting-places high over head by the fierce hurricane which seems ever to sweep the bleak summits of these mountains, ever and anon fill the gorge with the noise of a hundred thunders as they crash into the angry stream below. Many lives are annually lost by the fall of these rocks, and we passed a confused heap of ruins marking the spot where a cluster of houses, with all their inhabitants, had been overwhelmed by a huge fragment of cliff. After traversing ten miles of the gorge we spent the night in a kung-kwan built against the mountain-wall, and as the people said, rarely visited by the sunlight. Not ten paces from the door the torrent roared in all its fury; and it was impossible to get rid of the feeling that six hundred feet of cliff overhung the frail building, ready at any moment to roll down its death-dealing boulders. Ten more miles of the gorge were passed safely next day, and we breathed more freely when the mountains receded on either hand, and we emerged into a more open valley, and soon arrived at the town of Ta-tsian-loo. We took up our quarters at a Man-tsᵘ hotel, where rooms had been engaged by a servant of the Bishop's, who had been dispatched in advance from Hi-yan-ky. The proprietor was a soldier in the service of the old Man-tsᵘ King, and was absent on duty in the mountains. His wife, a handsome woman of thirty, did her best to make us comfortable, and having been told that a foreigner was to be her guest, had carefully swept out the two rooms reserved for my use. I was greatly surprised when she observed that her rooms were very small and consequently very cheap, the rent for each room being only ten chen per diem, including a daily supply of water.

The house, situated in the Chinese quarter of the town, was built partly according to the Chinese fashion, with four square main walls; the ground floor being used as a stable for the yaks, ponies, and mules; above it, and reached by means of a flight of wooden stairs, were the rooms for the family and guests, some of them lighted by small square barred windows without glass, and closed by shutters on the inside, while others were like ordinary Chinese rooms.

During the first night of our stay we discovered that vermin were unusually numerous, but the experience acquired since leaving Hankow had taught us to make light of this annoyance; and, on the whole, I was contented with the quarters in which I saw a prospect of remaining some weeks, as beyond this point our road was still rendered impassable by the snow.

The first few days were devoted to walking about the town and observing the manners and customs of the Thibetans, who form the majority of the inhabitants.

The town itself lies in a deep valley, between the snow-capped mountains, where they commence to slope back from the western mouth of the gorge. A stream runs through the middle, dividing the Thibetan quarter on the left bank from the Chinese quarter on the right. The height and abruptness of the mountains on either side of the valley

PART OF MANT-Z^E HOTEL IN TA-TSIAN-LOO.

render them naturally impregnable fortifications; while strong walls thrown across each end of the valley close the only approaches to the town.

The Chinese quarter consists of shops occupied by Chansi merchants, who trade in turquoise stones, tea, and snuff; which they exchange with the Thibetans for musk, hartshorn, drugs, gold, and various peltries, such as the skins of lynx, otters, leopards, wolves and bears. There are also numbers of silk shops, where China silks of all kinds are sold. The universal tea shop is not wanting, and numerous butchers' shops, are well stocked with pork, mutton, and Yak beef; the two latter being in great demand by the Thibetans, and exceedingly cheap—costing about twopence a pound. Provisions of all kinds are plentiful and cheap. We found a large and excellent white cabbage, pickled somewhat after the manner of sourcrout, a pleasant change from the wretched salted vegetables of China. Many of the Chinese residents in this quarter are Mahomedans, undistinguishable, however, from the rest of their countrymen by their dress; they did not seem to be much acquainted with the Koran, though rigidly observing its prohibitions of pork and wine. Their mosque, which was situated close to my hotel, is the handsomest building in the Chinese quarter, with dome and minaret after the model of those in India. It seemed well attended by worshippers, who were summoned to prayer morning and evening by the loud and dissonant blowing of a horn, which often broke my slumbers.

The Chinese garrison is composed of 250 foot, and 100 horse, who are daily drilled outside the western wall. The garrison is commanded by a blue button Mandarin, while the civil authority is exercised by a Taou-tai, who alone decides all cases of life and death. This is the only limit to the jurisdiction of the Man-ts^u King, whose position in relation to the Chinese government seems somewhat analogous to that of some of the native princes in British India. The present Man-ts^u Kwan, as the Chinese call him, is over seventy years of age, he is the lineal heir of the former native rulers of the country, and still exercises a limited sovereignty over the Man-ts^u or Thibetan population of the district already mentioned, between the Ya-long and Ta-tow rivers, and extending to the Lo-Lo country on the south. He pays an annual tribute to the Viceroy of Chen-tu, from taxes levied by him for the purpose; and is responsible for the maintenance of peace in his territory, appointing magistrates who adjudicate in all but capital cases. He also maintains a guard of several hundred soldiers. His palace, a large, rambling unadorned building, is situated in the Thibetan quarter, which is composed of the usual prison-like houses intersected by narrow dirty lanes, swarming with unwashed and uncombed children. The Man-ts^u population, besides soldiers and tradesmen, are woodcutters and cultivators; and, as already said, outnumber the Chinese, who are evidently only an immigrant class, engaged in business.

At each gate of the city stands a custom-house, where duty is levied on every article imported or exported, and all commerce between China and Thibet must pass this custom-house, which gives to the town its chief importance.

I had been several days in Ta-tsian-loo, without hearing anything from the authorities; when one morning the chief Lama of the Lamasery, situated outside the west gate, paid me a visit. He came mounted on a large white mule, with four Thibetan attendants; and on being shown into my room, introduced himself as one of the chief stewards of the Grand Lama at Lhássa. He was quite a young man, of fair complexion for a Thibetan, and very tall. His courteous bearing was remarkable, and he at once entered into conversation through interpreters with easy frankness; saying that he had only heard of my arrival a day or two before, and had taken the earliest opportunity of seeing the Palin (English) doctor; who, he understood, had travelled from a great distance to visit the land of Buddha. Philip having provided tea and pipes, the young Lama sat several hours with me, asking many questions, and at times, in spite of his perfect self-possession, betrayed an anxiety to draw from me some observation which would give him an opportunity to speak of my proposed journey through Thibet. Perceiving his wish to speak of my intended route, I observed that I had heard the Lamas were averse to French missionaries entering their Central kingdom; and added that I supposed it was on account of religious grounds; and was not surprised that a great religious country like Thibet or Tse-tsang, as it is called in the official dialect of China, should object to the introduction of a new religion. As I made this observation with apparent indifference, he looked surprised, and said: "Oh then, you are not a teacher of this new religion! May I ask then, what you are?" "Simply a traveller, who, having visited many countries, desires to visit and behold the country of Buddha," I replied; "neither teaching religion, nor troubling myself about anything, but such strange sights as may be witnessed in distant and unknown countries." "Wonderful!" answered the Lama. "Why, I had heard you were coming to open a road, by means of which your soldiers might come and take our country, and convert our people to the new faith! Are you not one of the new teachers?" I answered him by saying that I was a "Ta-Ing-qua jen," (Englishman); and not a "Ta-Fa-qua jen, (Frenchman); whose religion was not the same as mine, I being a simple believer in the law of Confudzu,* and quite indifferent to the teaching of new faiths. I was not a teacher; but respected the religion of all countries that I visited. My guest, on this, rose from his chair, and calling in one of his followers, spoke with him earnestly for a

* Confucius.

short time; then turning to me, he said: "I am very sorry to tell you that I have heard you are to be arrested, and sent back if you attempt to enter the Central Kingdom beyond Bathang, as you are represented to be quite a different person from what you tell me you are. However, I would advise you to proceed on your journey as soon as the road is open, and be careful to abstain from speaking of religion, or identifying yourself with the foreign teachers, *i.e.*, missionaries. He ended by asking me to return to his Lamasery with him. I was glad of such an opportunity; and had my little mule, Iron Duchess, saddled, and accompanied the Lama to his Lamasery, passing on our road thither numbers of little mounds, composed of flat pieces of slate, on which was inscribed the Thibetan prayer of "Om mani padme hum."

THIBETAN PRAYER: OM MANI PADME HUM.

It was a large square edifice, built of rough stone, with rows of square windows, admitting light to the numerous rooms or cells. In fact, the place more resembled a prison in its outward appearance than anything else. We entered through a large gate of massive woodwork, which opened into a dark archway, secured at the further end by similar gates. Along each side of the archway was a frame containing four wooden cylinders, about four feet high and a foot in diameter; each was fixed on a central pivot, and revolved with great rapidity as the Lama set them, one after the other, in motion as he passed, muttering a prayer, and telling his beads with the other hand. On each of the cylinders prayers were painted in large gold letters in the Thibetan character. Similar cylinders are found in the entrances of all lamaseries, and every Lama as he enters and leaves the building turns the cylinders and tells his beads.

Having passed through the inner gates, we entered a large square courtyard, whence we surveyed the four inner sides of the building, round which, level with the second story, ran a wooden covered balcony, about which numbers of Lamas were walking to and fro, counting their beads, and chaunting in a low, mournful voice the everlasting prayer of Omanee peminee, which, with one exception in the case of my friend the Chief Lama, was the only way in which I ever heard the prayer of Om mani padme hum, rendered during my travels in Eastern Thibet; nor could I ever, either from the Lamas or people, get any other translation of it than "glorification of the Deity," though it is otherwise translated by European scholars, "Oh, the jewel on the lotus!"

Crossing the courtyard, the Lama led me up a flight of stairs into his room, which differed from those occupied by the other Lamas only in its furniture and superior cleanliness. The other rooms were dirty, and contained nothing save a small stove in the centre of the floor, and a large wooden bucket, somewhat like an attenuated churn, and containing the everlasting butter tea of the Thibetans. My host's room, however, had in it several chairs of Chinese make, and round the stove was spread a thick woollen carpet, on which I was invited to squat. Having comfortably seated myself, a youth attired in Lama robes brought in silver cups, one of which my host filled with butter tea, and as an especial mark of hospitality, broke off from a huge pat of rancid butter a piece as large as his fist, and put it into my cup, which he politely handed to me; then filling his own cup in the same way, he invited me to drink with him.

Good manners obliged me to drink, and I succeeded in swallowing a mouthful of the greasy mess with well feigned pleasure, which my host observing, nodded his head, and bending gracefully forward with a flourish, stirred round the piece of butter in my cup with his little finger, and again pressed me to drink. I would have given worlds to have been spared this second trial, but calling up all my resolution, I made another gulp, and hastily relighted my pipe, while my hospitable host sipped his melted butter with as much gusto as an alderman would his full-bodied port.

Expressing a wish to view the lamasery, I was shown over it by the Lama, and visited the chapel or temple, where he daily offered his prayers to the Grand Lama, as he said; meaning, I presume, Buddha. It was a superb little place. At one end a railing, richly ornamented and gilded, fenced off intruders from a gilded image of Buddha, about five feet high, sitting in a contemplative posture, enveloped in a white drapery of silk gauze. Round the four walls were rows of niches like pigeon-holes, about a foot square, in each of which was a small Buddha of solid gold, about two inches high. There could not have been less than a hundred of these images, and my first impression was that they were only gilt; but the Lama pointed them out to me as gold, and several of them which I handled were made of the precious metal. We walked through several corridors with cells opening into them on either hand, from which the monotonous voices of the priests within chanting their orisons resounded. We then visited a large room used as a refectory, in which about forty Lamas were busy devouring tsanba and butter tea. The whole arrangements of this lamasery, and the religious hush which pervaded the building, made me feel as if transported back to one of the monasteries of olden times, where the monks, if not belied, lived on the fat of the land. In this respect at least they are quite rivalled by the Lamas of Thibet, who also, as all observers have remarked, by their monastic life and religious observances strongly remind the Western visitor of the monks and ritual of Catholic countries.

Quite in keeping is the appearance of the hundreds of priests, barefooted, with their clean shaven heads, wearing a costume consisting of a grey petticoat-like robe, reaching from the waist to the ankle, and a long shawl, worn like a Scotch plaid, across the chest, over the left shoulder, leaving the right arm and shoulder exposed. From the waist hangs a small leathern purse, containing flint and steel, and round the neck they wear rosaries of coral, turquoise, glass, or wooden beads, which they are constantly telling with the left hand, while the right is engaged in twirling their prayer wheels. These resemble a small stonemason's mallet, the thick part revolving round the handle, and are made sometimes of silver, but generally of ivory or wood, beautifully inlaid with precious metal, and inscribed with verses of prayers in letters of gold. Every time that the wheel revolves is supposed to count as a good action performed by the twirler, and both priests and people are everlastingly twirling their wheels, counting their beads, and chaunting the prayer of Omanee peminee.

I learned from Bishop Chauveau that before the Chinese conquest the Lamas used to marry, but that the Chinese, fearing the power of the sacerdotal caste, procured an order from Lhássa enforcing celibacy on all Lamas. Notwithstanding this, at the present time, out of the population of the three kingdoms of Thibet, more than one-third are Lamas. It may be imagined, therefore, what a power the priesthood has over the people. In almost every family one or more of the sons are Lamas, from compulsion. In a family of, say four sons, the Chief Lama of the district will generally insist upon two becoming Lamas, and at the age of between twelve and fourteen the boys are taken to the lamasery, where they are educated, and, when grown up, admitted into the priesthood. If the parents object to give up their sons to the priesthood, the threat of an anathema from the lips of the Chief Lama or the Grand Lama at Lhássa is sufficient to overcome all opposition; thus the ranks of the priesthood are constantly recruited and their power strengthened. The population, owing to this, is gradually lessening, and the lay people are the mere slaves of the Lamas, who live in luxurious idleness, for each lamasery possesses enormous estates, as well as the revenues drawn from the lay population in the shape of tithes on produce, both of cattle and grain.

A day or two after my visit to the Lama monastery I dined with the Bishop, and was glad to learn that he had news from Bathang, a Mission courier having succeeded in passing the snow, which he reported as fast disappearing in the valleys, while the avalanches were growing gradually less dangerous. This was good news for me, as my funds, like the snow, were daily melting away, and I had yet a journey of 1000 miles before me. Baggage animals and interpreters were to be procured, all of which was to be done out of the sum of 400 taels, or £130, all that now remained of the 600 taels with which I had started from Hankow.

The Bishop, after dinner, insisted on the necessity of my hiring an interpreter of some standing, and travelling with a drove of yaks as baggage animals; and estimated the cost of my journey to Lhássa, as likely to amount, at the very least, to 600 taels. On this I reminded his Lordship, that I possessed but 400 taels in the world, for which I produced the letter of credit given me in Shanghai. The Bishop was still incredulous, and at last told me, that although he believed I was a private traveller, yet up to this moment, he had been certain that I must have gold secreted about me. I reiterated my denial of this, and my assurance that I had only got 400 taels at my command; and at this he manifested genuine astonishment, and gave up the idea of a large caravan; advising me to purchase as many baggage animals, as would be required to carry the needful food and bedding, and kindly offering to lend me any further money I might need.

During our conversation, I happened to mention that I had seen numbers of lepers in Western China. Whereupon the Bishop communicated some fearful details of the prevalence of that horrible disease in Yunnan, which more than any other province in the Empire suffers from its ravages.

On one occasion, during his early missionary labours in that province, he was travelling on horseback, and as he rode leisurely along, his pony suddenly came to a standstill, and in spite of all his efforts, refused to proceed. At last he grew impatient (the more so that there was a very powerful stench in the neighbourhood), and applied his whip with such good effect, that the pony took the bit between his teeth, and started off full gallop. On turning a corner, a few yards off, the Bishop was horrified to behold, near the side of the road, a band of nearly fifty lepers, who had encamped there, and were preparing a meal. A number of the poor wretches held up their fingerless hands, and in mournful accents, warned the bishop to keep off; a needless warning, as his pony, with a wonderful instinct, seemed to know the nature of the horrible curse that lurked in the neighbourhood.

Very stringent measures are enforced against lepers in this province, they are not allowed to enter any town, or travel along highways, and the poor wretches, cut off from their fellow creatures, drag out a painful existence as best they can. The Bishop told me of several isolated villages, entirely inhabited by lepers, and to these places, all people, in towns and cities, attacked by leprosy, are immediately sent, lest contact with them should spread the fearful disease; for it is believed to be very contagious—an opinion in which, by the way, the Bishop coincided, though I believe it is contrary to that of European medical men.

Strange to say, the people of Yunnan implicitly believe that the curse of leprosy visited their country simultaneously with the advent of foreigners. This, however, can be little more than a popular prejudice, encouraged by the officials, who never fail, in their hatred of foreigners, to lay to their charge all the evils (and there are many) which visit the unfortunate Chinese.

The Bishop, before I left, reiterated his offer of assistance, and advised me immediately to set about making preparations for the road; this I was most ready to do, and at once posted an advertisement outside my hotel, to the effect that mules and ponies were wanted. This, however, produced no applications, owing, as I afterwards discovered, to the orders issued by the old Man-tsü King, that no animals were to be supplied to the Palin; the people of the hotel, however, promised me that as soon as the roads opened, and the country people came in, they would exert themselves to supply my wants. In the meanwhile, I practised that most essential requisite for a traveller in China, patience.

Shortly after leaving Hi-yan-ky, I had partly discarded my Chinese dress, replacing the turn-up-toed boots and uncomfortable leggings, by a pair of strong lace-up shooting boots and trousers. I had also allowed my hair to grow, but continued to cultivate the pigtail. Thus, on arriving at Tatsian-loo, my costume was calculated to puzzle any person, as to its nationality.

Now as both for convenience and expediency, I purposed to travel in Thibet dressed as an European, without any disguise, I took advantage of my friendly intercourse with my Man-tsu hosts, to leave my room one morning dressed as an Englishman; strange to say, I felt very uncomfortable, quite as much so as when I first assumed the Chinese costume in Hankow. On presenting myself in the large room, used as a kitchen and general room by the family and lodgers, my appearance, for a few moments, was greeted with a blank stare of astonishment from those present, followed by a roar of laughter, as they recognised Tang Koopah, looking very much ashamed of himself. There happened to be several women on a visit to my hostess, and true to the inquisitiveness of their sex, they commenced a most minute inspection of my, to them, extraordinary costume. My rough pea-jacket, from its want of skirts, was the cause of much merriment, and it was passed round the company, amid many remarks not at all complimentary to the English notions of propriety; my wideawake, however, was pronounced to be a very sensible and neat article; but my nether garments were referred to as decidedly comfortable, but quite inadequate for the purpose of clothing the extremities, without a skirt of some sort. Such was the freely expressed verdict of Chinese and Thibetans, with regard to the European costume. For my own part, it was several days before I became again reconciled to the change. I may as well pass from myself to the dress and appearance of my Man-tsŭ friends.

The Thibetan population of Ta-tsian-loo is composed principally of half-breeds, who are really very handsome, the females especially so. The men, who are mostly tall and strongly built, affect the Chinese costume and pig-tail; but the women adhere to the very becoming dress, of a long blue coat-like garment, with a yellow girdle round the waist, and a voluminous yellow turban; their love of jewellery amounts to a passion, showing itself in the wearing of silver rings on every finger, and massive gold ear-rings; their crowning glory, however, is a large saucer-like plate of gold, beautifully embossed, and worn at the back of the head, over the hair, which is gathered up, chignon fashion; by the poorer women, silver plates are worn instead of gold.

This costume is peculiar to the half-breeds all over Thibet, who profess to be superior to the pure Thibetans; but the gold head ornament is commonly worn by Thibetan women everywhere. The marriage tie among the half-breeds seems to be held in but light esteem. The women rarely marry, as a first husband, one of their own class, generally preferring to become temporary wives of the Chinese traders and soldiers, who reside in Ta-tsian-loo, a position which is regarded as quite honourable, and in which they observe the most scrupulous fidelity. They are laughing, light-hearted creatures, and make the homes of their Chinese masters very comfortable. Among themselves, they are connected by ties of kindred and friendship, which bind them, as it were in a large clan; and any woman who is deserted by her lord and master, readily finds a home, even if she has no near relations. Their social manners and habits, differ altogether from the secluded life and timid shyness of the Chinese women. They go about and pay visits as they choose, conversing freely with their male friends, without incurring suspicion, and their manner is marked by a child-like freedom from restraint, devoid of the least shade of impropriety. I remember an amusing illustration of this: One morning, four Man-ts^u ladies paid me a visit, and were ushered into my room, as I was preparing to wash my hands. I was immediately taken possession of, amid merry shrieks of musical laughter; one held Tang Koopah on her lap, while of the others, one washed my hands, another my face, and the third stood by with a towel; when this performance, which seemed greatly to amuse them, and certainly did not displease me, was concluded, I presented my fair visitors with some oranges; their dexterous fingers quickly removed the peel in an unbroken piece, which they then twisted in their jet black tresses, each in turn performing her coiffure before my looking-glass, this they told me was a sovereign preventive against sickness.

On the 24th of April, after I had been more than a fortnight in Ta-tsian-loo, several trading caravans arrived from Bathang. The traders came mostly from the Central Kingdom, and were fine specimens of the pure Thibetans, very tall, standing over six feet in height, of a dark brown, nearly black complexion, with a profusion of long black hair hanging over their shoulders. In feature they were totally unlike the Mongolian type, with aquiline noses, and straight deep-set eyes, overhung by shaggy eyebrows. They were dressed in the common dress of the country, consisting of a long sheepskin coat, worn with the wool inside, and bound with leopard or lynx skin; and a kind of half-boot, of woollen cloth, soled with sheepskin. From a belt round the waist, hung a keen-edged sword, four feet long, and of uniform width from hilt to point, encased in a wooden scabbard, generally very highly ornamented with brass and turquoise stones; and leathern cases, containing a small knife and needles, and flint and steel, attached to thongs, hanging from the waist-belt, completed the costume. Most of the traders carried long matchlocks, furnished with a kind of rest, made from the spiral horns of the common antelope. The Thibetans never fire from the shoulder, but always kneel to discharge their matchlocks, steadied by means of the rest, and at anything under a hundred yards are dead shots. These traders were accompanied by several of the savage watch-dogs of Thibet, resembling large sheep-dogs, and by others of a fawn-colour, very like an English mastiff.

The arrival of these men was a signal for me to hurry my preparations for a start. Having, by this time, been informed of the opposition of the Man-tsŭ King and Chinese Mandarin, I propitiated them both by means of presents of penknives, pencils, and pictures. This had such an effect on the old king, that he sent me a handsome white mule for inspection; but the price (eighty taels) was too high for my purse, so I returned it, with thanks. From this time the market was open to me, and I soon became the owner of two ponies and a mule, sufficiently good for baggage animals. My next care was to provide necessaries for the road, and I proceeded to lay in a stock of the articles most used in barter amongst the Thibetans, as, beyond Ta-tsian-loo, chen are perfectly useless, and silver is almost so, a few handfuls of tea often procuring more than silver or gold. Indian rupees, however, pass current throughout Thibet, and we exchanged a portion of our sycee silver for a hundred rupees.* A hundred and fifty taels were expended in the purchase of four baskets of tea, an assortment of glass, agate, onyx, and turquoise beads, needles and thread (both cotton and silk), and fifty yards of red cotton cloth, about a foot wide. Besides these, we procured a quantity of the silken net khatas, or scarves of felicity, which are in universal demand, both as presents and for sale,† throughout Thibet.

As the annual rains closely succeed the melting of the snows in spring, rain-coats were requisite; so Philip, out of two blankets, contrived a couple of garments that answered the purpose capitally, and saved us many a wetting.

Having completed all our own equipment, the next thing was to provide our mules and ponies with leather nosebags and pack-saddles, and to cover all our baggage with green cow-hides, as a protection from the wet. This done, we laid in a stock of provisions for ten days' journey, consisting of flour, butter, Chinese hams, and tea, and dried peas for our animals. Strong ropes, made of green cowhide, to be used in the passage of the snow-covered mountains, and a stock of horse-shoes and nails, which Australian life had qualified me to put on, in an emergency, were the last, but not the least important, item of our outfit.

We soon found a couple of half-breeds who were willing to act, the one as interpreter, and the other as muleteer, as far as Bathang, for a consideration of thirty taels and their food during the journey. All was now ready; but as I had expended nearly all my available funds in the outfit, it became necessary, in order to procure a fresh supply, for me to apply to the Bishop, who readily lent me two hundred

* See Appendix III. † See Appendix IV.

taels; and I determined to leave Ta-tsian-loo on the 30th of April.

On the 29th I took a farewell dinner with the Bishop, who, not content with having already done me so many kindnesses, pressed on me the loan of a horse to Bathang, as he foresaw that I should be placed in a dilemma if any of my animals were to knock up. I gratefully accepted this further mark of goodwill, and took my leave, promising to call as I left the town in the morning.

At the hotel, I was literally overwhelmed with presents of sweets and different articles of food, such as rice and pork; and this, my last evening, passed pleasantly among these kindly and sociable people, who had relieved the anxieties attendant on my stay, by their hearty and disinterested kindness to the English stranger. A curious incident marked the evening. As I sat smoking in front of the fireplace, which was exactly like a range, only built of stone instead of iron, I placed my feet on a raised hearth in front of the fire. All the women present at once threw up their hands, and screamed violently. I sprang up from my seat, thinking some accident had happened, and asked what was the matter. All then talking at once in a frightened manner, informed me that I had offended the household god, who dwelt on the hearth-stone. Seeing that my friends were really hurt, I took a small piece of silver out of my pocket, and threw it into the ashes. They were curious to know the meaning of this, so I explained that it was a present to appease the god, whom I had unintentionally offended, and that, if he would come to my room, I would give him some wine. At this they laughed uproariously, and were quite pacified by my *amende honorable* to the kitchen deity, and we parted in high good humour.

CHAPTER VIII.

EASTERN THIBET.

The Chinese Frontier—A party of Tea Traders—The Hokow Ferry—Mountains and Valleys—The Zandi Tribes—The Town of Lithang—A thieving Interpreter—The Tsamba Range—The Taso Valley—A welcome Resthouse—A perilous Swim.

ALTHOUGH we were up before daylight, all the inmates of the hotel were astir, and waiting in the large room to take leave of Tang-Tajen. Amongst those assembled were two soldiers sent by the old king as a mark of respect, with orders to accompany me out of the town. During more than an hour I was detained by the numbers both of Chinese and Thibetans, who came to wish me a lucky journey. Each had a word of advice or warning to give, useful to a traveller in the Inside country, as they called Thibet. I was to carefully avoid joining company with strangers on the road, and I was to look closely after my baggage, as the country people were great thieves. All the warnings proved with what terror the borderers still regard the mountainous country of Thibet.

At last all was ready, and so, taking a ceremonious leave of all in the hotel, I was escorted by the landlady and two of her brothers to the door, where again, according to Chinese custom, I bade them adieu, and, mounting, rode off, escorted by the two soldiers and the two brothers. I passed out of the west gate, where the Chinese guard turned out, and, with many kindly expressions, wished me a pleasant journey.

On reaching the Mission-house, we found all the Bishop's household assembled in the yard, while the Bishop himself stood at his door to receive me.

The kindness of the people of Ta-tsian-loo had made a deep impression on me, and in taking leave of the kind old Bishop, who, with tears in his eyes, invoked a blessing on me, my emotion checked all utterance. With a silent farewell, I galloped on, and soon overtook the party. Two miles from the town my honorary escort turned back, and my travels in Eastern Thibet were fairly begun. If it should prove feasible to proceed direct to Assam from Bathang, my journey would probably be concluded in two months. But both this prospect, and the alternative of being permitted to go by Lhássa to India, were most uncertain; time alone would show. For the present, I indulged in the excitement of travel in an almost unknown country. No longer cooped up in a chair, or embarrassed by the disguise of a Chinaman, with buoyant spirits I rode on through the wild, uncultivated country, so different from Sz-chuan. Not a house was visible; the road, however, was enlivened by droves of yaks and ponies, laden with brick tea for the marts of Thibet. Our path was bordered with wild gooseberry bushes, and wild roses in full flower. Camellias, too, displayed their beautiful red, white, and variegated blossoms in abundance; and the flowers were pleasingly contrasted with the glossy foliage of magnificent hollies. Huc has mentioned the extraordinary size to which the Thibetan holly-tree attains. I noticed many from twenty to thirty feet high, and of great girth.

After quitting the valley of Ta-tsian-loo, a tedious ascent of black and barren declivities covered with irregular masses of sandstone blackened by the weather, was rewarded by the splendid view from the topmost ridge of the Jeddo range. Away to the east stretched the vast empire of China. Hitherto it had been the boast of Frenchmen, that their countrymen alone of Europeans, had traversed China to Thibet; and as I stood alone on the summit of the Jeddo Pass, my exultation at the thought, that now at any rate one Englishman had crossed the Flowery Land, found vent in a cheer; and the mountains of Thibet for the first time echoed a British hurrah. Descending into the grassy valley below, towards sundown we reached our quarters for the night, in a tzan or courier post, 13 miles from Ta-tsian-loo. These tzans, which are found every 10 miles on the high road to Lhássa, are generally little more than small windowless, flat-roofed, cabins, built of stone and mud. They are tenanted by four couriers, or soldiers, usually half-bred Chinese, together with their families and ponies; the latter are used for forwarding the government despatches between the stations by a daily postal service. We pursued our route along the valley bordered by mountains four thousand feet high; here and there might be seen one of the square Thibetan houses, three stories high, with turrets at each angle, their shape and substantial appearance reminding one of old Border peels or Scotch castles, and indeed they are veritable strongholds. The entrance is secured by massive wooden gates, which when closed are only opened after the visitors have been jealously scrutinised from the prison-like windows or loopholes overhead; this precaution is rendered necessary by the daring of the numerous banditti who, in well organised bands, roam the mountains of Thibet.

At the end of three days' journey from Ta-tsian-loo we reached the first Thibetan village of Tung-olo, at the foot of the mountain of the same name. On the night of our arrival a heavy fall of snow rendered the road over the Tung-olo mountains impassable, and compelled us to remain two days in the village. After the snow had melted in the valley I strolled about the environs of the village; the hardy Man-ts"

TUNG-OLO VILLAGE.

women in their skin dresses, and wearing a cross of white beads on their backs, were busily engaged in weeding the crops of bearded wheat, now about six inches high; they worked in file, singing merrily as they plied their wooden hoes. The country looked lovely with the fresh spring tints. Some of the adjacent slopes were clothed with pine forests, from which the sweet monotonous note of the cuckoo rang out, while the air was full of the warblings of hundreds of skylarks mounting up to the sunlight. The people, all Thibetans or half-breeds, with the exception of two Chinamen, were most friendly, supplying us plentifully with yak buttermilk (which tasted like that of the cocoa-nut) and butter, in exchange for brick tea, and needles and thread.

On the third morning a party of traders and shepherds from the mountains reported the passes safe, and shortly after daylight we started, and by noon reached the snowy summit of Tung-olo, after a severe struggle up its steep and dangerous ascent. The snow lay three or four feet deep, and the dazzling light reflected from its surface obliged us to bandage the eyes of the mules and ponies, while the air was so rarefied that breathing became quite a painful labour.

We encountered in the snowy passes a party of Thibetan traders with a large drove of yaks and mules, bound for Tatsian-loo to buy tea.

The men, with their sheep-skin coats and long flowing hair, looked the very ideal of hardy mountaineers; and as we passed the cavalcade their watch-dogs made the mountain ring with their savage barks, and strained furiously at their leashes, struggling to attack us. The aspect of the country, as viewed from the western side of Tung-olo, was not inviting,—bare and rugged peaks rose in confused disorder, separated by deep valleys, covered with dense forests of white and yellow pine trees, growing to a height of eighty feet. As if to compensate for the wild and sombre character of the landscape, birds of different sorts, many decked in gorgeous plumage, abounded; just below the snow-line of the mountain were numerous crows and small daws, no larger than blackbirds; lower down, I noticed a bird of a species unknown to me, with beautiful light-blue body and wings, and two sorts of pigeons, one blue with white tail and another black, were cooing through all the woods; everywhere pheasants were more abundant than in the best-stocked coverts, and of

Q

several varieties, some resembling tragopans, the qua-qua-chee, speckled like a guinea-fowl with a turkey tail, and the ma-chee, splendid with its white body, crimson head, and black tail; overhead high in air was heard the barking croak of ravens of unusual size, which sailed about almost with the majesty of eagles. While on the subject of the feathered novelties, I must not forget the large yellow wild duck which is met with on all the Thibetan streams and mountain pools at a great elevation, these ducks were precisely similar to the Brahminee ducks of the upper waters of the Brahmapootra. I was anxious to secure a specimen, and fired at the first I saw, but luckily missed, for a Lama who was with us rushed up in great consternation—the yellow ducks were sacred to the Grand Lama, and to kill one would be a great crime; even to have fired at the sacred bird was an offence.

From the Tung-olo mountains two days' journey brought us to the little town of Hokow, situated on the left bank of the river Ya-long, a tributary of the Yang-ts^u. Our road led us through the wild country which we had seen from the summit of Tung-olo; at times we crossed high rugged mountains, and then descended through magnificent pine forests into beautiful fertile valleys, dotted here and there with the flat-roofed houses of the Thibetans, whose fields were green with spring crops of bearded wheat and white peas, and invariably planted round with fine walnut trees,—few countries in the world growing finer walnuts than those of the valleys of Thibet.

We arrived at Hokow early in the afternoon, but too late to cross the Ya-long that day, so we quartered ourselves at an hotel kept by a half-breed, and Philip applied to the resident Chinese Mandarin for the use of the ferry-boat to take us over in the morning. He was very civil, and in return for a penknife, and a few small coloured prints of pheasants, sent me some dried fish, smoked pork, and a packet of delicious tea, with a message that the boat was at my disposal.

Opposite the little town of Hokow the river Ya-long runs for about 400 yards in a deep unbroken stream, the milky hue of its waters bearing evidence of the limestone mountains, whose torrents feed it on the way from its source in Central Thibet, whence, too, it brings down the gold dust, with which its sands are everywhere rich. This Hokow channel affords the only place for a ferry that occurs for miles, as both above and below, the stream is interrupted by falls and rapids.

A large stretch of sandy shore, in front of the town, was covered with piles of brick tea on its way to Lithang, Bathang, and Lhássa, waiting to be ferried over by a somewhat novel contrivance: large circular baskets, six or eight feet in diameter, are covered with green hides, presenting the appearance of coracles, which when laden float lightly on the water, and are easily paddled across the rapid current by Chinese half-breeds, who are exclusively employed for ferry work on the Thibetan rivers, as the Thibetans themselves are afraid of the water.

It sometimes happens that these skin boats are carried down amongst the rapids by the force of the current; but so light and elastic are they that they rarely upset or suffer much damage from the sunken rocks, which would be fatal to boats of any other construction. The large wooden flat-bottomed ferry-boats, provided for the use of travellers of distinction, are never used for any other purpose.

The jurisdiction of the old king residing at Ta-tsian-loo, ends at Hokow, and beyond this point no female of pure Chinese blood is allowed to reside, not even the wife of the Minister at Lhássa. This is one of those strange restrictions illustrative of the peculiar relations existing between China and Thibet, which have to this day puzzled the ingenuity even of French missionaries. Although the eastern kingdom of Thibet, including the country from Ta-tsian-loo westwards to the Lan-tsan river, was annexed to the province of Sz-chuan about 1792, and the jurisdiction of the Viceroy of that province extended to the west of Bathang, where a stone described by Huc, was erected to mark the limits, it would seem that the eastern kingdom of Thibet has never been so incorporated as to be considered by the Chinese themselves as an integral part of China proper, the western boundary of which runs along the Jeddo range, coinciding with that of the province of Sz-chuan.

Some of my readers who have studied recently compiled English maps may be surprised at the boundary of China being drawn at the Jeddo range. In this I follow the authority of D'Anville's maps, which were based on the surveys made by the Jesuits for Chung III., as well as that of the Abbé Huc, our only recent informant on the subject of Thibet. This enterprising traveller invariably speaks of Ta-tsian-loo as the frontier town of China, and accurately describes the distinction between Eastern Thibet and Sz-chuan; indeed, the broadly marked difference in race, language, dress, and manners observable to the west of Ta-tsian-loo, must make it evident to the traveller that he has left the Flowery Land behind him. Even for the purposes of political geography the error of removing the frontiers of China proper to the banks of the Kin-cha, and including Bathang and Litbang in the province of Sz-chuan, could only be committed by persons ignorant of the fact, that in these cities the civil power is exercised by a Thibetan Mandarin—to whom even the few Chinese residents are subject. A Chinese military Mandarin commands the garrison, and represents the Chinese sovereignty obtained by conquest. The presence, however, of these Chinese soldiers no more makes Thibet part of Sz-chuan, than the presence of the Mantchu conquerors makes Sz-chuan part of Mantchuria.

I hope that this digression, necessary to make my readers clearly understand our whereabouts on the map, may not be considered irrelevant. Now let us resume our itinerary from Hokow. Having rested for the night, we were, early in the morning, ferried across the Ya-long with all our baggage-animals, in the ferry-barge. This was due to the courtesy of the Mandarin, who might have compelled us, like all traders and ordinary travellers, to leave our animals on the eastern shore, and hire or purchase others on the western—a curious obstacle to commercial intercourse between China and Thibet, —but such is the customary rule, from which we were happily exempted. We then skirted the river for some distance, its waters flowing 25 feet below the watermark which indicated their summer level. For four days we traversed a mountain country abounding in the most beautiful scenery. Occasionally, as we struck some deep valley, our road lay through forests of tea-oil trees, from a species of which the tea-oil of China is made; their beautiful, dark, evergreen foliage, was nearly hidden by their profusion of white flowers. At other times our path was lined with wild gooseberry bushes, laden with blossom; then leaving these pleasant spots, the road wound up the sides of steep mountains covered with thick forest, affording shelter to numerous herds of deer. The stillness was unbroken, save by the bells of our baggage-animals, or the occasional report of some hunter's gingal, repeated by answering echoes through the glens. The heat of the valleys was most oppressive, and alternating with the sharp cold of the snowy heights, was very trying; sometimes in the morning we would toil over perpetual snow, facing the keen wind, which blistered our faces, and in the afternoon descend into deep pent-up glens, where the heat was almost overpowering, and our muscles were so much relaxed that moving or standing became an absolute torture. Sometimes, indeed, the relaxation was so great, that neither Philip nor myself could rise from our seats. The country was very full of game, deer and bears, which latter were at that time still in their winter sleep; but I was always too tired after our day's march to attempt to go in search of venison, save on one occasion, and then I started on the track of a buck and two does, and after an unsuccessful stalk till dark, was glad to return empty handed, and by the time I made my way back to the station, was so done up that I turned in without eating my supper of damper and tea. Next day I was so unwell that for a time I feared that I had caught the cow-pock, from which all the people of the post were suffering; indeed, this troublesome disease was very prevalent among the people of Eastern Thibet, from the time that we left Ta-tsian-loo until we reached Bathang.

One night we put up at the house of a wealthy Thibetan, who maintained a domestic chaplain, in the person of a Lama. Our day's march not having been too laborious, we had some idea of sport, for the valley abounded with deer and pheasants; but we were forbidden by his reverence to shoot any bird or beast, or even to attempt to catch the fish with which the adjacent stream was plentifully stocked. All the *fera natura* had been taken under the protection of the chief Lama—the head of a Lamasery some way up the valley. The penalty attached to the breach of this pious game law would, the Lama said, be another predatory visit from the dreaded Zandi tribe, inhabiting the mountains forty miles to the south-west of this district. Only the year before, a party from this tribe had destroyed the house of my host, and carried off into slavery many of his relations.

These Zandi tribes, for there is another tribe in the country to the north, are the only Thibetans absolutely independent of the Chinese government. Under the rule of hereditary chiefs they cultivate their mountain glens with bearded wheat and white peas; but they are also bandits on a large scale. Every now and then they issue from their fastnesses, well mounted on hardy and swift ponies, and sweeping through the well inhabited valleys of the more peaceable Thibetans, surprise and burn the villages, and carry off crowds of captives, and herds of cattle and sheep to their mountains. The northern tribe is the most powerful; but their present chief is allied by marriage to the old Thibetan king at Ta-tsian-loo, and on friendly terms with the Chinese and Thibetan governments; abstaining from predatory excursions, but maintaining absolute independence, like the southern tribe. They are very warlike, and appear to be divided into several clans, constantly engaged in deadly feuds with each other, but uniting in one common cause against attacks from without. They also are cultivators, and rich in slaves, herds, and flocks.

Both tribes acknowledge the spiritual power of the Grand Lama at Lhássa, and maintain Lama priests.

On the fourth day from Hokow we ascended a very high range of mountains, and by noon entered a large plateau (on a level with the pass, beyond which rose snowy mountains of still greater height. The plain was about three miles long, and more than a mile wide in some places, in which lay the town of

Lithang. Nothing could exceed the dreary aspect of this plateau; not a sign of vegetation, except grass, was to be seen, and the walled town, built at the foot of the mountains, stood out on the plain, making the nakedness of the country still more marked, reminding me of those dreary landscapes seen along the shores of the Gulf of Kutch. As I neared the town, I almost fancied myself about to enter some city of the dead, for all was quiet; no sounds broke the stillness, save the distant monotone of the Lamas, chanting their prayers, while high overhead the lazy Turkey buzzards and huge croaking ravens sailed in circles over the city, ready as it were to swoop down, and gorge themselves on their prey. Once within the town, I was immediately struck by the solemn air of the people. Numbers of Lamas, dressed in their flowing green robes, were passing to and fro, devoutly twirling their prayer-wheels, and muttering the prayer of Omanee peminee (as they pronounce "Om mani padme hum.") And this solemn demeanour characterised not only the Lamas, but even the few rough tea traders, dressed in their sheep skins, and the townspeople, who one and all twirled their wheels, and joined in the everlasting chorus of Omanee peminee.

On arriving at the hotel, both Philip and myself were in a sad plight. The alternate heat and cold of the mountains and valleys had blistered our faces frightfully. On entering the plain of Lithang, a keen wind, driving before it a heavy hail-storm, literally cut our faces to pieces; and when we entered the hotel, the blood was pouring from our wounds, and excited the sympathy of the inmates, who flocked round us with exclamations of pity. However, after cleansing the blood with warm water, an application of fresh butter afforded some relief, and we managed in a short time to make ourselves as comfortable as the universal dirt and discomfort of a Thibetan hotel would permit.

It was needful, in order to rest the wayworn animals, to halt a day in Lithang, as well as to lay in provisions for the ten days' journey to Bathang; but beyond a few pounds of dried peas to serve as fodder, nothing could be procured, owing, as I afterwards learned, not to the scantiness of the townspeople's stores, but to the hostility of the Lamas, who secretly forbade the merchants to supply us with provisions. This proved a serious disappointment, and was the cause of much subsequent hardship.

The morning after our arrival, both the Thibetan and Chinese officers sent to inquire who I was, and demanded my passport, which proved satisfactory. An interpreter from Lhássa also called, and on seeing me, at once recognised me as a Palin, or white conqueror of India, as the Thibetans call the English. He had been to Darjeeling and described his visit to a Palin house, which from the description he gave of it, must have been either a police guard-house, or a traveller's bungalow. He was a native of Lhássa, and besides Thibetan and Chinese, spoke several languages, Nepaulese amongst the number. The Grand Lama of Thibet had employed him as interpreter to the party of Lamas, who annually repair to Lithang to receive the present of tea, sent by the Emperor of China to the Grand Lama.

In the afternoon I went for a walk, and my European costume attracted a great crowd, who followed me wherever I went, but without even so much as addressing me. I visited the celebrated Lamasery, with its golden dome. The building, with its surroundings, covers a great extent of ground, and contains over 3,500 Lamas.

My intention of entering the main building was defeated

by a number of scowling Lamas posted at the gateway, who warned me to keep off. I was, therefore, obliged to be content with the view of its exterior, and sauntered back to the hotel, discouraged from making any further examination of the town, as every Lama met me with a scowl of hatred. One thing during my walk, however, struck me very forcibly, and that was the peculiar physique of the people, differing from that common amongst the people of Thibet, who are very tall and large framed, having dark complexions, and a profusion of black hair hanging over their shoulders; many of the Lithangites, on the contrary, were thick sturdy fellows, with short woolly hair, and light complexion. I tried in vain to obtain any explanation of these racial peculiarities; though it was said that some of these people had come from countries to the south of Lhássa.

During my absence, Philip discovered that all our packages of beads, needles, and tea, &c., had been plundered. On his reporting this discovery, I at once pitched upon our half-breed interpreter as the thief, for his knavery had already appeared on our journey from Hokow. I had been compelled to hire two baggage-ponies from the wealthy Thibetan at whose house we had stayed one night, and having paid the interpreter four rupees as the price for two days' hire of ponies, the fellow pocketed two rupees, and engaged yaks, which could only travel eight miles a day. On my objecting to take them, he insolently refused to exchange them, and told me to go on without him. I was obliged to give him a thrashing, which brought him to his senses, and the ponies at once were brought out of the forest. However, for the rest of our journey to Lithang, I made him ride in front of me, and as a precaution had the baggage, every night, packed so as to make a bed for Philip.

It was necessary to check this plundering, so he was summoned, and required to submit his baggage to a search; upon this he became very noisy, and soon created a great disturbance; however, I held him over his baggage, while Philip, one after the other, extracted several bricks of tea, more than four pounds of beads, and several articles of our missing property. As each stolen article was held up by Philip, the curious crowd who filled the house shouted with indignation, and on my helping the culprit out of the room with a kick, they hustled him into the street, and the last I saw of the scoundrel was as he fled up the street, pursued by the jeers and hooting of the excited mob. We were well rid of him, as the muleteer answered our purpose much better as an interpreter, and was an honest hard-working lad.

Of all the rogues one encounters in Thibet and the frontier towns of China, the professional interpreters are the greatest, and should be carefully avoided. Their profession is a lucrative one, and their appearance, generally speaking, is very respectable; indeed, without some previous knowledge of the class, one might take them for petty Mandarins, whose air and manners they generally assume.

After a day's rest I was heartily glad to leave Lithang; owing to its great altitude, the rarefied atmosphere rendered breathing so difficult, that during the night I several times awoke with a most painful feeling of suffocation; besides this cause of discomfort, my arrival in the town had created great excitement amongst the Lamas, who, taught by the Chinese officials, looked upon my coming as the forerunner of the annexation of their country by the Palin, and met me everywhere with muttered curses.

Leaving the town by the road by which we had entered it, we traversed the plain, accompanied by two half-breed soldiers who joined us, under pretence of availing themselves of our escort, but really sent as spies. We then ascended a snowy range opposite; a more wild and desolate country than that now entered it is impossible to conceive,—huge masses of quartz and granite lay scattered over the sterile surface, and blocks of grey granite, piled one on the top of the other, rose into gigantic pyramids crowned with snow, the melting of which fed numerous torrents; as we crossed their beds, and the hoofs of our cattle ploughed up the sand, abundance of scaly gold was visible, tempting unsuspicious travellers to stop and gather the treasure. But gold, like all else of a yellow colour in Thibet, is sacred to the Grand Lama; at least so the soldiers informed me, and I was forbidden even to take up a handful of the golden sand.

We travelled for five days through these desolate mountains, with flagging spirits, and pinched by cold and hunger. Our provisions scarcely allowed us six ounces of food per diem, and the two hams left from our Ta-tsian-loo stock proved to be flyblown and useless. The poor animals, beyond a daily pint of peas doled out to them, had nothing to eat, and became a great source of anxiety as day by day, from hunger and exposure to the cold, they became weaker and weaker until they staggered under their loads. At the end of the first day's journey from Lithang, we put up in a courier's hut built in one of the passes of the mountains, and half-buried in snow and ice. It was a little place about twenty-four feet square, constructed of mud and stone, and in it the courier, his wife, and two grown children, myself, Philip, our muleteer Lowdzung, the two soldier spies, a cow-yak and calf, and four ponies, were crowded together for the night; the place swarmed with ravenous vermin, but to their powers of tormenting we were soon rendered insensible by the fatigue of our day's journey, and we slept comfortably because warmly. The third day I was obliged to journey on foot to spare our tired horses. In the forenoon we passed a succession of grassy hills, the pasture ground of thousands of sheep, tended by nomad shepherds dwelling in tents. At the foot of one of the hills a hot salt spring bubbled out, the favourite resort of the yaks and sheep. In the afternoon the grassy hills were succeeded by rocky mountains sparsely wooded, and containing frequent veins of white and yellow marble; on our right rose higher mountains, an offshoot of the great Tsanba range; at last, having turned the flank of these, we came in sight of the mighty peaks of the main range, seeming to bar our further progress. Turning to the north, the road wound along a broad flat valley, which, although lying at a great elevation, was comparatively free from snow, and afforded pasture for numerous droves of yaks; it was walled in on one hand by the Tsanba range, whose countless peaks towered one after the other in white grandeur, looking in their unsullied purity like fit thrones for angels; and on the other by the huge wavelike mountains covered also with snow, along whose base we had been marching: at last we reached the Tsauba station at the foot of the pass.

Round the fire of the little courier hut where we put up for the night, we were joined by a Lama, who was, he said, *en route* for Bathang. Since the unwelcome addition of the soldier spies to our party, it had become necessary for me to wait till all were asleep, to write up my journal. I was hard at work about midnight when the Lama returned to the room, pretending to have left his prayer-book behind; and seeing me engaged in writing he became very curious to know what I was doing. Had I owned to recording a simple narrative of the day's journey, he would have reported that I was taking notes of the country for some sinister purpose, so I replied that I was writing my prayers, a ceremony which I performed every night. This is a very common occupation of the Lamas themselves, but he was surprised that a merchant should write prayers; so I told him that I always recited them after they were written, and would commence as soon as I had finished. He waited, and I soon commenced to read my journal over in a monotone like that in which the Lamas recite their litanies. After reading thus for nearly half an hour, I stopped and asked my friend to recite his prayers for my benefit, promising to pay him for the service, —and off he started and kept it up without ceasing until daylight next morning, when he awoke me, and received his fee of one rupee. He declared that I must belong to the Yellow religion, but I assured him to the contrary, merely saying that my religion much resembled his own. He was evidently puzzled, but pleased at my having made use of his services as a priest, and begged me to allow him to keep under my escort to Bathang.

At an early hour we commenced in a fall of snow the ascent of Tsanba, which was dangerous in the extreme, and very exhausting to our already weak baggage animals; they groaned and laboured under their loads in the most painful manner, tottering ten yards or so they would rest with their distended and bloody nostrils touching the snow, from which they inhaled the thin air with spasmodic gasps. By two o'clock we attained the summit, and across a deep narrow valley beheld the still loftier chain of the Great Taso range. The lower cliffs were bare perpendicular walls of yellowish limestone, above which the snow-covered peaks towered into the clouds which veiled their summits. These two mighty ranges, uniting to the north of this valley, extend for about

100 miles north-eastwards, feeding the head waters of the Ya-long and Kin-cha-kiang by innumerable torrents; to the southward they extend in parallel chains for about 50 miles, finally losing their height and uniformity before reaching the Sui Shan, or snowy mountains, in Yunnan. Near the western base we entered a magnificent forest, the same which Huc describes as the finest he had seen in Thibet. The cedar and pine trees were of singular magnitude and beauty, the latter rising straight as "the mast of some tall amiral" to a height of 100 feet; from the branches hung weird-looking masses of withered moss like a giant's scalp-locks. Emerging from the gloomy shades of this forest, we descended into the long grassy valley formed by the fork of the ranges; which is a great breeding place for yaks. And while thousands of the queer-looking long-haired cows and their calves were grazing, the black tents and huts of the shepherds, with the wreaths of smoke curling up from the yak-dung fires, gave a promise of rest and refreshment which was not fulfilled. Anxious as we were for a day's rest to recruit our starved and jaded animals before attempting the heights of Taso, we found it impracticable, for we could procure nothing but tsanba, or meal made of bearded wheat roasted and ground, and butter tea. We still had plenty of tea, and flour enough to last for four days; but I was afraid of losing my cattle, which had been starving for three days on half a pint of peas, and what they could pick up during an hour or two that we left them out to graze, for the cold at night was so intense that we were forced to tie them under the lee of the huts where we slept; if they perished, my funds would not suffice to replace them and carry me to Lhássa or Assam; so there was nothing for it but to push on, but it was with great misgivings that we started the next morning to scale the inaccessible-looking

Taso mountains in a heavy snow-storm; the only pass was along a fissure in the wall of rock, not more than eight yards wide, forming the now dry bed of a mountain torrent. Up this steep ascent we clambered, and after a mile or two of very severe toil struck a path opening into a wide grassy plateau leading to the pass; the mountain seemed literally alive with the large silver-grey hare common to Thibet, and numerous pheasant-like birds were running about on the snow, uttering calls which resembled the hysterical laughter of a woman, but we could not stay to secure specimens. After passing the snow-line the danger of the ascent increased; at times we crept along glaciers overhanging frightful chasms, at others we floundered along through snow drifts in which the poor struggling baggage animals sank down utterly heart-broken, and refusing to move, compelled us to shovel away the snow and literally carry them out. No words can describe the labour and suffering we thus underwent; for we had the greatest difficulty in drawing breath, and after every effort to extricate our nearly frozen animals the whole party, including the Lama and spies, would throw themselves flat on their faces, unable to articulate a single word; by this means recovering their breath much sooner than by sitting down or standing. A keen cutting wind blew in fierce gusts down from the snowy heights, splitting our faces into gaping wounds, for it was impossible in the difficulty of breathing to cover them, and in this condition, the blood often pouring from our gums and noses, we struggled on for eight hours.; at last we reached the summit of the mountain, all but dead, and too exhausted to risk resting in the snow, lest we should become stiff and unable to proceed. In this sorry plight men and animals staggered down the descent, and by 5 P.M. emerged from the snow, and descending for another hour reached a Tzan. Fortunately it was a superior station, comprising not only the house of the courier but four others occupied by Chinese soldiers, forming a post stationed to guard the pass of Taso. The hospitable inmates of the Tzan soon made us comfortable, and our sinking spirits and exhausted bodies were speedily revived by a capital feed of rice and boiled chicken, washed down with samshu. My worn-out ponies and mules were housed in a warm well-built shed, where for nearly an hour they stood with drooping heads, too exhausted to eat the hay with which the people of the house had liberally supplied them.

None but those who have travelled for days, pinched by hunger, with starving cattle constantly appealing to their pity, can understand the pleasurable feeling aroused by seeing the poor dumb brutes comfortably stabled, with an abundance of provender before them; and this was enhanced by the unexpected relief from the fear of losing the all-essential services of the poor companions of my travel.

The evening I spent at the guard-house on the Taso mountains will long be remembered by me. The Chinese soldiers seemed to vie with each other in making us comfortable after our terrible journey, and, tired as we were, we sat round the fire, burning on a hearth in the centre of the room, until a late hour, sipping our hot samshu and listening to the tales of mountain adventures, which our rough but kindly hosts took turns in relating.

Before turning in, I went to take a look at my animals, and found them still eating, but less ravenously. The full moon was shining brightly, and lighted up with her soft silvery beams the snowy peaks of Taso, which towered, as it were, perpendicularly above the little station, forming a scene of indescribable grandeur.

Next day we continued to descend the mountain, and by 11 o'clock A.M. struck the source of a mountain stream, and kept on our way along the ravine, down which its waters, in gradually increasing volume, foamed some hundred feet below, on their way to the Kin-cha-kiang.

The road, or rather path, was hewn out along the face of the almost perpendicular cliff, and unprotected by any kind of fence; it was so narrow in some places that there was not room for two persons to pass clear of each other, and it became necessary for our guides to keep up a continued shouting to warn any party ascending, that they might stop at a broader place until we passed.

While threading our way down one of these narrow passes, I happened to be in front of the baggage ponies, when one of them was struck by a mass of rock, which rolled from above; the frightened animal rushed madly down the path; and I had only time to look back and perceive my danger. A collision seemed inevitable, which would have hurled us all down the precipitous side of the mountain into the foaming torrent below. In a moment I threw myself flat down across the path, the frightened animal leaped over me, and cannoning against my saddle pony, slipped and fell, rolling over the precipice, with a scream of agony, into the stream. I made sure that he was killed, and looking down, I saw him being rolled over and over in the water, till he at last brought up against a large boulder, still carrying his load; the poor brute, however, scrambled to his legs, and stood apparently little the worse; but it seemed impossible to get him up, so steep was the cliff, and my followers proposed to descend and bring up the baggage, and leave the horse to his fate. To this, however, I objected, as we were not more than a mile from the plain of Bathang, through which the stream flowed, and I fancied that it would be possible to get the pony down the stream to some accessible landing-place; I therefore went down with the guide and Lowdzung, and succeeded in recovering the baggage and pack-saddle off him, and with the aid of the ropes, by which we had descended, got them safely hauled up to the narrow path above; I then asked the guide to get the pony down-stream the best way he could, but the poor fellow turned pale at the very idea; there was nothing for it but to set to work myself, for I was determined not to lose the animal, without making an effort to save him. The atmosphere was quite warm, so I stripped to it, and, mounting the pony, plunged into the raging torrent. The first shock of the ice-cold water, as the pony boldly jumped into a deep, clear pool, was terrific, and I yelled, on coming to the surface, as though I had jumped into a cauldron of scalding water; but I had little time to think of it, for we were swept down a small rapid, and then the pony, with wonderful pluck, recovered himself, and scrambled over a bed of rocks, underneath which the water rushed with a deafening roar. For nearly a mile we alternately scrambled over rocks, and were being swept along with fearful force, sometimes being caught and spun helplessly round and round in a deep eddy. Whenever we got into a deep place, I always slid off, and laid hold of the pony's tail. At last we reached a good landing place, and once more got the pony up to the path, where the rest of the party stood trembling and muttering prayers. Looking back on this adventure, I suppose I ought to have been dashed to pieces; but strange to say, beyond a few slight cuts and bruises, neither the pony nor myself were at all the worse for it. Some Thibetan men and women who had joined us at the guard-house, were charmed with the proceeding, and whooped and yelled in answer to my repeated cheers, as I succeeded in getting safely over some more than ordinarily dangerous part of the stream; and when I once more stood dressed in the path amongst them, they seemed positively to imagine that I was some superhuman creature dropped from the clouds, the whiteness of my skin having entirely bewildered them. This adventure delayed us a long time, but at last we all resumed the order of march, and continuing down the valley, soon reached the plain, and by 4 P.M. entered the town of Bathang.

CHAPTER IX.

BATHANG.

Making Friends with the Mandarins—A Morning's Trading—A Thibetan Turf-man—My Friend Tang—The Golden-roofed Lamasery—Small-pox in Thibet—More Frightened than Hurt—An Intrigue Discovered—Route to Assam—Tz Ta-Lowya—A Mandarin in Difficulties—Change for Yunnan.

OUR arrival in Bathang caused great excitement; as we passed through the long streets of two and three-storied houses, with their prison-like windows, which composed the town, men, women, and children formed inquisitive groups, anxious to see the "Palin," to whom rumour had already ascribed the most sinister intentions. Numbers of Lamas hurried from group to group, earnestly addressing the people, with most excited gesticulation. I however passed on without receiving the slightest insult, and at last reached the only hotel, situated at the further end of the town, where I was soon comfortably quartered, and my poor half-starved cattle provided with an abundance of provender in a shed attached to the building, which was more Chinese than Thibetan in its arrangement.

Before I had time to settle down in the hotel, three missionaries, Messrs. Fage, Goutelle, and Desgodins, arrived, to inform me, that at their instance, the authorities had provided a house for my residence in Bathang, and they strongly urged me to remove into it at once. But as free quarters are only provided by the Thibetans for officers of distinction, I thanked the Fathers for their kind offices, and declined to move. The Bishop's last word of advice had been that I should stop at hotels only, avoiding all assumption of such importance as would be at variance with my description in my passport as a travelling merchant. And I felt that the officious kindness of the Fathers in demanding free quarters for me, was likely to rouse an ill-feeling on the part of the authorities, besides leading them to suppose that I was connected with the missionaries. A proof was soon given that the authorities, both Chinese and Thibetan, were greatly incensed against me; for on sending my passport for examination, with the customary trifling presents, the latter were returned, without any message—a very intelligible hint that my presence in the town was unwelcome.

The excitement consequent on my arrival, lasted all the afternoon, so I kept out of sight. The next morning, about eight o'clock, I went on the flat roof of the hotel, overlooking the street; an immense crowd, assembled below, greeted me with loud shouts of "Pebunza, Pebunza," (Nepaulese, Nepaulese), "Palin, Palin," (Englishman, Englishman). Though rather startled at this outcry, without losing my presence of mind, I bowed politely, and seating myself on a wooden bench, in full view of the crowd, proceeded to light my pipe, and calmly surveyed them. After taking a good stare at the stranger, the crowd dispersed, without any sign of hostility, and from this time forth my presence ceased to attract any attention.

During the morning the Chinese Mandarin sent to inquire if I had anything for sale, so I informed his man that I had some watches and revolvers to dispose of. He soon returned, to say that his master desired to look at my merchandise; whereupon I sent Philip with my rifle, revolvers, and a couple of watches, with instructions to offer them at prohibitory prices. On his return, Philip informed me that the Mandarin had been very indignant at the idea of having to provide me with free quarters; but, on hearing that I had refused to take them, was greatly mollified, and intimated that he would now accept the presents, which he had returned. I was glad thus to have come to a good understanding with the chief authority of the place, and hastened to gratify his desire for the presents. In the course of the day the Thibetan officials sent me presents, taking care to instruct their messengers to let me know that they had only refused my offering because the Chinese Mandarin had done so. Thus the evil impression produced on the minds of the authorities by the unfortunate, though well-intentioned, interference of the missionaries was removed, much to my relief; for I knew that at this point the fate of my expedition must be determined, since the next stage would take me out of the direct jurisdiction of China into the Central Kingdom of Thibet, and, in case of trouble, the Bathang authorities would be my only protection.

After I had been two days in the hotel, without going out, I accepted an invitation from the missionaries to breakfast with them. There, for the first time, I heard from a Chinese tea trader of the existence of a trade route from Bathang to Rooemah, a town in the Thibetan province of Zy-yul, situated near the borders of Assam, twenty days' journey distant. This information was most satisfactory; and it seemed as though I was about to accomplish the object of my journey— the discovery of a route direct from China into our Indian possessions. One great difficulty, however, remained to be overcome; my passport laid down my route as from China to

India viâ Lhássa; and new passports from the authorities of Bathang would be required to enable me to proceed to Assam. Whether these would be granted to us remained to be seen.

The good Fathers gave us an excellent breakfast of roast fowl and vegetables, with what, to me, was the greatest treat of all—some wine. In the enjoyment of their cheerful and profuse hospitality, the fearful hardships we had endured in the mountains were forgotten; and after the meal we adjourned to smoke our pipes on the flat roof of their house.

From our elevated position we looked down upon the valley of Bathang, which lay stretched out before us in all the luxuriance of its young crops of bearded wheat and peas.

The little plain, about three miles in circumference, watered by a branch of the Kin-cha-kiang, which runs through it, forms a perfect oasis in the inhospitable mountain country, and lies like a green jewel in the setting of bare mountains which enclose it on all sides. The fertility of this little Eden of Eastern Thibet is wonderful,—two crops are annually reaped. Various vegetables, such as potatoes, cucumbers, Chinese cabbages, a long turnip-flavoured root, pumpkins, leeks, onions, and spinach grow in great profusion; and fruits of great size and flavour—pears, peaches, walnuts, and water-melons—ripen in abundance. Fowls, mutton, and fish from the neighbouring tributaries of the Kin-cha, are plentiful and cheap, large supplies being easily obtainable for a skein of silk thread, a few handfuls of tea, or a dozen needles.

The town, containing probably 6000 inhabitants, including the Lamas living in the famous Lamasery, is of considerable importance as a market, to which the central Thibetans and Mongols bring their produce of musk, borax, peltries, and gold to exchange for tea and snuff, of which latter they are great consumers.

There is a superior military Mandarin, exercising civil functions, and an inferior officer in charge of a detachment of 180 Chinese soldiers. Besides these, there are two Thibetan officials, who take cognisance of all matters concerning the native population, having supreme power except in capital offences, which are disposed of by the Chinese Mandarin.

After spending a very pleasant morning with the Fathers I returned to the hotel, where I found a number of visitors from amongst the townspeople. Their motive was pure curiosity; but, as an excuse, they professed a desire to purchase a variety of articles, such as emeralds, turquoises, and agates, with holes for stringing: red and pink corals were also eagerly asked for; and European toys, such as kaleidoscopes, were in great demand, and, strangest of all, nearly everybody asked for photographs. The Nepaulese ambassador and his attendants, in passing through the town on their way to China, had evidently done a large trade in these articles. Indeed, I was told that the traders in his party had sold an immense quantity of coral, procured in the salt lakes to the north of Lhássa, at a price which threw the ladies of Bathang into a perfect coral fever. This article is highly esteemed by them, and, previous to the ambassador's arrival, had sold at weight for weight in gold. The excitement which therefore prevailed when the Nepaulese traders sold it at weight for weight in silver was intense; and, unfortunately for the traders, they did not find out their mistake until they had disposed of nearly the whole of their stock.

My visitors were apparently so eager to buy that I produced my beads, turquoises, onyx, and agates, thread, needles, and silks, determining to amuse myself with a little bargaining. Just as I expected, however, nothing suited their fastidious taste; but I was bound to uphold my character as a trader, and produced a packet of photographs of friends, collected in Shanghai; and these were no sooner exhibited than a dozen buyers at once entered into lively competition, and I did a brisk business. The ladies sold at prices varying from a fowl, to three fowls and a bundle of hay for the best-looking, average articles meeting with ready sales at a rooster or two bundles of hay a-piece. Thus, in exchange for two or three dozen portraits I procured a supply of food for my party and cattle, nearly sufficient to last us during our stay in Bathang.

Our bargaining afforded, at my expense, an instance of the astuteness both of the Chinese and Thibetans. While in Ta-tsian-loo I had purchased from a Chen-si merchant a quantity of what I thought to be real turquoises at a very low rate; the corresponding price at which I now offered them awoke the suspicions of my Thibetan customers, one of whom, having purchased a single stone, immediately crushed it to pieces beneath his heel. This conclusive proof of the spuriousness of some of my wares elicited murmurs of disapproval, and I should have lost my character for fair dealing, had I not at once, with loud anathemas on the rogue who had taken me in, crushed in the same way all the porcelain beads which he had palmed off on me as real turquoises; whereupon the Thibetans, with loud laughter, assured me that I was no match for the sharp Chen-si traders. Their ridicule was, however, infinitely preferable to being taken for a vendor of spurious articles on my first introduction to the Bathang public. Towards evening several Lamas paid me a visit; though extremely polite, they could not refrain from asking many questions about my intended movements, and, when they saw the passport authorising me to proceed to Lhássa, unanimously declared that such a thing was impossible. I appeared, however, to think that they were mistaken, and quickly changed the conversation, not wishing as yet to open the question.

I had now been several days in Bathang, and, beyond the inquiry made by the Chinese Mandarin as to whether I had anything for sale, had seen or heard nothing of the authorities. I was, therefore, agreeably surprised when, on the morning following my sale of photographs, the second Thibetan Mandarin, accompanied by several of his officers, paid me a visit. He was a middle-aged man, dressed in the full costume of a blue-buttoned Chinese Mandarin, with shaven head, and tail, and spoke Chinese fluently. He was very friendly; and we were soon on such good terms that he invited me to accompany him to his house, where we dined.

He happened to be a very horsey individual, and showed me through his stable, which contained many fine specimens of the Thibetan pony as well as mules, all in splendid condition, and groomed to perfection. Mine host, in showing me through his stable, had an eye to business, knowing that my stud was in bad condition. He asked me if there were any animals amongst his lot that I would like; and, having ascertained that I really did want to buy, asked prices ranging from one to three hundred taels each, so that I concluded he had only offered his animals out of politeness. When we returned to the house, I learned that he was particularly anxious to possess one of my silver watches, one of which had cost me a hundred taels in Shanghai. This was an opportunity to trade for baggage-animals, so I pretended not to wish to sell my watch.

I had a capital dinner served *à la Chinoise*, and took leave of my host, Min Ta-lowya, with a promise to visit him again on the following day. At the hotel I found the chief Thibetan Mandarin waiting for me. He also was dressed in Chinese costume, and, though an old man, was very erect, and, unlike Min Ta-lowya (who was rather small for a Thibetan), exceedingly tall, standing fully six feet two. We had a long chat, which ended in his asking me to dine with him some day. He spoke of my intention to go to Lhássa, and assured me that, as far as the Bathang officials were concerned, I need fear nothing, but that beyond the frontier of the Central Kingdom he felt certain I should be either stopped or maltreated. I did not force the subject of my departure, as I proposed to rest at least a week longer in Bathang. My guest had scarcely taken his leave, when I received a visit from the missionaries, who were very anxious that I should not alter my intended route, but push on at once towards Lhássa, and tried hard to discover what I had determined to do. I told them plainly that I would make an effort to reach Assam by the road from Bathang to Rooemah, * and not attempt the Lhássa route. The good Fathers were somewhat selfishly, though naturally, disappointed at this determination, for if I should succeed in reaching Lhássa, there would then be no excuse for the authorities to keep *them* out of Central Thibet; and it was natural to suppose that if the Thibetans maltreated me or arrested my progress, the British Government would resent such interference with one of its subjects, and teach the Thibetans to respect peaceable Europeans.

Though sorry to disappoint the good Fathers after all their great kindness, I still felt that, as the object of my journey

* See Map.

was to reach our Indian possessions by the most direct route, it was my duty to exhaust every effort to reach Assam from Bathang before attempting to penetrate to Lhássa. After their departure, and just as I was on the point of settling myself for the night, Philip ushered in another visitor in the person of Tang Ta-lowya, an officer of the Chinese Commissariat Department, who, besides being a namesake was a fellow-lodger, and quite a character. He was nearly sixty, but carried his age remarkably well, and affected the man of extraordinary constitution, to whom nothing was impossible, and was a passionate admirer of the fair sex. He wore spectacles, and was particularly proud of his huge leather thigh-boots, with the toes most fashionably turned up. His hands were very delicate, with finger-nails of great length; and long practice in stroking his moustache enabled him to perform this little vanity to perfection.

He entered into conversation with the most perfect ease, and very soon showed that he knew all about me and my affairs. There was something about the man at once so comical, and yet clever, that I readily accepted his invitation to supper, having first, at his earnest desire, promised to accompany him to Lhássa, if I should be going that way, while I took care not to let him know of my wish to go to Assam.

It so happened that, according to the internal economy of our hotel, every lodger was obliged to cook for himself. Philip so far had acted as *chef de cuisine* for me, and offered his services to Tang. He, however, would not hear of it, and assured me with a wink, and expressive elongation of his comical face, that *he* knew how to cook, and that I should have such a supper as would surpass anything on this side of Chen-tu-foo. So we adjourned to the kitchen, where the Thibetan inmates of the house showed, by the profound respect with which they treated my companion, that he had fully impressed them with a sense of his wonderful importance. He had ordered the materials for his supper, and fowls, pork, and vegetables were all ready to undergo a transmogrification into savoury messes under his skilful touch.

The three Thibetan women and a boy were engaged at their evening meal of butter, tea, and tsanba, but they all flew about with great alacrity to minister to the wants of Tang, who, with the skirts of his long Chinese coat fastened up behind him, sleeves rolled up, and spectacles nicely balanced on the tip of his nose, solemnly and majestically brandished his knife, and set to work. Fowls and pork were soon reduced to proper Chinese cookable size, and converted into savoury stews by the accomplished Tang, who, amidst his occupation, frequently paused to instruct me in the mystery of his peculiar style of cooking, which, he assured me, was only to be attained by careful study. As I watched this strange character, and listened to his dissertation on the art of cooking, I could almost fancy that the ghost of Soyer had visited Thibet in the person of Tang; and, indeed, the fellow dwelt with such force on good eating, that, in spite of myself, I grew awfully hungry, and my mouth watered as I watched the progress of our supper, which, when served up, proved worthy of his encomiums, and we sat until a late hour.

Tang informed me that he intended to start for Lhássa in a few days, and it was agreed that we should travel in company; an arrangement that proved so gratifying to him that the copious libations of samshu with which he ratified the agreement, caused him, while bowing me out, to tumble down-stairs, and come in violent contact with the door-post, thereby completely closing up one of his eyes.

Next morning, just as I was mounting my pony to pay a visit to the Lamasery, Tang made his appearance in a woful plight. A bandage over his unfortunate eye concealed nearly the whole of his countenance; but, in spite of his disfigurement, he had lost none of his importance, and, on being joked about his misfortune by the women of the house, gravely assured them that their house would, sooner or later, prove fatal to him, as it was built in a style quite unfit for the habitation of a Chinese gentleman.

Having promised to return and dine with Tang, I started for the Lamasery, accompanied by Philip. We had not far to ride, as the building is situated less than a quarter of a mile from the west end of the town. My arrival at the gates of the Lamasery caused a great hubbub. Hundreds of Lamas swarmed on the flat roof of the buildings which composed the square block enclosed by a high wall, while numbers hurried to and fro through the courts and passages in a state of great excitement.

Dismounting outside the gate, I left my pony in charge of the gate-keeper, and entered. Scarcely, however, had I passed the inner gate, when a Lama, addressing me in Chinese, inquired my business. I informed him that I was desirous of seeing the building, and, giving him my card, desired him to present it to the Chief Lama, with a request for permission to view the Lamasery. He requested me to remain at the gate until his return, and took my message to the Chief Lama.

As he was absent nearly a quarter of an hour, I amused myself by talking to those Lamas whom curiosity had collected around me.

From where I stood I could see but little of the interior of the building. As much, however, as was visible proved that the fame of the Bathang Lamasery was justly deserved. In the centre of the block of buildings the roof of the sacred temple was plainly visible, its massive gold covering flashing and gleaming in the sunlight with dazzling brilliancy. On the roofs, and, indeed, everywhere, the place was literally alive with roosters, which kept up an incessant crowing, blending in a chorus with the chants of the Lamas. These birds are sacred to Buddha, and number, I was told, more than a thousand. None are ever killed, and their ranks are constantly swelled by the donations of the country people, who bring the chickens to the Lamasery as religious offerings. The birds are all capons, and, like the Lamas, live a life of celibacy. Not a single hen is allowed to come within the building. Everything in the sacred edifice is dedicated to the worship of Buddha, and supposed to be free from the contamination of the outer world.

I noticed several nuns about, with shaven heads, but dressed in the ordinary garb of Thibetan women, with this difference, that the colour and material of their dress were the same as those of the priestly robes of green stuff. These nuns are the abject slaves of the Lamas, performing all the drudgery of the house in common with youthful novices or deacons. They, however, in the outer world enjoy, like the Lamas, a superior social position, and command considerable respect from both sexes of the lay people. They do not shut themselves up entirely in Lamaseries, like cloistered nuns of the Romish religion, but often live with their families, and work at the household duties and in the fields. These nuns, like the priests, profess the strictest chastity, dedicating themselves entirely to the worship and service of Buddha. But, from my own observations, and from the openly-expressed opinion of the lay inhabitants of Thibet, which I had frequent opportunities of hearing, virtue is a thing unknown amongst the priesthood, and the Lamaseries are little better than dens of debauchery.

Just as I had begun to be a little impatient at his long absence, the Lama returned with a message to the effect that my presence was not desired within the building, as it would unsettle the priests at their devotions, but if I wished to leave an offering, in the shape of money, or anything else, it would be accepted. As this concession on the part of the Chief Lama was meant as an expression of goodwill, I gave the messenger a tael of silver, and, with a feeling of disappointment, returned home.

I afterwards found that I had reason to congratulate myself on my exclusion from the Lamasery, as many of its inmates were suffering from small-pox. This fearful disease commits great ravages amongst the Thibetan population; of whom almost every fourth person is disfigured by its effects. It sometimes becomes quite an epidemic, and an outbreak of small-pox excites the greatest consternation amongst the people. When cases occur in a town, the Lamas compel the families attacked to remove to the mountains, and seal up their houses. Should the sick persons be unable to bear removal, they are shut up in the house, all communication with them being prohibited, and are left to die or recover, as the case may be.

At the hotel I found Tang awaiting me, with a triumph of his culinary skill in the way of dinner. By way of adding my share to the pleasures of the table, I produced a bottle of port, which the good missionaries had sent me the day previous. Mr. Tang pronounced it excellent, and declared, with a solemn shake of the head, that people who could make such wine as that, must know how to cook. While we were smoking our pipes, the two Thibetan Mandarins joined us, and the chief dignitary invited Tang and myself to breakfast with him the next day but one. His deputy had brought a large black mule for me to look at, which he offered to "swap" for my watch, if, on trial, it suited me, of which he was confident.

As I had now been a week in Bathang, it was time to broach the topic of my departure, so I informed the Mandarins that I intended to leave in three or four days. They silently exchanged significant glances, and the chief official remarked that he feared I would meet with some trouble if I attempted to proceed to Lhássa, the precise nature of which, however, he professed himself ignorant of, save that he had heard the Lamas say that I should not be allowed to enter the sacred kingdom. I was satisfied with having announced my decision to proceed, feeling sure that if the Lamas and Chinese had determined to stop me, I should hear more before long.

The mule proving satisfactory on the trial next day, I handed over my watch, with which the Mandarin was as pleased as a boy with a new toy. During the morning which we spent in looking over his house and stables, he pulled it out, to examine it and listen to the ticking, nearly a hundred times, handling it as delicately as though it were made of glass. Next day, when I met him at the Chief Mandarin's house, he pulled out the watch with a very long face, saying that it had stopped speaking, and he was afraid to wind it up lest he should break it. Nothing could exceed his delight when I had once more set it going for him; and during the rest of my stay in Bathang he brought it every morning to be wound up.

Our breakfast, consisting of fragrant tea, cold roast mutton, stewed fowl, fish, and a variety of vegetables, was suddenly interrupted by the entrance of a Thibetan slave, who, trembling and in breathless accents, informed his master that Tang Koopah's gun had gone off, and killed Min Ta-Lowya's son-in-law. This announcement, as may be imagined, threw the whole party into the greatest confusion, and I started off for the hotel, foreseeing out of this unlooked-for accident a long detention, if not absolute danger. However, just as I was leaving the room, my Thibetan boy, Lowdzung, presented himself, and from him we learnt the true state of affairs. It appeared, that soon after I had left the hotel, Min Ta-Lowya's son-in-law, in company with two Lamas, had called, and not finding me at home, had determined to await my return; and by way of beguiling the time, they had commenced to examine my baggage. Having found my rifle, which I kept loaded, under my blankets, they had submitted it to the closest examination; of course the poor fellows were utterly ignorant of their danger, and were horror-stricken when the rifle went off, knocking over and stunning the young man who held it, and inflicting a severe blow on the face of one of the Lamas. Fortunately the ball, passing through the window, lodged in the opposite wall, without doing further harm.

The two Lamas fled, leaving their companion as they thought dead, and hence the story which was brought to us. As to the young fellow, even after he had recovered his scattered senses, it was some time before he would believe that he was not shot; and when at last he was convinced to the contrary, he ran home, and mounting his pony, rode off to a distant village to hide his shame.

Long before we had heard the whole of the story through, the absurdity of the affair made us all laugh, and we resumed our seats at the breakfast table, greatly relieved.

In course of conversation, I related how we hunted and

raced on horseback in England, and then, for the first time, I learnt that the Thibetans are passionately fond of horse-racing; both the Mandarins were enthusiasts, and owners of rival racing stables, which were always competing for the supremacy. Our turf-talk soon became exciting, and ended in an adjournment to the race-course, about a quarter of a mile from the village. We all rode down, and the two Mandarins each had two of their racing ponies brought out on the ground.

The course was a good level piece of turf, about 500 yards square, which also served for a parade ground for the Chinese troops.

The ponies equipped with the heavy Chinese saddles, with immense flaps and short stirrups, were led up to the starting point, where they were mounted by Thibetan servants, huge men, weighing not less than fifteen stone. At a signal given by a Chinese soldier, off the plucky little animals started, doing their 500 yards at a tremendous pace, the legs and arms of their riders flying about like the sails of a windmill. Each pair of ponies ran three heats, the first in two heats being declared winner. Ta Ta-lowya's stable won the day, much to the chagrin of Min Ta-lowya, who however, as the races were not public, soon regained his temper, and backed his ponies against those of his rival, for the forthcoming races in the summer.

These annual races are quite an important affair at many of the larger towns in Thibet. On these occasions the people assemble in their best attire, pitch tents near the course, and keep up a regular pic-nic festival during the few days of sport; while at night, dancing and singing succeed to the day's sports of horse and foot racing.

Fortunately for the racing ponies, the course run over

never exceeds 500 yards, pace for that distance being the desired object; and considering the weights carried, the pace is splendid; indeed, for their size, which rarely exceeds thirteen hands two inches, these Thibetan ponies might challenge the world to produce their equals either for speed or endurance.

After spending a very pleasant day with Ta Ta-lowya, I returned to the hotel, where I found my friend Tang, whose black eye had kept him at home, in a very solemn mood, shaking his head, and acting altogether in a very mysterious manner. At last, after indulging in a series of pantomimic performances, he signified that he had something of very great importance to communicate; having carefully closed the door and windows of my room, he informed me that during my absence, the writer, or chief man of business of the missionaries, an old friend of his, had called to see him, and in the course of conversation had hinted, first that he had better not allow the Englishman, Tang Koopah, to travel in his company to Lhássa; and then, after supplying Tang with some excellent samshu, had asked him as a favour to break the engagement between us, whereby Tang was to escort me to Lhássa, and assist me as far as possible. The reason for this request was, that he wanted me to be stopped by the Thibetan authorities, by whom, indeed, he hoped that I should be maltreated, as in that case the Indian Government would go to war, and open up Thibet; and then the Christians and missionaries would be able to go to Lhássa, whence he and his brother had been expelled as Christians, and obliged to leave their drug shop, in the hands of a knavish Chinese, who had robbed them. So I was to be the cat to pull the chestnuts out of the fire for the Christians in general, and Tang's friend in particular. Greatly surprised at this revelation, which threw a light on many things, I at once sent Philip to the Mission, to request the presence of the individual, whom I found so unexpectedly interfering in my affairs. Philip had strict orders to say nothing of what we had heard, and the fellow, evidently not suspecting that Tang had betrayed him, soon made his appearance. I at once taxed him with his perfidy, and he was so completely taken aback, that for some time he could not speak, and when at last he found utterance, it was to beg me not to tell the missionaries.

I considered for some time, as to whether I should inform the Fathers or not. On reflection, I thought it best not to trouble them with the matter, feeling, of course, certain that they were not privy to their employé's scheme; so contented myself with forbidding the man to visit the hotel again, unless sent by his masters, during my stay in Bat-hang.

I knew too much of the Chinese character not to understand that Tang had betrayed his countryman, in the hopes of being handsomely rewarded, and in the evening I presented him with a silk coat; he, of course, refused it, according to Chinese etiquette (for a Chinese gentleman always refuses a direct gift); however, I sent the coat up to his room and heard no more of it.

Next day I received a card from the chief Chinese Mandarin, Tz Ta-lowya, with a message that he would visit me on the morrow. I felt certain that this visit meant much more than mere ceremony, and that the struggle with the authorities was now about to begin; for it was pretty well known throughout the town, that I intended to leave in a day or two. No trouble had been spared to let me know, indirectly, that I would not be allowed to go on to Lhássa; even the missionaries, while they pressed me to make the attempt, seemed, from expressions which fell from their lips, to consider it hopeless. The officials had expected that I would make the first overture. I knew, however, that if it were resolved to prohibit my journey to Lhássa, I must have notice to that effect, and was quite prepared, and, indeed, waiting to hear from the authorites. My friend, the Thibetan Mandarin, had evidently declined to meddle in the matter, and now the Chinese Mandarin was obliged to interfere. One thing I had made up my mind to, and that was not to return unless actually forced to do so.

My purpose now was really to go to Assam. If forbidden to proceed to Lhássa, my professed goal, I might by way of compromise, and to apparently avoid complications, offer to take the Rooemah route, and thus attain my object without appearing to do so; for should the Chinese suspect me of wishing to go to Assam, I should be stopped at all hazards. Nothing is more contrary to the policy of the Chinese Government and Lamas, than the introduction of Assam tea. The Chinese on their part dread the loss of their valuable wholesale monopoly, to maintain which they give the Lamas the monopoly of the retail supply; who, by this means, hold in absolute subjection the people, to whom tea is a prime necessary of life. The Lamas, on their part, fear that with the introduction of British trade, the teachers of the new religion would come, and free trade and free thought combined would overthrow their spiritual sway. A proof of their hostility to the opening of the Assam tea trade, had been already afforded by the prevalent rumour that a quantity of tea had been destroyed by order of the Lamas on the frontiers of Zy-yul; and though this proved to be false, yet it is a fact, that a guard is maintained to prevent all such importation, and I myself was destined, both now and in a subsequent journey, to experience their determination to prevent the intrusion of the detested Palin.

I was too anxious all night to sleep, and at an early hour next morning, before I had finished dressing, the advance guard of ragamuffins, which compose the escort of a Chinese Mandarin, arrived at the hotel; gongs were beating, and the crier, who always precedes the procession, stood in front of my door, ordering, in a loud voice, all idle persons to stand aside, as Tz Ta-lowya, the magistrate, was coming. I had only just time to put on my coat, and go into the outer room, to receive his honour, who throwing aside all Chinese etiquette, rushed up to me, holding out his hand to shake mine "English fashion," and commenced bowing and scraping like a dancing monkey. When seated in the inner room, he grew calmer, and the following conversation took place, which I give, as noted in my journal immediately after his visit.

Mandarin.—Iyaw! so this is the great English merchant? Ah, I am glad to see him; his people are the dear friends of China; they always help China; very good, very good.

Myself.—Your honour is very condescending to call us the friends of China, it is too great an honour; while your very great kindness in coming to my poor hotel, shows me that you are a great and good man.

Mandarin.—Iyaw! you speak like a Ta-jen. Ah! a great people the English; their merchants are as rich as viceroys; they are not like Frenchmen.

Myself.—Your honour has travelled a great deal, and perhaps seen much of my countrymen.

Mandarin.—I came here direct from Pekin, sent by the Emperor. I saw the British minister[*] at Pekin last year.

[*] Sir R. Alcock.

Ah, a great man! But I have forgotten to tell the English merchant what I have come for. When you first arrived I was sick and could not come to see you; yesterday I heard that you intended to start in the morning. Iyaw! I could not let you go without coming to see you, and now that we know each other, will you not stay four or five days that I may have you to dine with me, that we may become great friends, and show the Lamas that you are not a Frenchman?

Myself.—I am exceedingly sorry, but I have been so long away from my friends that my heart is sick to return to them; besides, I am at a great expense every day, living at an hotel.

Mandarin (putting a hand affectionately on my shoulder). —I look into your face and my heart is glad; I must be your friend. To speak truly, I understand that the Lamas intend to stop you at Kyan-kha, four or five days' journey from this place; now if this happens the Viceroy at Chen-tu, myself, and the Mandarin at Kyan-kha, will lose face.* I have only heard that you are to be stopped. I do not know for certain; but I like Englishmen, and feel it my duty to help you. If you will remain five days here I will send to Kyan-kha and inquire, and in the meanwhile see the Thibetan Mandarins and Lamas here, and hold a council with them. Perhaps you can be sent by a small road, an out-of-the-way path, to Lhássa; if not, then you will have to return to Pekin, but I hope the Lamas won't interfere.

Myself.—Your honour speaks cleverly. Of course I will stay here five days to oblige you, and in order not to cause trouble at Pekin. I hope, however, that your honour has been misinformed. The Emperor's people in Thibet would not dare to disobey the Chen-tu Viceroy's order. As to going

* A Chinese expression signifying disgrace.

back, that is impossible. If I do so it would be an insult to the Viceroy; and, besides, if I return from Bathang, when I complain to the government, the Thibetans will say we know nothing about the man; he never was in our country, but returned from Bathang. Your honour will therefore see that I must go on until I am either killed or imprisoned; and if the Emperor's people kill or imprison me I fear it will cause trouble.

Mandarin.—Iyaw! don't talk in this way, you make my heart ache. Ah! this is dreadful. I will make it all right if you will only stay here five days. If an Englishman is stopped in this country there will be dreadful work at Pekin.

Myself.—Your honour understands that I cannot go back unless I am arrested. I should be very heart-sore to cause you trouble above all people, but you know as an English merchant I have a right to travel in the Empire of China, and I cannot give up that right unless I am made to do so by force.

Mandarin.—Yes, yes, I know if you are stopped there will be serious trouble, but do not fear, I will make it all right. Will you come to my house? What do you eat? I will order my cook to furnish you with meals. Iyaw! I am glad to see an Englishman—a great people—only traders—not coming to insult the religion of the country, like the Frenchmen, who are the cause of all the trouble in this country.

With these flattering remarks, and a repetition of his grotesque bows and scrapes, Tz Ta-lowya took his leave, and having seen him into his chair I returned to my room, quite convinced of one thing, that I should not be allowed to go to Lhássa.

THE MANDARIN IN DIFFICULTIES.

The Mandarin sent for me next day, and after a good deal of small talk, he asked me if I had thought about proceeding. I replied that I was now only waiting for the five days to expire to continue my journey. Upon this he told me that he had received a private letter from the Chinese minister at Lhássa, saying that the Lamas had given him notice that I should not come further than Kyan-kha. I replied that I was sorry to hear it, but would certainly go on, and if the Emperor's people stopped me it would be no fault of mine. The Chen-tu Viceroy had given me a passport authorising me to go to Lhássa, and I would go on until arrested. Poor Tz Ta-lowya grew very much alarmed at this, and begged me to help him out of a difficulty by going to Burmah through Tali-foo; saying, if I would do so he would send Chinese soldiers with me to Tali, and I should travel free of expense. This seductive offer I refused, alleging the clause of our treaty, which forbade me to travel in rebel country. I told him, however, that in order to keep him out of trouble I would go to Assan-qua (as the Chinese call Assam) if he liked. On hearing this he jumped up and embraced me, saying I was a good man—he had never thought of this road—I should have a guard, which I could send back on reaching the frontiers; and he would have passports drawn out at once; and my visit ended on his asking me to dine with him.

I left the Ya-mun full of hope. All accounts gathered from traders, who travelled regularly between Bathang and Rooemah, agreed that Assam was distant but twenty days' journey, and if all went well, I might perhaps in another month reach Calcutta. This dream was soon dispelled, for two days after my visit, the Mandarin called to tell me that the Lamas would not hear of my going to Assam, or Adzara as they call it, since the road lay through part of the Central

Kingdom, and they were determined that I should not enter it. In the evening he came to see me himself, and appeared disappointed that our little arrangement had fallen through. He then flatly informed me that I must either go to Burmah *viâ* Tali-foo, in Yunnan, which he assured me was free from rebels, or go back. I could go on to Kyan-kha at my own risk, but it would be useless as troops were already stationed on the frontiers of the Central Kingdom. I replied at once that I would go to Yunnan, provided he would give me a passport, and a letter saying that I could not go through Thibet. This he would not do, but offered to give me a pass if I would give up that of the Chen-tu Viceroy. This I refused. He grew excited, and fairly entreated me to agree to his terms, saying that the Chinese minister at Lhássa receives large sums of money from the Lama government to keep out foreigners (this I had heard both from the missionaries and townspeople), and if any evil befel me in attempting to enter the Central Kingdom, I should get no help from the Chinese authorities. I adhered to my determination, and Tz Ta-lowya left me quite crest fallen.

It was the 31st of May. Summer was advancing, and I had yet a long journey before me. I had made up my mind to go to Yunnan, rather than risk detention at Kyan-kha and the failure of my funds—now reduced to 150 taels; and I now became anxious for a start. My baggage-animals were quite fresh. A mule which had become useless from a sore back, I had given to Min Ta-Lowya's son-in-law, in return for a capital mule which he had sent as an apology for having entered my room in my absence,—with this and the animal I had purchased from Min Ta-Lowya I was now well off, having one animal to spare. The few preparations I had to make were soon completed. I laid in provisions for six days, changed some good Chinese sycee for the inferior silver in use in Thibet,* and, finding it impossible to hire a man, as few Thibetans will work as servants, if they can help it, Philip engaged an elderly female as a general servant, who was also to act as interpreter; for Lowdzung, my Thibetan boy, could not understand the dialect spoken beyond Bathang. In hiring this servant I took care not to say where I intended going, so as to lead the Mandarin to believe, until the last moment, that I intended to go to Lhássa. Directly, however, that he heard I was ready for a start, he sent for me to the Ya-mun. He once more pressed me not to attempt to go to Lhássa; and offered to give me a passport and guard for Yunnan, and allow me to keep the Chen-tu Viceroy's pass. To this arrangement I agreed, much to Tz Ta-lowya's delight, who promised to let me have my passport next day. On returning to the hotel I found the good missionaries waiting for me. They were greatly disappointed at hearing that I intended to go to Yunnan; but, of course, there was no help for it. And Father Desgodins took leave of me to return to Yen-gin, a mission station on the right bank of the Lan-tsan-kiang, five days' journey from Bathang.

There remained but one day more for me in Bathang; and as I had nothing to do, I devoted the greater part of it to exercising all my baggage-animals: saddling them all, I mounted my new mule, which I christened Jacob, and rode a few miles round the suburbs of the town. The road led me along the bank of the small stream which I had followed down the valley from the Taso mountains, and which joins a larger stream flowing through the plain of Bathang to the Kin-cha-kiang.

* Appendix III.

In this ride I had an opportunity of witnessing one of the two modes by which the Thibetans dispose of their dead.

Several bodies, exposed on the banks of the stream, were being devoured by crows and buzzards, which soon leave nothing but the skeletons, which are washed away by the summer rise of the stream. The Thibetans believe that as each buzzard, gorged with its foul repast, soars into the heavens, a portion of the spirit of the deceased is taken up to heaven. In the case of rich people, Lamas are employed to divide the body into small pieces, and carry it up to the top of a hill, where the vultures and buzzards soon dispose of it. Interment of the dead is also practised; but only amongst the poorer people, who cannot afford to employ Lamas to perform the ceremony of exposing the body.

Next day, according to promise, I received my passports,—a Thibetan one for Atenze, on the Lan-tsan-kiang, eleven days' distant, and a Chinese pass for Weisee. The messenger was accompanied by Sz Ta-lowya's cook, bearing a large tray, on which were about twenty dishes, forming a dinner which he begged me to accept as a mark of friendship. And in the afternoon I received like presents from each of the Thibetan Mandarins, who came to say good-bye, and to arrange about my guard, which I now found would consist of Thibetan soldiers instead of Chinese—a change that I did not object to. In the evening my old friend Tang dined with me, who, taking advantage of the occasion, drowned his sorrow at our parting in plentiful potations. And, alas! for human nature, just as he had finished embracing me for the hundredth time during the evening, he subsided under the table, from beneath which he was lifted by his servants, and I never saw him again, as I started the next morning before he had slept off his samshu.

CHAPTER X.

BATHANG TO ATENZE.

I am Married unawares—Matrimonial Devotions—Robber Hill—Robbed of our Stores—A Soug, but no Supper—Stopped on the Boundary—Refused Food at Tsung-tza—Banditti Repulsed—The Musk-hunter of Jessundee—A Terrible Woman—Tsali Shan—Passing a Snow-drift—First View of the Lan-tsan-kiang.

THE promised escort made its appearance at an early hour in the persons of two half-breed coolies, who, for the occasion, had assumed the swagger and bullying air of Chinese soldiers; to me, however, they were very attentive, and we were soon ready for a start.

Quitting the hotel amidst the loudly-expressed good wishes of a large crowd assembled to take leave of "Tang Koopah," we passed through the town. Before almost every house a small group stood waiting, and with bows and waving of hands saluted me, reiterating kindly expressions and prayers for my safety.

Once clear of the town, my little caravan settled down to the march; and in two hours we struck the left bank of the Kin-cha-kiang, running southwards in a deep, swift, but muddy stream, about 100 yards wide. Hovering over the stream were hundreds of small bluish gulls, such as I had seen at Hankow and far inland on the rivers of India.

At noon we halted for breakfast near a large grove of walnut-trees. Before I had time to dismount, a group of young girls, gaily dressed and decked with garlands of wild flowers, came out of the grove and surrounded me: some of them held my mule; while others assisted me to alight. I was surprised at their kind attentions; but at once concluded that I had come across one of the pic-nic parties of which the Thibetans are very fond. So, without the least hesitation, I followed my little guides into the grove; there, on a patch of velvet sward, near a beautiful little spring, another party of girls and two elderly women were busily arranging a feast of cold roast mutton, flour cakes, tea, sugar, sweetmeats, and walnuts; while the grove echoed with peals of merry laughter. The great attention paid to me by the group of girls, who had at once constituted themselves my handmaidens, and their familiarity with my name, left me little room to doubt that my arrival had not been unexpected. The whole scene was so arcadian, and the romantic effect so irresistible, that, though struck by the remarkable absence of the male sex, I gave myself up to the influence of the situation, and waited with languid curiosity for the *dénoûment* of this pleasant little adventure.

The little waitresses at once supplied me with pipe, tobacco, and a light; and when, at last, one of the elderly females announced, in Chinese that, "food was ready," I sat down in a circle of merry, joyous girls, who vied with each other in anticipating my wants.

A brisk morning march had fully prepared me to do justice to the viands, as well as the samshu, in which I pledged my sylph-like attendants. When their pressing entreaties failed to make "Tang" eat any more, they handed me my pipe; and I threw myself back on the grass, and yielded to a fit of castle-building. From this state, however, I was soon roused by the girls, who came up in a group, pulling along in their midst a pretty girl of sixteen, attired in a silk dress, and adorned with garlands of flowers. I had already noticed this girl sitting apart from the others during the meal, and was very much astonished when she was reluctantly dragged up to me and made to seat herself by my side; and my astonishment was considerably heightened when the rest of the girls began to dance round us in a circle, singing and throwing their garlands over myself and my companion.

I was beginning to feel that it would be as well to move, and rose for the purpose of giving orders to saddle, when Philip came up, looking very foolish, and, with a long face, said, "Well, sir! this is a bad business. That young girl, sitting beside you, has been sent instead of the servant I hired; and they have *married you* to her!!" My first impulse was to roar with laughter; but the next moment I realised the serious awkwardness of my predicament. That I had become a victim to a custom of Thibet, of which I was not altogether ignorant, was apparent; and the idea of encumbering myself with a useless girl was dreadfully startling. The grove, before so cool and pleasant, became dark and stifling; the limbs of the walnut trees, which I had been placidly admiring for their gigantic proportions, seemed transformed, as by enchantment, into the arms of demons uplifted to clutch me. For a short time I sat utterly bewildered. At last, however, I called up the two elderly women, who proved to be the aunts of my bride, and informed them that it was not the custom of Englishmen to marry strange women or buy them; and that they must take back their niece. Upon this they set up loud lamentation, and in which all the girls joined. The clamour soon brought several men and women from a neighbouring house; and I was unanimously pronounced to be a great scoundrel, who wished to cast disgrace upon a respectable family who had given me their daughter.

It was plain that I was in a fix. To cast off the girl would probably give dire offence to the Thibetans; so, I decided at once to choose the least of two evils, and take her with me, purposing to hand her over to the Catholic Sisters in Calcutta, in the event of my arrival there.

The poor girl was quite willing to remain behind; but the people around and her aunts would not hear of it. The latter scolded her soundly for daring to hint at it; so that at last, she added her entreaties to me to take her, lest she should be beaten when she got home for having cried. My consent, however, at once restored good humour to all but myself, and all parties prepared to go. With a bad grace I handed over ten taels to the sisters as a dowry; and then, in the hearing of all, addressed Lo-tzung, for such was my bride's name, desiring her to regard and address me in future as "Foo-chin," father. Thus, in the space of two hours, I was married and possessed of a daughter.

Thoroughly oppressed with the responsibility of looking after my new charge, I hurried from the scene of my misfortune. Having placed Lo-tzung on my mule, we recommenced our march, escorted for nearly a mile by the little bevy of girls who had acted as bridesmaids. They then took leave of us, each, in turn, embracing Lo-tzung, and then handing me a small bouquet of flowers, accompanied by a short speech, generally to the effect that I must take care of my wife and be kind to her.

This scene of leave-taking was very affecting. It was accompanied by an abundance of tears on the part of the young girls; and its conclusion was a great relief, the more so, that I was painfully conscious that the rascally guards, and even the boy Low-dzung, were enjoying the discomfiture evident on my countenance. Indeed, the guards every now and then gave vent to their mirth in bursts of laughter, which made me feel a strong desire to give them something to cry for.

Our female escort left us at the foot of a high hill, which we at once commenced to ascend, and, having gained the summit, Lo-tzung dismounted for the purpose of praying at the foot of one of the large mounds of stones which, as usual in Thibet, marked the summit. These cairns, sometimes thirty feet high, are erected by travellers, who, when passing over the summit, add a few stones which they have collected in the ascent, and mutter prayers. Lamas, passing, erect poles, with pieces of silk, or Khatab* cloths attached, to resemble flags; and no Thibetan ever passes a cairn without adding a stone or two to the heap, and saying a prayer. These piles, besides reminding the traveller of his duty to Buddha, are very useful to point out the passes to strangers traversing the mountains.

Lo-tzung, having contributed her quota of stones and prayers, gave me to understand that, in order to secure our future happiness, she must have a couple of Khatah cloths to attach to the flagstaffs; and there was nothing for it but to unpack one of the baggage-animals, and get out the "scarves of felicity" (?). Having given them to the young lady, I was inwardly congratulating myself that now, at least, we should be able to continue our march, for the afternoon was wearing, and our station for the night was still distant. But my matrimonial embarrassments had not yet ended. It was necessary for ME to tie one of the "scarves of felicity" to the flagstaff, and kneel in prayer with my bride. This I peremp-

* See Appendix IV.

torily refused to do; but poor Lo-tzung shed such a torrent of tears, and informed me in such heart-broken accents that if I did not do this we should not be happy, and that she especially would be miserable, that there was nothing for it but to comply. And there, on the summit of a Thibetan mountain, kneeling before a heap of stones, my hand wet with the tears of a daughter of the country, I muttered curses on the fate that had placed me in such a position.

About 5 P.M. we reached the village of Soopalong, a ferry station on the left bank of the Kin-cha-kiang. The place is famous for fish,* numbers of half-breeds being engaged in the fishery in the winter, and acting in summer as ferrymen, using small skin-boats for the purpose. Next morning we crossed the Kin-cha by means of the large wooden ferry-boats maintained by the Chinese government, and having followed the right bank of the river for about six miles, struck off to the south-west, and ascended the famous Robber Hill.

Our two guards, who, up to this point, had never laid aside their swaggering demeanour, subsided the moment we left the river, and during the ascent of the hill were absolutely dumb from terror. About half-way up the ascent we perceived two heads stuck on bamboo-poles. Their owners had belonged to a gang which at this spot had, the week before, murdered a party of Chinese tea traders on their way from Yunnan to Bathang. The Soopalong military Mandarin, on hearing of the outrage, had gone forth with his garrison and given battle to the banditti, two of whom had been captured, at the cost of the lives of ten of his soldiers, and the heads of the robbers had been set up the week before, to terrify their comrades.

The banditti of this neighbourhood are famous throughout

* A kind of Mahseer.

Thibet, and defy alike the Chinese and Thibetan authorities. Living in the fastnesses of the mountains, they hold the more peaceable inhabitants in complete terror. Nothing will induce them to betray the robbers, and in order to secure themselves from the depredations of the freebooters, they screen them in all cases from the authorities. When accused of sheltering the banditti, in order to save themselves from the consequences, whole families flee to the mountains, and swell the robber ranks. To make matters worse, it is a well-known fact that all the chief Thibetan authorities, even those at Bathang, have a secret understanding with the freebooters; for a fee to any of them will generally reproduce stolen property, and even pass a traveller unmolested through the robber district.

Fortunately for us, on this occasion we ascended the robber hill in safety, and now entered a cold, wintry climate. On all sides rose huge rounded mountains of limestone, covered with grass, relieved here and there with sombre pine-woods. We put up for the night in the village of Kung-ze-din, at the house of a Thibetan chief, or head man, and were hospitably treated. Poor little Lo-tzung was the envy of the young ladies of the house. Her silk bridal dress became the centre of attraction; and when, following out the plan that I had adopted on the previous night, I left her in charge of the chief's wife, the surprised looks of the young daughters of the house plainly showed that they thought me a very cold bridegroom. My behaviour was, however, more favourably viewed by the more influential members of the community, for, during the evening, a Lama, in high repute for piety, who lived near, sent a present of hay, tsanba, eggs, and a fowl, with a message, that it was because he had heard that I acted as a father to a daughter of his country. In this house we came across, for the first time, what we afterwards found common in the Thibetan houses, namely, the use of pine splinters as a substitute for candles. Every room has an iron utensil, like a gridiron, hanging from the rafters, on which the pine splinters are burned. The smoke from these primitive lamps is very offensive, and with that of the fires, which are generally lighted in the centre of the room under the opening in the roof which alone serves as a chimney, renders the Thibetan houses almost unbearable, and produces much smoke-blindness amongst the elderly people.

By the smoky light I tried to take the portrait of a Lama resident in the chief's household, but, on discovering my intention, he was much discomfited, and, with strong expressions of dislike, left the room, and would not again venture into my company. Whether it arises from religious scruples, or superstitious dread, I know not, but I invariably experienced the same invincible repugnance on the part of all Lamas to have their portraits attempted. Our party was reinforced next day by two women, sent by the chief as guides, according to the terms of my Thibetan passport, women being substituted for men, on Lo-tzung's account. The cooly guards should here have quitted us, but volunteered their company, to which, unluckily, I made no objection.

We continued our journey through a gradually rising country, wooded here and there, and about noon, emerging from a dense pine wood, entered on an elevated and extensive grassy plateau. We had scarcely cleared the trees, when, about a mile distant, we descried a small band of horsemen bearing down on us at full gallop. Immediately calling a halt, I turned to inquire of my guards the probable intentions of the approaching party, when, to my surprise, I saw the scoundrels, who had remained at the edge of the plateau, and unloaded my baggage-pony, just disappearing into the forest, carrying between them our stock of butter, flour, and dried fish, which we had laid in at Bathang for the journey to Atenze, now eight days' march distant.

In the face of the approaching cavalcade, pursuit was impracticable, nor dared I fire upon them, well knowing that if I once shed blood, I should never carry my life out of the country. The strange horsemen were rapidly nearing us, and there was only time to get all the baggage-animals together, and secure them head to tail, before they dashed up to us with a chorus of yells. Without appearing to notice them, I placed myself at the head of my little party, and marched on, Philip guarding the rear with my double Enfield, Lo-tzung perched behind me, and my boy, Low-dzung, leading the string of baggage-animals. We proceeded in this order for nearly a quarter of a mile, while the others kept galloping round us in circles. At last one of them rode up alongside, and commenced to shout at me, accompanying his oration with insolent gestures, and, seeing that I was not inclined to notice him, put his hand on his sword. Without betraying any sign of haste or fear, I drew my revolver, and, cocking it, calmly looked at him, still proceeding at a slow walk. Seeing me thus prepared, he galloped off, and joined his party, who wheeled to the right about, and made for the village of Pa-moo-tan, now just visible, nestled at the foot of the mountain barrier which stretched across the plateau.

As soon as our eccentric visitors were well out of sight, I called a halt, and held a council with Philip. The loss of our provisions was at this juncture a most serious calamity. We still had two baskets of brick tea, but tea would scarcely serve to keep us alive during eight days' march. To divide our party by pursuit of the fellows who had robbed us, was out of the question; and, to add to our anxiety, little Lo-tzung told us that, by their dress and features, she had recognised the armed party who had just left us, as soldiers from Lhássa. However, I determined to continue onwards, and, after a hasty breakfast of hot tea, we again fell into the line of march.

About 4 P.M. we arrived at the village of Pa-moo-tan, which we found full of Lamas and armed men. The villagers, instructed by the Lamas, would not open their doors to us, and, after trying in vain at every house in the place, we at last discovered a door open which led into a yak stable under a large house. Into this I marched my party, and sent off Lo-tzung to the head man with my Chinese and Thibetan passports.

The girl shortly returned, accompanied by a servant of the head man, who ordered the people of the house to give us straw for our animals, which they furnished at once. He then delivered a message from his master, to the effect that he knew nothing of me, but that for the sake of my wife he had ordered straw to be given to our cattle. As for myself and servants, we might get provisions the best way we could, but no one in his village should supply us. So here we were, in an evidently hostile district, with an eight days' march before us, and absolutely without a morsel of food.

Strange to say, in the face of this great difficulty, my spirits rose, and I felt determined to push through, at all events, to Yunnan. If the worst came to the worst, I could always kill one of my baggage-animals, and get a supply of food that way; so, in order to keep up the spirits of plucky little Philip and the boy, Low-dzung, I lighted my pipe, and, between occasional whiffs, made the rafters of the old yak stable, now my palace, ring again with the tune of "Rule Britannia." The people of the house and several Lamas came to see what was the matter, when I changed my tune, and sang them "Slap bang, here we are again!" accompanied by comical gestures, which apparently mollified their feelings, for one of the Lamas spoke kindly to Lo-tzung, and, as the evening wore on, some women, accompanied by the Lama, brought her six eggs and a cup of milk. These she, like a dutiful daughter, presented to me, and joined the women of the house at their evening meal of tsanba and butter tea.

The boy Low-dzung had, fortunately, a pound or two of tsanba with him, and, like a true child of nature, sat down to a meal of tsanba and water, in which he consumed his whole stock. Philip and I took a raw egg and half a cup of milk each for our meal, and, settling ourselves comfortably, commenced a long and anxious watch for morning, not daring to sleep both at once lest our animals should be stolen; for Lo-tzung, on joining us after her supper, had told us that the people of the house suspected that we would be attacked by the Lamas and soldiers during the night. We had a number of suspicious-looking visitors, but a resolute display of my revolver kept them quiet.

Poor little Lo-tzung was very unhappy, and cried nearly all night, for she was afraid we should all be murdered. She had heard that the Lamas had prohibited the people from supplying us with provisions, and that three hundred soldiers were waiting for me on a hill that we should have to pass next day. However, when daylight appeared we were all in capital spirits, and, shortly after dawn, left the inhospitable village of Pu-moo-tan, accompanied, as before, by two women sent by order of the village head man as guides.

As we left all was quiet, and we kept on our way unmolested; and having ascended the hill which frowns upon the village, we entered on another grassy plateau between two high ranges of grassy wave-like mountains.

The Lhássa route here turned sharp to the north, and, as I expected, the range of hills on our right proved to be the

THIBETAN SOLDIERS.

boundary between the Central and Eastern kingdoms of Thibet. Shortly after we entered on the plateau, a party of some two or three hundred mounted soldiers slowly descended the boundary mountain, and halted at the foot.

In order to test their real intentions, I made towards them, as though intending to ascend the mountain. On this they drew up across the path, and waited until I approached them to within fifty yards, when they hailed me, and, presenting their matchlocks, with matches burning, ordered me to halt, or they would fire.

Halting, as desired, I dismounted, and lighting my pipe, walked up to them in company with Philip, and entered into conversation, inquiring the meaning of their behaviour in a cool but pleasant manner. They were greatly astonished at what they termed the Palin's audacity, but, on being informed that I did not mean to force a passage to Kyan-kha, and really intended to go to Yunnan, a number of them dismounted, and having extinguished their matches, seated themselves beside me, while the rest kept their position.

I displayed the passports, authorising me to go to Yunnan, and told them that they were foolish to hinder me from going to Lhássa or Assam, as I was nothing more than a peaceful trader, and asked them why so many soldiers had been sent to arrest one man. This question made them smile, but at first elicited no direct answer. They, however, evinced a timorous curiosity about the wonderful guns, which they said had been described to them as terrible death-dealing engines, and begged that I would fire my revolver. On doing so, each discharge was greeted with shouts of "Al-lay!" a favourite Thibetan exclamation of admiration or surprise. I reloaded in their presence, of course telling them that I had put in enough powder for a thousand shots. My evident friendliness thoroughly won these children of the mountains, and they became quite confidential, saying that my avowed intention of going to Yunnan had given them great pleasure, as their orders were to stop me at the risk of their lives, but not to hurt me; and they had fancied, from the description given them of my weapons, that I should have killed a great number of them.

After smoking a couple of pipes with them, we separated.

The soldiers retraced their steps half-way up the mountain, and then rode parallel with our course until we turned southward again for Yunnan.

As we proceeded we were tantalised by the sight of pheasants and deer in abundance; but though the temptation to stock our empty larder was painfully strong, we dared not go in pursuit, lest we should give a pretext to the Lamas for attacking us. So with longing looks we pushed on, and gradually descended into a less elevated country, the grassy limestone mountains being succeeded by bare hills of a clayey sand, with huge square masses of sandstone imbedded, the lower sides of these boulders being rippled with watermarks.

During the conference with the soldiers, the two female guides had quietly decamped, and it was not until we came to the spot where the track turned off to the south that I missed them. I was almost glad to be rid of them, as they had been forced to accompany us, and did so with an ill grace; but, ere long, we had reason to regret the absence of the guides, for we soon lost our way amidst the numerous yak-tracks which crossed each other on the mountains. However, by keeping a southerly course, towards nightfall we came upon the village of Tsung-tza, which, luckily, happened to be the first station from Pa-moo-tan on the road to Yunnan.

At the entrance of the village, we met a party of young girls returning from a pic-nic party, who seeing Lo-tzung, who still wore her bridal dress, accompanied us to the head man's house, singing and dancing.

This reception led me to hope that I might here procure supplies, but alas, I was doomed to bitter disappointment. The whole male population seemed to turn out, and evince a desire to become violent; they, however, thought better of it, and towards dusk left us alone. Neither for ourselves nor our animals could we get a bite, though we offered to purchase tsanba for its weight in silver. The two days' hunger and want of sleep, had so told on me, that I fainted from sheer exhaustion, while poor little Philip, too tired even to make himself some tea, bathed my forehead with water. I soon recovered, and a pipe of tobacco allayed for a time the pangs of hunger.

After considerable trouble, we brewed about four gallons of tea, and gave our baggage animals three pints each, which the poor things eagerly sucked up, and then resignedly laid down, utterly worn out.

Next morning, after another night of watching and anxiety, I again begged for some provisions, but the people continued obdurate, and we were obliged to prepare for a start nearly dead with hunger. A Lama, to whom I applied, pleading that I was dying of starvation, merely answered that I should not have come into their country.

As soon as the jaded baggage animals were loaded, I applied to mine host for two guides, and at first he indignantly refused my request; but when I informed him that I would remain and die in his house, and commenced to unload the baggage, by way of carrying out my threat, his son volunteered his services.

Just as we were starting, a messenger arrived from an uncle of Lo-tzung's, who lived in a village a few miles distant, and my little charge, who had yesterday begged me to send her back, as she was afraid of dying, sorrowfully bade me good-bye, and left for her uncle's house; it was a great relief to be rid of my poor little daughter, especially as Lo-tzung's absence left me a spare mule, in case I should be compelled to kill one for food: an alternative that I reserved for the last extremity.

The head man's son, having conducted us out of the village, coolly told us to be off, and by way of expediting our movements, threw a stone at me, hitting my saddle-mule on the head, which drew from a crowd of men, who had followed us, roars of laughter, and a shower of stones.

Hunger had rendered me somewhat savage, and it was with a great effort that I managed to keep cool, and ride off. The villagers, however, emboldened by this apparent submissiveness, charged after us in a body, with savage yells. Matters now looked serious, and I at once wheeled about, ordering Philip to fire over the heads of our assailants, while I drew my revolver and did likewise; this display of fight on our part, had the desired effect, for the enemy fled, and we were left alone to pursue our weary march.

Our position was apparently becoming hopeless. Hungering and without a prospect of food, we ran the risk of losing our way, for the bewildering yak-tracks rendered it impossible to distinguish the right path. Yet neither my brave Philip, nor the boy Low-dzung, even hinted at turning back.

I had observed, when holding the conference with the soldier at the foot of the Boundary mountain, a gigantic range of snowy mountains, running almost due N. and S., rearing their white peaks and ridges far above the surrounding mountains, and at once recognised them for the range described to me by Father Desgodins, in Bathang, as forming the right bank of the Lan-tsan river, and according to my Chinese map, the road to Yunnan led along the left bank. These mountains were now visible, towering above us on the right, a lesser range only intervening, which I concluded formed the left bank of the Lan-tsan. As long as I could keep them in view, I had little fear of actually losing myself, and we carefully followed the broadest track.

About noon we came to a large wooden bridge, spanning a stream of considerable size, flowing to the S.E., marked in the Chinese map as a tributary of the Kin-cha-kiang. Its waters were *vermilion coloured;* so in the absence of any name assigned to it by the Chinese, I named it the Vermilion River. Having crossed to the right bank, we followed the stream for several miles along its course, between lofty hills rising on either hand, at an angle of 75 or 80 degrees.

We were slowly proceeding, sullen, and indifferent to everything but the desire of reaching the next station, when the whistling of a bullet, within a few feet of me, simultaneously with the report of a gun, quickly roused all my faculties. In the direction of the report a large party of men appeared, high up, near the mouth of a cave on the opposite bank of the stream. I had scarcely time to make the observation when we were greeted with a volley; we were evidently out of range of the matchlocks, but several balls dropped amongst us, and one hit Philip's mule, which resented the liberty by throwing up its heels and depositing him on the ground; following up their volley with frightful yells, the banditti, as they evidently were, charged down the mountain towards us.

I confess that for a moment or two I felt very much like making a bolt, but a moment's reflection showed me that I could not do so without losing my baggage animals, and I determined to fight for it; so, dismounting, I made a barrier of the body of my mule Jacob, an example quickly followed by Philip and Low-dzung. In this order we waited until the robbers got within a hundred yards of us, when laying my double Enfield over Jacob's back, I took a steady aim at them and pulled trigger. If a thunderbolt had fallen amongst the band it could not have created greater consternation. I distinctly saw the splinters fly from the wooden stock of one fellow's matchlock, and another scoundrel threw up his arms, evidently hit, but not so severely as to prevent him following his companions up-hill at double quick time. I thought I would just give them a further proof of the power of my weapon, and waited until they had got away three or four hundred yards, when sighting at seven hundred yards, I fired and struck the mountain some distance above them; this made them stop for a second or two, when again taking heart of grace they hurried on, and reaching their cave dashed in pell-mell like so many rats down a sewer.

My delight at the result of this engagement was slightly dashed by the thought that I had probably mortally wounded one of the robbers; in which case it was not at all improbable that I should be followed and shot from behind a tree or rock: however, by this time the constant expectation of coming to grief had settled down into a dogged indifference that I had felt once before in my life, when in a gale of wind in the Southern ocean. The ship, in which I was the only passenger, sprang a leak; for several days the water, despite the crew's exertions, kept gaining on the pumps, and as the truth gradually forced itself upon us that our sinking was merely a question of time, we grew perfectly indifferent, eating and sleeping as though nothing unusual had occurred, only the quiet and serious expression of all countenances spoke of the absence of hope in our hearts. Thus it was with our little party now. We kept on doggedly, much oppressed with the excessive heat, and in the evening reached the station of Jessundee, consisting of two musk hunters' cabins, in one of which we found shelter for ourselves and animals, and above all a kindly welcome from the hunter. Our host was very poor; a long run of ill luck had left him without musk to buy powder, and to add to his misfortune, his wife had died a few days before, leaving to his care four small children. The poor fellow was heart-broken, and seemed, like ourselves, reduced to the last extremity; his chief article of subsistence was a sort of creeper growing on the mountain; but he possessed two she-goats, and the milk from these he divided between Philip and myself, giving us each about half-a-pint. This with a couple of hard-boiled eggs served us for supper, and was the first food we had tasted for forty-eight hours. Low-dzung shared the host's tsanba, and I added a present of brick tea; for this the gratitude of the hunter knew no bounds; he would have killed one of his goats for us, but this I would not permit. I was glad, however, when I saw him lop off several large branches from a walnut tree growing near his cabin and give them to my starved cattle; the poor brutes looked at the glossy green leaves for a moment or two as if they doubted their own eyesight, and then fell to on them, crunching up the branches, some of which were an inch in diameter, as if they were straws.

The aspect of the country was extremely dreary; bare limestone mountains rose abruptly everywhere around us in chaotic confusion; no cultivation was visible, but in some places patches of withered scrub clothed the mountain sides, affording cover for numbers of pheasants and tragopans,— occasionally the summit of some more than usually lofty peak covered with forest would stand out in bold relief to the surrounding barrenness, and in such places as these the hunters stalked the musk deer.

After a watchful night, for we still dreaded the banditti in the neighbourhood, who as the hunter informed us with a laugh were brother sportsmen, we continued the march, our host's son, a lad of ten years acting as guide, to the village of Tsali, where we were told provisions could be had in plenty. From the hunter's cabin our road gradually led us upwards until we entered a finely wooded country; we passed several houses, but the inhabitants were either abroad or disinclined to admit us, for every house was locked, and but for the barking of watch-dogs all was perfectly still.

About ten o'clock we came across a large flock of sheep. The sight of them made our mouths water; and, on coming up with three or four men in charge of them, we at once entered into negotiations for the purchase of a lamb; but the fellows treated the request with scorn, and told us to be off. So Philip threw them three rupees, and, bending down, without further ceremony, lifted a nice young lamb on to the front of his saddle. The owners picked up the rupees, apparently quite indifferent; and we continued on our way rejoicing.

Shortly after noon we stopped at a road-side house, and were at once admitted by a woman, who turned out to be the only person at home. Philip immediately prepared to kill our lamb, while I attended to the boiling of two eggs which the woman gave me. It seemed as if, with the prospect of a good meal, all our cares had vanished; and I was sitting, patiently waiting for the eggs to boil, when suddenly I heard an agonising cry of, "Mr. Cooper! come quick, sir." Rushing to the door, I saw Philip, with bared arms, a knife in one hand, and holding on to the lamb with the other; while a stalwart Lama was trying to drag it away from him.

On seeing me the Lama dropped his hold of the lamb, and commenced yelling at me in a frantic manner. As soon as he stopped to recover breath, Low-dzung informed me that the fellow claimed the lamb, and insisted on its being given up. This I refused to do, saying I was starving, and had paid three times its value; but, as I did not wish to have a row, I would give three rupees more.

During the altercation numbers of men, armed with matchlocks and the long Thibetan knife, seemed to spring from the ground, and, while I was in the act of taking the rupees from my pocket, a fellow suddenly pinioned my arms from behind. An elderly virago, of huge proportions, planted herself in front, and commenced a furious assault on me with a cudgel, aiming vigorous blows at my head, which I avoided only by moving my head from side to side, thus allowing the blows to fall upon my shoulders. The giant, who held me, almost made me frantic by yelling in my ears; and I was decidedly getting badly used, when Philip at last abandoned our precious lamb, and came to my rescue. Having got my rifle, he pointed it at my captor's head, causing him to let go his hold, when, turning sharply round, I stretched him on the ground by a well-planted blow on the nose, receiving, at the same instant, a frightful blow from the female fury behind me, which laid my head open, and for a second it seemed to bring all the stars into my eyes. She was about to repeat the dose, when, with the little remaining strength I possessed, I poked her in the stomach and stretched her along side her assistant in the fray.

Low-dzung, whom until now I had always looked upon as rather soft, had, during the encounter, with wonderful sagacity, replaced the packs, which we had unloaded to rest our animals; and, the moment I was free, both Philip and myself mounted and rode off: not before, however, both men and Lama had disappeared, together with the lamb. Thus, in the place of a meal, I got a severe beating, and, what was worse than all, in my haste to be off, forgot the eggs which the good woman of the house had given me.

Hurrying away, as quick as possibly, from the scene of the disaster, and followed by the screams and curses of the terrible female, we continued our march for the village of Tsali, about ten miles distant, fearing every moment that some of the armed men, who had so suddenly appeared on the scene, might quietly pot us from behind some rock or tree. Nothing happened, however; and towards sundown we reached the village, situated in the centre of one of those plateaux so common in Thibet.

In size Tsali might almost be called a Thibetan town, numbering, probably, 100 houses. On our arrival the place was extremely quiet, and we tried nearly half the houses before we could gain admittance; but at last an old woman opened her door, and we soon found ourselves housed in a yak-shed, where we stowed ourselves away along with the baggage-animals. A present of two taels induced the old woman to give us about twelve pints of barley for our animals, which, with the exception of dried sticks, yak-dung, and the few walnut branches, given them by the musk hunter, was the first "square" meal they had eaten for three days. For ourselves she brewed some butter tea, and served it up with tsanba, which we converted into porridge and eagerly devoured, in spite of the horribly rancid butter used in the tea.

About eight o'clock in the evening a Lama and two men entered our shed by the light of the yellow-pine torches. They at once asked, in a peremptory tone, for tea. Thinking that a liberal present of tea might convert our self-invited guests into friends, I ordered Philip to give the Lama a brick, giving the men, at the same time, a handful each. Having carefully stowed this away, the fellows demanded more; and, on this request being refused, they coolly laid hold of the remaining basket, and were turning to leave the room. This would not do; so I quietly, but quickly, repossessed myself of the basket. Whereupon out flew their knives and my revolver; and a shot from the latter, fired close past the ear of my nearest assailant, produced a startling effect. I had drawn the weapon and replaced it in my bosom so quickly, after firing, that in the uncertain torchlight, they had evidently not seen it; and, after staring at each other for a moment, with a cry of terror they fled, dropping, in their haste, the tea which had been given them at first.

Feeling certain that they would return with reinforcements, we set to work at once to barricade the door of our shed, piling up baggage, pack-saddles, and straw, of which there was an abundance.

Thus secured against a surprise, we felt more at ease; but, our pine-splinters becoming exhausted, we were soon left to keep an anxious watch in the dark. A wretched half-breed cooly, who had followed in our rear all the way from Bathang, and had joined us this evening, cried with fright the whole time.

Philip, about cockcrow, discovered the end of a Chinese candle in his saddle-bag. By the light of this we quietly proceeded to saddle-up, and, when we were all ready to march, cleared away the rest of the barricade and left the place.

As we silently, but quickly, made our way through the village all was still. The stars were shining brightly overhead, and the fresh, cool breeze of morning seemed to lend us vigour.

For two hours we kept steadily on, the half-breed now doing good service as guide; and when daylight broke we rested awhile at the foot of a high mountain, which bounded the Tsali plateau on the south, and partook of a slight meal of dry tsauba, washed down with a draught of clear cold water from a mountain torrent close by.

By noon we had nearly accomplished the ascent of the Tsali Shan or mountain. In a hollow, near the summit, we overtook two officers of the chief Thibetan Mandarin in Bathang, who immediately recognised me; and, seeing the worn-out condition of the party, at once gave orders for a halt.

They were escorting a caravan of several thousand baskets of tea to Atenze, and had with them a large party of mounted soldiers, and about 500 tea-laden yaks, besides a great number of half-breeds, as drivers, and coolies.

Our friends soon prepared tea (real flowery Pekoe, brewed expressly for me), rice, and roast mutton. It need not be told how great a blessing was this meal, and I could literally have hugged my hosts on sitting down to it.

As soon as the cravings of hunger had a little subsided, I related the unpleasant adventures which had lately befallen us, and as I described each incident, with Low-dzung's help, to the motley crowd of soldiers and drivers scattered, in various attitudes, around me, some lying down, and others leaning on their long matchlocks, in eager attention, they gave expression to their astonishment and admiration in a chorus of "Al-lays."

After an hour or so thus spent, the word was given to march. We soon, however, came to a regular stand-still near the summit of the pass. A large hollow, about 100 yards across, full of snow, softened by the spring thaw, presented an almost impassable barrier; for, the moment either yaks or mules put their feet on it, they sank up to their bellies, and lay after floundering for a few minutes, utterly helpless.

High, overhanging cliffs made it impossible to go round; the only pass lay 100 yards in front of us, through a cleft in the mountain-ridge. There was nothing for it, therefore, but to get through the snow somehow ; so we halted and unloaded the string of yaks, spread in a moving black mass far down the side of the mountain. This operation was completed in a very short time, soldiers and coolies going to work in right good earnest. Then, about 100 yaks were driven, pellmell, into the snow, with the aid of stones hurled from the slings which the drovers carry, and use with unerring aim and effect on the hind-quarters of the patient yaks, which, in the present case, evidently thought a quiet seat in the snow preferable to the stinging sensation of the stones; for they plunged into it, and, those unable to proceed, quietly lay down, while others walked over them, and lay down in front. By this means the whole herd got over; and their passage across having trampled the snow into a hard mass, they were marched back and reloaded; then the yaks, followed by the soldiers and ponies, all got safely over, and we surmounted the crest of Tsali Shan.

The caravan made its way down the mountain so slowly that we pushed on ahead, and striking a mountain-stream which took its rise near the summit, followed its descending course. The path, if so it could be called, led over irregular masses of rock. Riding was impossible; and our poor animals picked their painful steps with difficulty over the rugged surface. Occasionally the mountains closed in, leaving but a narrow channel for the stream, in the bed of which piles had been driven, and supported a narrow timber causeway. One magnificent gorge, winding between its walls of rock for seven miles, I named Duncanson Gorge, after a kind friend in Shanghai. Where the glens widened out between the gorges, the less precipitous slopes were covered with tea-oil trees; while, over the white masses of flowers, hovered clouds of the common white butterfly.

In the afternoon we came to the banks of another torrent, falling into the first; and the united waters formed a considerable stream. The wooden bridge, by which the road crossed, proved to be broken; and it was necessary to ford the stream, a work of some difficulty to the tired men and ponies of our party.

Towards evening the rays of the declining sun lit up what, at first, seemed to be a line of clouds; but were soon made out to be snow-clad summits, on the western horizon, far over-topping the intervening mountains. This was the great range west of the Lan-tsan. Eighteen hours of toilsome marching were brought to an end by our arrival, at 7 P.M., at the village of Tong, on the right bank of the stream which had been our companion from Tsali Shan.

Whether from the effects of the long strain of fatigue or anxiety, I know not, but on arriving at a house and receiving a cordial welcome from the inmates, I staggered into the room where the family were taking their evening meal, and fainted. Nothing could exceed the kindness of my hosts: some of them carried me out, and bathed my face at a spring running close to their door; while others attended to Philip, who had become hysterical, and ended by vomiting violently.

The attentions of our good-hearted hosts soon revived us; and we were comfortably stowed away in a straw-shed (there being only one room in the house), where we were served with a large basin of boiled rice and milk.

As for our cattle, they were up to their knees in fresh-cut green wheat, enjoying themselves to their heart's content. Sleep, of which we were so much in need, seemed a long time in coming to our relief; and it was not till nearly midnight that I fell into a deep slumber, from which the women of the house did not rouse me until next day at noon, when they brought me another basin of rice and milk.

The border town of Atenze was only eight miles distant; I therefore, much against the wishes of our entertainers, determined to start for it, and about one o'clock left them, amidst kindly expressions of sympathy and grateful acknowledgments for a liberal present of tea.

The kindness of these people, compared with the hostile behaviour of those amongst whom we had lately been travelling, confirmed a suspicion which had been aroused in me, when we overtook the Bathang Mandarin's officers at the Tsali mountain, viz., that to their misrepresentations we owed all the ill-will displayed by the people, who, doubtless, had received instructions to throw every obstacle in our way. Indeed, I afterwards had positive proof that, in spite of the apparent friendliness of the Thibetan Mandarins, they had exhausted every means within their power—short of taking my life—to hinder me from proceeding beyond the village of Pa-moo-tan.

From the summit of a high hill, which we ascended shortly after leaving Tong, the Lan-tsan river first opened to our view, running in a deep, muddy, and impetuous stream, 150 yards wide, at the foot of the gigantic snowy range which had served as our landmark from Pa-moo-tan. A slow march of some four miles gradually led us into the mountains from the Valley of Tong, and we entered a fine undulating country, beautifully wooded: grassy slopes, like ornamental lawns, were dotted with the gnarled oak and luxuriant chestnut trees; wild strawberries were abundant, and gooseberry and red currant bushes, in great numbers, were laden with blossom.

When descending the western slope of this mountain we

seemed to walk on beds of sweet-scented wild flowers. Snowdrops, towards the summit, peeped from the grass in myriads, and, lower down, buttercups and a large species of wild hyacinth, with blue bell-like flowers, grew in the greatest profusion.

Half way down the mountain we halted under the shelter of a large oak, until a passing shower spent itself. In a few minutes the rain-cloud passed away, giving place to brilliant sunshine, which soon cleared the haze caused by the rain, and displayed to our view the town of Atenze, lying at our feet in a hollow, formed by four ranges of lofty hills running down to the same point.

A prettier view than Atenze and its environs, as beheld from this spot, had rarely met my eyes; and it was with an effort that I at last tore myself away from contemplating the lovely landscape spread, as it were, at our very feet.

As we rode down the mountain countless numbers of large silver-grey hares scampered about, disturbed in the act of nibbling the wet grass; and flocks of large bronze-winged pigeons uttered their soothing notes from almost every tree and shrub on the mountain-side. I was charmed with the approach to Atenze, and entered the town rejoicing at the prospect of a rest and freedom from anxiety.

We soon found quarters at an hotel, and, thanks to the half-breed landlord, a capital dish of ham, eggs, and potatoes was soon forthcoming, which, as mine host remarked, we disposed of like proper travellers. Immediately after dinner I sent Philip to the Chinese Mandarin with my passports for examination; and while he was absent, I turned into bed at 4 P.M., and did not wake till eight o'clock next morning.

CHAPTER XI.

THE TRIBES OF THE LAN-TSAN-KIANG.

Trade of Atenze—The Goueah Tribe—Hogg's Gorge—Sagacity of the Mules—Tz-coo Mission Station—The Lu-ts⁰ Tribes—The Moso Tribe—The Ya-ts⁰ Tribe—The Mooquor Chief—Deer-stalking at Compo—A Hunt Supper—Village of Kha-kha—Weisee-foo—The Tartar General—Soldier Robbers—A Yunnan Mahomedan.

THE following morning Philip informed me, that on presenting my passports and reporting the treatment we had received along the road, at the Ya-mun, he had been sent away with much abuse, and a message that I had better return by the way I had come.

We had numerous visitors from amongst the townspeople, who appeared very friendly, and the greater part of the day was spent in disposing of our remaining stock of needles, thread, cloth, and beads, which beyond this point would have been comparatively useless,—iron chen and sycee taking the place of barter. Among the rest several Chinese merchants called, in company with whom I took a walk through the town. Atenze, like Ta-tsian-loo, is a border town and frontier Customs station, being under the jurisdiction of the Imperial Viceroy of Yunnan; it possesses what is called the Chinese quarter enclosed by a wall, containing however many Thibetan houses inhabited by Thibetans and half-breeds. Through the centre of the little town a street runs north and south, with two rows of Chinese houses principally inhabited by Chinese soldiers engaged in various trades, as blacksmiths, carpenters, and furriers, the latter establishments being the most common—indeed the town is famous for its bleached lambskins; and besides the Chinese, hundreds of half-breeds are engaged in curing and dressing skins. In one of the drug-shops, which abounded as in Ta-tsian-loo, I discovered the ground caterpillars, which are found in great abundance in the hills about Atenze. The Chinese use them as medicine, attributing to them the property of reproducing youthful vigour; and in the eastern parts of China they are sold in bundles of a dozen, at the rate of twelve taels the dozen.

The body is yellowish like the Australian edible grub, and resembles a common caterpillar, about an inch and a quarter long, but with a seeming trunk, an inch and a half in length, exactly like a stem of dried grass, from which the Chinese give it the name of "Grass Caterpillar." When these caterpillars were first shown to me by the Chinese druggist, struck with their extraordinary appearance, I questioned the old Chinaman about them. He informed me that the insect grows in the ground an inch or two below the surface, its whereabouts being easily discovered from the grass blade which springs from it; and with all the gravity imaginable solemnly assured me, that from the blade there buds in spring a tiny white flower, which in due course ripens and drops a seed, and this falling into the ground produces another caterpillar. My evident disbelief of this strange tale so irritated the old druggist, that he angrily gave me to understand that I could leave his shop if I had no further business.

I am indebted to the courtesy of Mr. G. R. Gray, of the British Museum, for further and more correct information respecting this strange little insect. A larger species is common in New Zealand; and what seems to be the grass-like trunk of the insect is a species of fungus, *Spheria Sinensis*, which grows from the head.

Before the Mahomedan war in Yunnan, Atenze held considerable importance as a mart to which the Thibetans brought large quantities of musk, which they exchanged for a very fine description of black tea which grows in Yunnan, sugar, snuff, and tobacco, which articles grow to greater perfection in Yunnan than in any other province of China. Of late years, however, owing to constant warfare between Mahomedans and Imperialists the trade has dwindled almost to nothing.

In the afternoon I got all my baggage animals shod, having so far worked them without shoes; but as our road now gradually descended into a warmer climate it was necessary to protect their hoofs more than in Thibet, where mules and ponies are scarcely ever shod, the coldness of the ground and the dryness of the atmosphere evidently preserving the hoofs.

Just before I turned in for the night the landlord ushered into my room a remarkably fine-looking half-breed, tall, with an enormously muscular frame. After a few excuses for presenting himself at so late an hour, mine host informed me, that the stranger was his brother-in-law, whom, according to my instructions, he had hired in the morning to act as my guide to the town of Li-kiang in Yunnan. He then informed me that the Chinese Mandarin having heard that Dandy, as the guide was named, had hired himself to the foreigner, had sent for him, and having got the poor fellow into the Ya-mun, gave orders to the soldiers to give him one hundred strokes of the bamboo, for not having first obtained the consent of the authorities. The soldiers laid hold of Dandy to execute the Mandarin's orders, but before the punishment was completed the infuriated giant broke loose, and after committing great havoc amongst them, left the Ya-mun in triumph. It so happened that Dandy, though nothing more than a musk hunter by profession, was the hero and oracle of the town, where his word was as the voice of a prophet, and soon the news of his ill-treatment in the Ya-mun spread through the town. There was a general rush to arms for the protection of Dandy, and the Mandarin, in order to quiet the disturbance, was obliged to issue a notification to the effect that Dandy was not only forgiven, but commissioned by the Mandarin to escort the foreign merchant, Tang Koopah, to Weisee.

The poor fellow took off his coat in my room and bared his magnificent herculean shoulders and back, bleeding from frightful gashes. He did not speak, but a deep smothered sigh told how keenly he felt the shame of the blows.

As I intended leaving Atenze at daylight I gave my guide an opiate, and he soon fell asleep, but apparently only to dream of his disgrace, for his slumbers were broken by moans and deep sighs.

Next morning we were off just as daylight was breaking, and leaving Atenze by the south gate passed through about a quarter of a mile of suburbs, consisting of Thibetan houses and small Lamaseries, for Lamas swarmed even in the little town of Atenze like rats, and lived on the industry of the people. We descended through a broad fertile valley, watered by a small stream falling into the Lan-tsan, and rich with luxuriant crops of bearded wheat and peas, interspersed with groves of walnut trees, till about mid-day, when we reached the left bank of the Lan-tsan, a turbulent muddy stream, a hundred yards in width, flowing between steep mountains in a due southerly direction. Quitting the entrance of the valley, which opened like a huge portal in the mountain wall, the road now turned due south, winding along the side of the mountains, which rose from the river bank at an angle of 75 to 80 degrees. At times we crept along a path about eighteen inches wide, worn in the mountain, a few feet above the highest water mark, indicating the summer rise of the river thirty-five to forty feet above its present level. At other places a dangerous fissure compelled us to ascend nearly to the summit of the bare slaty mountain, and from the enormous height, often fifteen hundred to two thousand feet, we gazed down upon the river at our feet in the depth below like a tiny brook. So steep and smooth were the mountain sides, that a large stone set in motion rolled from the highest point down into the river.

After eight hours' march from Atenze, we reached a valley running up from the river, and halted at the village of Goneah, inhabited by a peculiar race of half-breeds, closely resembling the Thibetans in feature and stature, but much lighter in complexion.

Their manners and customs and religion are peculiarly Thibetan, as is also their dress, with this exception, that the men's coats, instead of being sheep skin, are made of a very coarse kind of wool. Their language is a mixture of Chinese, Thibetan, and Lei-su, to which tribe they claim to belong, though differing altogether in religion, manners, and customs.

The head man or chief of the village pays a yearly tribute to China, otherwise maintaining complete control of his people, having full power over them, excepting in cases of life and death, which are disposed of by the Chinese Mandarin at Atenze.

The chief gave us quarters in his house, and we stayed the next day with him, receiving the kindest hospitality from himself and his household.

All the people, without a single exception, from the old grey-headed men to the youngest children, suffered from goître, or swelling in the throat. Though this disease is common everywhere in Thibet, nowhere else had I seen it so frightfully developed as at Goneah, and I was besieged by applicants for medicine to cure it.

My store of medicine consisted solely of quinine, chlorodyne, purgative pills, and a few pounds of Holloway's ointment, so I distributed some of the latter, more to please the people than in hopes of benefiting them, and nothing could exceed their gratitude. Milk, fowls, butter, and horse feed poured in upon us, until at last a teaspoonful of ointment was worth a fowl and any quantity of peas, and the demand became so great that I was obliged to lock up the small remaining stock of ointment, about six ounces, and beg the chief to tell his people that no more could be spared.

A younger brother of the chief was suffering from fever, and on the first night of my stay I doctored him with such good effect that he was a different man next morning. This no sooner got abroad than I was again besieged by people in quest of fever medicine. The excitement became so great, that I was obliged to bribe the chief with some quinine to exert his authority, and relieve me from the crowd of eager inquirers who filled my room during the greater part of the morning.

The poor creatures begged so piteously for medicine, that I could scarcely refrain from sharing my precious store of quinine amongst them; however, the interference of the chief soon put an end to their entreaties, and secured quiet for the remainder of the day.

Wishing to give my poor baggage-animals a rest, I hired five mules of the chief for three days' march for the trifling sum of three taels, and this included the attendance of the chief himself as guide.

During our day's rest at Goneah the summer rains set in with a heavy thunder-storm, and henceforth we had the prospect of being constantly wet during the march.

On the 14th of June we left Goneah, escorted by nearly all the villagers, who accompanied us for a quarter of a mile or so, until the road once more led us along the precipitous bank of the Lan-tsan, where, amidst loud shoutings and the firing of matchlocks, they took their leave, and we continued our march till near mid-day, when we stopped for breakfast on a kind of terrace cut from the mountain, at the mouth of a gloomy gorge.

Another party had just camped before our arrival, and were preparing their meal, while their string of twenty baggage mules were arranged along the terrace. Our animals having been disposed of in the same way, we sat down to breakfast.

The river at this point formed a regular basin nearly a hundred yards across, the outlet being the mouth of the gorge, which was not twenty yards in width. On the right bank, opposite to us, the mountain rose several hundred feet in a bare, perpendicular wall from the river, and then sloping upwards terminated in a lofty peak clothed with pine trees.

As soon as our mid-day meal was finished, the Goneah chief and his mule driver started ahead through the gorge to the lower entrance, where he posted his man, to prevent any other party from entering the gorge at the same time as ourselves, as the path in many places would not admit of two mules passing each other.

On the chief's return to us we saddled up, and commenced our passage through the gorge, a portion of which is shown in the frontispiece, and which, in the absence of any local name, I called "Hogg's Gorge," in honour of the gentleman who first pointed out to me the enormous advantage which would accrue to our Indian possessions in the event of a route being discovered by which India could supply Thibet with tea.

The path, cut from the solid rock, which we now followed, sometimes ascended to a great height, and again led close to the river, which foamed down its narrow channel, over beds of jagged and pointed rocks, with a deafening roar, which echoed in strange unearthly sounds from the cliffs on either hand.

A mile or so from the upper entrance we arrived at the worst part of the gorge. The rock-hewn track now gave place to a gallery, as represented in frontispiece, supported by wooden struts fixed in the rock. Like every public work in China, it was out of repair. The flooring in many places was rotten and in holes, and gave us an opportunity of witnessing the great sagacity of our mules, which with lowered heads and outstretched feet tried each board before trusting their weight to it.

The Goneah chief had not warned me of the nature of the path before us, and I rode into the gorge only to find when once in that I could not dismount, owing to the narrowness of the path. My feelings, therefore, on finding myself riding along the rotten balcony—suspended, as it were, in the air, over a cauldron of seething water a couple of hundred feet below me—were anything but pleasant. My mule, Jacob, possessed great courage and sagacity, yet during the passage I several times felt him tremble under me, while the perspiration poured from him. The "Iron Duchess," which from her great courage and sagacity I had made leader of our string, greatly distinguished herself on this occasion. She hit upon a more than ordinarily rotten board, and refused to proceed until the chief, who led the way, marked it by placing on it some stones carried for the purpose, apparently following a practice common with the travellers who frequent the gorge, for many places were marked in the same manner.

The sagacity of the "Iron Duchess" as a bell mule had rendered her a great favourite with every person that had travelled in her company from Ta-tsian-loo. Out of a hundred mules it is often difficult to procure a good leader that the rest of the string will follow with confidence; and it is a curious fact that in large droves the steadiest and most sagacious animal finds her way to the front, as it were, by common consent of the rest—a trust which the clever animal discharges faithfully, but with great additional labour, for the leader has always the heaviest load to carry, so that where she passes her followers are quite safe.

On issuing from the gorge, we halted to rest our animals on a terrace similar to that at the upper entrance. The river below the narrow mouth of the gorge opened out considerably, in some places being over 200 yards across. The water-mark visible in the gorge showed a summer-rise of at least thirty feet above its present level, and a flood had already set in, for the rain had never ceased since the day we left Atenze. A similar peak to the one already mentioned as marking the upper entrance of the gorge marked the lower one, and I named them Winchester Peaks, after Mr. C. H. Winchester, her Majesty's consul at Shanghai, to whose kindness I am much indebted for being enabled to start on these travels.

About sundown we reached the village of Wha-foo-pin, having from the gorge travelled through a lovely country. The mountains, which sloped back from the river, were covered with verdant woods, affording cover to great numbers of golden pheasants, whose shrill call sounded on all sides of us, while every now and then their gorgeous plumage flashed across our vision as they whirred up from their evening meal.

The inhabitants of Wha-foo-pin were chiefly Christian converts gathered from among the Lei-su and Lu-ts^u tribes. They were very kind to us, evidently taking me for a missionary. Their houses still resembled those of Thibet, though the people spoke a mixed language of Chinese, Lei-su, and Lu-ts^u, and in dress and manners were quite Chinese, though their tall figures and regular features made it impossible to mistake them for Celestials.

We were most hospitably entertained, and next morning, led by a party of the villagers, I paid a visit to the little Mission Station of Tz-coo, eight miles distant, on the right bank of the Lan-tsan, here 200 yards wide, which we crossed by means of a bamboo rope stretched from bank to bank.

The rope at the taking-off side is made fast, at a much greater height up than at the opposite landing-place, so as to form an inclined plane. Ascending a small platform, the passenger secures himself in a sling of leather thongs made fast to a sort of skid of hard wood fitted on the rope, and lifting his feet off the little stage, shoots with the rapidity of an arrow across to the opposite bank, where on another little stage he gets out of the sling. For the purpose of recrossing, there is another rope fastened in a corresponding manner. By means of these bamboo ropes even mules and cattle are transported from bank to bank.

People unaccustomed to this mode of crossing rivers are apt to become giddy, from the rapidity with which they shoot through the air, especially if they look down, for the ropes are often 100 to 200 feet above the water.

Having safely crossed this novel bridge, I was warmly greeted on the little stage by the French Fathers Biet and Dubernard, missionaries of the station, and conducted by them to their modest house, a short distance from the rope bridge. They would not hear of my leaving them that day, so I sent word to the Goneah chief to camp, and I would join him in the morning.

ROPE BRIDGE ON THE LAN-TSAN-KIANG.

At the Mission Station I met a motley group of Mosós, Lei-sus, Ya-ts", Mooquors, and Lu-ts", all connected as converts or tenants with the mission, for the Fathers own a large district, including the village of Wha-foo-pin, having purchased it of the Ya-ts" chief, who resides at a village of the same name, two days' journey from Tz-coo; and the Lei-su population of this Church estate are nearly all Christians. This mission was established some thirty years ago, for the purpose of converting the neighbouring tribes, especially the savage Lu-tsŭ, who inhabit a strip of country about fifty miles in length, between the Lan-tsan and Nou-kiang rivers, stretching from the neighbourhood of Wha-foo-pin in the north, to Weisee-foo in the south.

These Lu-tsŭ are most barbarous in their habits. In saying this, I must be understood to except the few Christian converts in the neighbourhood of Tz-coo, who have adopted the ordinary Chinese costume, and whose pursuits are those of industrious and peaceable cultivators. The majority of the tribe, however, are still nomadic, and utter savages. They build no houses and raise no crops, depending for their subsistence on the chase and predatory excursions amongst the neighbouring tribes, to whom they are an absolute terror. Armed with cross-bows and poisoned arrows, they are bold and successful hunters of deer, mhitton,* wild boars, wild goats, bears, and leopards. In religion they are utter heathen, sacrificing fowls to propitiate the evil spirit. In appearance they are darker than the other tribes of the district. But this may be partly owing to engrained filth. They also tattoo their faces and bodies with a kind of blue dye, and wear their hair in long matted locks. Their costume, if it may be so called, consists of a girdle of cotton cloth or skins; at least, the warriors of the tribe, whom I afterwards saw on their way to fight the Mahomedans, had no other garments, except a few of the leaders, who wore a kind of cloak of leopard, goat, or fox-skins. Their arms consisted of the crossbow and poisoned arrows, tipped with a species of aconite

---

* Wild cattle of the same species as are found on the Assam hills, resembling a cross between the bull and the buffalo, but being a distinct species.

THE LU-TSU TRIBES.

known in Assam as Mishmee-bee, spears, and knives * about eighteen inches long, increasing in width from the hilt, and terminating in broad blunt ends.

The Lu-tsu owe no allegiance and pay no tribute to China, though they occasionally serve under the Imperial banner. The Chinese Mandarins, fearing the bold spirit of this tribe, who muster something like twelve hundred fighting men, are careful to maintain friendly relations with them, and, for the purpose of gratifying their predatory inclinations at the expense of the Mahomedans, annually invite them to take part in a grand raid into the enemy's country.

The Lu-tsu, being unable to read or write, have arranged with the Chinese a sort of code of signals or tokens, by which important messages are carried to and fro between them. For example, a piece of chicken liver, three pieces of chicken fat, and a chili wrapped in red paper, means " Prepare to fight at once."

They rarely cross to the east of the Lan-tsan-kiang, excepting to make war on the other tribes or the Mahomedans. Little, therefore, is known of this savage tribe by either Chinese or anybody else, excepting, perhaps, the Catholic missionaries, who, at the time of my visit, seemed to be on the most friendly terms with them. One of the Fathers had only just returned from visiting a sick member of a Christian Lu-tsu family on the banks of the Nou-kiang; a visit which he informed me led him through the very heart of the principal tribe. This tribe is distinct, and appears to differ in some respects from the Lu-tsu inhabiting the country bordering the west bank of the Lan-tsan river, who have been

---

* The author while lately travelling amongst the tribes in the neighbourhood of the Bramakund, on the Bramapootra river, discovered that these knives were identical with those made by the Kamptee tribe, inhabiting a district adjacent to the north-east borders of Assam.

subjugated by the Ya-ts" chief, serving him as tributaries, and have adopted a few habits of civilisation, such as cultivation and living in small log-houses.

The history of the Tz-coo Mission may, from the date of its establishment, be traced in the blood of numbers of brave and noble-minded missionaries who have fallen by poison and the knife in the cause of their religion. Self-banished to this country, without a hope of return, the French missionaries have worked on, and, in spite of massacres by the savages, incited by the implacable hatred of the Chinese Mandarins, which even now often drives them to seek protection in the mountain fastnesses, their devotion has been rewarded by hundreds of genuine converts; a result which strongly contrasts with the known ill-success of the Protestant missionaries in their less dangerous field on the eastern coast of China.

Having spent a pleasant night with the Fathers Biet and Dubernard, I bade them good-bye, and re-crossed the Lantsan early next morning. From Tz-coo to a Moso village which we reached in the evening, we rode through dense woods, in which the chestnut-trees grew to magnificent proportions, and along the banks of the river, which was foaming over dangerous rapids, down which immense quantities of drift-wood were swept by the rapidly rising flood, swollen by the unceasing rain.

At the Moso village we were kept a long time in the rain before any one would admit us into a house; but the good offices of the Goneah chief at last procured us comfortable quarters for the night.

The Mosos are apparently the remnant of a once powerful tribe, fast losing their identity and becoming merged into the Ya-ts" tribe, whose chief governs them. They are quite

Chinese in appearance, the men wearing the common blue cotton jacket and short wide trousers of China, shaving their heads, and growing the pig-tail. The costume of the women is fantastic, but graceful. It consists of a very becoming little cap of red and black cloth, with pendant tassel, jauntily worn on the top of the head, inclining a little to one side; a short loose jacket, with long wide sleeves, over a tight-fitting cotton bodice, covering the breasts; with a kilt-like petticoat of home-made cotton stuff, reaching from the waist to the knee, and gathered in longitudinal plaits. Instead of stockings, their finely-shaped limbs are swathed from the ankle to the knee with white or blue cotton cloth, while leather shoes, turned up in a sharp point at the toe, complete the *chaussure* of the Moso ladies, who, though not quite so fair as the Chinese, are generally well-proportioned and good-looking, and unembarrassed by the shy reserve of the fair Celestials. As ornaments they wear huge silver ear-rings (resembling in shape the handle of a common key), silver rings and bracelets, and bead necklaces. In religion they profess both Buddhism and the Chinese worship of ancestors.

They have a language of their own, but no written character. Chinese is perhaps more used than Moso, and in their schools Chinese reading and writing alone are taught; so that in time the Moso, in common with the language of other tribes in this part of Yunnan, will probably die out.

Their houses are principally built of wood, and are quite Chinese in appearance. They cultivate rice in terraces up the sides of the hills, the climate being exceedingly genial during the day, but cool at night.

From the Moso village we journeyed through a beautiful country. The mountains had given place to gently sloping hills; and towards mid-day we approached the Ya-ts^u village situated in the centre of a little plain. I was much struck with the luxuriant cultivation. A good deal of ripe wheat was still standing, spoiled by rain ; and herds of a remarkably fine breed of black cattle, of which the tribes possess large numbers, were fattening amongst it. Rice-planting was just commencing, and the pea crops were being harvested. A few patches of opium looked very thriving ; and, altogether, the little plain of the Ya-ts^u village smiled again in its richness.

Our arrival at the village attracted little or no attention ; and as we were proceeding through the streets, we met a party of men, whom I took to be husbandmen, returning from the field. They, however, stopped us ; and one of them, quite a young man, asked me in Chinese, with a subdued air of authority, who I was. The Goneah chief dismounted on his approach, and, after a ceremonious salute, informed him who I was ; whereupon he told me to go and put up for the night in a joss-house near the high mud wall which surrounded the village. Similar walls defended all the villages that we had passed since leaving Tz-coo.

When we had made ourselves comfortable in our novel quarters, the Goneah chief informed me that the individual who had addressed me in the village was no less a person than the great Ya-ts^u chief himself, and during the afternoon a great number of soldiers came from the chief with presents of rice, fowls, and pork.

There is nothing in outward appearance to distinguish this tribe from Chinese except the peculiar dress of the females, which is exactly like that of the Moso women, with the one exception that they sometimes substitute a red cloth hood thickly braided with cowrie shells for the neat little Moso cap. Their religion and religious edifices are peculiarly Chinese, as well as their habits and customs; although they have an unwritten language of their own, all the men that I saw could speak and read and write Chinese. In the school attached to the joss-house, as is common in other and more civilised parts of China, only Chinese was taught; and the only apparent difference between the Ya-tsu and Chinese is, perhaps, that the former are if anything more dirty-looking than the general run of the latter.

The chief of the Ya-tsu is by far the most powerful chief of all the tribes of the Lan-tsan, for besides governing his own tribe, he is chief (by virtue of the conquests of his ancestors) of the Mosos, and the more numerous tribes of Lei-sus. Great quantities of gold are found in his territory, both in the sands of the Lan-tsan, and in the hills, whence it is extracted by means of horizontal shafts. The chief alone has the power of granting permission to work gold, and one-third of the gold procured is taken by him, out of which he formerly paid tribute to the Chinese government; this of late years he has omitted to pay, owing, as he says, to the curious fact, of the former Mandarin at Weisee having destroyed the official seals under which the tribute was formerly collected. This is the excuse which this chief, and many others, urged as a plea for non-payment; it is, of course, a mere pretext, the real fact being that since the commencement of the Mahomedan war the Chinese authorities have been afraid to call in the tribute.

The Ya-tsu pay their chief a tax in the shape of produce, and supply him with labour; his sway is quite despotic, his people being to all intents and purposes his abject slaves,—indeed, all the chiefs of this country keep slaves in their houses.

His relations with the Chinese, from whom he holds the rank of blue button, require that he should refer all questions touching the life of his subjects to the Mandarins in Weisee;

but this, like the tribute, has, of late years, become a dead letter. For this chief, with his near neighbour the Mooquor chief, have been known to talk very loudly to the Chinese authorities of their intention, in the case of the latter pressing the question of tribute, to join the Mahomedans. And this threat has so far settled the matter at once.

On the morning after our arrival at the Ya-ts^u village the Goneah chief took his leave of me and returned to his village. I, however, was obliged to remain; one horse had died the day before from sheer privation, and the incessant rain had so softened the hoofs of my two Thibetan ponies that they had been scarcely able to travel. One, which was quite disabled, having fever in all four feet, I was glad to sell for $2\frac{1}{2}$ taels; the other, disabled in his hind feet, was just able to travel unloaded. The loss of their services obliged me to hire two mules of the chief for three days' march to Weisee, for $1\frac{1}{2}$ taels; and leaving Ya-ts^u, in one long march we reached the village of the Mooquor chief, who received us most kindly, giving us the best room in his house, which was a fine new building after the better Chinese style.

He would not hear of my leaving him for a few days, and as I had suffered from fever the last day or two, I gladly consented to rest the next day with him. The Mooquor village, like that of Ya-ts^u, is situated in a small plain running in from the river, and bounded by wooded hills, which extending eastwards form the lower ranges of the great Sui Shan, or snowy mountains, which tower in the back ground above the village, forming the watershed of the Lan-tsan and Kin-cha rivers, and attain their greatest height near the city of Li-kiang-foo in Yunnan, whence gradually diminishing in height, they lose their identity amongst the irregular mass of hills bordering the great plain of Tali-foo.

In the neighbourhood of Compo, the Mooquor village, blackberries grew in great quantities, and I enjoyed a capital dessert of them after a dinner consisting of fat capon, ham, and some delicious little wheaten cakes, prepared by the chief's handsome Ya-ts" wife in honour of her guests. Nothing could exceed the kindness of my hosts, and we sat long after dinner; the chief entertaining me with many interesting particulars relative to the Mahomedan war. On one occasion La-won-quan (such was the chief's Chinese name and title) joined the Chinese in an attack on the city of Koking or more properly speaking Ho-chin, then occupied by the Mahomedans. In accordance with the usual cowardice displayed by Chinese generals, La-won-quan and his soldiers were sent to the front to bear the brunt of the battle, and so effectually vigorous was his assault that he took the city. The Mahomedan garrison fled, but being unmolested by the Chinese army, and strongly reinforced, became the besiegers in turn; and after an investment of three months, during which the Chinese general made no effort to relieve his allies, undermined and blew up the defences. La-won-quan, with eight of his soldiers, cut their way out, and succeeded in getting back to Compo. The chief had evidently had a rough time of it, for his arms, legs, and breast were covered with the scars of what must have been ugly wounds. He interlarded his narrative with many expressions the reverse of complimentary to Chinese Mandarins; indeed he, in common with all the other chiefs, cordially detested them. But when I spoke of the Boy Emperor at Pekin, the stern hard features of this battered warrior relaxed, and the tears glistened in his eyes as he remarked, that it was no use for the Emperor to be good when all his servants were scoundrels.

Like the Ya-ts" chief, La-won-quan has received the

Chinese rank of blue button from the Emperor, of which he is very proud.

His relations with the Chinese government are precisely the same as those of his brother-in-law, the Ya-ts^u chief; and the two being allies both by marriage and policy laugh at the authority of the Chinese Mandarins.

There is nothing in the appearance, manners, and language of the Mooquors to distinguish them from the Ya-ts" or Mosos; and my visit to their village, which struck me as peculiarly Chinese in its appearance, happened just after the rice planting was finished, a period when all the people devote themselves to holiday making, so that I had ample opportunities for carefully observing them. During the evening my arms were produced and minutely inspected by the chief and his brother, a young musk hunter, and a discussion naturally followed on the respective merits of the matchlock (with which these Mooquors are equipped, and in the use of which they are very expert) and the foreign gun, the latter being by no means regarded amongst these Yunnan borderers with the same respect that it had commanded in Thibet. Before we separated for the night it was arranged that I should start with the young musk hunter in quest of sport in the adjacent mountains, and so practically test the comparative merits of matchlock and rifle.

Long before daylight next morning I was roused from a comfortable sleep in the chief's own bed which he had insisted on giving up to me, by his brother, who intimated that it was time to be moving. The toilet is never a very long performance for the pioneer in wild countries, and by 3 A.M., in company with Philip, I was following the young musk hunter through a dense pine forest, covering the lower slopes of the mountains to within a few hundred yards of the village.

After travelling about three miles, we reached an eminence, from which we looked down into a long valley, through which leaped a mountain torrent, fed from the snows lying in white grandeur away to the east, some 6000 or 8000 feet above us.

Up this valley the young man led the way, following the course of the torrent upwards until we reached the grassy slopes above the range of pine forests. As we stepped out on to the velvety grass, the keen air sweeping down from the heights above had a most invigorating effect, for I have generally found that walking briskly through forests even at these elevations, is attended with more or less oppressiveness. As it was not yet daylight, we retired amongst the pines, and, lighting a fire, smoked our pipes over its comfortable blaze. As soon as the first dawn of day appeared the young hunter left us, and we had not waited many minutes when he returned, saying that two hundred yards from our fire he had come across the tracks of a solitary buck ta lut-s^n.* The slots were fresh, and tending towards a ridge of bare peaks, lying about a mile to our right. To knock the ashes from our pipes and shoulder our guns was the work of a moment, and, our stalwart guide leading the way, we picked up the trail, and silently in Indian file followed the game.

The buck was evidently unsuspicious, for in many places the hunter pointed to trees against which he had stopped to rub the velvet from his horns, while often his zig-zag course showed that he was in no hurry. At the end of half an hour's silent progress the young hunter stopped us with a backward wave of his hand and pointed to several fresh tracks which had joined those that we were following. On examination they turned out to be those of two does. Our game

---

* *I. e.*, "large deer," which proved to be the bara singh of the Himalayas.

was now easy to follow, for in the damp mossy ground the tracks were fetlock deep. Caution was now the order of the day, and we kept on, guided by the houndlike sagacity of our leader. The great stillness was only occasionally broken by the hoarse cry of the ma-chee (a bird of the Tragopan family) and the argus pheasant as we disturbed them at their morning meal.

We soon gained the edge of the forest, through a break in which we looked out on the green slopes before us (rendered still more green by contrast with the bare limestone peaks in their background), and saw a noble buck within seventy yards of us, the two does having apparently kept on their way, for he was alone. The young hunter silently pointed to the noble animal in front of us, signing for me to fire, while he kneeled in readiness with the match of his long matchlock already lighted. To level my double Enfield and fire was the work of an instant. The noble buck, struck too far behind the shoulder, gave a single bound, then for a second looked back; but before he had time to make another bound a flash from my companion's weapon sent forth an iron bullet, this time with more certain aim, for with a bound or two the buck rolled headlong to the ground, and lay dead within eighty yards of us. The young hunter, with a smile of disdain at my rifle, then walked up to his prize—for such it proved to him, the horns alone selling afterwards for no less a sum than 150 taels, equivalent to £50 sterling.

The work of skinning we left in his hands, while, with appetites sharpened by the keen morning air and exercise, we set about making tea, and preparing our fire for a roast. Our young Nimrod soon joined us, bringing with him the horns—carefully taken off with part of the skull and encased in a coating of clay—and some venison steaks still smoking.

Cooking these on the embers, we made a hearty breakfast, and started back for the Mooquor village, the young hunter making the mountains ring again with the echoes of his loudly-sung Thibetan hymn of praise,—the "Omanee peminee," which he had learned in his frequent hunting excursions amongst the mountains of Thibet.

Shortly after noon we got back to the village, where the chief and his elders met us with the inquiry of "what luck?" On seeing the horns which his brother carried, he loudly congratulated us on our good fortune, and invited us to partake of a substantial meal, during which I was good-naturedly quizzed about the boasted superiority of my rifle.

In the evening we wound up with a grand banquet of roast sucking pig, which Philip's culinary skill had cooked to perfection. The pig was served whole, and I carved it with my knife and fork to the intense admiration of all present. The chief was so charmed with my performance that he insisted on employing the knife and fork himself,—his clumsy but effective handling of them causing all the guests, especially his wife who sat by him, great amusement.

Our supper having ended, spirits followed, and, on being pressed by mine host, I sang an English song or two in a loud voice, which, probably, from the great noise I made, more than anything else, delighted every one; and it was long past midnight before we got to bed.

On the following morning I took leave of La-won-quan's household, and the chief accompanied us about a quarter of a mile along the road, for the purpose of showing me one of his gold mines.

A number of his people were hard at work: some bringing the auriferous earth from horizontal shafts in the side of the hills; others washing it in long troughs, made of hollowed trees, into which a constant supply of water flowed from a little stream.

The gold mines, the chief informed me, were very rich; indeed, the country lying between Atenze and Weisee may be called the gold field of China; for, although gold is so plentiful in Eastern Thibet, the religious prejudices of the Lamas allow but very little of the precious metal to find its way to China.

I was shown some scaly gold, of a rich deep colour; and the chief gave me a handful, as a sample, to show to the merchants of my country, saying that he would be glad to trade with them. Now, for the first time, I learnt that he knew all about the foreigners in Assam. For many years he had hoped that some of the rich foreign merchants from Assanqua (as he called Assam) would come to his country; and he looked upon my arrival as a partial realisation of his hopes.

Hearing La-won-quan speak with so much knowledge of Assam, I at once proposed that he should send a party of his soldiers with me straight across country for Sudiya, or Man-chee, a town immediately on the borders of Assam, and about eighty miles to the west of Compo; but he shook his head at this proposal, saying a direct route was impossible owing to the number of tribes to be passed through, and that I could only go either *viâ* Tali-foo or from Bathang by Rooemah.

On taking leave of this kindly-disposed chief, he placed in my hands three letters: one for his brother-in-law at the next village, and one for a relation in the village of Kha-kha, and another for an hotel-keeper in Weisee-foo. These letters, he said, would ensure me a kindly reception, and let people know that I was a great friend of La-won-quan. Heartily thanking him for his kind thoughtfulness, I continued my march in sight of the Lan-tsan, in the waters of which numerous fishermen plied their nets and lines. All day we traversed a garden, planted by Nature's hands: wild pears, egg-plums, peaches, sloes, and hazel-trees, laden with green fruit, grew in the greatest profusion. About 5 P.M. we reached the Mooquor village of Sheow-weisee, and proceeded to the house of La-won-quan's brother-in-law, whose first churlish refusal was at once changed by a perusal of the chief's letter into a hospitable welcome.

The country now was quite open to the west of the Lan-tsan; the hills receded in gentle slopes, teeming with luxuriant crops of wheat, peas, rice, barley, and opium.

Shortly after leaving Sheow-weisee, the road quitted the Lan-tsan, and we proceeded on, south by east, till we halted at Kha-kha, a Lei-su village, where, again, La-won-quan's letter procured us the greatest hospitality from a Lama, the only one of his cloth that I had seen since leaving Goneah. The country now wore the ripe smile of summer. The tobacco, opium, and wheat crops were astonishing; indeed, the people of Kha-kha informed me that the harvest was unusually abundant, and that much of their opium and tobacco had been allowed to run to seed for want of hands to harvest it. Everywhere dragon-flies of enormous size and gorgeous blue and scarlet colouring danced in the warm sunshine; and near this village I noticed, for the first time, the "pa-la" or "white-wax" insect, which produces the famous so-called vegetable wax of Sz-chuan. The branches of the smaller trees and shrubs, along the road for a great distance, appeared to be covered with snow, from the quantities of these insects resembling small moths of a very delicate white colour, with a fluffy tail curling over the back.

From the village of Sheow-weisee, and, indeed, from the vicinity of Compo, the country showed unmistakeable signs of Mahomedan inroads; great numbers of houses lay in ruins, blackened by fire.

In one Lei-su village that we passed through, more than two-thirds of the houses had been burnt, and the mud wall surrounding it was breached in many places. I shall not soon forget our passage through this village, for we were attacked by a pack of dogs of the common Chinese species, and our baggage-animals so severely bitten, that I was obliged to make use of my revolver, and shoot several of the assailants before the villagers would call them off. As may be imagined, the death of their dogs enraged the people, who, in turn, attacked us with sticks and stones. Fortunately, a Mooquor happened just then to enter the village, on his way to Weisee, who told the people that I was a great friend of La-won-quan's, which immediately turned the tide, and everyone started off, as if to see who could first hide his diminished head under the roof of his cottage.

Not far from Kha-kha we exchanged our track for a paved road, like the common roads of China, a change which was anything but agreeable to our horses' feet; and a short march through a country, the smiling aspect of which was deformed by the blackened ruins of detached houses and villages, brought us to the city of Weisee-foo.

The town, which ranks in the first class, is built at the foot of a steep hill, which separates the valley of Weisee from the Lan-tsan. It contains a mixed population of Lei-sus, Chinese, and half-breeds, numbering, probably, six thousand inhabitants. The pure Chinese portion is very small, consisting almost entirely of soldiers and officials. Formerly, it was surrounded by a brick wall, which was all but destroyed when the town was taken by the Mahomedans a few years before, and had been patched up with hard red mud, of which material most of the houses in the place, like those of the villages of the neighbourhood, are built.

Before the Mahomedan rising, Weisee was of great importance, as the city to which the chiefs of the numerous tribes of the surrounding country annually repaired with their tribute; but the prevailing anarchy has left it only the questionable advantage of being the head-quarters of the Chinese general commanding the so-called Imperial Army, which is supposed to be gradually overwhelming the Mahomedans, but which, in reality, is nothing more than a well-organised body of banditti, numbering, probably, three hundred men.

On our arrival, we found the hotel to which the chief, La-won-quan, had directed us, and, presenting his letter, were made as comfortable as possible, the largest room in the house being reserved for my sole use.

An hour after, both the civil and military Mandarins sent their cards, thinking I was a Chinese Mandarin; so, in return, I sent Philip with my passports to the Ya-mun. In the evening, the landlord of the hotel, a half-breed Lei-su, came to my room, and, after hesitating a little, informed me that, in coming to Weisee, I had run into great danger; the town was utterly demoralised; and most of the respectable people had long since quitted the place, and the chief portion of those remaining were but a community of plunderers. The Mandarins had for two years received neither their own salaries nor the soldiers' pay, which was embezzled by the Chen-tu functionaries charged with the payment of the frontier army. The soldiers accordingly had become banditti, who roamed the country under different chiefs, nominally to make war on the Mahomedans, but really to plunder the peaceable inhabitants of the Imperial territory; while both the civil and military Mandarins received large sums from the bandit chiefs for their connivance. This state of things, as may be imagined, often led to reprisals on the part of the people, who, when denied justice in glaring cases of murder committed by the Imperial soldiers, armed themselves, and siding with the Mahomedans, would take fearful revenge. In this manner Weisee had twice fallen into the hands of the Mahomedans, who, after pillaging the place, had retired, before the united forces of the Ya-ts" and Mooquor chiefs, to Li-kiang-foo, their great stronghold in Northern Yunnan.

Such was the state of affairs in Weisee, as described by mine host, Low-ling, who strongly advised me either to return, or proceed towards Tali-foo at once, before the news of my arrival attracted the attention of the soldiers. He further warned me never to stir without arms, and, above all, to boast loudly of my friendship with the chief, La-won-quan.

Acting on this advice, I went to the Ya-mun next day, to get my Bathang passport changed for one authorising me to pass through the district under the command of the Tartar general, Leang-Owhan. In reply to my application, he sent out word, by a ragged satellite, to say that I could not proceed, and that he did not wish to see me. To this I replied by a lofty wave of the hand, saying, "What! not see me, who have talked to his superiors all the way from Pekin? Impossible! You must be mistaken. Take back my card to the Ta-jen, and say that I have important business with him. Quick! Do not keep me waiting in the sun." My demeanour so overawed the man, that he disappeared, and in a minute returned, saying, "The Ta-jen will see you;" and forthwith I was ushered into the august presence of the Tartar general, who received me with the dignity belonging to his race,

He apologised for having declined to see me, as he could not speak my language, and wished to save me the trouble of an interview. Thanking him, I produced my Chen-tu passport, which he had not yet seen, and asked his advice about proceeding further towards Tali-foo. My asking advice from the old officer (who was a fine, intelligent man, fully sixty years of age), seemed to please him, and he at once said that there would be a little danger from robbers, but as I had doubtless seen a good deal of these gentry in my long travels, I would not care much for them, in which case he thought I might proceed, as fighting had not yet commenced, and he would give me a passport through his district, which extended two days' journey from Weisee. Beyond this point, however, the Mahomedan jurisdiction commenced, and he could not be responsible. Having thus disposed of business, the general ordered tea, cakes, and tobacco, and entered into a long conversation. He had been absent from Pekin for twenty years, and made many inquiries about his beloved city. Philip, during the conversation, told him, unknown to me, that I was accustomed to see the princes and great men in Pekin; a statement which, as I had never in my life been at Pekin, rather horrified me, especially when the general asked me where the Chinese Minister for Foreign Affairs lived. However, I answered at once, " In the Sung-le Ya-mun ;" and, in answer to his question as to where I lived in Pekin, I told him about one Li from the same place. He appeared satisfied with my somewhat vague answer, and grew very polite, saying that it was a great pleasure to see any one who had recently visited the great city; and we parted on mutual good terms.

Outside the hotel we found a great crowd assembled, and, on entering, the first thing I saw was a soldier coming out of my room into the court-yard, with my rifle over his shoulder, while others followed, each carrying some article of my property. Marching up to the leader, I knocked him down, and drew my revolver and long Swiss hunting-knife, both of which I had concealed in my Chinese coat when starting to the Ya-mun. Of course this was the signal for a free fight. The soldiers drew their knives, and at it we went, my assailants yelling like demons, and brandishing their knives, carefully, however, keeping out of reach of mine. I soon found myself surrounded on all sides, so I fired my revolver twice into the ground. At this there was a rush for the street. Philip and myself quickly followed, and, on gaining the street, another discharge of my revolver over the heads of the mob opened a passage, through which we made tracks for the Ya-mun, followed to the very gates by a hooting crowd.

Panting and out of breath, we rushed into the Ya-mun, and got behind the general, who rose as we entered. Our story threw the good general into an awful passion. He raved and stamped about the room, until I thought he would go mad; but presently a subordinate came in, and informed him that the soldiers had taken me for a foreigner going to Tali-foo, to help the Mahomedans to make guns, and wished to kill me. Hearing this, I said I would remain in the Ya-mun until the men were quieted; and the general immediately gave orders for a proclamation to be issued, stating who and what I was, and that any one molesting me should be flogged.

After waiting for about three hours, the general told me that I might safely return to the hotel, where I would find all my property secure, and five of the plunderers in the Keang* before the door.

* Keang or Cangue.

The general's writer escorted us back. Scarcely a soul was to be seen in the streets, but outside the hotel we found five of the ruffians in durance vile. Within, all was quiet, and all our property restored.

Such were my first day's adventures in the town of Weisee; which, coupled with some experiences of the Chinese mode of warfare during the Taeping rebellion, and the state of the country round Shanghai wherever fighting took place, enabled me to form some idea of the danger attached to any attempt to pass from Chinese to Mahomedan territory. Yet, in spite of the knowledge of the danger before me, I could not abandon the attempt. My brave little Philip scorned to give up the hope of reaching India without at least one effort; so we determined to start for Tali-foo on the receipt of the passport. For this we waited three days, well cared for by the landlord, Low-ling, who was unceasing in his attentions.

Fortunately, the living here was very cheap; the daily maintenance of the whole party (four men and five animals) not exceeding twenty-five cents.* But it was hard to wait patiently, especially as it was by no means certain that the lawless population would respect the general's order. However, we were comparatively unmolested, except for an attack made on the hotel by the wives and concubines of the soldiers who were in the keang at the door. They were, however, speedily dispersed by the arrival of soldiers from the general, who brought me a message to the effect that Philip was to call next day for the passport.

In the hotel there were numbers of petty traders in skins, ironware, &c., waiting for the event of an expected fight between the Imperialists and Mahomedans near Li-kiang-foo. They informed me that it was an invariable rule

* Equal to 1s.

for the Mahomedans, who were, it appeared, always successful, to enjoy three days' pillage after a victory; after which, any Mahomedan soldier found plundering would be beheaded, according to a standing order of Dow-win-sheow, the Mahomedan Emperor. The traders accordingly wait for the fourth day to commence their journey to and fro between the "Pa-chee" and "Hung-chee" (or White and Red-flag) countries, as the Mahomedan and Imperial territory are respectively called by them. Thus, during the intervals of warfare, a considerable trade is carried on between Mahomedan and Imperial Yunnan in skins, opium, iron pots, cotton goods, and tobacco, on which both governments levy duties, the Mahomedan king fostering trade as much as possible, both by the imposition of light duties and a rigorous administration of justice, to which the traders bore ample testimony, lauding the security of the Pa-chee territory. Indeed, a flourishing trade had existed for two years previous to my arrival between Weisee and Tali-foo, Imperial Chinese having had free access to Mahomedan territory, and *vice versâ*. Even at the period of my visit there were a great many Mahomedans in the town, wearing their long hair, the Mahomedan badge, living in apparent indifference and security, which led me to surmise correctly that the Mahomedan Government had until lately been recognised by the Imperial officials in Yunnan.

When Philip called at the Ya-mun next day, the general sent me a present of some flour and a ham, with a kind message to the effect that he would send a guard of soldiers as far as Tung-lan, the Tze-fan chief's residence. This offer I declined with thanks, my past experience of such guards having decided me never again to place myself under their protection. I also sent him a common silver watch as a return present, which pleased him greatly, and this little interchange of courtesies commenced a friendship between us, of the sincerity of which on the general's part I had afterwards ample proof.

Having received the passport, which authorised me to travel through Yunnan, viâ Tali-foo, to Ava in Burmah, I hired a guide in place of Dandy, who had mysteriously disappeared on the night of our arrival in Weisee, and determined to start next morning.

In the evening a visitor was introduced by Low-ling, in the person of a Mahomedan merchant. He was a splendid specimen of the Yunnan Mahomedan, standing over six feet. His appearance was singularly haughty and noble; a long black moustache ornamented his upper lip and hung down to his chest, while his thick black hair was gathered into an enormous tail, which rolled from under a massive blue and white turban, and almost touched the ground. The man's manner was peculiarly gentle and dignified, seeming at once to inspire both confidence and respect.

He commenced talking to me about my visit to Tali-foo, and told me that there were five Europeans like myself already there, three engaged in casting guns for the Emperor, and two as teachers of the Koran.*

He further said that the only chance of reaching Tali-foo was to push boldly for Tung-lan, whence the Tze-fan chief who had been acting as border customs officer for both Imperials and Mahomedans for two years, would, if possible, forward me on. He had himself written to this chief about my intended attempt to reach Tali, and I might trust him, as he was a

---

* These men were not, as might be imagined, any members of the French Expedition, but rowdies from the Eastern ports, two of whom had gone within my own knowledge.

friend of the Mooquor chief, La-won-quan. On the road to Tung-lan the dangers to be guarded against were poison and attacks from Chinese soldiers disguised as Mahomedans.

I asked him how it was that he lived in Imperial territory with long hair. At this question he smiled a little scornfully, and observed that Mahomedan subjects had been well received in Weisee for two years past, and there had been no restriction on the intercourse between Tali-foo and Weisee.

My Mahomedan friend took his leave after we had taken supper together, the religious prejudices prevalent among the Indian Mahomedans being unknown to those of China.

At bedtime I received a visit from the general's factotum, who came ostensibly to say good-bye, but in reality to receive the customary present. He proved very talkative, and I learned from him that according to the report in the Ya-mun I was supposed to be a Mandarin sent from Pekin to investigate matters, and see what the authorities were about; and I verily believe that the peaceful relations which had so long existed between Tali and Weisee were suddenly interrupted by my arrival; and further, that this report was carefully circulated by the Mandarins, in order to excite against me the hostility of the Mahomedans, and prevent my visiting their capital. My visitor was very anxious to know if I really was a Mandarin, and if so, what was the object of my visit. I referred him to the passport, which stated who and what I was; if he did not believe it, he could write to his Government for further information, as I had none to give him. On this he took his leave, and I soon forgot all anxieties for the future in a sound sleep.

CHAPTER XII.

AMONGST THE TZE-FANS.

Sz-se-to Village—The Lei-sus—Arrival at Tung-lau—My Politics Tested—Night Attack—The Tze-fan Village—The Mahomedan War—A Traitor Viceroy—Mahomedan Progress—The Scorpion Fly.

THE landlord aroused me at daylight, having himself been up long before, in order to prepare an excellent breakfast of stewed fowl, potatoes, and tea.

Poor Low-ling! Had I been his son, he could not have shown me greater kindness. Nothing seemed too much for him to do for "Tang Ta-jen." While I was eating my breakfast he was praying fervently to the household god, before whom he had lighted fresh joss-sticks, and every now and then interrupted his devotions to help me to tea, at the same time reiterating his instructions for the perilous journey before me. Both he and the Mahomedan merchant, whom I had invited to breakfast, warned me against the attacks of Chinese soldiers disguised as Mahomedans. They said that I was about to travel with the knife at my throat, but perhaps the God whom I worshipped would protect me, for their gods seemed to delight only in bloodshed. Primed with cautions against all kinds of treachery, on the 28th of June I left Weisee for Tali-foo, accompanied by Low-ling, his brother, and the Mahomedan merchant for nearly a mile. As a last word of advice, Low-ling told me to boast everywhere and to every one of friendship with the Mooquor chief.

At last, left to ourselves, Philip and I rode side by side, under a deluge of rain, and talked over our position, till the guide interrupted us with the information that he had lost the road. I at once suspected that the fellow, who had received an advance of wages, intended to desert. This became evident when, in answer to my remonstrances, he turned to retrace his steps, saying, " Go and find the road for yourselves." Somewhat angry, I galloped after him, and placing my revolver to his head, shouted, " If you act the scoundrel I will shoot you like a dog!" At the time I meant this, and he evidently knew it, for down he went on his knees, abjectly entreating for mercy. A sharp admonition with a riding-whip soon made him rise, and resuming his lead, he speedily found the right road.

About noon, just as we reached the summit of a high hill, thickly wooded, we were suddenly surrounded by a score of armed men, whom I at once recognised as Chinese soldiers. Their leader, a villainous-looking brave, ordered me to halt, saying, " We have been sent by the civil Mandarin of Weisee, Tien Ta-lowya, to inspect your box." We halted, and a momentary glance at Philip showing me that he had covered the leader with his rifle, I replied that they should not examine my box, and told them to be off. They, however, persisted in demanding my passport and a present of chen, whereupon I quietly remarked, " I have two passes, one for robbers, and one for the authorities. This "—presenting my revolver—" is for robbers like you, and the chen are inside it, and if you do not be off you shall have them." Without more ado they made off, and disappeared amongst the trees, taking with them the honest guide, and as we rode forward their laughter resounded through the forest.

From Weisee our road followed a south-east course, through

a country altogether changed in appearance from that to the north of Weisee. We crossed range after range of low, steep hills, covered with a rank vegetation of bamboos, except where cultivated by the Lei-sus, whose crops of opium, wheat, barley, and potatoes just beginning to flower, testified to the richness of the soil and industry of the people.

Fortunately, after the guide left us the path led straight to Sz-se-to, a Lei-su village one march from Weisee, where we arrived in the afternoon without further adventure.

The village consisted of a cluster of about six square log-built houses, roofed with slabs of timber, and we had but little difficulty in finding the residence of the head man. As we approached he was sitting smoking in front of his door, but on observing us rose and entered the house. This was not promising, and Philip, who followed him in to prefer a request for quarters, soon came out again to report a decided refusal at first; curiosity, however, brought the churl out to have another look at the strangers, when, fairly driven to my wits' end to know what to do for shelter from the driving rain, I made him the sign of a Master Mason, which produced an immediate effect. He at once stepped up, and catching hold of my bridle, desired me to dismount and enter his house. I of course imagined that I had discovered a "brother," but on questioning him, it appeared that he had taken the signs to mean that I had some secret message for him, or was a Mahomedan agent.

Calling to mind Low-ling's advice, I asked my host if he knew the Mooquor chief, to which he replied, "Who does not know La-won-quan? He is the father of the Lei-sus; he is the same as my eldest brother." Upon this, Philip produced La-won-quan's letter to Low-ling, which the latter had given him to show if required, and my position as a distinguished personage was at once established, for our host, having read it, roused his household to prepare supper and a bed.

I should have exhibited my credentials on arrival, but I felt it necessary to be cautious about boasting of any acquaintances in Imperial territory, now that we were nearing the Mahomedan country.

We were most hospitably entertained by the Lei-su chief, and next morning he accompanied me with two of his soldiers to a Lei-su hut, where we put up for the night, after a wretched day's march amidst a perfect deluge of rain.

The chief carried with him round his waist an iron chain, about three feet long, with manacles at each end, an emblem of authority, the use of which became apparent when, as occurred twice during the day, we changed our escort of soldiers. On the first occasion the chief, after entering a house, from which, as it happened, the men were all absent, dropped his chain on the floor; a girl at once silently picked it up and left the room, while we remained smoking for a few minutes, and chatted with the old woman, who brought us each a cup of mead—for this is the only name that can be given to the sweet, rather strong liquor, resembling in appearance muddy pale ale, which the chief told me was made from wild honey.

Having resumed our journey and proceeded for a mile or so, we were overtaken by two Lei-su men, who, coming up out of breath, saluted the chief and handed him the chain, which the latter received with a bow, and fastened again round his waist.

In the evening we were made very comfortable at a Lei-su hut; and over our mead after supper I drew from the chief some information with regard to his people, their manners and customs, and political relations with the Chinese.

THE LEI-SUS.

The Lei-sus, prior to the occupation of their country by the Chinese, were a powerful tribe, inhabiting an extensive tract of country round Weisee-foo. According to their traditions, they had come originally from the west of Yunnan, and settled in the Valley of Weisee as cultivators of rice, opium, and tobacco. Under the rule of successive chiefs, distinguished both as wise rulers and great warriors, they held their acquired territory against all attacks from the neighbouring tribes of Ya-ts^u, Mooquors, and Tze-fans, until the Chinese, coveting the wealth acquired by their industrious habits, in conjunction with the other tribes made war upon them, and eventually became masters of all the Lei-su country, and built the stronghold of Weisee-foo.

From that period the Lei-sus seem almost to have lost their unity, and are now divided into villages or communities, each governed by a chief or head man, who collects the annual tribute for the Chinese Government.

The Mooquor and Ya-ts^u chiefs, in reward for their help during the war which established the Chinese supremacy, received grants of chieftainship over several Lei-su villages or districts, from which they collect tribute, paying a certain head-rent to the Chinese Government.

In dress the Lei-sus closely resemble the Chinese, the men wearing, like the Sz-chuanites, large turbans of blue cotton cloth. The women in some cases wear the short petticoat and jacket of the Mosos, and little caps ornamented with cowrie shells, but more frequently adopt the ordinary Chinese female costume.

Their religion is Chinese Buddhism, and in the schools attached to their religious edifices Chinese alone is taught. They still, however, preserve their own language, which, like the other tribal dialects, is unwritten.

At the last village on the frontier of the Tze-fan country the chief took leave of me, but sent two men as guides to the house of the Tze-fan chief, at the village of Tung-lan.

While travelling through the Lei-su country we had observed no signs of disturbance amongst the people, but about ten miles from the last Lei-su village, before entering a Tze-fan village, we met numbers of men, women, and children, laden with articles of household furniture, hurrying away to the hills, and to all our inquiries they merely replied that "the soldiers were coming."

The village itself presented a very curious scene of excitement. Women and children were running about crying and shouting. From some of the houses men were throwing all kinds of utensils to women, who were loading themselves with them; the inmates of others, as we passed by, levelled gingalls from the windows, and greeted us with yells of defiance, and one or two blank shots were fired, apparently with the object of frightening us. From other houses men and women brought us presents of tobacco and samshu, saying at the same time that they were "Hung-chee," red flag, or Imperialists, and begging me not to hurt them. Our assurances that we were only peaceable travellers were of no use; all seemed convinced that we were the advance-guard of a Chinese army. Our position was becoming every moment more embarrassing, so I insisted on seeing the head man, to whose house we were at last conducted by a trembling crowd. I at once told my Lei-su guides to explain who and what I was, and when at last the Tze-fans understood that I was not a soldier mandarin, and had examined my half European costume, nothing could exceed their joy.

The head man told me that early in the morning a Chinese soldier from Weisee-foo had passed through the village with the news that a great Chinese mandarin had arrived at Weisee from Pekin to report upon the progress of the Mahomedan war, and that a great army was following him to Tung-lan, where he intended to fight the " Pa-chees," white flags, or Mahomedans. This accounted for the terror of the villagers, while it plainly showed that the Chinese Mandarins at Weisee had taken this means to prevent me from reaching Tali-foo.

I had seen this soldier pass the door while we were at the village of Sz-se-to, and had asked the chief who he was; but having seen me, the fellow disappeared so suddenly that he was nowhere to be found, when the chief sent some of his people to make inquiries about him.

It seemed only too probable that all hopes of passing across the Imperial frontiers were now vain; however, leaving the village where our presence had caused so much excitement, we pushed on for the Tze-fan chief's house. During the afternoon we met a Tze-fan soldier, who stopped and asked us who we were. On hearing that I was going to Tali, he said, "Oh, you are too late. Our chief has turned 'Hung-chee,'"—red flag—" and is going to fight the Mahomedans in company with the great Chinese army, now on its way." This, if true, destroyed my last chance of proceeding towards Tali, and I reached Tung-lan only to find my worst fears realised.

On arriving at the chief's house he received me most ceremoniously. Several hundred fighting men, drawn from the surrounding country, were in the village, and all the head men accompanied the chief as he came to the door of his courtyard to receive me. His eldest brother led my pony into the yard, and when I dismounted at the house door the chief stepped forward, and bending his knee, bade me welcome to the house of "your servant." I at once raised the chief from his kneeling position, and said in a loud voice, "I am not a Chinese Mandarin, nor is there any army coming from Pekin. I am a foreigner on my way to Ava, and seek from the Tze-fan Ta-jen food and guides to Tali-foo." This statement created a great stir amongst the assembled chiefs, who at once commenced a loud and angry discussion amongst themselves, during which I entered the house, and gave the chief a truthful account of myself, at the same time producing the Sz-chuan Viceroy's passport. Great was the wrath of the chief as it dawned upon him that he had been duped into forsaking the Mahomedan cause by the wily Weisee Mandarins, who had availed themselves of my arrival to spread the report that a secret messenger had arrived from Pekin, announcing the coming of a large army.

The chief only the day before had eaten pork, a ceremony of recantation which publicly announced that he was no longer a Mahomedan, and he told me that it was now too late to undo the mischief, for he had allowed a party of Chinese soldiers to pass through his territory towards Li-kiang-foo three days before.

I asked him if he knew La-won-quan the Mooquor chief. The name of my old friend seemed at once to restore the Tze-fan to good humour—and he replied, that La-won-quan and the Ya-tsu chief were the peace-makers of the country. So I told him of my relations with La-won-quan, whose name again proved a talisman, for he at once promised me his protection which subsequently saved my life.

Our conversation was at length interrupted by the entrance of the chief's eldest brother, who brought a message from the assembled chiefs, desiring that I should at once eat pork and declare my true character; to this the chief replied, that I should be served without delay in their presence. As soon as his brother's back was turned, he whispered that half of his people were for holding to the Mahomedans, and half advocated the Chinese cause for the sake of prospective plunder. He then left me for a few minutes; but during the short time thus gained for reflection, I decided that I would refuse to eat pork, and state at the same time that I was a foreigner, interested neither in Mahomedans nor Imperialists.

I had scarcely made up my mind to this course, when the chief re-entered and desired me to take a seat before the door, outside of which were gathered in a crowd all his head men, intent on putting me to the proof of my political partizanship. Having seated myself as desired, the chief came out of the house accompanied by his brother, carrying on a tray a fowl, a basin of boiled rice, and a piece of boiled pork, and approaching to my right side, he kneeled and tendered me the fowl and rice in turn. I rose and received each with a bow; there was then a second or so of painful and breathless silence, during which the chief took the pork off the tray and presented it to me.

I fixed my eyes full on his, and again stood up raising my left hand high above my head to arrest attention, and said loudly in Chinese, "I do not eat pork; I am not a Pa-chee; I am not a Hung-chee, I am an Englishman," and then sat down again. The chief turned to his people outside and laughed loudly; at once a great hubbub arose, the Mahomedan party shouted "Pachee-jen, Pachee-jen," "White flag man, white flag man," and chaffed the Imperialist party, who in turn lavished all kinds of abuse upon me, the noisiest of all being the chief's brother; but it was plain that the Mahomedans were the strongest, and I knew that my conduct would be favourably reported in Tali-foo.

After our evening meal in the house, the chief told me that his people were desirous to hear from my own lips a statement as to my object in visiting their country; accordingly, about eight o'clock we adjourned to a large room reserved for councils, where about fifty Tze-fans were assembled. I was seated next the chief, and at his invitation gave a simple account of my travels, and explained my purposes in endeavouring to pass through their country, finally, requesting their convoy to Tali-foo, promising to recompense the service by a gift of all my horses and money. In answer to this, I was assured that it was impossible for me to proceed; the story of my being a Chinese official had preceded me, and the Mahomedans would certainly kill me, for which the Tze-fans would be held responsible.

The Chinese party who were strongly represented at the council, scowled menacingly at me, and the chief's brother after a long and angry speech drew his knife and shook it in my face, but with a quiet smile at the assembly I drew my revolver, an action which was greeted with a triumphant laugh by the Mahomedan party; this so enraged the others that they all got up and left the room, and I sat with the chief until a late hour.

In the conversation that followed, I learnt that the Chinese party were furious now, as they had been boastful before in the prospect of the approach of the mythical Chinese army, and the chief easily made me understand, that to proceed further into Mahomedan country would be sheer madness. Having promised to sleep upon his advice, and drunk a cup of samshu in good fellowship, I retired to the room prepared for Philip and myself, which was next to the chief's own chamber. When we were left alone, I threw myself on the bed without undressing or laying aside my weapons, and for two hours courted sleep in vain; anxiety about my present position, and the frustration of my cherished hopes of reaching Tali, only sixty miles distant, combined to keep me awake and alert; and well for me this involuntary vigilance proved. Suddenly, when the whole household appeared to be buried in sleep, the door of my room was burst open, and in rushed the chief's brother and two others; the former threw himself on me before I could spring from the bed, and grasping me by the throat dragged me on to the floor. By a tremendous effort I got my arms round the fellow's chest, and held him in a bear-like hug till I fairly felt his ribs bend, and the pain forced him with a yell to let go his hold. The next instant he was on his back, while I kept him down with my knee, and placed my revolver to his breast. In the meantime the other ruffians were busy, one holding Philip by the throat and all but strangling the poor little fellow, while the other ransacked my box.

The chief's brother finding the pressure of my knee intolerable, roared loudly, and roused the chief, who rushed into the room, followed by three or four men, who, seeing the state of the case, attacked our assailants with drawn knives; in the *mêlée* the candle was overset, and a free fight ensued in the dark. The two robbers were much cut about, although they made a good defence, inflicting one or two cuts on the chief's assistants. At last, however, they were expelled, and a light having been procured, showed us the chief's brother lying apparently insensible on the floor; when he did get up the chief abused him violently, and lifted his knife as if to strike, but suddenly checking himself, literally hurled him out of the room. Peace having been procured, my sycee, which the robbers had dropped, was restored to me by the chief, who apologised for his brother's conduct, and assured me that we need have no further fear as he would himself sleep in our room. From his remarks it appeared that even the Mahomedan party among his people, though they would not hurt me, were indignant with me, as being the innocent cause of their joining the Imperialists.

He then told me, that he knew me to be a European, as he had seen some of my countrymen in Tali-foo, who were employed in casting big guns for the Emperor Dow-win-sheow, and teaching the Koran. If the Chinese partizans knew me to be a foreigner, they would assuredly do me some harm, and he strongly urged me to return to Weisee, and wait there for more tranquil times, when, if I returned, he would forward me into Tali-foo; in the meanwhile, he undertook to report my visit to the Mahomedan General, who resided at Ho-chin or Ko-king, about twenty miles distant. He candidly avowed his intention to turn Mahomedan again, as soon as it was certain that no great Chinese army was coming; and passing his hand over his forehead, with an air of weariness, he said with a sigh, that he had a difficult policy to play, in order to save his country from the alternate ravages of Imperialists and Mahomedans; so far, he had indeed been very successful, always having managed to keep on the winning side, but that this time he had been fairly out-manœuvered by the cunning Mandarins of Weisee, with whom however he vowed he would soon be even.

After this conversation we were joined by the two Chinese soldiers who had brought the false intelligence from Weisee. Their position was not pleasant, for they asked the chief's protection against his Mahomedan head men, who had sworn to kill them. In their presence the chief at once became reserved and almost silent, and at day-light left us in charge of some of his head men.

Before he left me, I told him that the prospect of having to return was worse than death, and begged him to try and pass me on to the next Mahomedan Mandarin, offering in return my rifle and all my cattle. At this request his countenance suddenly lighted up, and he told me not to fear; he would think about it, and if I had a stout heart, perhaps he could send me on. I had already determined to start for Weisee that morning, but this slight hope given me by the chief, combined with the very heavy rain to induce me to remain with him until next day.

I saw no more of the chief until the evening, when he came to me about six o'clock, saying that my chance was not good; he could not send me on, for the risk was too great. Unwilling to retrace my steps, I then begged him to let me remain with him, as I felt safe under his protection. I could see that this confidence evidently gratified the Tze-fan's pride. He hesitated for a moment, but at last said, it could not be, for the Mandarins at Weisee would be jealous, and for his own sake he dared not let me remain; so it was decided that I should return in the morning with an escort of his Mahomedan soldiers.

During the day several petty chiefs arrived with their followers, and the village was full of warriors, more than five hundred in number.

The Tze-fan village, the houses of which are built principally of wood after the Chinese style, some, however, being composed of rough logs, is beautifully situated on the side of a densely wooded hill, covered with an undergrowth of almost tropical vegetation. In this district the famous yellow thin-leaved Yunnan tobacco is largely cultivated, the leaf of which is very delicate, about eight inches long and as many wide, growing from a very fine stalk; when dried, it is of a pale yellow colour, and in smoking resembles the finest kind of Manilla tobacco, but to my taste is greatly superior in delicacy of flavour and aroma; in fact I know no tobacco superior to it. Both as regards the quantity and quality of this product, the tobacco trade alone of Yunnan will be enormously valuable if opened to the European merchants in Burmah, whenever the country shall have recovered the devastating effects of the Mahomedan civil war, which has destroyed, or driven from their homes, half the population of that magnificently fertile province. The importance of this Mahomedan revolt, as affecting the intercourse of Europeans with the west of China, makes its origin and progress a subject of interest, though the extreme difficulty of procuring information has hitherto veiled it in obscure uncertainty. The direct influence it had in closing the country against myself, is a sufficient reason for a short digression on this subject.

The rise and gradual growth of Mahomedanism in China are shrouded in mystery; though the mythical tales of a plantation of auxiliary troops, sent by a neighbouring Mahomedan monarch, may probably contain a very small nucleus of truth; and the intercourse carried on, both by maritime and overland traders with India and Central Asia, quite sufficiently accounts for the propagation of Islamism, at an early period in the several provinces of China. As an instance of the various accounts given by the Chinese Mahomedans themselves, it was told me in conversations with one or two on this subject, that long ere European voyagers visited China, Mahomedans from India settled on the northern shores of the gulf of Tonquin, and thence found their way by the Tonquin river into Kwei-chew; however, and whenever introduced, Mahomedanism spread far and wide throughout the Empire. The Chinese toleration of any religion which did not attack the fundamental principles of their polity, or seemed to bring foreign domination in its train, heeded not the successful proselytism to the faith of the Prophet, whose votaries are at the present day counted by millions. There is scarcely a town of any importance where Mahomedans or Hwai-ts", as the Chinese call them, are not to be found. The great strongholds of the Mahomedan Chinese have always been Yunnan, Kwei-chew and the north-western provinces of Kan-soo and Chen-si, and in these are found the two areas of the present revolts, those of Yunnan and Kan-soo. In western Yunnan especially, previous to the war, or about the year 1850, the Chinese Mahomedans formed fully half the population, and were distinguished by their wealth and energy;* it must however be clearly understood, that although some of them affect an Arab descent, the majority of Mahomedans were of Chinese race, and, save in religion, differed in no respect from their fellow-countrymen. There seems to have been no disaffection among them, nor any oppression exercised towards them on religious grounds, nor was there any reason to apprehend a Mahomedan any more than a Buddhist revolt. An able paper communicated to the Asiatic Society of Bengal in 1867, by the talented Chief Commissioner of Burmah, General Fytche, traces the first outbreak to the silver miners of Loo-soon-foo, "who exasperated by unjust treatment had recourse to force, and murdered every Chinese officer they could find." This account was furnished from Burmese sources, and probably contains substantial truth, but General Fytche himself complains that his information is vague and meagre. The opportunities for inquiries during his residence in Yunnan, possessed by Monseigneur Chauveau, give him a right to be considered an authority on the affairs of the province, and it was my good

* For the condition of Yunnan at that time, see Appendix V.

fortune to obtain from him an account of the outbreak and subsequent events up to the period of my visit, which was independently confirmed by several intelligent Mahomedans. Some years previous to the revolt, the Mahomedan community containing, as has been said, the wealthiest and most influential class of the people, were thoroughly organised under twelve elders, resident in the principal towns. These men chosen not for their learning but for their influence, acted as the representatives and guardians of the religious interests of the faithful. The attraction of the religion, or perhaps the idea of using to his own advantage the power of the Mahomedan community, induced the Imperial Viceroy of Yunnan, resident at Yunnan-foo, to embrace the religion of the Prophet, and the example of so illustrious a proselyte was numerously followed. He, however, by some arbitrary interference with the established rites, which he wished to alter according to his own ideas, gave great offence to his new co-religionists. One of the twelve elders more daring than the rest, who resided at Li-kiang-foo, a small city lying at the eastern foot of the Sui-Shan, or snowy mountains, denounced the conduct of the Imperial Viceroy as contrary to the freedom of their religion. This remonstrance, in which he was joined by the other elders, was treated with contempt by the haughty official, whose conduct soon brought matters to a crisis.

In 1855 the white flag of rebellion was first unrolled from the walls of Li-kiang-foo, whose elder called the Faithful to arms, and the call was soon responded to by all the elders. The war thus begun was vigorously carried on by the Mahomedans, and success from the beginning appears to have continuously attended on their arms, until the white flag floated over every town in Western Yunnan—even over the famous and wealthy city of Tali-foo itself, the holy city of the western tribes; and Mahomedan armies closely invested Yunnan-foo, the provincial capital.

During the few years of continual warfare which led the Mahomedan armies to the gates of Yunnan-foo, Dow-win-sheow, the elder presiding over the district of Tali-foo, had greatly distinguished himself, both as a general and ruler. He had previously been a wealthy merchant of Tali-foo, known amongst his fellows as a shrewd and far-seeing man, and shortly after the commencement of the war he was chosen by a majority of the elders to lead the armies of the faithful.

In the meanwhile, the Imperial Viceroy at Yunnan-foo had been writing to Pekin constant reports of victories gained by himself over the rebels; and although he had been ordered to repair to Pekin, and an official sent to supersede him shortly after the outbreak of the rebellion, he had excused himself under the plea that he was just about to administer the final blow to the revolt and could not give up his governorship at that critical moment. Repeated dispatches from Pekin were unheeded by him; the Mandarins sent to supersede him, either glad to escape the responsibility of governing a province almost entirely in the hands of rebels, or bought off with heavy bribes, made no effort to displace the Viceroy, and so matters went on, till Dow-win-sheow thundered at the gates of Yunnan-foo.

The Imperial Viceroy, foreseeing the imminent surrender of his stronghold and his own certain destruction, opened negotiations with Dow-win-sheow, and finally concluded a treaty, according to the terms of which Dow-win-sheow was to hold Western Yunnan, extending from the Burmese frontiers to within thirty miles of Yunnan-foo. Peace having been thus established, Dow-win-sheow withdrew to Tali-foo, the Mahomedan capital, and the Imperial Viceroy wrote to

Pekin to the effect that the rebellion was crushed, and peace once more restored to the province. A year or two of tranquillity followed, which the Mahomedans made use of to consolidate and regulate their Government, and under the skilful rulership of Dow-win-sheow, who had been made Emperor, the ravages of war were repaired, and trade gradually increased between Western or Mahomedan Yunnan, and the neighbouring Imperial provinces.

When the Pekin authorities were at last made aware of the real nature of the peace which existed in the favourite province of the Empire, a Mandarin was at once despatched to supersede the traitor Viceroy; but on arriving at the capital the Pekin official received a very strong hint not to interfere; and after having been hospitably entertained for several months by the disaffected Viceroy, was sent back to Pekin with a message to the effect that it was not just then convenient to make any change in the government.

Having thus defied the Pekin authorities, it was necessary to strengthen his position against a possible attack from Sz-chuan; so the Viceroy acknowledged Dow-win-sheow as Emperor of Western Yunnan by a proclamation under the Viceregal seal. Dow-win-sheow, in return, engaged to support the Viceroy in case of an Imperial attack, and supplied him with money to buy over all the officials and troops sent to Yunnan-foo to oust him from his viceroyalty; and up to the time of my visit nothing beyond sending an occasional useless draft of Imperial soldiers to Yunnan-foo from Sz-chuan had been done towards crushing the power of the Mahomedans.

Thus at this period the Imperial Viceroy at Yunnan-foo was virtually king of Eastern Yunnan, and while keeping up the mockery of calling himself the Imperial Viceroy, was as much an enemy to the Emperor of China as Dow-win-sheow himself, while with the enormous wealth at his command he bought off all opposition on the part of the troops sent against him from time to time.

Since the period of my visit accounts have from time to time come from the Pekin officials, according to which the Imperial authorities seem to have exerted themselves with success to put down the Mahomedan rebellion. From what has been already said, it will be evident that such accounts are not in themselves to be relied on; and the fact that the Viceroy of Kwei-chew* now exercises authority over what remains of Yunnan as an Imperial province, coupled with the information brought by Panthays, or Mahomedan Yunnanese, to Rangoon, that "Yunnan is perfectly tranquil," seems to show that the Mahomedans now hold possession of Yunnan-foo itself. If this be the case, an attack on Sz-chuan by the Mahomedan king, in concert with Abdul Jaffier, the Mahomedan chief in Kan-soo, may be imminent. At all events, accurate information as to the actual state of affairs is most desirable, in view of the present attempts to establish routes for overland trade with Yunnan.

It may seem incredible to many that the Pekin authorities should have been so long defied by the Viceroy at Yunnan-foo; but this is only one of the many evidences of the weakness of the Chinese Government and the utter demoralisation of the Mandarins; while the means of communication throughout the Empire are so inadequate to the requirements of a well administered Government, it is useless to look for any improvement. Bribery and falsehood have so long usurped the place of truth and justice, that the people are totally estranged from any sympathy with their

* In Kwei-chew itself at the present time a Mahomedan rebellion is widespread and deeply seated, though the recapture of Tsi-kung-ting, a strong city, is reported, up to Feb. 15.—*London and China Telegraph*, April 2, 1871.

rulers. The exclusiveness, unprincipled extortion, and absolute power of the Mandarins and their satellites combined, seem to have broken the spirit of the people, and rendered them indifferent to the affairs of Government. There are few men of thought amongst the Chinese who do not acknowledge that their country is in a bad way, and this feeling is very prevalent amongst the educated and governing classes. Instead, however, of arousing them to seek for internal reforms, it vents itself rather in animosity towards foreigners, in whom they recognise a stronger people than themselves, and arguing according to their own ideas of human nature, naturally conclude that the foreigners will sooner or later attempt to take their country. That they are to be got rid of, therefore, is the cry which sounds from every Ya-mun in the Empire.

Although, as I have said, the people possess little sympathy with their Government, nothing is more repugnant to the Chinese mind at large than the idea of being governed by any foreign power; and while round the eastern seaboard of China, where foreign power is justly estimated, the people might hesitate to rise *en masse* against foreigners, there are, beyond the reach of consular and gunboat influence, millions of people whose ignorance regards all foreigners as mere barbarians, hitherto allowed to remain in their country; these, once excited by superstition, and encouraged by half-fulfilled prophecies* promulgated by the Mandarins, would flock to the

* A pseudo-prophecy most zealously circulated by the Mandarins at the present day, is one relating to what is called the four "Ts^u" wars, viz. the MAN-TS^u, MIAOU-TS^u, HWAI-TS^r, and YANG-KWAI-TS^u, in which the great Central Kingdom is to be successful. The impression left on the popular mind by the past history is that the MAN-TS^r, or Eastern Thibetans, and the MIAOU-TZ^u of the hill districts of Kwei-chew, have in turn been conquered. At the present the people are told that the HWAI-TS^u, or Mahomedans in Yunnan, are yielding to Imperial arms, and when they are subdued, there will remain but the YANG-KWAI-TS^r, or foreigners, to be disposed of.

banner raised for the expulsion of foreigners, and every act of forbearance on the part of foreign governments will only tend to encourage the unfortunate people in the belief that foreigners may be injured or expelled with impunity.

My own personal experiences of Mandarin treachery gave ample food for unpleasant reflections during the day of forced inaction at the Tze-fan village, and I obeyed with alacrity the chief's summons to rise and prepare for a start next morning before daylight.

After a hasty meal of fowl and cold rice, the chief led me from his house by a by-path to the outskirts of the village, where the escort and baggage animals were all ready waiting. It was still quite dark when, bidding the kind Tze-fan farewell, we commenced our return to Weisee, and ere dawn were several miles away from Tung-lan.

About noon we met a party of Tze-fan scouts, returning from Li-kiang-foo, lying about twenty miles distant on the right. They reported a skirmish near Li-kiang-foo, in which the Imperialists had been worsted. We all breakfasted together, and having smoked a friendly pipe, once more commenced our march, and late in the evening were welcomed by our old friend in the village of Sz-se-to.

THE SCORPION FLY.

During this day's march the baggage animals had been much annoyed by the attacks of a kind of scorpion fly. The stings drove them nearly frantic, and many times we had to reload the baggage kicked off by the poor beasts in their frenzy of pain. We had experienced this pest previously in a lesser degree, and for some time had been utterly unable to account for the unusual restiveness of our mules. Philip had been thrown twice, and my usually steady Jacob seemed to have been transformed without apparent reason into a vicious kicker. The flies, which only attack the bellies of the horses or mules, for a long time escaped our notice, until I discovered them by accident. While resting by the roadside, the mule, which I held by the bridle, suddenly gave a squeal and commenced kicking and plunging madly, and then for the first time I saw the fly sticking to his belly. After apparently stinging the mule, it fell off to the ground, where I killed it as it lay seemingly stupified. Its jointed body was of a reddish brown, and covered with a scaly coat of mail, while the flexible tail was armed at the tip with a long sharp sting, and it fully deserved by its appearance the name I have given to it. The Chinese term it the Wen-s^u fly.

One march from Sz-se-to, under the escort of the Lei-su chief, brought us back to Weisee on the 3rd of July, and we again took up our quarters with Low-ling, who welcomed me back as one whom he had never expected to see again.

He had succeeded in apprehending the guide who had deserted us on our way to the Tze-fan country, and had handed him over to the General, who before bed-time sent the fellow to cool himself in the keang before the door.

After a good supper, prepared by Lowling, I turned in, and soon buried all feelings of disappointment and anxiety in a deep, refreshing sleep.

CHAPTER XIII.

IMPRISONMENT AT WEISEE.

Tien Ta-lowya—In the Ya-mun—Rifle Practice—The Black-Nose—Tien Drunk—Lending a Mount—A Forced Loan Resisted—The Mandarins and the Revolver—Little Sen—Tien Dangerous—Playing with Edged Tools—Our Escape—Recaptured—Rescued by the Chiefs—Last Night in Weisee.

GREATLY refreshed by a night of undisturbed rest, I set about making the necessary arrangements for a retreat to Chen-tu, in case Weisee should prove an untenable residence.

Philip was despatched to the General with a request that he would exchange his passport for another, which should make it optional for us either to proceed to Tali-foo, or to return to Sz-chuan by a direct route leading from Tsung-tain, a city situated on the banks of the Kin-cha-kiang, three days' march from Weisee, and thence by a due north-east course to the city of Ya-tzow, so as to avoid the hostile country between Atenze and Bathang.

The old General expressed great pleasure at my safe return, and gave orders for the necessary passports to be prepared. He also sent a message to the effect that he was going to leave in two days, and I had better start before him as after his departure he could not be responsible for the conduct of his soldiers. My reply to this was, that I could not leave at present; and as to the soldiers I was not afraid of them.

To do the old man justice he certainly expressed great anxiety for Tang's safety, and without a doubt his advice was dictated by his foresight of what was likely to happen after his own departure.

In the evening the civil Mandarin, Tien Ta-lowya, sent for Philip, and inquired if it would be agreeable to his master to come and live in the Ya-mun, where he would be secure from attack. As this proposition seemed to be made in good faith, it was accepted, and he was informed that he might expect his guest on the morrow.

When Low-ling heard of this arrangement he shook his head, and declared that Tien Ta-lowya was a great scoundrel, and had certainly some sinister purpose in this proposal. By way of testing his sincerity Low-ling advised me to frame some excuse and politely decline to stay in the Ya-mun, which would, he predicted, result in my being annoyed in some way.

From Low-ling's manner it was plain to see that he knew more than he chose to say, and I decided to send an apology, declining to take up my quarters in the Ya-mun, on the ground of the great trouble that our presence would cause him.

Next morning, just as Low-ling predicted, the hotel was mobbed by a crowd which loudly threatened the foreigner; my door was smashed in and broken to atoms, and there was such an air of fearlessness about the mob that it seemed certain they had been instigated by the authorities, so I at once drew my knife and cleared the room just as some soldiers from my friend the General arrived and dispersed the crowd outside. When all became quiet again, Low-ling assured me that Tien Ta-lowya had been the instigator of all the attacks made upon me in Weisee, and had evidently some deep motive for his conduct. We had scarcely settled down after the fracas when a message came from him, that he was much occupied with the General, but requested that I would come to the Ya-mun next day.

About seven in the evening I was surprised by a visit from Tien Ta-lowya himself, who came, as he said, to see if I wanted anything; and then, referring to the attack of the morning, remarked, " Well, you see I told you it would not be safe for you out of the Ya-mun, and you had better move in to-morrow." The appearance of Tien Ta-lowya at first sight was calculated to leave a very pleasant impression: quite young, probably about seven-and-twenty, and rather above the middle height, his figure was slender, and his bearing peculiarly graceful, while he spoke with a soft and languid drawl; his complexion was very fair, almost white, and his skin smooth and delicate as a woman's; large drooping eyelids gave to his eyes a sleepy appearance, which vanished the moment that the eyelids were lifted, and a pair of restless bright black eyes glittered snake-like for a second or two, and then disappeared behind the drooping lids, while his countenance resumed its habitual sleepy look, well calculated to mislead a careless observer.

His hands were very delicate, and the tips of his slender fingers ornamented with fashionably long nails, to show which he usually sat with one elbow on the table or on the arm of his chair, with the hand hanging listlessly across his chest. Such was Tien Ta-lowya in appearance. In spite, however, of his pleasant and engaging manner, I felt that he was dangerous, and hesitated for a moment between the alternatives of abandoning all hopes of reaching Burmah, or running the risk of going to the Ya-mun. I chose the latter, and told him I would move into his Ya-mun next day. At these words his eyelids lifted for a second and he fixed his eyes on me, with a look that was absolutely hideous in its snake-like coldness, but I met his look with a full gaze, and his eyes disappeared behind the drooping eyelids.

He took his leave with great politeness, and after he had gone Low-ling and the Mahomedan merchant came in to see me. They both agreed that the Mandarin meant mischief, but that if I really was determined not to give up my hope of reaching Burmah, there would be more security in the Ya-mun than at the hotel, exposed to the attacks of the Mandarin's satellites; and, moreover, if the Mandarin intended to rob me he could do so with greater impunity if I left Weisee just then, as he could easily order his banditti to shoot a traveller and plunder his baggage, while he would thus escape detection; whereas so long as I remained in the Ya-mun he would be responsible for me.

This line of argument on the part of my friends proved the correctness of my decision to become a guest of Tien Ta-lowya, in whose house on the seventh of July I took up my abode. My host had gone to escort the General (who left in the morning) out of the town, but his younger brother did the honours with ceremonious politeness. The Ya-mun was a fine group of buildings and courtyards, enclosed by four high walls, originally built as a joss-house, but now appropriated as a temporary official residence. From the street a massive arched gateway, over which was a room formerly used as a theatre, opened into a large square courtyard, on the opposite side of which, facing the first gate, was another large folding door, giving admittance to a second court which we crossed, and through another door entered a passage with a small room on either side; this led into a smaller court surrounded by rooms, a large one facing the doorway being used as a joss-house, containing a number of huge images with joss-sticks burning in front of them.

On the right as we passed through the inner door was the Mandarin's private room, and into this I was ushered by his brother, while my baggage was stowed in one of the small rooms in the passage between the two folding doors, and the baggage animals stabled in the outer court-yard.

In the afternoon, just as Tien's brother and I had finished dinner, Tien himself made his appearance, and the cordiality of his welcome would perhaps have quieted my suspicions but for Low-ling's warning, and his evident knowledge of Tien's real intentions. In the evening he ushered me into one of the rooms opening off the passage, which he told me to consider as my own; it was a dingy little apartment about eight feet square, containing a solitary table and a wooden bench to sleep on. Daylight dimly found its way through two wooden gratings made in little squares covered with thin white paper extending from about three feet from the floor to the eaves of the roof, and occupying two opposite sides of the room. One window opened on the inner court facing one end of the joss-house, and the other opened on the middle court; the third wall of the room was formed by the main wall of the Ya-mun. Any person standing outside of either of the windows, could observe all that took place within the room by making a small hole in the paper. This at once forced itself on my notice, and did not add to my comfort; however the chance of reaching Burmah was not to be given up, and I made myself as comfortable as possible.

A short residence in the Ya-mun convinced me that earnest preparations were being made for an attack on the Mahomedans; messengers were constantly coming and going with despatches, and a party of Ya-ts^u were sent to the chief of the Lu-ts[u] tribes on the Nou-kiang river, with a packet containing a green chili, three pieces of fowl fat, and a piece of liver, tied up in red paper; as already stated, this packet was an emblematic telegram, directing him to repair at once to Weisee with his warriors.

The Ya-ts[u] and Mooquor chiefs were also summoned to Weisee with their fighting men, and Tien languidly informed me that in less than a month he would eat up the Mahomedans.

For four days Tien's hospitable behaviour evinced his desire to inspire me with confidence in him, and his repeated protestations of friendship were apparently most sincere.

On the fifth day the Mooquor chief, La-won-quan, arrived in company with the Ya-ts[u] chief. My old friend was delighted at our reunion, and spent a great part of the day in my room. Tien made himself particularly agreeable, and proposed a little rifle practice to amuse his guests.

One of the Chinese soldiers in the Ya-mun was a famous marksman with the gingal, and Tien backed him for 1,000 chen to shoot with his weapon against the Englishman with his rifle; so we adjourned to the outer courtyard, where a leaf about the size of a man's hand was stuck against the wall, and thirty paces marked off. The chiefs, with a number of their followers and the people of the Ya-mun, composed the crowd of spectators, while Tien constituted himself and La-won-quan the judges.

We drew lots for first shot, which fell to the soldier, who, kneeling as our riflemen do when firing at long ranges, fired and grazed the outer edge of the leaf. Tien smiled, and asked what I thought of that? It was evident that my antagonist knew how to shoot, and as I had no confidence in myself it seemed that I stood but little chance of winning;

however I stepped forward and made an effort, which placed my ball in the hole made by the ball from the soldier's gingall. This seemed to balance opinions amongst the bystanders, but as I had taken a very careful aim at the leaf, I felt that it was a bad shot. The soldier fired again and missed the leaf by three inches, leaving a mark on the wall bigger than a five-shilling piece; when I again stepped forward a sudden whim seized me, and instead of firing at the leaf, I let fly at the mark just made by the soldier's ball, and hit well on the edge of the mark. Though I felt conscious that it was a fluke, I smiled knowingly, and to the eager inquiries of many of the bystanders, including Tien himself, whether I had aimed at that spot, the only answer vouchsafed was a still more knowing smile.

My soldier friend again took up his position, and hit the leaf nearly in the centre. This performance was greeted with loud applause; and, on stepping forward, I could see that the result of my shot was anxiously looked for,—I fired, —another fluke! My ball had touched my adversary's bullet mark again; there appeared to be no mistake about my shooting powers now, and La-won-quan suddenly giving vent to his feelings, cut a caper, and told Tien that his soldier was shooting against the devil. The effect of my last shot on the soldier was visible when he prepared for his next attempt; the fellow was quite unsteady, but managed to hit the point of the leaf. The three flukes had given me such confidence that I jauntily stepped forward and added another to the list, placing my ball in the same hole as the soldier's last shot! This was too much for me, and I nearly exploded with laughter. It was, however, quite a settler for Tien and his champion, and the former handed over 1,000 chen, which I gave to the soldier, who was very downcast.

This little incident gained me great celebrity, and I was regarded as a sort of fire-god, and frequently afterwards asked by the Ya-mun people to exhibit my skill, but always declined on the plea that I could not waste my ammunition.

In the evening the two chiefs and myself dined with Tien, and when we retired I gave up my bed to La-won-quan, who sat up till nearly daylight smoking opium and talking.

During the early part of the night Tien joined us in my room to smoke his pipe. He told me he was very anxious to lay his plan of attack in the coming campaign before me, for the benefit of my opinion on it. I replied that I was engaged in mercantile pursuits, and my opinion on such matters would be worth little; but he, with a polite air of disbelief, declared I was one of those foreign fighting mandarins employed by the Pekin authorities. I assured him that he was mistaken, and added that with such a clever head as he had, his plan of attack must be good. He had been drinking rather deeply, and spoke several times about Yang-kwai-ts^u, which La-won-quan afterwards pronounced to be a gross breach of etiquette; however he soon left us alone, when the Mooquor suggested that I had better return to his village and await there the result of the coming fight. I at once jumped at his offer, and arranged to accompany him back.

The next morning the two chiefs met Tien in the public room of the Ya-mun to discuss the coming fight, and afterwards they ceremoniously sent me their cards; this was looked upon by the Ya-mun people as a great mark of distinction, and it was followed by an invitation for myself and La-won-quan from the military Mandarins of the town to a dinner, where we met three other petty Lei-su chiefs. After dinner the Ya-ts^u and Mooquor chiefs led the van in a very angry discussion with Tien and the military Mandarins, the latter being told pretty plainly that it was all very well calling the tribes to fight, but unless arms and ammunition were forthcoming this state of things would not last long. It was a great relief when at last the dinner was over, and La-won-quan and myself were seated quietly together in our room. The chief told me that both he himself and the Ya-ts^u chief had determined not to fight unless supplied with arms, and suggested that I had better remain in the Ya-mun instead of returning with him; as it might only create a quarrel between him and Tien if I showed a preference for himself.

The good fellow cautioned me not to leave the Ya-mun, under any pretence, by myself, and never to be without arms for a moment.

We spoke of the shooting exhibition on the previous day, and I told him that it was all chance; whereupon he told me not to tell any one else, as the reputation for skill I had acquired would be a great safeguard.

Next day I gave a dinner to the military Mandarins and a petty chief called Black-Nose, while Philip entertained the secretaries and chief subordinates of the Ya-mun.

During the morning the Ya-ts^u and Mooquor chiefs, after a violent quarrel with Tien, had departed for their villages; so that at dinner Tien was obviously very ill-humoured, and drank rather deeply. The dinner was by no means agreeable, and the departure of the guests was most welcome, enabling me to enjoy a reflective smoke in my own room. This, however, was soon interrupted; for the Black-Nose returned, and volunteered to smoke a pipe with me. He gradually led up to his subject, and at last intimated that if I wished to go to Tali-foo, he would, for a proper consideration, take me there. A secret sign from Philip warned me to be on my guard, and I declined his proposal, with polite expressions of thanks, and regrets that my stock of cash was only one hundred taels. Black-Nose, having finished his pipe, took himself off, going straight to Tien's room; and Philip then told me that he was one of Tien's instruments in all shady transactions, and one of the Ya-mun writers had hinted to Philip that Tien wanted money, and that the Black-Nose would take me to Tali-foo if I paid him well enough. Temptingly baited as the trap had been, it had failed to catch the bird, and the Black-Nose was doubtless disappointed in not having the pleasure of quietly disposing of me on the road to Tali-foo, in which city he was, as I afterwards learned, a marked man, for he had been once a Mahomedan, and had assassinated the Mahomedan Mandarin at Kien-chuan, when that city fell to the Mahomedan arms, and then had deserted to the Imperialists. He had been also concerned in the murder of two Chinese Mandarins, while a partisan of the Mahomedan cause; but, being a useful agent to Tien, he had so far managed to keep his head. Such was the character of the Black-Nose, whose kind offer I had refused.

There was no longer any doubt as to the intentions of Tien. It was evident that he wanted my money, the amount of which his imagination doubtless exaggerated. However, I could not bring myself to believe that he would venture on actual violence.

My feelings on lying down to sleep were not pleasant; and from thenceforward Philip and myself determined to keep alternate watches of six hours during the night.

Philip took the first watch, and soon aroused me from sleep, announcing Tien, who staggered into the room, considerably the worse for liquor. The difference between Tien drunk and Tien sober was most remarkable. In his present state he was quarrelsome, rude, and blustering; when sober he was listless, polite almost to dandyism, and very quiet. On this occasion he told a long rigmarole story about his getting money from Chinese merchants for orders on Chen-tu, and then broke forth into a violent tirade against the Ya-ts" and Mooquor chiefs, and alluded to them as "your friends" (meaning mine), and wound up by declaring that, after the fight, he would cut their heads off, as well as those of other people, enumerating, with the most horrible minuteness, all the heads that should roll on the ground when he had finished with the Mahomedans; and then, in a mock-maudlin manner, asked if I should like mine cut off. His absurd way of asking the question made me laugh, which seemed to irritate him, and he asked me what I thought my head was worth; when I replied that I valued it at the price of the Chinese Empire. On this he got up, stared for a moment, and left the room.

For the next five days I saw nothing of Tien. Due supplies were furnished us of rice and pork, which Philip cooked and served in my own room, the door of which, since the day after Tien's drunken visit, had been closely guarded by soldiers, who kept a sharp watch on me, and prevented my walking in the outer courtyard.

On the same evening that these guards were posted, the head writer of the Ya-mun came to my room with a request from Tien for the loan of one hundred taels. The request was conveyed in a manner so much resembling a command, that I peremptorily replied that I could not comply with it, inasmuch as all my money only amounted to one hundred taels. I then demanded the reason for placing the guards at the door, and prohibiting me from walking in the outer courtyard. The reply, given with an air of mockery, was in effect that Tien Ta-lowya had ordered me to be well guarded, lest any person should enter the Ya-mun and do me some injury. Of course, I knew the meaning of this, and quietly informed my visitor that he could go.

The next day I was allowed to walk in the inner courtyard in front of the joss-house, the extent of my promenade being not more than thirty yards; and I paced up and down for several hours, passing the time between smoking and talking to my soldier-guard, who, fortunately, was a jovial sort of fellow, and greatly appreciated sundry pipes of tobacco. Philip seemed to be almost unnoticed by the Mandarins, for he was allowed to leave the Ya-mun whenever he chose, for the purpose of buying provisions ; and no restraint was placed on the attendance of my servant, Low-dzung.

Several days passed in this manner, and nothing of interest occurred ; indeed, my presence seemed to be quite forgotten. Tien visited me once, and treated me with the greatest politeness. Alluding to the guard at my door, he told me that he was very anxious for my safety, for he was responsible for me while in his Ya-mun ; and as to my not being allowed to go into the outer yard, that had been quite a mistake, which should be rectified : I was not to consider myself a prisoner. The cool insolence of the fellow was something marvellous ; and he wound up his visit by telling me that he must have fifteen or twenty taels. It was no use my saying that I had only one hundred left. He told me I should have the money returned next day ; so, not wishing to irritate him, I was glad to get rid of my visitor at the price of twenty taels.

Immediately after his visit I found two of my ponies standing, saddled, in front of his room, the door of which opened into the inner court. I at once inquired the meaning of this, and was told that Tien required my animals, to carry an express to the General. Tien's brother was my informant; but I gave him to understand that I objected to this proceeding, and by way of proving that I was in earnest, took off the saddles myself. Several of the writers of the Ya-mun came out of Tien's room to ask what I meant by this conduct. I briefly told them that I meant to fight if my cattle were interfered with; and drew my knife with such an air of determination, that Tien himself was obliged at last to come out, and beg that I would lend him a horse, as he wished to visit the military Mandarins. Of course, I expressed myself only too delighted to oblige Tien with a mount. In fact, I begged that he would use my cattle whenever he liked, if he would only let me know.

This was a great let-down for my accomplished gaoler; and although I felt completely in his power, something seemed to tell me that he dared not touch my life. Thus matters went on till the 22nd of July; and, beyond the effects of close confinement and anxiety, I suffered but little.

At this season—now nearly midsummer—the climate of Weisee was not altogether enjoyable. The summer rains, which commence in June, and break in the beginning of August, made it very damp; and a hot sun, which occasionally shone for an hour or two in the middle of the day, caused everything to steam again. But the nights were cool and pleasant. Mosquitoes, however, were very numerous, and, in the absence of curtains, rendered sleeping somewhat difficult, especially in my prison chamber, which was altogether without ventilation, except for a few holes which I made by pushing my fingers through the paper windows.

It happened to be my watch, from 12 to 6 A.M., on the 22nd. Philip had relieved me, and I had just fallen asleep on my boards, when I was aroused by a hand laid on my shoulder. It was Philip, who, placing his lips to my ear, whispered that something was wrong. The two military Mandarins had come to the Ya-mun with several soldiers, and desired him to call me at once, as they had two letters from the General for Tang Ta-jen. There was no one else about but the guard at the door, and he had observed that the soldiers who accompanied the Mandarins had their knives concealed in the legs of their long stockings, and one of them carried a gingall. All this Philip communicated in a rapid whisper, and then said aloud, in Chinese, that two letters had arrived from the General.

I was up in a moment, and ready to receive the Mandarins; for, since the guard had been placed at my door, I had never undressed, or laid aside my arms, when lying down to sleep. Philip ushered in the two Mandarins, Ho Ta-lowya and Min Ta-lowya by name. They entered with an air of great importance, followed by five soldiers, and seating themselves on my bed, handed Philip the letters, desiring him to read them. The first one ran as follows:—"Just now there is a great fight. The General, Leang-Owhan, wants money. He desires that the English merchant, Tang Koopah, will lend him two thousand five hundred Leeang,* which shall be repaid after the fight. If he lends this money, he will sooner be able to go to Ava; and, if he has the money, he must not say nay." The second letter was to this effect:—"Leang Ta-jen hears that the English merchant has a foreign gun, and a wonderful little gun, which shoots five times without fire or powder. For the general good of the people and country, these must be lent to the General, in order that the Mahomedans may be frightened with these foreign guns."

* Chinese term for taels=about eight hundred and thirty pounds sterling.

When Philip had read the letters, he told me that they only bore the seal of the General's writer, and were without date.

Laughing in very bitterness of soul, I told the scoundrels that I had no money to lend, for eighty taels was all I possessed, and barely sufficient to enable me to reach my country. Ho Ta-lowya, then, in a bullying manner, declared that he did not believe it, and would search me, and at once gave orders to his soldiers to examine my baggage. I told him, quietly, that I should not allow this; then, seeing that they really intended violence, I asked them to call Tien, and said that if he ordered me to show my baggage, I would consent. To this they agreed, and Tien was called. He soon made his appearance, and innocently asked what was the matter. The farce of explaining matters to him was gone through, when, with a friendly air and voluble assurances that no harm was intended, he advised me to let the General's messenger see that I really had not got the money, and to give them what I had, which would soon be returned.

It was evident that a robbery was intended, and it was equally plain that the loss of my remaining eighty taels would render it impossible for me to reach either Burmah or Bathang. I resolved, therefore, to stick to them till the last; and, pretending to agree with Tien, I suggested that the soldiers should be sent out, to make room for Philip to display all my possessions. My cunning friends were duped: they ordered the soldiers out of the room; and, when the last one had passed out, I sprang to the door, shot to the wooden bolt, and, drawing my revolver, covered Tien's head. My blood was up; and, as I stood glaring at the frightened scoundrels cowering before me, I felt a devilish inclination to blow out first their brains, and then my own. For several seconds no one spoke; and, at last, I said to Tien, "Ah, you have got me in your Ya-mun, and think to rob me more easily. Good! Now, listen. I will show you everything I have, even to my eighty taels; but if one of you puts a finger on them, I'll shoot you all, and then destroy myself." When I had done speaking, Ho Ta-lowya called to the soldiers to shoot me through the window; and the end of a gingall was shoved through the paper. I hesitated for a second to fire at Tien; and then, finding that the soldier did not fire, I told Tien, still pointing my revolver at his head, that the moment I was struck my revolver would go off, and shoot him. His terror, on hearing this, was perfectly sickening: he screamed at the soldier (who was busy trying to light the match of his gingall by the aid of a flint and steel) not to fire, and to take away his weapon. The long snake-like barrel was drawn back, and I breathed more freely; while the three cowardly wretches in my room begged me not to be angry. How scornful I felt as I watched their terror! I positively felt myself swell with the pride of superiority; and, in spite of reason's warnings not to irritate the cowards, I told Philip, with an air of mockery, to show the robbers our baggage. How I loved my brave little follower for the smile of contempt which he cast on his countrymen, and the air of mock reverence with which he took every article from my bags, and held it up for their inspection! a needless piece of politeness, for they were blind to everything but the gaping muzzle of the revolver, which I still kept pointed at them. When my skin box had been turned inside out, and its contents spread on the floor, I asked the Mandarins if they were satisfied, and dropped the muzzle of my revolver. All three spoke at once, saying that they were quite satisfied, and hoped I would not be angry; they had performed an unpleasant duty, and were sorry that it had annoyed me. I merely replied, that it would be as well to drop unnecessary falsehood, and warned them that any further attempt to rob me would be useless and dangerous. During this conversation I kept a close watch on them. Both Philip and myself were slightly at a loss what to do with our prisoners, for such the Mandarins had really become. Afraid to move lest I should fire, they sat huddled together. However, we both agreed that they dared not kill us in the Ya-mun, which was a sacred edifice, lent by the town to the Mandarin until the proper Ya-mun, which had been destroyed by the Mahomedans, was rebuilt. And, besides, everybody knew that I was travelling under protection of the Sz-chuan Viceroy.

Having come to this conclusion, I informed Tien that they were at liberty to leave the room, a permission which they immediately availed themselves of; and I bowed them out, each, in his turning, making his exit with most ceremonious obeisances.

When the door was fairly closed on them, I sat down on my bed, and for a moment or two gave way to melancholy forebodings. The Mandarins had now committed themselves by an act of violence, and they would be afraid to let me go free (especially as I had retained the forged letters), lest I should report them at Pekin. If I left the Ya-mun to return to Sz-chuan, they would, in all probability, have me disposed of on the road. The only chance of safety, therefore, was to remain where I was, though at the risk of being poisoned: a danger which struck Philip so forcibly that, on mentioning it, he covered his face with his hands, and utterly broke down.

I was not left to indulge long in painful speculations, for in less than an hour Tien came to my room wearing a very rueful countenance. He entered with a very humble air, and seating himself on the bed, said, "Ah! this is a bad business. I have been told that the officers Ho and Min desire to rob you, and have forged those letters from the General. I shall punish them for this affair; and I want the letters, that I may have evidence to convict them." In reply to this, I told my friend that I preferred keeping the letters myself, and desired him to give me an escort to the General next day, before whom I would lodge a complaint against these officers. I had no intention of quitting the Ya-mun, but merely said this to confuse Tien, who at once declared it to be impossible for me to go to the General, who could not be troubled with me. I then told him that I would start for Bathang next day, and take the letters to Pekin. This was too much for the villain; he grew furious, and, throwing off all disguise, roared out that I should not leave my prison until I had kissed the sole of his boot. I drew my revolver, and Tien made a hasty retreat.

Five days more passed without a sight of Tien. Philip was not allowed to leave the Ya-mun, and we were daily supplied with a cup of raw rice, some salt vegetables, and a piece of raw pork, thrown into the room, as if to dogs. For two days both Philip and myself refused to eat, being afraid of poison; on the third day, however, one of the writers of the Ya-mun came to my room, accompanied by a soldier bearing some boiled rice and chicken stew, and, sitting down to dinner, took mouthful for mouthful of the stew with me. Anxiety and long fasting had made me quite ill, but this revived me, and during the remainder of our detention some of the Ya-mun people ate with me at every meal.

An occasional present of chen and tobacco quite won the hearts of the guards, who relaxed their vigilance a great deal, and allowed me early in the morning, before Tien was out of bed, to walk in the outer courtyard.

My fearless treatment of the three Mandarins seemed to have struck everybody about the Ya-mun with awe. Previous to this affair, I was scarcely noticed; but now no one ever passed me or entered my room without making a profound obeisance, and I was always addressed as "Ta-jen."

One very old man, a writer, paid me a visit every day, and to him I was indebted for many little acts of kindness. He invariably brought presents of fruit, eggs, and tobacco, which my old friend Low-ling and many of the townspeople sent me. The old man had a son, who was also a writer, and he also visited me daily. But a visit that I always looked forward to with the greatest pleasure was that of the old man's grandson, a pretty child about eight years of age. This little fellow lived in the Ya-mun with his grandfather, and every afternoon on returning from school the child came to my room, bent on one knee before me, and held out his books that I might touch them. This is one of those customs growing out of the Chinaman's reverence for his elders, and is certainly a graceful act on the part of youth. He never came without some childish offering: sometimes a peach or a plum would be bashfully offered, accompanied by a whispered request for a little piece of foreign paper to write on; on these occasions, when he had got his treasure, he would dance out of my dull chamber, and rush off to his grandfather, under whose guidance he would write some complimentary lines in honour of Tang "Ta-jen," and send them to me. Poor little Sen! he was the only bright thing I saw during my stay in the Weisee Ya-mun.

On the 28th of July, six days after Tien's unsuccessful attempt at robbery, a great commotion in the Ya-mun made me aware that something unusual had happened; and on inquiring of my guard the cause of the unusual stir, I learned that the Mandarin from Atenze had arrived with a party of soldiers, *en route* to join the General, and throughout the day there was a continual clatter past my door, which was locked on the outside, to prevent my showing myself, as the guard said, with a wink, when he brought in my dinner and sat down with me. In the evening Tien and the Atenze Mandarin dined together, and while they were at dinner, Philip, who was allowed to roam all over the Ya-mun, managed to creep under the window of their room, and succeeded in gaining a very practical illustration of the proverb which tells us that "listeners never hear any good of themselves;" for he came to me pale as a ghost, and related the following conversation, which he had overheard between the two Mandarins.

Just as Philip took his place under the window Tien asked the Atenze Mandarin if he had seen the foreigner who had passed through Atenze on his way to Tali-foo, adding, "We have him here in the Ya-mun." His guest replied, "No, the cursed barbarian; what is he? I heard he was writing all the time he was in my town, and drawing the country. The son of a dog, too, writes with a pen that requires no ink.* I suppose he has come to see the country; and his people will come and take it by-and-by. You have got him here; why don't you kill him?" To this my friend Tien replied, "Why, it's no use to kill him; he has no money. We have searched him; he has nothing; and now we are considering what to do with him." When Philip had got thus far, he was so completely overwhelmed, that it was several minutes before he could proceed; when he had recovered a little, he

* Patent manifold writer, which I used in writing my Journal.

went on to relate what the Atenze Mandarin said in reply. The ruffian evidently hated foreigners, for he said, "Oh, kill him. You dispose of him; and when I return from the fight, I will kill those sons of dogs, the missionaries on the Lantsan-kiang: they are fast converting the Lu-ts", and they will very soon be masters of the country, and we shall be killed; so kill them all, I say." Tien did not seem to join in these sentiments, for he took time to consider, and then proposed that they should dine together next night and talk the matter over. When poor little Philip had finished his startling communication, I sat and trembled violently for a few minutes; in spite of myself, all the nerves of my body seemed to give way, so that I could not lift my hand. This horrible feeling, however, soon gave place to passion, and I felt inclined to rush in on the Mandarins, shoot them, and take the consequences; but, with an effort at self-control, I sat down to deliberate. Tien and his companion might get drunk the next night, and work themselves up to commit any violence. If I could escape, it was just possible to reach the Mooquor chief. I was weary of close confinement, and the thought of once more treading the mountain paths caused a thrill of pleasure, and I decided upon making an attempt to escape on the following night. The excitement attending this resolution kept me from brooding over my position, and when, towards midnight, Tien came staggering into my room he found his prisoner in capital spirits. This was his first visit for a week. I suppose the amount of samshu he had drunk at dinner made him brave, for he commenced to talk about foreign devils, and the taking of Pekin by the French and English, whom he cursed frightfully for having destroyed the Emperor's palace. He also told me that his eldest brother was in the capital when it surrendered, previously to which he had suffered severely from starvation; and then, looking at me with a sneer, he hiccoughed forth that it was very curious that he should have a foreign devil with him now; and suddenly remembering what his Atenze friend had told him about my having written a description of the country, he demanded my journal, which was concealed and securely strapped under my waistcoat. I merely laughed at his request, and told him to find it; and he soon forgot its existence.

The idea of his having got a foreign devil in his power seemed to tickle him amazingly, and he indulged in repeated bursts of laughter, which caused his attendants at the door to shake their heads and look serious. I sat without taking the least notice of all his taunts, hoping that he would grow tired of talking to himself, and go to bed. But he had no idea of giving up the pleasure of tormenting me so soon; on the contrary, he mistook my quiet manner for fear, and drew his long, heavy, silver-handled knife, desiring that I would feel the edge of his weapon, which I pronounced to be sharp as a razor. This statement he emphatically endorsed, and further informed me that it was used for cutting off the heads, ears, and noses of prisoners. Having delivered himself of this terrible fact, he proceeded to go through the Chinese sword exercise, which consists of a series of mountebank-like contortions, during which the sword is whirled round the body with great rapidity. During this performance he frequently pretended to make a cut at me, trying to make me betray fear for his enjoyment; but he was not successful, and this made him very savage—so much so, that I feared he might make a real cut at me, so I stood up and drew my knife, amidst a general entreaty on the part of his attendants that Taug Ta-jen would not hurt Tien Ta-lowya, who had visibly subsided the moment that I drew my blade; but, beyond entreaties, not one ventured to interfere. I assured them that I was only going to play with the Ta-lowya, and proceeded to say that in my country we had a custom of fencing with naked weapons, the rule being not to give mortal wounds, but to cut each other about the arms and legs; and I asked Tien to play a little, at the same time placing myself on guard. This sobered my gentleman, who sheathed his weapon, and began to talk in a maudlin way about his great friendship for Tang; but it would not do to let him off so easily, and I made my blade whistle round him until his terror became so great that my laughter obliged me to desist, and allow the poor wretch to rush out of the room—not, however, till I had told him that I intended to leave the Ya-mun, and if any one attempted to stop me I would fight; but he seemed to take this as a joke, and informed me that if I did I should, in all probability, be killed on the road.

Next day we arranged a plan of escape, and, without being observed, secreted about our persons as much of our valuables as we could stow. The guard at the door was one of our greatest difficulties, and it was decided to overpower him if he offered any resistance, which, however, was not likely, for he had already offered to let me out of the Ya-mun for a bribe of ten taels. Low-dzung was to have two of our ponies saddled just before daylight in the morning, and wait in the courtyard until joined by Philip, when, if the guards gave the alarm, he and Low-dzung were to make their escape, go to the Mooquor chief, and beg him to come to my rescue.

One obstacle, however, which we had overlooked until it was almost too late was the watchman at the outer gate. He was an old man, and an inveterate opium-smoker; so I immediately suggested that Philip should make him a present of his favourite drug, and the old man was forthwith supplied with enough opium to last him for a week, and when he got it he set to work with his pipe at once.

About seven in the evening the Atenze Mandarin came to dine with Tien, and the two worthies kept it up until a late hour, when they retired utterly incapable, as the guard told us.

The excitement attending on our premeditated flight kept us wide awake, and about three in the morning I opened the door of my room and found the guard asleep on the step; he jumped up, however, in an instant when I put my hand on him, and asked where I was going to. Instantly putting my revolver to his head, I said, "I am going to Bathang: do not make a noise, or I will shoot you." He at once understood matters, and went with me to the room on the opposite side of the passage, where his companion was drowsily smoking. Here I showed him the Chen-tu Viceroy's passport;—when he had read it, I drew my knife and, kissing the blade, said I would kill him if he prevented my leaving the Ya-mun, at the same time offering him a handsome present if he was quiet. He was at first inclined to be rusty, and aroused his companion; so, dropping my knife, I suddenly knocked their heads together with such force that they were half stunned. Taking them both along with me, I joined Philip outside the gates, and soon reached the outskirts of the town. The two soldiers had followed me like lambs, and never once attempted to give an alarm as we passed through the streets. I at last dismissed them with a present of 2,000 chen, which pleased them greatly, and they volunteered a promise not to give the alarm at the Ya-mun until Tien got up. The fellows even asked me to forgive them for having had to guard me, and took leave with many expressions of gratitude. By them I returned the two forged letters to Tien, hoping by this means to rid him of one great cause for alarm at my escape.

From the time of leaving my room until we found ourselves outside the town, everything had passed so quickly as to give no time for reflection, and I could with difficulty realise the fact that I was free. After dismissing the soldiers I almost regretted not having made them accompany me, but second thoughts suggested that they would have been likely to give the alarm at some of the villages on our road, and, feeling the necessity of putting as much distance as possible between myself and Tien, I hurried forward. Philip narrated, that on taking the ponies out of the courtyard, the watchman had called out from his den to inquire what was astir; so he put his head in at the door and asked him how he liked the opium,—on which the old man merely remarked that it was very good, and returned to his beloved pipe.

After riding at a good pace along the highway until daylight, we struck off into the hills and picked our way through the forests, hoping by this means to avoid being retaken by pursuers from the Ya-mun; but, after floundering along for several hours over the rough sides of the hills, we once more descended to the main road, and reached Kha-kha about three in the afternoon, with our animals completely exhausted. I went to the house of La-won-quan's friend, where I had put up on my previous visit, and in less than an hour the Lama procured a messenger, whom I despatched to Compo with a letter telling the chief how I was situated, and intending to rest at Kha-kha until sundown, I gave my ponies a feed, and set about getting a meal for ourselves. About five o'clock, just as we were saddling up for a start, a soldier arrived, accompanied by a dozen others, all armed to the teeth, and, coming straight to me, produced a warrant for the arrest of

Tang Koopah, addressed to all the head men and chiefs of the country between Weisee and Atenze, under the seal of Tien Ta-lowya. The soldier was very civil, saying he was sorry, but must obey orders, and begged me not to resist, as his instructions were to bring back my body, dead or alive. Of course resistance was useless, and I was again made prisoner. Poor Philip quite gave way now, and in accents of bitter grief declared that we should have our heads taken off to a certainty. I confess to feeling very uneasy, but kept my trust in La-won-quan, who would get the letter next morning, and hasten to my relief; and with this assurance I cheered up poor little Philip as much as possible.

With the first dawn of day my captors were impatient to start; and by five o'clock I marched out of Kha-kha a prisoner closely guarded. A more horrible ride I never had in my life, for I expected, every moment, some treacherous assault from our guards; and I was still more depressed by the tears of poor Philip, who varied his lamentations by vociferous prayers, calling upon the Virgin and all the saints to protect us.

About noon we re-entered Weisee, and rode through the main street, which, as it was market-day, was crowded with people. Among the crowd many recognised and saluted me. When passing the hotel, Low-ling attracted my attention by waving his hand. Beating his breast energetically, and drawing himself up with a shake of the head, he intimated that I was to keep up my heart. Strange to say, the moment we entered the town my spirits rose, and I acknowledged the kindly salutes of the people with friendly smiles and bows.

At one or two of the hucksters' stalls I was stopped, and a number of hands were stretched out to me, each holding a present of some sort, such as an apple, plum, or new-laid egg.

These little marks of kindness had a cheering effect; and I entered the outer court of the Ya-mun with a haughty, indifferent air, that silenced all remarks on the part of the surrounding crowd of underlings. Dismounting at once, I strode through the crowd straight into the Mandarin's room, Philip delaying to follow for a minute or two. Tien was sitting alone, and asked me, with a sardonic grin, if I had enjoyed my ride. Without noticing his rudeness, I quietly told him that he was very foolish to keep me in prison, and demanded to be sent to Bathang. This he refused, with a burst of insolent laughter. Still controlling myself, I asked him what he intended to do. He replied, in a languid manner, that he was considering whether he should put me in chains, or cut my head off. With a bitter laugh, I grasped him with my left hand, and was in the act of drawing my revolver to shoot him, and put an end to the oppressive agony of suspense. Just at this critical moment, as Tien was struggling to free himself from my grasp, Philip entered, and told me not to shoot Tien, as he had heard outside that some of the neighbouring chiefs had sent deputies that morning to the Ya-mun for the purpose of demanding my release. Upon this, I burst into a loud roar of laughter, exclaiming, " Ah, Tien, now I know the meaning of all this business. You thought I was a Mahomedan agent. You did not want my money; you only wished to examine my baggage, to see if I was taking anything to the Mahomedans. Well, well, I will wait here until you write to Bathang, and inquire who I am. You don't seem to believe my passport, so I'll remain till you hear from the Bathang Mandarin, who received a letter from the Sz-chuan Viceroy about me." When he heard this, Tien was unmistakeably pleased. He admitted that what I had said was true, and begged me to let him go into the next room, and not be angry with him. He came out of the room again almost immediately, accompanied by his two accomplices, Ho Ta-lowya and Min Ta-lowya, the soldier Mandarins, and laughed at them for taking me for a Mahomedan spy; and they appeared intensely pleased at the idea, saying, now that we all understood each other, they would write to the General, and ask him to let me go.

Aware that the Mandarins feared to let me depart under the impression that they had intended to rob me, Philip's announcement prompted this happy thought of persuading them of my belief that they had only detained me on suspicion of being a spy. That they swallowed the bait, is certain; for they at once composed a letter to the General, saying that I had been detained in the Ya-mun for some time, under suspicion of being a Mahomedan spy, but that now all doubts were cleared up, and, if the General had no objection, they would give me another passport enabling me to go. This letter was forthwith dispatched. And then Tien cunningly told me that he would also have to get the consent of all the head men of the neighbourhood to my departure. Matters had now taken an unexpected turn. I felt safe, and retired to my room in high spirits. Philip was enchanted with my cunning mode of removing the Mandarins' anxiety about their attempted robbery; and the brave little fellow fairly laughed himself to sleep.

Next morning when I awoke, after a refreshing sleep of six hours, all was still in the Ya-mun, and I smoked an early pipe in the outer courtyard, whither I went without encountering a soul; for all *surveillance* was apparently at an end.

Between ten and eleven I was sitting alone at breakfast (Philip having been forced, against his will, to go to the house of the Mandarin, Ho), when a great commotion was heard in the middle court. I was conscious of a slight tremour, as the jarring sound told almost at the same instant that the bolt of my door was drawn on the outside; and, to add to my fear, I fancied I heard Philip call out, "Master!" Nearly an hour, however, passed without any intrusion, though I heard loud and angry voices in Tien's room, and, occasionally, the words "Tang Ta-jen!" "Ta Ing-qua!" (great England) distinctly reached my ears. Something was evidently taking place with reference to myself; and my anxiety had almost become unendurable, when the uproar increased, and the door was suddenly burst open. In a moment I was on my feet, and levelled my revolver at the intruders, the foremost of whom advanced a step into my room, and, bending on one knee, said, "Don't fear, don't fear, Tang Ta-jen; you shall not die in this country." For the moment I glared on my fancied assailants without recognising them. As soon, however, as the first one spoke, I recognised him for La-won-quan's brother-in-law. The relief experienced was almost too much for me, and I raised the Mooquor with a few warm words of sincere welcome. The other men outside, who were deputies from the Ya-ts^u, Tze-fan, and Lei-su chiefs, then one after another came and bent their knees before me, repeating that I need not fear, for they would protect me as far as Atenze, and I could leave the Ya-mun whenever I liked. After chatting for a little time, they all took their leave, promising to detach some of their people to take care of me; and, accordingly, a number of Mooquor and Ya-ts^u soldiers remained in the Ya-mun, and, in the place of a Chinese guard at my door, several Mooquors attended on me, taking as much care of Tang Koopah as though he had been an emperor.

When Philip returned, about an hour after, he told me

that Ho Ta-lowya had sent for him, under the pretence of wishing to buy some turquoise stones ; but had only talked to him, apparently, without any other object than that of keeping him out of the Ya-mun. After leaving Ho's house, he had met the deputies, who told him about their stormy interview with Tien, and its result. It appeared that Tien told them he had tried to get money from me for the purpose of protecting *their* country against the Mahomedans, and, in order to succeed, had used violence. If, therefore, I was allowed to return to Pekin, I would report the whole affair ; in which case all the chiefs, as well as himself, would be punished, and, under these circumstances, he proposed that I should be quietly disposed of. This proposition had enraged the deputies, as it displayed an intention on Tien's part to make their chiefs to some extent his accomplices. The deputies, one and all, emphatically repudiated all complicity on the part of their chiefs, and gave Tien to understand that I should not be killed in their country. They also expressed their belief that foreigners were good men, who paid for everything as they went along, and they had little fear but that Tang Ta-jen would speak the truth when he reached Pekin. Tien flew into a passion when he was told this by the Mooquor deputy, who suddenly ended the conference by defying Tien, giving emphasis to his defiance by banging his fist on the table, and rushing off to my room, as I have described.

When Philip had finished his report, we went to Tien's room, and found that worthy closeted with Min Ta-lowya. I asked if the General had given orders for my release, and whether the head men objected to it ; in answer to which I was told by Tien to mind my own business : when the order for my release came from the General, I should be set free.

I spent the next day on my bed, very unwell with fever, the results of a wetting during our ride to Kha-kha. In the evening, Tien sent for Philip, to say that now everything had been explained, and the General had sent orders for my release, so I could leave whenever I liked for Tali-foo. I, of course had long since abandoned all hope of reaching Burmah; and any attempt to pass into Mahomedan territory would give Tien an opportunity to take his revenge, and my life would not be worth a day's purchase. It was with a heavy heart, therefore, that, on the 5th of August, after nearly five weeks of imprisonment and painful anxiety, I commenced preparations for retracing my steps towards home.

In the evening I called on the two military Mandarins, to take my leave. They were both from home, and I left my card for them. This ceremony was a little piece of humbug on my part, for the purpose of making them imagine that I was sincere in the belief that they had mistaken me for a spy.

Tien came to my room late at night, and brought a passport for Atenze, telling me that he was "quite sorry to lose the pleasant society of Tang Ta-jen." We bade each other a ceremonious farewell; and I turned in, to sleep for the last time in the Weisee Ya-mun.

CHAPTER XIV.

RETURN TO TA-TSIAN-LOO.

Departure from Weisee—A Ministering Angel—Return to Atenze—Thibetan Dairies—Bursting of a Rain-cloud—Renewed Hopes—Disappointment—Baffled Banditti—Tea-ferry on the Kiu-cha-kiang—Cold Reception at Bathang—An Act of Justice—Thibetan Necessity for Tea—Burmah and Yunnan Trade—Difficulty about the Despatches—A Wild Night.

THE morning of the 6th of August was lovely; the summer rains had broken, the heavy curtain of mist which so long had hung over the valley and mountains had disappeared, and the morning sun shed its undimmed light on the surrounding country, fresh and smiling after its long summer bath.

It was a glorious morning to enjoy our newly-acquired freedom, and by six o'clock my party, all ready, waited in the outer courtyard, while I received the tedious good wishes of the subordinates of the Ya-mun. At last I fairly turned my back on them and rode through the town; at the hotel a large crowd of people, headed by Low-ling, fairly blocked up the way, and I was again detained by leave-taking. This is always accompanied by great ceremony amongst the Chinese, but on this occasion it appeared interminable. My position in the Ya-mun had been well known and fully canvassed amongst the townspeople; and the fact of my being a foreigner, to say nothing of my rescue by the chiefs, had caused great excitement, and now that I was about to leave in triumph, many people whom I had never seen before were anxious to go through the ceremony of leave-taking with Tang Ta-jen; and there was such a bending of knees and reiteration of compliments, that it became at last necessary to cut it short by orders for a move; so, escorted by a large crowd to the very outskirts of the town, I there finally took leave of my staunch ally, Low-ling, and settled down to the march.

In three days we reached La-won-quan's village, having met the chief himself, in company with the Ya-ts^u chief, on their way to Weisee, at the head of a large body of fighting-men. The Ya-ts^u chief merely bowed as he passed, and sent a man to inquire if I was all right, by whom I returned a message to the effect that I was greatly indebted to his interference for my safety. About half-an-hour afterwards I met the Mooquor; he dismounted the moment he caught sight of my party, and advanced on foot to meet me. Paying him the same mark of respect, I dismounted, and the good fellow expressed his joy at my safety, saying that he had heard of Tien's behaviour, and at once sent his head man to Weisee. He apologised for his needful absence from his house, where, however, he had left orders for our entertainment.

Referring to Tien's assertion that he had tried to get my money for the purpose of carrying on the war against the Mahomedans, La-won-quan assured me that he and the Ya-ts^u chief had time after time supplied him with money for the war, which had always been squandered by Tien and his associates in riotous living; and the chief particularly requested that Tien's conduct might be reported at Pekin, in order that he might be punished.* With a promise to report

---

* In November, 1868, I reported my imprisonment to Sir R. Alcock, her Majesty's Minister at Pekin; but up to the present time, more than two

all that had taken place to the proper authorities, and to do my best to have Tien punished for his misdeeds, I took leave of my friend and protector.

I was sorry that we could not spend more time together, but our interview interrupted the march of the chief's little army, which numbered about 400 fine-looking fellows, nearly all armed with gingalls, in this respect differing from the Ya-ts^u chief's followers, who, though greatly superior in numbers, were not so well armed; not more than one in twenty possessed a gingall, while the rest had only their knives, crossbows, and poisoned arrows. The Ya-ts^u chief had declined to call out many of his own people, and had contented himself with summoning his Lu-ts^u subjects, to avoid the charge of disloyalty to the Chinese. Neither he nor the Mooquor were at all pleased at having to repair to Weisee, and, according to subsequent information, the Mahomedans were not much troubled on the Weisee side.

Arriving at Compo, I was received as an expected guest by La-won-quau's wife and family. From the time of leaving Weisee I had been suffering slightly from fever, and now felt thoroughly ill, and in less than two hours after my arrival was quite insensible. For two days I laid unconscious of everything. When at length I regained consciousness, the chief's wife and Philip were bending over me, the latter murmuring prayers, and the former wringing out a wet towel which she had just taken from my head. Beyond extreme weakness, I felt little the worse, and in a couple of hours was able to eat some boiled rice.

Philip told me that I had suddenly become insensible, and

years since this report was received at Pekin, her Majesty's Government have never received the slightest explanation from the Chinese authorities.— March, 1871.

continued in violent convulsions for a long time, accompanied by purging and other symptoms. The people of the house had suspected poison, and administered emetics in the shape of salt and water; however, it could not have been anything serious, for I was able on the third morning to get up, and after a hearty meal commenced another march. I record this incident in order to bear testimony to the gentle kindness and motherly care of my hostess, to which my recovery then was owing, and who proved herself a ministering angel.

A couple of marches brought us to the bridge leading to the missionary station of Tz-coo, and I hailed the Fathers across the river, but after waiting in vain for an hour, we went on to Wha-foo-pin, and put up with my former friends. From them I learnt that a party of soldiers had been sent from Weisee, to escape from whom the Fathers had fled to the hills, so that they also had been suffering from Tieu's hatred of foreigners.

About two in the morning I was suddenly awakened by hearing some one in the room and Philip's voice demanding who was there, when, to my great surprise, the intruder replied in Latin. A light was speedily procured, and revealed two Lu-ts^u Christians, who had been sent by the missionaries with a letter, stating that Tien had sent a party of officials, attended by a number of soldiers, to the Mission-house, with a demand for 1200 taels; and on the request being refused, the party had threatened to return next day and burn the place down unless the money was forthcoming. This state of things had compelled the good Fathers Biet and Dubernard to take refuge in the mountains in order to save at least their lives.

Some native Christians who remained at the station had heard me hailing, but were afraid to answer before communicating with the Fathers, who, learning that I had gone on to Wha-foo-pin, sent the letter in explanation of their absence.

From Wha-foo-pin we reached Atenze in three marches. The people of Goneah as we passed through their village flocked round with entreaties for more ointment. Poor things! it was hard to disappoint them, but my store had long since been exhausted. The chief in person escorted me to Ateuze, and I was glad to hire some of his mules, as my cattle were knocked up, the result of having been fed on nothing but green grass in Weisee.

From the point where the road left the Lan-tsan-kiang and entered the valley leading to Atenze, I was struck with what appeared to be signs of a terrific flood, and on inquiring of the Goneah chief, he told me that about a week after our departure from Atenze a frightful flood had torn down the valley, sweeping everything before it. Not a trace of the luxuriant wheat fields, walnut groves, and Thibetan houses, before noticed, now remained. Near the town itself, where the valley narrowed, the ravages of the flood were more apparent. The extensive Thibetan suburbs had entirely vanished, and where we had formerly passed along a path bordered on either hand by numbers of houses, we now picked our way along the bottom of a deep furrow, which looked as if it had been formed by the passage of some giant plough. Part of the town itself, with a portion of the wall, had also been washed away by the flood, which had in the space of three hours risen, wrought all this fearful havoc, and subsided.

Our entrance into the town was a signal for the population to turn out *en masse*, for rumours of the proceedings at Weisee had already reached them. Though perfectly respectful, the people thronged round us with open-mouthed curiosity, and the two Mooquor guards seemed to attract considerable attention. Our arrival at the hotel placed the landlord in a quandary. Imagining me to be still under surveillance of the Mandarins, he at once said that he could not admit me without an order from the Ya-mun; but I quickly disposed of his objection by telling him to get one for himself, and took up my quarters as before, while he rushed off to the Ya-mun for the required permit. He soon returned, saying all was right, and set about discharging his duties as host with due alacrity.

We had now once more reached a great elevation, and drawing breath produced the same suffering that we had experienced when ascending the mountains after leaving Ta-tsian-loo; however, though painful, it was sure, as experience had taught us, to wear off, and we determined in spite of it to continue on next day.

In the evening the mother of the Mandarin who had so strongly urged Tien to put the "foreign devil" to death sent to beg a little ointment for her leg, which was very sore. By dint of scraping, the jar yielded enough to satisfy her request, and I received in return a present of tobacco, rice, and dried venison, with a message that Tang Ta-jen was to be of good heart, as he was now safe. She probably did not know how very much her son had wished to kill me, or perhaps she would not have been so pressing in her entreaties.

At this place the faithful Mooquor guards were to leave me, and accordingly next morning they bade me good-bye, refusing to accept any present for their services. Their departure considerably lessened my sense of security, and it was only too probable that we should meet fresh troubles in the hostile country before us. However, before leaving, they procured me two trustworthy Thibetan guides to take us to Bathang.

Although, in order to avoid the journey between Atenze and Bathang, I had induced the General to alter my passports, so as to give the option of travelling by Tsung-tain to Ya-tzow, it seemed safer not to attempt that route against the advice of the Mooquors and the strongly-expressed objections of Tien when he heard of my intention, and we resolved by forced marches to avoid stopping at the places where the people had formerly manifested their hostility. This was rendered easy by our having laid in a capital stock of provisions for the road, in the shape of ham, flour, dried venison, and tea. So on the 17th of August, having quitted Atenze amidst a deluge of rain, we passed the night at Tong, where our former hosts treated us very kindly. Arrived at the foot of Tsali Shan, we found the road obliterated, and the mountain torrent, along whose banks the road ascended from Tong, fearfully swollen, while the bridge by which we should have crossed together with several hundred yards of the pathway had been entirely swept away. An attempt to ford it proved a failure, for the rush of water was too great, and the animals refused to face it; so there was nothing left but to make a detour up the mountains, and we commenced the ascent on our left. For several miles we toiled up the lower flanks of Tsali Shan, picking our way through the forest without any track to assist us, and towards sundown emerged from the pines and tea-oil trees on to the grassy slopes of a mountain piled in huge swelling masses above. Wave after wave of the mountain was ascended, until at last, just as it was getting dark, we reached a herdsman's hut, nestled in a valley high up amongst the clouds, just on the line of perpetual snow. Here we were admitted, and our animals turned loose to graze with the yaks belonging to our host.

Next day we were obliged to remain at the hut, for Philip

in his turn was down with high fever, and for several hours was quite delirious; but towards night the beneficial effects of a purgative and liberal doses of quinine were visible in his decided improvement.

I amused myself during the day by examining the interior of the hut, which was ornamented by tiers of iron milk-pans all round the walls, while large hides full of butter took up the greater portion of the floor, and then I watched the herdsmen making butter and cheese. Three men churned from morning till night, using long barrels about four feet high and one foot in diameter, in which they worked a dasher, made of a round, flat piece of wood, with holes in it, and a long handle. These dashers they worked up and down one after the other, keeping time to a monotonous tune.

There were ten men belonging to the hut, who were employed in milking about a hundred cow yaks, and making butter and cheese; while four others travelled daily between the grazing ground and Tong, with the produce of the dairy, which was transported on yaks.

The Thibetans consume large quantities of cheese, but their manner of making it renders it anything but palatable. Their iron milk-pans are never washed, and, accordingly, their cream and milk are always very sour. The acidity of the cheese makes it uneatable; and, as the buttermilk is never squeezed or washed out of the butter, I found it too rancid for use, unless when it was possible to buy it fresh and wash it, and pick out the hairs myself.

Our hosts were exceedingly kind and liberal with their butter, and in the afternoon I accompanied them to their milking-ground, about a quarter of a mile from the hut. All the yaks were waiting, and appeared very tame. Each man carried with him a small basket of salt, a handful of which was given to each. It seemed to have a great effect upon the animals; for, as soon as they had eaten their salt, they stood patiently to be milked.

The calves, which were allowed to run with the mothers, had on halters, studded with spikes, to prevent them from sucking; and, as soon as each cow was milked, her calf would shove up its little head, to have the halter taken off. The herd were in magnificent condition; as fat and glossy in the coat as stall-fed oxen.

August and September are the two best months for the Thibetan herdsman, for then his herd, having fed their way up the mountain from the lower valleys, which they leave about the middle of May, have grown fat on the young and tender grass, which shoots up with wonderful rapidity as the snow gradually melts. About the beginning of October the yaks, of their own accord, commence feeding downwards, as the snow begins to lie on the heights, and by the middle of November they are all down in the lower valleys again, where they soon lose their condition, and pick up a precarious livelihood, contending against the snows of the Thibetan winter.

After a day's rest, Philip found himself able to travel, and we continued our ascent. It rained in torrents all day, and we camped at night in another grassy valley, just below the snow-line, taking up our quarters in the ruins of an old hut. Part of the mud walls remained, affording but scanty shelter from the driving rain. However, a traveller is fertile in expedients, and one of my blankets was soon converted into a fairly comfortable tent; while our guides, muffled up in their huge skin-coats, defied alike both rain and cold. A wretched night of cold and rain was succeeded by a fine sunrise, and we saddled up early, glad to warm our numbed bodies by exercise. This valley led us up to a pass in Tsali Shan, about ten miles to the north of our former route. From the summit of the pass a splendid panorama of mountain scenery unrolled itself before us. All around, far and near, gigantic snow-capped peaks towered heavenwards in the wildest disorder, forming a scene of desolate grandeur as we ascended above the boundary-line of vegetation. But we could not stay to enjoy the prospect, for our guides begged me to make haste, and descend, pointing, with looks of fear, to a line of black clouds rising in the west. We hurried down the mountain, and reached a long grassy glen, down which a tiny stream flowed peaceably on its way to the lower valleys. Here we stopped for breakfast; and while we were engaged on our butter tea and damper, the guides called my attention to the clouds, which were now approaching the pass. Just above it towered an enormously high peak; and when the cloud reached this peak it immediately seemed to dissolve into smoke, and a peculiar subdued roar soon reached our ears. In a very few minutes a white line showed the water tearing down the mountain to join the stream, a hundred yards from which we were camped; and presently, with ever-increasing roar, the body of water forced its way past us. As the torrent rushed down the valley, it tore up the bed of the original stream, excavating a deep channel for itself, some thirty feet deep and fifty wide, with banks formed of earth and stones, as if piled up by navvies. In less than an hour all was still again, and the stream running quietly at the bottom of its enlarged bed. Bidding my party continue on, after breakfast I rode back towards the foot of the peak, which was still partially, as I thought, enveloped in a dense mist. In an hour, however, I reached the pass, and, to my amazement, found that the peak had been reduced into a huge mound, shorn of two-thirds of its former height, while both the eastern and western slopes of the mountain were torn up and strewn with the *débris*, in the shape of boulders and stones. This rounded eminence alone remained to mark the place of the giant peak; and I had thus an opportunity of observing how these rugged mountain peaks are gradually transformed, by the destructive power of water.

Throughout the mountains of Eastern Thibet, the rounded appearance of some of the heights is very remarkable, and it is doubtless to be attributed to the agency of deluges such as that I witnessed in actual operation.

Thankful at our own escape, and awe-stricken by the view of this great feat of Nature, I hurried down the mountain, and picking up the tracks of my party, soon overtook them near the village of Tsali. We passed through without stopping, and camped out in the open, a few miles from the hut of the musk-hunter at Jessundee, to whom next day we paid a flying visit, only to find the friendly owner absent, and the hut closed. Beyond Jessundee we left the main road, and struck into a by-path leading to Pa-moo-tan, finding a night's quarters and a warm welcome in the house of a Thibetan acquaintance of one of our guides, who, for less than a half tael, sold us the half of a fat sheep, weighing about thirty-six pounds, which our party of six disposed of before starting the next morning. The house of our host was situated in one of those beautifully fertile valleys that the traveller so often meets with in Thibet. Peas, turnips,* and the now ripe bearded wheat were flourishing luxuriantly; and our store of luxuries was enriched with an abundance of new walnuts.

During the evening our host told us that on the morrow the "Pebunza," or Nepaulese Ambassador, was expected to

---

* Or rather vegetables strongly resembling turnips, both in leaf and root.

arrive at Pa-moo-tan, on his way back to Lhássa. This was good news indeed. Juggut Share had asked me, in Chen-tu to accompany him back to Lhássa, but the date of his return was then so remote, that I could not wait. Now, however, there was nothing to prevent my acceptance of his offer; and there seemed to be a chance of reaching India after all hope of success had been given up. Excitement banished sleep; and Philip and myself sat up smoking until daylight, when we roused our party, and started for Pa-moo-tan, where we arrived early in the afternoon, and put up at the head man's house. He was absent, but his servants informed me that the Ambassador would arrive at Kung-ze-din village, one march distant, next day. So, after another night of restless impatience, we again resumed our march.

My poor baggage-animals by this time were nearly all done up; the two ponies were mere skin and bone, dead lame, and unable to carry a load. I had, in consequence, marched on foot for two days, having transferred their loads to my own mule, Jacob. Fortunately, Philip's mule was able to carry him, for his late illness had left him very weak, while I had quite recovered. All attempts to hire some baggage-animals at Pa-moo-tan proved fruitless, for every animal in the country had been pressed for the transport of the Ambassador and his suite; so there was nothing for it but to tramp on again. Our arrival, in the afternoon, at Kung-ze-din produced great excitement. The van of the Ambassador's party had already arrived, and many of them were standing at the doors of the houses as I passed, and their stare of astonishment, at the foreigner dressed in European costume, was most amusing. They all greeted me with "Salaam, Sahib!" and several of them accompanied me to the house of the head man. The whole house was engaged for the Ambassador, but the owner found me comfortable quarters in a house belonging to one of his slaves, whither I was followed by the Nepaulese, who were very anxious to learn all about me.

About an hour after, a great stir in the village announced that Juggut Share had arrived; and in less than ten minutes one of the principal officers of the Embassy came with a message from the Ambassador that he would be glad to see me after he had dined. I can safely say that the interval which passed before I saw Juggut Share was the happiest time I had spent since leaving Hankow, for I felt confident that I should now be able to go on to Lhássa, and, reaching India, be rewarded for all my troubles and privations.

While thus indulging in pleasant anticipations, a Goorkha came to say that the Ambassador was ready to see me; so off I started for his quarters, where (a great mark of distinction in this country) he received me at the door. When closeted together in his room, I narrated all my misfortunes, and requested permission to join his party, and travel with him to Lhássa. With many expressions of regret, the Ambassador informed me that he dared not let me accompany him, for the Thibetan Government had already given him notice that they would not permit any strangers to join his party. He, however, kindly told me that if I was in need of money he would be glad to supply my requirements, and would also give me a horse. Thus my hopes were again blighted; and for a moment or two I was unable to speak, so great was my disappointment. In Chen-tu the Ambassador had, with such apparent sincerity, proposed to me to accompany him, that I never dreamed of his now refusing. It seemed improbable that the plea of inability could be genuine, for the Thibetans were unmistakeably afraid of the Nepaulese, and I at once naturally concluded that he was afraid to take me with him without the orders of His Royal Highness Jung Bahadoor the Nepaulese Regent, whose jealous dislike of English intrusion into Nepaul was too strong for him to relish the idea of introducing an Englishman into the Thibetan nest, where he, in conjunction with the Chinese, finds so many golden eggs.* Subsequent information, however, convinced me that Juggut Share would gladly have acceded to my request if he had dared; and I take this opportunity of placing on record my sense of gratitude for the great kindness experienced at his hands.

The Ambassador and myself spent the greater part of the afternoon together, and arranged to remain at Kung-ze-din next day for the purpose of writing letters, which we were to exchange and deliver at our respective destinations. On my return to our quarters, I was at once assailed with eager inquiries from Philip, who was very anxious to know when we were to start for Lhássa, and was bitterly disappointed to hear that we could not go. It was no use, however, to grieve, and we sat down to a supper of mushrooms and green chillies fried in butter, a deservedly favourite dish amongst the Thibetans, whose grassy mountains in the autumn yield incredible quantities of delicious edible fungi, resembling, but far exceeding in size, our English mushrooms.

Early next morning I repaired to Juggut Share's quarters with pens, ink, and paper, and we both set to work writing; I to her Majesty's representative at Khatmandoo, stating my imprisonment and forced return; and the Ambassador to Jung

* To do Jung Bahadoor justice, I must state that on my return to Shanghai I learnt that he, at the request of the Indian Government, had sent instructions to Juggut Share to bring me to Lhássa, and thence to send me under an escort into Darjeeling. These instructions, however, had not—I believe— reached Juggut Share when I met him at Kung-ze-din.

Bahadoor, from whom he had not heard for several months, as the Chinese had kept back all his despatches. While thus engaged, Juggut Share could not refrain from expressing his utter astonishment in the most amusing manner; every now and again looking at me, as I sat dressed in full European costume, he would say, "Ah, you Englishmen are wonderful men! who but an English Sahib would travel alone in such a dreadful country as this, so far away from any of your countrymen?" from such remarks as these, which both he and his officers frequently made during the day, I learnt that whatever may be the jealous dislike of the Nepaulese towards the English in India, they certainly respect and admire the courage of "the Sahibs." It was at last time to return to dinner, for, as Juggut Share remarked, with polite apologies, "his caste" could not allow of our eating together; but he had already shown his thoughtful care by sending a live sheep to our quarters; and I left him with a promise to call for his letters, and take leave of him, as I passed through the village in the morning. After I had dined, several officers of the Embassy called upon me, nearly all of whom spoke Chinese, which they had acquired during their two years sojourn in China; several who did not speak Chinese, understood Hindostani, and this served as a medium for conversation.

As I intended to march betimes next morning, Philip and myself soon turned in, but alas, our favourite diet of fried mushrooms had brought on severe indigestion, which cost us both a restless night, and early morning found us astir and speedily ready for the road; our cavalcade having been increased by the addition of the sheep, which followed us like a dog, trotting merrily along, and became a great favourite, so much so that, be it said in passing, its life was spared for three weeks, and only at last unwillingly sacrificed to dire necessity. At the Ambassador's quarters we found himself and his whole staff waiting to see us off, so having taken charge of his despatches, and thanked him for the handsome horse he had sent me the day before, I rode out of the village, after exchanging many cordial farewells, mingled, on his part, with warnings to beware of the banditti at Robber's Hill, who had recently attacked and routed the advance-guard of his party. Robber's Hill was in our line of march, and would have to be crossed during the day, so that there was the pleasing excitement of a possible encounter with Mongol banditti; and my former experience of their daring when firmly opposed, had not impressed me with much fear of these gentry.

About midday, we had finished the descent of the famous Robber Hill, without seeing any signs of the freebooters, and were quietly pursuing our way through a defile, along the banks of a small stream, a feeder of the Kin-cha-kiang, which was visible at the end of the defile. Suddenly several dismounted Mongols stepped out from behind a pile of granite boulders; and with their long matchlocks (on which the matches were burning) thrown over their arms, stationed themselves across the path. I was leading my little party, the three baggage animals following next, while Philip and Low-dzung, closely followed by Billy, the sheep, brought up the rear. Seeing the Mongols take up an evidently hostile position, I threw forward my rifle, so as to bring it to bear on them, and rode up to within a yard of the suspicious looking strangers; I then cocked my rifle, asked them in Chinese to stand aside, and without waiting for an answer, rode at their line, which at once opened to let me pass; having thus broken their line, I reined up, and remained at the side of the path while the rest of my party passed on.

The sturdy Mongols seeing the plunder about to escape them, closed in upon me, and roughly asked for some tea. "We are hungry and must have it." Pointing to several sheep which lay securely tied near their place of concealment, I raised my rifle a little and replied, "You are not hungry with so much sheep's flesh at your disposal, and there is some tea in this foreign gun that will stop your hunger for ever, if I let you have it, so you had better go away." The impudent fellows laughed outright at this, and asked where I was going to, and whence I came. I told them that was my business, and rode on. Two of them then followed for a few paces, but as I pulled up and presented my rifle, they retreated, whereupon I galloped after my party, first having thrown the outlaws a little pouch, containing about half-a-pound of tobacco, and I saw no more of them.

Having cleared the defile, we struck the right bank of the Kin-cha-kiang, and continued on for the ferry at Soopalong.

Late in the afternoon we overtook a party of Chinamen, driving an immense flock of sheep, which they had purchased in the Central Kingdom of Thibet, and were taking to Ta-tsian-loo for sale to the dealers who annually repaired thither to buy sheep. The poor fellows mistook me for a Mandarin, as I was muffled up in my blanket-coat, and immediately began to fall on their knees, complaining that they had been robbed early in the morning, at the foot of Robber's Hill, of half a basket of tea and five sheep. When they found that I was only a common wayfarer, and had, like themselves, encountered the robbers (but with a far different result), they were loud in their expressions of surprise at our escape.

They told me they had nearly two thousand sheep with them, which they had purchased in the neighbourhood of Kyan-Kha, for about three mace each, equivalent to one shilling and tenpence, and hoped, allowing for death and other accidents, to get about a thousand to Ta-tsian-loo, where they would realize two and a half taels a-piece. The sheep were very large, short legged, and carrying a great quantity of very long fine silky wool. Wishing my Chinese friends better success for the future, we proceeded on, and reached the ferry near Soopalong, about five in the evening. The ferry-boat had been removed from its former place opposite the village, to a spot about a mile below, on account of the swollen state of the river; and the man in charge of the boat refused to take me across, without an order from the Mandarin; however a judicious display of wrath removed his hesitation, and we and our animals were soon landed on the opposite bank of the river. During our passage across, a drove of about five hundred mules swam over the river, the tea which they were carrying into the Central Kingdom, being piled in a heap, as big as a small house, on the bank, where it was left to be ferried over in skin boats, numbers of which were plying to and fro. The muleteer tried to cross the river on pony back, and came to great grief, his pony unable to bear up under the weight of its rider, who appeared to lose his presence of mind, sank from under him, and was drowned, while the poor fellow himself was picked up insensible by a man in a skin boat. This ferry-place presented a very busy scene, with its numerous boats, immense stacks of tea, bustling traders, and droves of cattle. It was now the height of the season, when the traders buy their tea at Bathang, and the ferry-boats were constantly in requisition.

We halted at Soopalong for the night, and started next day for Bathang; about midday stopping for breakfast at a house near the walnut grove, in which I had been unintentionally married to the little girl Lo-tzung.

The people of the house at once recognised me, and asked after my bride; they knew that she had left me to go to her uncle, and the woman chaffed me severely for letting her go. This woman, by the way, was a wife common to three brothers and their father, a complicated connection, and recognised as legal by the social laws of Thibet, where, in many families, the wife of the elder brother is common to both the father and other brothers; this custom, however, does not extend to the wife of the father, unless she be the wife of a second marriage, and not the mother of his sons. Mine hostess was so hard upon me for parting with my wife, that I turned to her nominal husband, the eldest of the three brothers, and bantered him on the fact that his wife belonged to no man; I thought I had made a good hit at my dusky, but good-looking tormentor, but it only elicited a roar of laughter from all present, including the dame herself; and the nominal husband made such an admirable defence in favour of the custom, that I was obliged to confess myself vanquished. He said, "You say that my wife belongs to nobody; why she belongs to my father, myself, and my brothers; and besides being a good wife to all of us, she is a capital worker, and always merry. She has no other women in the house to quarrel with, she is sole mistress, and we enjoy perfect quiet; but if each of us had a wife, they would be always fighting, we should have more women to clothe, more children to feed, and we should be miserable men." I was completely sold in my attempt at sarcasm, and dropped the subject.

There were several Lamas in the house, who suspiciously watched me during my stay, and one of them caught sight of my note-book, which lay on the floor alongside of me, and on his taking it up, out dropped the Ambassador's despatches, which were deposited in it for safety. The fellow at once recognised the Nepaulese handwriting, and called his companions to look at the letters; after conversing together in whispers for a few minutes, the one who had first taken up the letters placed them in his girdle, and rose to leave the room. Rising at the same instant, I asked for the letters, when he told me that I could not have them, as I had no business with them, and he would himself take them to Bathang; in reply to this, I drew my revolver, made it click, and held out my hand for the letters, which were quietly placed therein, and thence safely transferred to my pocket; after which I finished my meal, and bidding good-bye to the wife of many husbands and her lords, we started for Bathang, and entered the town about six in the evening. At the bridge over the little stream which flows near the outskirts of the town we saw the head of a Mongol, who had been beheaded in the morning for being concerned in a robbery at the famous Robber Hill.

On our way through the town to the hotel I was recognised by a good many people, who, however, to my surprise, took no notice of me; and on arriving at the hotel, I was more astonished when the landlord refused to admit me. He was so persistent in his refusal, that at last I became angry, and thrusting him on one side, entered his house and took possession of my former quarters. Before an hour had elapsed Sz Ta-lowya sent me his card, expressing his great concern at my having been obliged to return. The missionaries, Messrs. Fage and Goutelle, joined by my friend Father Careau, who had just arrived from Ta-tsian-loo, also came to see me. They had heard through the fathers at Sz-coo that I was in prison at Weisee, and warmly congratulated me on my escape. Shortly after they left, there arrived a bottle of port and some delicious leavened bread from the Mission-house; the wine was a great treat, and in a bumper of it I drank to the health of the French missionaries in Thibet, and the kind Fathers next day repeated their most acceptable present of precious liquor from the medical stores of the mission. In truth, it was a restorative that even a teetotaller would have appreciated. Sz Ta-lowya also sent me an elaborate dinner, consisting of more than twenty dishes of Chinese delicacies, such as birds'-nest soup, pigeon egg soup with edible sea-weed in it, sharks' fins, and jellies made from deer sinews; so that this day was spent by Philip and myself in feasting.

On the second day after I arrived Min Ta-lowya, the second Thibetan Mandarin, called upon me; he was very polite, but ill at ease when I spoke of the treatment I experienced from the people on the way to Atenze; and when I observed that the guards supplied by his orders had decamped with my provisions, he protested that they had already been severely punished by him. This, of course, was not true, but I dropped the subject, and wishing to get rid of him, I started on a visit to the Chinese Mandarin, who in receiving me pretended to be very angry with the Weisee Mandarins, and called his writer to take down a report from my lips, which he might at once send to the Sz-chuan Viceroy. When this ceremony had been performed, he sent for a courier, and despatched him along the road to Lithang, with orders to have three baggage animals ready, at every tzan, or stage, between Bathang and Lithang. This was a great boon, as another of my ponies had been disposed of as unable to travel.

The afternoon seemed a fitting opportunity for performing a stern act of duty, which I had resolved on at Pa-moo-tan. A Chinese cooly, who had been engaged at Weisee to cook for me on the road to Bathang, became very insolent, and on the evening of our arrival at Pa-moo-tan sat down before the charcoal fire in my room, and refused to stir, replying to my orders to him to leave the room, "Who are you that order me as if I were your servant? Remember, you were a prisoner in Weisee, and if I mention that in this house the people will turn you out." I was dreadfully savage at the time, but contented myself with promising the fellow a thrashing in Bathang. Lowlo had apparently forgotten this, and on my return from the Ya-mun he made his appearance, and claimed five taels, which he said I had promised him on our arrival at Bathang. The impudence of this statement reminded me of the promise made to myself in Pa-moo-tan; so by way of reply I caught him by the tail, and gave him a good thrashing, the result of which was that he fell on his knees and struck the ground with his forehead, in token of submission, and begged me to allow him to accompany me to Chung Ching, his native town, promising that if I would only give him his food, as before agreed on, he would do anything for me. This I agreed to, and had no reason to find fault with him again; and the same evening I hired another Chinese cooly on the same terms to accompany me to Ta-tsian-loo. This addition to my party relieved both Philip and myself of much hard work.

The missionaries came to see me before bedtime, and told me that the Lamas were very busy in the neighbourhood promulgating a prophesy, which they say is written in their sacred books, to the effect that if foreigners are allowed to enter the sacred kingdom there will be a great famine; and the people of Bathang were, in consequence, just then very cool towards the missionaries. This, I presume, accounted also for their evident change of manner towards myself, and determined me to quicken all preparations, so as to leave for Ta-tsian-loo on the morrow.

When I had seen all my provisions properly packed, and everything ready for a start next morning, I went out, accompanied by Low-dzung, for a stroll round the town, which was full of traders from all parts of Thibet and Mongolia. Those traders from the latter country were not in any way distinguishable from the Thibetans, save in their language. Their stature, complexion, dress, manner of wearing the hair, and weapons, were precisely the same; and had I not been told by Low-dzung that they were Mongols, I should never have recognised them as such. It was with great difficulty that we passed through the streets, which were thronged with a never-ending stream of yaks and mules laden with tea for the Central Kingdom and other distant parts of Thibet.

Immense stacks of tea were piled up all round the suburbs of the town, and testified to the enormous demand for that article, which at present is entirely supplied by the Chinese from the district of Ya-tzow-foo. When I left Ta-tsian-loo, on my way to enter Thibet, there was little or no tea in transit, as the snows had not sufficiently melted, and grass was scarce; now, however, that the snow was all gone, excepting on the highest passes, and the grass had had time to grow, hundreds of yaks and mules were daily arriving in Bathang with tea.

A few remarks on the trade of Thibet may not be out of place here, seeing that my travels were undertaken for the purpose of finding a route between India and China by which the people of these two countries might engage in trade with each other.

The readers who have followed me in the description of the 200 miles of country between Ta-tsian-loo and Bathang must, like myself, have arrived at the conclusion that the nature of the country, with its terrible mountains and snows, is against the probability of any lucrative trade being carried on between

India and China by this route. Trade might exist, but the consumption of piece goods in Eastern Thibet would never maintain a flourishing trade in that article; and besides tea, there is no other article of trade which India could supply to the Thibetans, whose only, but pressing wants, that their own country cannot supply, are summed up in one word—tea. This is their prime necessary of life; to their need of it may be ascribed the final success of the Chinese conquest of Eastern Thibet. Their whole business in life seems to be to procure a sufficiency of it; and it is no cheap luxury, for the Lamas, keeping in their hands the retail, as the Chinese monopolise the wholesale trade, by this means reduce the people to absolute dependence on them, exacting in return for the precious article labour and produce. Grain, yaks, sheep, horses, and even children, are given to the rapacious priesthood in payment for tea.

Amongst a people whose necessity for tea is so great, it is easy to see how very valuable must be the monopoly of its trade; and the Chinese, rivalling the policy of our Indian Government with respect to the dooars of Bhootan, have taken advantage of this necessity, and guard their tea trade with the most scrupulous jealousy. Little as it has been imagined, the Chinese maintain at this moment the strictest watch on the frontiers of Assam, lest tea from that fertile valley of the Bramapootra should find its way into Thibet, and give rise to the only trade which, in my opinion, can ever really flourish between our Indian possessions and the adjacent Chinese dominions. If once the teas of Assam and the Himalayan plantations could gain admittance to the Thibetan market, the Indian Government would thence derive a revenue that would replace any falling off in the profits arising from the opium trade.

That with an open trade route our Assam teas could compete with the Chinese supply with advantages which would speedily transfer the monopoly in the Thibetan markets, is plain, when we consider that the Assam planters can lay down brick-tea, made from the refuse of their crops, at a point on the Bramapootra, but a day or two's journey by steamer from the gardens, and twenty days' journey from Bathang; while four annas per pound at that point of delivery would yield them a handsome profit, a statement which is made on the authority of several influential planters. On the other hand, the Chinese tea is sold at Ta-tsian-loo at eight annas per pound, and having been transported by coolies, yaks, or mules to Bathang, sixty days' journey distant, is sold there at one rupee eight annas per pound; if, therefore, as there is no reason to doubt, the Assam tea can rival the Chinese article in quality, it is plain that it can undersell it in the Bathang mart.

It will not be deemed presumptuous to assert that the advancement or retardation of the transfer of the Thibetan tea trade to our Indian planters depends mainly on the policy adopted by our Government. If a vigorous determination to protect British subjects be shown, it will result in securing to them the same freedom of access to the now closed markets of Thibet that is already enjoyed by the Nepaulese and Chinese.

As in this journey I made an attempt to traverse from the Chinese side the route now commonly known as the Bhamo and Tali-foo route, from Burmah into Yunnan—in association with which the name of its original advocate, Dr. Clement Williams, should be always mentioned—it may not be out of place here to record a few observations on this subject.

Although the existence of this route was first introduced

to public notice by Dr. Williams, on his return from the exploration of the upper waters of the Bramapootra, more than ten years ago, a large trade had existed between Burmah and China by this route for hundreds of years, which flourished up to the commencement of the Mahomedan rebellion, in 1854-5, when the province of Yunnan teemed with a prosperous and industrious population, busily engaged in developing the resources of its fertile soil and mineral wealth.* Since that time the trade has ceased to exist, and the disastrous change which has overtaken this province, and the fearful decrease of population, compel me to think that the importance of the trade which would revive were the route again opened has been greatly over-estimated by those whose interest is most closely connected with the restoration of unrestricted intercourse between Burmah and China. That, however, any such revived trade would benefit the British possessions in Burmah is certain, for taking Rangoon as the seaport through which commerce would find its way, *viâ* the Irrawaddy river, to Bhamo, and thence to Yunnan, it is natural to suppose that British Burmah would be benefited by the transit of goods along her great water-highway. It is, however, utterly improbable that Calcutta, as an emporium, would be in any way benefited, seeing that the real vitality of the trade will spring only from the demand for piece goods in Yunnan, and that this demand will be supplied directly from England through Rangoon.

Looking forward to the probability of small steamers some day ascending the river Yang-ts" to Chung Ching, I have little hesitation in saying that, beyond the province of Yunnan, the trade with Rangoon in piece-goods will never extend. And this ought to remove from the minds of our

* See Appendix V.

merchants in China the fear that their interests would suffer by the opening of the Tali and Bhamo route.

That the trade of Yunnan will be of great importance to British Burmah, is not to be disputed; and it may be reasonably expected that when the restoration of peace, either under Mahomedan or Chinese rule, shall have again re-peopled the province with busy workers and energetic traders, a flourishing trade will be carried on between the two countries.

There is one other proposed route for commerce between Yunnan and British Burmah—that advocated by Captain Sprye. Of the difficulties or facilities of this, however, I know nothing, beyond the fact that it is proposed to carry a line of rail, *viâ* Kiang-hung, from British Burmah into Yunnan, avoiding the territory of the King of Burmah. This fact alone seems worthy of consideration whenever the time, not now far distant, may arrive for deciding upon the most eligible line of communication.

When I returned from my walk, the Thibetan Mandarin, Min Ta-lowya, was waiting at the hotel, in company with three or four followers, and among them the Lama who, as before described, had tried to possess himself of Juggut Share's despatches. On my entrance, all my visitors rose with most ceremonious politeness; but upon recognising the Lama I at once divined the object of their visit. Returning their salutes as scrupulously, according to proper Chinese etiquette, I ordered in tea and tobacco. My friend Min was evidently very anxious to unburden himself of the object of his visit, but I was determined to lead them a dance; and so, whenever Min spoke, I at once interrupted him, and commenced with some irrelevant remark. This game went on for more than an hour: and the Lama kept looking at Min, who fidgeted about in his seat with half-suppressed rage, contending with his studied air of politeness. At last, when I had tantalised him to my heart's content, I asked him if he had any communication to make; upon which he eagerly replied, that the Bathang Mandarins had been informed that the Nepaulese Ambassador had intrusted me with despatches to take to his country, and, as I travelled slowly, if I would give them the letters, they should be forwarded by an express courier. I expressed myself greatly obliged for the kind offer, but informed Min Ta-lowya that I preferred to take them myself. For a minute or so Min seemed rather puzzled how to proceed; then, assuming a very friendly air, he said, "In our country merchants are not allowed to do these things, and interfere in the affairs of Government: it would be better, therefore, if you do not wish to get into trouble, to hand over the letters to the authorities." "Very clever of you, Min Ta-lowya," I replied, "but you must understand that I do not mean you to have these letters; and, what is more, if anyone attempts to take them, he shall die." And, to make my meaning plainer, I drew my revolver; whereupon the whole party bowed themselves out, maintaining their politeness amid their discomfiture.

In the evening the missionaries came to say farewell. My old friend, Father Careau, was in very low spirits; and I felt very sorry to bid adieu to the young priest, who had visited me twice or thrice every day during my short stay at Bathang.

On the following morning, the three baggage-animals promised by the Mandarin made their appearance at an early hour, and we were off for Ta-tsian-loo. In the streets there was not a soul to be seen, but from every house curious eyes peeped out through the holes in their windows. This was an evident sign of fear, that made one feel rather uncomfortable, for it was plain that the people must have a strong motive for behaviour differing so much from their friendliness on my previous visit. When clear of the town I was joined by a comely Thibetan dame, of some thirty-five summers, carrying a large bundle. She introduced herself as the mother of the little girl Lo-tzung, and told me that as I had been obliged to part with her daughter, she had come to supply her place, with the consent of her husband. I laughed outright at this astounding proposal, and, still smarting under the remembrance of the ludicrous figure I had cut in the walnut grove, gave my kind mother-in-law to understand that I was not a marrying man, and, at the same time, advised her to return to her home. The good lady appeared half inclined to take forcible possession of me, as her daughter had done; but on my threatening to return to Bathang, and apply to Sz Ta-lowya for protection, she affectionately kissed me on both cheeks, and departed, leaving me to congratulate myself that I was still left in a state of single blessedness.

The snow-clad Taso and Tsanba ranges were re-crossed without difficulty or adventure, and, on our fifth day from Bathang, we reached the little plain of Lithang. A forced march on that day found us, when daylight closed with a thunder-storm brewing, still several miles from Lithang. The night became so dark, from the heavy clouds over-head, that we lost our way; and, to add further to our confusion, there were in the distance a number of traders' tents on the plain, from each of which a small light twinkled. We blundered along for more than an hour, amidst a deluge of rain and deafening peals of thunder, accompanied by terrific lightning, which every now and then lighted up the plain, disclosing immense herds of yaks, belonging to the tea traders, all round us. Occasionally we got amongst a herd, which, frightened at our voices, would make a stampede, and rush madly off into the darkness; once or twice stray animals darted through our ranks, creating the greatest confusion, and I was heartily glad when at last we arrived at a tent.

In answer to our hail, three rough-looking individuals made their appearance, one of whom I asked to guide me to Lithang; after some little demur, one fellow agreed to show me the way for five mace; which, however, he insisted on having in advance. No sooner had Philip handed him the money than the rascal calmly told us to be off, or he would let loose his dogs, several of which were chained round about the tent. I did not quite see this, and insisted on his fulfilling his bargain, to which demand he simply replied by letting loose three enormous dogs, which flew at us in the dark like wild beasts. Several of my baggage animals and my Thibetan boy were severely bitten, and the former commenced kicking until all their baggage was off. In self-defence I was obliged to shoot one of the dogs that was tearing at the flanks of the patient Jacob, and Philip, who carried my rifle, followed suit by putting a ball through another dog that seemed intent on making a supper off poor Low-dzung. The scene as witnessed by the dim light of the tent fire was very savage; the huge figures of the Thibetans looming in the murky light, the savage tearing and baying of the dogs, and the struggling ponies and mules, made up a picture not easily forgotten. The sudden warlike turn of affairs, and the boom of the rifle across the plain, terrified the Thibetans, one of whom immediately threw himself on the remaining dog, to save it from the fate of its companions, while his comrades fell on their knees by the side of my pony, entreating me to come with them, and they would show the way. Having reduced the enemy to terms of capitulation, I dismounted, and drawing my knife, took a swarthy Thibetan by a lock of his long black hair, and marched in triumph off the field of battle towards Lithang. When we at last arrived at the gates of the town my guide again fell on his knees, and prayed for his release. Glad to be rid of the prisoner, I let him go, and after knocking some time at the gate, was admitted by some Chinese soldiers, who eyed me suspiciously, and kept me waiting nearly half an hour, drenched to the skin, while they examined my passport. When at last they discovered that I was Tang Koopah, they were loud in their astonishment at my return, and forthwith conducted me to the hotel, where I was soon made comfortable by a change and some hot rum and water, the last of a bottle given me as a viaticum by the good missionaries in Bathang.

On instituting a review of our baggage and baggage animals next morning, some of the former was found to have been lost in the nocturnal scrimmage, while several of the baggage animals were very much torn; not so seriously, however, as to cause any unnecessary delay. The Chinese coolies and poor Low-dzung (who, though badly bitten, seemed to care little about it) went in search of the missing articles, and were fortunate enough to find everything as it had fallen from the frightened beasts, our discomfited enemies of the night before having decamped early in the morning, apparently afraid to touch any of the property.

One day's rest at Lithang was necessary for both man and beast, and that was devoted to procuring provisions and cleaning ourselves, a ceremony it had been impossible to perform anywhere but in an hotel, and then only under great difficulties, as we were always watched by curious people, intent on studying the manners and customs of the foreigner.

From Lithang five marches brought us to Ho-kow, where we were again ferried across the Ya-long-kiang—not, however, before the Chinese ferryman, who was at his evening meal, made me very angry by keeping us waiting for a length of time which seemed interminable, but which he, with true Chinese *sang-froid*, calculated to be only equal to the time occupied in drinking two cups of hot tea. This mode of reckoning time vaguely by cups of hot tea and meals of rice is exceedingly irritating to any person in a hurry, but very characteristic of Chinese indifference to the lapse of time.

After leaving Lithang, and, indeed, all the way from Bathang, we saw numerous parties of Thibetans engaged in gold digging; but all were under the superintendence of Lamas, who appeared to keep a strict guard over the diggers, who were mostly slaves belonging to the Lamaseries.

On the night of our second day's march from Lithang, a sheep-dealer, who travelled in company with us, had camped outside the village with his flock. During the night he was attacked by robbers, and a number of his sheep carried off; next morning the robbers were traced to a number of graziers' tents, which we had passed in a grassy valley the day before. Recovery, however, was impossible, for the tent people showed fight at once, and drove off the dealer and his party. The nomade inhabitants of these tents are all given to plunder. Having no fixed abode, they wander from place to place with their flocks and herds, and are not easily brought to account for the numerous depredations which they commit on travellers and the more settled and industrious people of the country.

From Ho-kow Ta-tsiau-loo was reached in six marches—not, however, without an adventure which, I fear, proved fatal to one of our party, and at one time seemed to threaten the safety of us all. The night before our arrival we halted in the grassy valley at the foot of the Jeddo range of mountains.

It was a lovely autumn evening, the air cooled by the rain which had accompanied a thunder-storm in the afternoon; the cultivators in whose house we lodged had only that day gathered in the last of their harvest of bearded wheat, while their flocks and herds showed the fattening powers of the rich pastures which covered the valley and lower slopes of the mountain. Before sundown I strolled into their wheat-fields, and to my surprise put up several large packs of a grouse-like bird. They were very tame, and rose almost from under my feet. When I mentioned these birds to the people of the house, they told me that their congregating in the stubbles was a sign of approaching winter, and that in all probability before eight-and-forty hours the country would be buried under its winter covering of snow. It was only the 17th of September, so I thought that this foretelling of winter from the habits of the birds was probably little more than a local superstition. Next morning, on turning out, I found, to my great surprise, the valley and mountain covered with half a foot of snow. This indeed was sudden winter, and I felt anxious lest we should be snowed up. The people of the house urged me not to start for Ta-tsian-loo, as more snow was certain to fall during the day, and we might lose our way in crossing the Jeddo range. None of the men would accompany me as guide, so it became necessary either to remain for an uncertain period or face the snow at once. I chose the latter alternative, and we soon commenced the march. A little before noon we were more than half way up the mountain, and could see the mound on the summit, embellished with its numbers of poles and little flags, so that I felt little anxiety about losing our way. I had reckoned without my host, however, for a heavy cloud shortly rose over the mountain from the east, driven before a furious gale, which blew in cutting blasts down the western slope, a heavy fall of snow commenced, and we were soon unable to see ten yards in front of us. Our baggage animals refused to face the driving storm, and becoming quite unmanageable, commenced to stray aimlessly along the slope. The two Chinese coolies, after a vain endeavour to keep them together, gave up the task in despair. My Thibetan boy, Low-dzung, for the first time showed the white feather, and after begging me to return, took himself off, only turning up in Ta-tsian-loo on the eve of my departure thence. I was compelled to undertake the job of getting the bewildered animals together, and after wearisome efforts, at last succeeded in tying them head to tail, and again commenced the march up the mountain. The storm seemed every minute to increase in violence, the snow fell in enormous flakes, and was perfectly blinding. After toiling upwards for about two hours, the dreadful truth that we had wandered from the track was forced upon me, by suddenly coming on the edge of a ravine, which lay far to the right, below the pass. In this dilemma the Chinese coolies, perfectly panic stricken, sat down in the snow and cried like children, and even Philip begged me, with tears in his eyes, to descend again. This course, however, was obviously likely to be attended with as much danger as going forward, for it was just a chance whether or not we should reach our last night's resting place, at least ten miles behind us, and we might wander about until night-fall without finding it, all traces of the road being obliterated. I knew that the landmark could not be far from us, so giving the leading rein of our caravan to Philip, I ordered him not to stir until my return. I walked along the side of the mountain for two or three hundred yards, scraping away the snow, and carefully sounding for the deep tracks made by the droves of tea yaks; at last feeling the ground uneven I knelt down, and after a careful examination, to my great delight found traces of the path. I was up in a moment and, marking the spot with my hat, retraced my own footsteps in the snow, and led my party back to the path, minus, however, one of the Chinese coolies, who, on my departure, had suddenly started off down the mountain, apparently out of his senses, neither Philip nor the other cooly daring to follow him, against my positive orders to remain in the same spot. When I learned what had become of the poor fellow, I commenced to shout, but without any reply, and I never saw him again; it was impossible for me to go in search for him, for the preservation of our remaining party demanded all my care. I literally felt for the path, and carefully picking my way, at last came upon the landmark on the summit. The eastern descent proved easy, for the path wound in a zig-zag form downwards for several miles, and although covered with snow, was easily discernible amidst the rough boulders which encumbered the sides, in strong contrast to the smooth counterslope of the mountain. After a few miles of descent we got out of the snow, and late in the evening arrived greatly fatigued at Ta-tsian-loo.

On the following morning I called on Bishop Chauveau, and found a letter waiting me from my friend Hogg, in which he informed me that her Majesty's Minister at Pekin had sent him 300 taels, to be forwarded to Ta-tsian-loo, in case of my being forced to return. This act of timely forethought on the part of Sir Rutherford Alcock was a perfect godsend, as I had only ten taels left, and had determined, rather than lay myself under any further obligation to the good old Bishop, to sell off my mules, ponies, and weapons, and walk the rest of the way to Hankow.

I was now about to quit Thibet for the Flowery Land, and exchange the exciting insecurity and adventurous travel to which I had been for so many months accustomed, for the more monotonous, but secure, journeying under the absolute jurisdiction of the Viceroy of Sz-chuan, whose passport would always be respected. Accordingly it became necessary to put off my European costume, and don the pig-tail and petticoats again; so after a few days' rest at the hotel, the barber was summoned, and with head and face closely shaven, and a new piece of hair plaited into my tail, I resumed the petticoats, and once more became a proper Chinaman.

The next thing was to dispose of my superfluous stud; one of the ponies, which was completely worn out, was mercifully despatched; another, which the Ambassador had given me, I sent to Father Careau at Bathang; and provided myself with a Thibetan sheepskin coat, in exchange for a mule, thus materially reducing the stable expenses, and freeing myself from unsaleable incumbrances.

While dining with the Bishop, a few days after my arrival in Ta-tsian-loo, he told me that a letter from Chen-tu had enlightened him as to the nature of the instructions sent from Lhássa to Bathang, with reference to my exclusion from the Central Kingdom. The Chinese Minister, acting in concert with the Lamas, had sent orders to stop me at all hazards, but not to hurt me in any way. That the Bishop's information was correct, is proved by the tenor of the petition sent from Lhássa to the Emperor at Pekin, in anticipation of my visit, a copy of which document will be found in the Appendix.* I have little doubt that to the nature of those instructions, which were inspired by a fixed determination to stop my progress, combined with a wholesome fear of injuring an

* Appendix VI.

Englishman, I was indebted for my safety in Thibet, where, but for the dread entertained by the Lamas of the British power in India, I should have been ruthlessly butchered by them, acting on the instigation of the Chinese. On my way home from the Bishop's house I met a Lama, dressed in yellow, with his face veiled, as too sacred for the profaning gaze of common men, being the countenance of one in whom resided a portion of the essence of the spirit of Buddha; this spiritual rank is only attained by years of secluded contemplation, by which the devotees are supposed to raise their minds above the world, and reach a sublime sanctity.

A fortnight pleasantly spent in Ta-tsian-loo prepared me for the homeward journey through China; chairs and chair-coolies were engaged, and Philip was sent to the Ya-mun to make a report about our missing cooly, and to deposit ten taels and his bundle of clothes, in case he should re-appear. And in the evening, for the last time, I dined with the excellent Bishop, and took leave of him, carrying with me a never-to-be-forgotten remembrance of him, as the ablest man and kindest friend I had found in Western China. Late in the evening, a Thibetan came to the hotel with a number of knives for sale, of the famous Pomi make, that is, made in the Thibetan territory of Pomi, which lies on the north of Assam; from the iron of this province the finest steel is manufactured, and it is also extremely rich in gold, silver, copper, and quicksilver. The owner of the knives assured me that any of his long knives would cut my Swiss hunting knife in two, being of much superior quality. He had asked ten taels for his best weapon, and so when he talked about its cutting mine in two, I proposed to give him ten taels and my knife for his, if it was better than mine, but if mine proved better than his, then he should give me his weapon for two and a half taels; to this he readily agreed, and we drew lots to see who should have the first cut at the other's knife; I won and took a cut at the Thibetan knife, making a notch in it about a quarter of an inch deep, and on examination my knife was found to be uninjured. The poor Thibetan was completely sold, and tears of rage stood in his eyes when I proceeded to hand him over two and a half taels, and take possession of his sword. Several bystanders, who watched the contest, seemed amazed at the quality of the foreign knife, and expressed their belief that it was a magic blade; they, however, enjoyed a hearty laugh at the expense of the sword dealer, and I retired in triumph, the possessor of what they pronounced to be a very cheap article. I confess that I felt rather afraid that the dealer might accuse me before the mandarin of dealing in magic swords to get back his weapon; but as I intended leaving Ta-tsian-loo at daylight, I kept the sword and risked the consequences.

CHAPTER XV.

HOMEWARDS.

A Cooly Riot—Respect for Parents—The White Wax Country—Dog ham—Gypsum Pits—Kia-ting-foo—Thibetan Trade-tricks—Salt Wells—Appointed an Arbitrator—The French Expedition—General Tin—Chinese Chess—The Hairy Tortoise—The Modern Army of Martyrs.

THE sixth of October beheld us once more threading the Ta-tsian-loo gorge, the prevailing gloom of which was now relieved to some extent by the still lingering effects of summer, for the winter had not yet descended from the heights of the surrounding mountains, where it seemed to hover preparatory to throwing its darkening shades over the lower valleys.

Two marches brought us to the chain-bridge of Loo-din-chow, at about six in the evening. By this hour the afternoon winds had spent their force, and the bridge-keeper allowed us to cross, a feat, for such it really was, owing to the vibration and swinging of the roadway, which we performed with difficulty. Our two mules had been brought with us from Ta-tsian-loo, in the hope of selling them in Sz-chuan, and it was a fine sight to see the sagacious animals picking their way over the loose boarding, and steadying themselves against the swinging of the bridge. As to Philip and myself, before we had proceeded twenty yards, we were obliged to call in the aid of some of the numerous coolies, who are constantly in attendance at the gates of the bridge, and earn their livelihood by conducting passengers across. These fellows, who by long practice have, so to speak, got their sea-legs, and are used to the motion of the unsafe structure, render great assistance to passengers, most of whom find it difficult to preserve their equilibrium.

We halted for the night at the town of Loo-din-chow, and were now fairly out of Thibet and its jurisdiction. Late at night the chair-coolies commenced to fight amongst themselves, and carried on the fray with so much noise, that a crowd of ruffians seized the opportunity and joined in, really to plunder; presently a general rush was made towards the inner part of the hotel, which happened to be full of well-to-do travellers; the crowd seemed bent on looting the place, but the inmates, including ourselves, had taken the precaution, in the early part of the fight, to shut and securely barricade the large doors of the outer public room, used by chair-coolies and such like gentry. Repeated attempts, fortunately to no purpose, were made to burst open the door, behind which some twenty fellow-lodgers and myself were drawn up in battle array, ready to fight for our property. Of course no officials appeared on the scene of action during the row, and the crowd, which had gradually yelled itself hoarse, melted away by degrees. When all had been quiet for an hour or so, and we were once more settling down to sleep, the house was again disturbed by the arrival of a squad of Chinese soldiers, accompanied by a petty, but self-important Mandarin. We were all unceremoniously knocked up by the soldiers, who, entering all the rooms, one after the other, took the inmates into custody for creating a disturbance; an attempt to serve me as they had done the other guests, and lay hands on our baggage, was not patiently submitted to, and the two most forward plunderers suddenly found themselves quoited out of the room; one of them in his passage through the door collided, as the Yankees say, with the Mandarin, who performed an unexpected prostration. Soon recovering his feet, for an instant he was speechless from anger; then he burst forth into a perfect yell, and set to cursing and abusing me at the top of his voice, gesticulating like a maniac. I joined him at this, and by dint of out-heroding him, both in loudness of tone and violence of gesticulation, I fairly reduced him to silence. Philip then displayed to his frightened gaze, the vice-regal seal of Chen-tu; never was impudent bully so completely cowed. Without staying to read the passport he ordered the soldiers to go outside, and turning to me with a request that his conduct might be overlooked by Ta-jen, asked me to let him know all about the disturbance, which had really commenced in a drunken argument between two of my chair-coolies. The Mandarin, evidently bent on showing great courtesy, asked me if it were my pleasure that the ringleaders should be punished; but I declined this kind offer, as it would have interfered with my leaving the town next morning. We however decided, after talking it over, that they should pay the landlord 2,000 chen as damages for the breakage of his furniture; and Mr. Foo, the Mandarin, bowed himself off, amidst the astonishment of my fellow-lodgers, who seemed to think that I had delivered them from the jaws of the lion, for they testified their gratitude to Tang Ta-jen, by bending before me and uttering the most lavish praises of my august person.

From Loo-din-chow we traversed a hilly country, yielding immense crops of Indian corn, but bearing signs of heavy floods; several villages had been completely washed away. On our fifth day's march, we re-crossed the Fei-yue-ling range; there was no snow in the pass, but the higher peaks were covered. This giant mountain range of China, by its wildness and dangerous precipices, rivals any of the mountain ranges in Eastern Thibet, and in crossing it I could have imagined, as Huc says of his own experience, that I had suddenly been transported back again into the wilds of "The Inside country." During our descent of the western slope of the mountain, I overtook an old Chinaman, picking his way down the path, and sustaining himself with a long staff; a long white beard gave to his tall, but slightly bent figure, a venerable air, which made him look like an ancient sage. When overtaken by us, he stopped with a groan, and deposited a somewhat heavy bundle on the ground, with an air of weariness that excited my pity, so I addressed him, saying, "Father, I see you are ill; give your bundle to my chair-men, who are behind, and they will carry it for you." Instead of appearing pleased at the offered kindness, the old man looked at me for a second or so, and then, in a voice tremulous from indignation, said, "Have you no respect for your father, that you call everyone you meet father? I am not your father; go on your way, I don't want you." Rather disgusted at this new view of filial respect, and seeing that he was really hurt and angry, I passed on, feeling in spite of myself, annoyed at his incivility. Theoretically the Chinese do attach great importance to respect for elders, and it is a common habit among them to say that so and so is like a father to them, or is like an elder brother. Sons do also provide for aged parents; but as far as my experience goes, little real love or respect enters into the performance of this duty, which owes its origin, less to real feeling, than to the Chinese law of inheritance, which besides dealing with the succession of property, confers on the heads of families certain powers and privileges, which they hold and exercise towards their families until death. Indeed nothing is more glaring than the indifference, and even cruelty, often practised by children towards their aged parents, whose dependent condition is generally taken advantage of, to show to the world how good they are in providing for their parents; thus making a virtue of necessity, at the same time that they make the poor old folks (as long as they can work) mere household drudges.

From the Fei-yue-ling mountains our road gradually descended through a more fertile country, with occasional patches of rice cultivation, and in two marches we arrived at the city of Ya-tzow-foo. So far I had retraced my steps, but as I intended to descend the Ya-ho, and visit Kia-ting-foo, instead of returning by Chen-tu, we here left the main highway, and followed the banks of the Ya-ho river for two days' journey, through a beautifully undulating country, devoted to tea cultivation, forming the district where the best brick-tea for Thibet is grown. The whole country formed a series of large gardens, without a single fence to divide the different plantations, and kept in the most scrupulous order, the trees, which stood about four feet high, being neatly trimmed, and planted in rows four feet apart. The numerous homesteads which were visible were surrounded with belts of large tea trees, growing to a height of twelve to fifteen feet.

On the third day we entered the White Wax country, so named from its producing the famous white wax of Sz-chuan, which has been erroneously called vegetable wax. This district was less undulating than that of the tea gardens, and presented to the eye a view of extensive plains surrounded by low hills. The plains were all under wax and rice cultivation, the wax trees being planted round the embankments of the small paddy fields, which were at most thirty yards square. The country thus presented to the passing traveller the appearance of extensive groves of tree stumps, each as thick as a man's thigh, and all uniformly cut down to a height of about eight feet, without a single branch.

The cultivation of wax is a source of great wealth to the province of Sz-chuan, and ranks in importance second only to that of silk. Its production is not attended with much labour or risk to the cultivator. The eggs of the insect which produces the wax are annually imported from the districts of Ho-chin, or Ho-king, and Why-li-tzow, in Yunnan (where the culture of eggs forms a special occupation) by merchants who deal in nothing else but Pa-la-tan, "white-wax eggs." The egg-clusters, which were described to me as about the size of a pea, are transported carefully packed in baskets of the leaves of the Pa-la-shu, "white-wax tree," which resembles a privet shrub, and arrive in Sz-chuan in March, where they are purchased at about twenty taels per basket. The trees by the middle of March have thrown out a number of long, tender shoots and leaves, and then the clusters of eggs, enclosed in balls of the young leaves, are suspended to the shoots by strings. About the end of the month the larvæ make their appearance, feed on the branches and leaves, and soon attain the size of a small caterpillar, or rather a wingless house fly, apparently covered with white down, and with a delicate plume-like appendage, curving from the tail over the back. So numerous are they, that, as seen by me in Yunnan, the branches of the trees are whitened by them, and appear as if covered with feathery snow. The grub proceeds in July to take the chrysalis form, burying itself in a white wax secretion, just as a silkworm wraps itself in its cocoon of silk. All the branches of the trees are thus completely coated with wax an inch thick, and in the beginning of August are lopped off close to the trunk, and cut into small lengths, which are tied up in bundles and taken to the boiling houses, where they are transferred, without further preparation, to large cauldrons of water, and boiled until every particle of the waxy substance rises to the surface; the wax is then skimmed off and run into moulds, in which shape it is exported to all parts of the Empire.

It would seem that the wax-growers find that it does not pay them to reserve any of the insects for their reproductive state, and hence the necessity of importing the eggs from Yunnan. In the districts of Ho-chin and Why-li-tzow, where the culture of the eggs is alone attended to, both frost and snow are experienced, so that it would not be difficult to rear the insect in Europe ; and considering its prolific nature, the production of white wax might repay the trouble of acclimatising this curious insect.

After travelling for a day and a half through the wax district, we arrived at the city of Hung-ya-chien, situated about a mile inland from the left bank of the Ya-ho river. A cooly was despatched to the river to hire one of the rafts which are exclusively used in navigating the Ya-ho between the city of Ya-tzow-foo and Kia-ting-foo. These rafts are very simple in their construction ; a number of large bamboos about thirty feet long and three inches in diameter, are lashed side by side to cross pieces, forming a floor about seven feet wide, along the centre of which is erected a kind of stage, two feet wide, made also of bamboo work, and raised two feet above the floor ; on this stage cargo and baggage are stowed. Some of the larger rafts can carry one and a half tons of cargo, and when thus laden do not draw more than three inches of water. They are managed by three men—two stationed forward with paddles, and one at the stern with a long oar, by which the raft is steered in deep water, and guided in the shallows and rapids. These craft, for descending rapids, are perfect, being easily handled, very buoyant, and of light draught; even if they strike a stone or rock in shooting a rapid, there is no danger, and it is simply impossible to upset them. The bamboos, from being constantly immersed in water, become very slippery, and slide over the shingly bottom, if they happen to touch, without damage.

While waiting for the return of the cooly, Philip and myself breakfasted at a fine tea shop, the proprietor of which, thinking that his customer was a Mandarin, prepared an elaborate meal, consisting of a number of dishes, and among others, fried dog ham! When this delicacy was put on the table mine host made his appearance, and informed me that I was in luck, for he just then happened to have a dog ham in cut, which he had only received from Chung Ching a few days previous. Though aware that the Chinese considered dog hams a delicacy, I was scarcely prepared to be brought into contact with it; it may be imagined, therefore, that I was somewhat startled when informed that the unclean flesh was actually before me, and, worse still, had positively made my mouth water by its savoury odour. For a few minutes prejudice carried all before it, and I was on the point of ordering away the horrid dish, but as Philip seemed to enjoy it, reason put in an appearance, and argued so strongly against prejudice, making such a strong point of the fact that I was a traveller, seeing and noting everything with an impartial eye, that, in order to prove myself an impartial judge between reason and prejudice, I proceeded with stoical fortitude to taste doggie; one taste led to another, and resulted in a verdict for reason; for in summing up, after a hearty meal, I pronounced the dog ham to be delicious in flavour, well smoked, tender, and juicy. The landlord having heard that the Yang-jen, as that test had discovered me to be, had conquered his prejudice, brought in the ham to show me. It was very small—not much bigger than the leg of a good-sized sucking-pig; the flesh was dark, and the hair had been carefully removed, while the paw had been left, as a stamp of its genuineness, as the proprietor remarked. Dog hams are justly considered a great delicacy in China, and as such bring a very high price, costing as much as five taels per pound. They are chiefly cured in the province of Hoonan, where dogs of a peculiar breed are fattened for the purpose. Hoonan is also famous for its pigs, and possesses a large trade in bacon and ham, especially in pig hams which have been cured in the same tub with dog hams, and are considered thereby to have acquired a finer flavour.

As soon as we had finished breakfast, I wrote a letter to the Bishop at Ta-tsian-loo, which Philip (for though I could now make myself understood in Chinese, I could not write it) addressed and posted at one of the numerous post-offices which are common in every town in China, and kept always by private individuals or companies, not under the supervision of the government. Although the letters often take months to reach their destination, especially if it be in a distant part of the empire, they rarely miscarry. Post-offices, however, are not favourably viewed by the officials, who recognise in them a principle capable of being developed into a great benefit to the people. The government rarely or never make use of the post-offices, beyond impressing the couriers for its own use, in which case, the post-office proprietors are responsible for the honesty of their servants, and the public may wait for their letters. The rates of postage are moderate, 250 chen being the charge for my letter to Ta-tsian-loo. Soon after, the cooly returned to announce the raft as ready, and I walked down to the river, first despatching two coolies with my mules overland to Kia-ting, two marches distant.

We were soon comfortably stowed away on the raft, and commenced to descend the swift current of the Ya-ho, the course of the river carrying us through a beautiful country entirely under wax and rice cultivation. During the passage to our port of Kia-ting-foo, where we arrived early next morning, we met hundreds of rafts laden with samshu, oil, cotton-cloth, tobacco, and sugar for Ya-tzow-foo, which were being towed up stream by two men each, and we occasionally passed strings of them a quarter of a mile in length. Gypsum is largely worked in the neighbourhood of Kia-ting, and we passed numerous pits on the river bank. This article is the staple of a large trade in China, and is extensively used in the preparation of a kind of pea cake. The pea flour, mixed with powdered gypsum in the process of grinding, is made into cakes, which are kept till mouldy, and then eaten as a relish with rice, the flavour of this compound much resembling that of strong decayed cheese.

As soon as our raft was made fast to the steps of the Kia-ting custom-house, an officer came aboard, demanding my name, destination, and business. To which we answered: "Ta Ing-qua, Tang Koopah, tow Pa-chin." Literally, "Great England countryman, Tang Koopah, to Pekin." At this statement, the worthy appeared greatly puzzled, repeating, "Ta Ing-qua, what country is that! Is it near Pekin?" "No, beyond the sea." "Oh! I understand! Yang-jen, oh! well, give me his card?" With which he took himself off; and, having landed, we passed the custom-house, without a word, and took up our quarters at an hotel.

I had heard so much of the fame of Kia-ting during my travels, that I determined to halt for three days, and see something of the famous city; but unfortunately the rain which set in shortly after my arrival, and continued more or less during the next three days, deprived me of an opportunity of seeing the famous sacred mountain, Omee-shan, situated two days' journey to the south of Kia-ting, and conferring on it much of its celebrity. Omee-shan was described to me as a conical mountain, and of immense height, its summit covered with perpetual snow, and, according to Chinese description, the pilgrims who scale its heights pass through in succession the four seasons on its sides, at least during the months of June, July, and August, when its lofty summit is covered with perpetual snow, and its base is clothed with the luxuriant summer verdure. Hundreds of magnificent Buddhist temples are built at intervals up to the very summit, to which thousands of pilgrims annually resort from Mongolia, Corea, Pekin, Lhássa, and all parts of China, and all these passing through Kia-ting, spread the fame of that city far and wide.

As seen from the river, Kia-ting presented a picturesque appearance, covering the point of a hill which divided the Chentu River, as the Min is called above this town, from the Ya-ho, and Ta-tow-ho; the town was surrounded by a fine stone wall, built on the low sandstone cliffs, in which were carved colossal representations of Buddhist divinities, while the wall itself was thickly covered with an evergreen creeper, from which in places peeped the battlements, forming a picture that reminded one of the old ivy-clad towers of England. The interior of the city, however, presented the same narrow dirty streets, ruinous-looking buildings, and filth, which characterise most Chinese towns. European piece goods, and shops for the sale of drugs, are numerous. A considerable traffic in medicines is carried on between the Kia-ting drug merchants and the Lolos and other tribes inhabiting the country to the west of the Min river, and the numerous and, for Chinese, very fair hotels are constantly filled with pilgrims. The trade of Kia-ting, however, is not so great as might be expected from its position as chief city of the great wax and silk district of Sz-chuan ; indeed little or no silk or wax is exported from it. Hung-ya-chien, and other large towns on the Chen-tu and Ya-ho rivers, export the produce of the district to Chung Ching, and other parts of China, while Kia-ting-foo merely collects the duty *in transitu*.

On the second day a Chinese Christian called upon me, from whom I learned that a Protestant missionary had visited the city in the early part of the year, and had distributed a good many religious books ; one of which, in the possession of the landlord of the hotel, proved to be a copy of the New Testament in Chinese. The owner produced the volume, and adjusting his spectacles with a solemn air of wisdom, turned up the passage which runs as follows: "It is easier for a mule (the camel in English version) to pass through the eye of a needle than for a rich man to enter the kingdom of heaven." Having read the words, he looked over his spectacles at me, and asked in a very contemptuous voice, if it were possible for any man to believe such a statement, and if foreigners really did believe the statements made in this book? It had been my invariable custom since commencing to travel in China, to avoid religious discussions, and always to proclaim myself a disciple of Confucius, so I now replied that I was not a teacher of religion, but only a humble disciple of Con-fu-dzu, but as to the statement about the mule passing through the eye of a needle, I thought I could explain that; and then proceeded to interpret the word "needle," as used in the passage referred to. This somewhat mollified mine host, who remarked that he had no doubt that English teachers found great difficulty in writing the flowery language, and it would perhaps be as well if they did not write religious books for the Chinese under such circumstances. When I was alone I could not but regret that the praiseworthy efforts of the missionary in Kia-ting had not been more successful. However, as soon as it becomes safer for Europeans to travel in China, there is little doubt but that the self-denying, and hard-working, Protestant missionaries will enter upon a new and extensive field of labour, in which their energy, devotedness, and well known *pacific* influence will doubtless win for them, if not success, at least admiration from their supporters at home. The inhabitants of Kia-ting were so kind and polite, that I walked about the city alone with perfect freedom, and on the last afternoon of my stay strolled into the silk quarter of the town. The term Kia-ting silk, is so well known to the European merchants in Shanghai, that I hoped to see something that would repay a visit to the looms. It appeared, however, that only an inferior quality of silk is manufactured in Kia-ting, all the finest raw material being sent to Chen-tu and Chung Ching, to be manufactured into the beautiful tissue known as Kia-ting silk, which obtains its name from the so-called district where it is grown, rather than the city. So that in this matter also the importance of Kia-ting fell short of my expectations. During my rambles, Philip, who had remained at the hotel for the purpose of delivering the mules to a purchaser, tried to sell some deer horns which he had bought in Thibet. The young and velvety horns of deer, are, as I have already stated, much used by the Chinese as a strengthening medicine. When pulverized, the horn is made into pills, which are fried and eaten by the aged and infirm, who ascribe to them the property of restoring youthful vigour. Philip hoped to sell his stock in Kia-ting at a profit of three or four hundred per cent., but unfortunately, when submitted to the scrutiny of the drug merchants, many of them were found to be counterfeit; instead of being young horns, they were old ones skilfully covered with fawn skin, the seams, which were beautifully sewn, having been disguised by the mud with which the young horns are always smeared, for the purpose of preserving them. Poor Philip became the laughing-stock of the hotel, but fortunately the few genuine horns amongst his stock sold well, and left him a handsome profit on his investment; but that the affair rankled in his memory often appeared from his frequent remarks that the Thibetans were great thieves. I was intensely amused, for I had objected to his investment in horns, not wishing to add to the loads of our baggage animals, and, moreover, perceiving that some of the horns were covered with hair unlike the velvet of young horns, had expressed a doubt of their genuineness, but Philip had scouted the idea of an imposition, saying that the Thibetans were not cunning enough for such tricks.

After three days' stay in Kia-ting, we embarked, with about half-a-dozen other passengers, on board a small, deeply-laden junk, drawing four feet six, and started to descend the Min River to Chung Ching. As we glided easily down with the current, through a beautiful country, we noticed numerous salt-wells in the red sandstone which formed the river-banks. These wells are among the wonders of China; and as in the evening we brought up to the river bank for the night, I was enabled to visit several of them close to our moorings. One of them was fourteen hundred feet deep, sunk through the red sandstone, with an orifice or mouth only three to four inches in diameter. I was at once struck with this narrow mouth, and began to wonder how the wells had been bored. I was, however, soon enlightened on this matter, for the men at the well pointed to another in process of sinking, which had been carried only to a depth of a hundred feet. The workmen employed a round bar of steel, five feet long and an inch and a half in diameter, with a ring at one end and a broad flat edge at the other. To the ring was attached a strong bamboo rope, working over a kind of windlass above the hole, by means of which the bar was drawn up a foot or two and then allowed to drop; a process which gradually wears away the rock at the rate of from two to six inches a day, according to the hardness of the rock. For the purpose of bringing up the *débris* from the bore-hole, about two feet of water is always kept in the shaft, and when this becomes thick with the loosened sand, the steel bar is drawn up, and a long bamboo tube (with a sucker like the tongue of a pump-box at one end) is let down. On meeting the water the sucker opens and allows the bamboo to sink to the bottom of the hole. When drawn up, the weight of sandy water in the tube forces down the sucker; and in this manner the hole is cleared, and fresh water having been poured in, it is again ready for the borer. Many of these wells occupy several years of patient toil in sinking, and entail a great risk of capital and labour, for it often happens that the well fails to tap a salt-spring, which, of course, causes the shaft to be abandoned; or, as sometimes happens, the rope attached to the steel bar breaks, and then months are occupied in drilling past the bar. Salt, however, is so valuable that, when once a spring is struck, the profit is enormous. The brine is lifted by means of bamboo tubes such as I have described, and bullocks are used in turning an enormous drum-wheel, over which the rope attached to the tubes is wound. In some parts of Sz-chuan a combustible gas often bursts from these wells, and, catching fire, renders them unworkable; in which case salt-pans are erected over the jets of flame, and the water from other wells is conducted to them for evaporation. In the district of Lu-tzow, not far from the mouth of the River Min, salt is very cheap, and acres of ground are covered with the salt-wells, the water from which is evaporated by the agency of fires issuing from abandoned wells. Huc, in his "Chinese Empire," gives a fine description of these salt and fire-wells.

The country on either side of the stream was richly cultivated with sugar-cane and saffron, and showed, as yet, no traces of autumn. The days were sunny and warm; while a delightful cool breeze prevented the atmosphere from being oppressive, either by day or night. We passed several large towns and villages, all apparently in a thriving condition, though the ruined suburbs of some on the right bank showed traces of the passage of the rebels who, in 1860 (while the first English explorers, Blakiston, Sarel, and Barton, were on the upper waters of the Yang-ts^u), rose in a body at Swi-foo, and, being driven from that city, marched up the right bank of the Min to Kia-ting, which they took, but were shortly after overpowered by the loyal inhabitants. From this rebel raid also dated the numerous fortifications which, from time to time, became visible on the cliffs of the river, some of which were exceedingly picturesque. Among the most remarkable was the village of Kien-cho-chee, perched on the square summit of a high cliff, and unapproachable save by a long zig-zag flight of steps cut out of the rock, and leading up from the river.

After a passage of two-and-a-half days down the Min, which flowed in a deep broad stream, often a mile wide, and unbroken by a single rapid, we reached the city of Swi-foo, situated on its right bank, at the point of junction with the Yang-ts". Swi-foo is the last city of importance on the Upper Yang-ts", which becomes unnavigable at a point about one hundred miles above. During the war carried on by the Chinese against the Lolos and other tribes inhabiting the country lying between the Min and the Kincha-kiang, Swi-foo was the base of Chinese operations, and afterwards for many years continued to be the city to which the conquered tribes annually repaired with their tribute. It has now a considerable trade in oil and sugar, which are exported to Chung Ching, the great central market of Western China. After a stay of an hour here, which was devoted to laying in a stock of provisions, we again got under way, and glided out into the stream of the Yang-ts", which carried us downwards at the rate of five knots. The river was very high, for the season of the year unusually so, and I looked forward to hearing at Chung Ching of unusual floods in Hoo-peh, especially after the tremendous floods that had done so much injury in Thibet and the west of Sz-chuan.

While floating down the tranquil waters of the River Min I had felt comparatively safe in our deeply-laden junk, but on entering the Yang-ts", with its rapids, eddies, and whirlpools, this feeling of security gave place to continual alarm. Every now and then, in places where the current of the river was interrupted by deeply-sunken rocks, the water seemed to boil up with a deafening roar, as if from a sub-aqueous explosion, and huge pyramidal waves would sometimes lift our junk up by the stern and plunge her bows under, which, as her decks were within three inches of the water, was anything but pleasant. The day after leaving Swi-foo our craft was caught in a whirlpool, and spun round and round with such velocity as to make us perfectly giddy. We shipped a great quantity of water, and lost four oars, which were jerked out of the men's hands. Fortunately, the whirlpool was not a stationary one, so that after being whirled about for some time, we were suddenly shot out into the main current of the river, with the junk all but water-logged, and sinking. We managed, however, to make for the shore just in time, and commenced to discharge her cargo, which was principally composed of oil and drugs. The owners of the cargo, who were our fellow-passengers, never opened their lips until safely on land, when they burst into a chorus of abuse of the Lowder for his carelessness; this lasted all the afternoon, which they spent in unpacking their drugs and drying them in the sun. The row at last became so hot between the Lowder, his crew, and the merchants, that they appealed to me to settle the matter. The Lowder swore that the merchants, who had chartered his junk for the voyage, had insisted on cramming her so full of cargo that she was almost unmanageable. The merchants admitted that the junk was over-laden, and proposed to send some of the cargo in another boat to Chung Ching, provided that the Lowder would pay the freight, as he was to blame for allowing them to load his vessel so deeply; this, of course, he refused to do, saying that the merchants had continued to ship cargo even after he had warned them that the junk was not safe, and it was on the question of the liability to pay the extra freight that I was constituted arbitrator, both parties agreeing to abide by my decision, which was not, I trust, biassed by the natural fear of continuing the voyage in the over-loaded junk. All parties adjourned to a tea-house on the river bank, where, as soon as we were all supplied with tea and tobacco, I adjusted my large green spectacles with an air of wisdom befitting my years (for my readers will remember that my pig-tail and petticoats gave me a very venerable appearance), and assumed my judicial office, premising that as it was impossible for me to know which statement was true, I would proceed to decide the dispute by aid of reason. I delivered judgment to the effect that as the merchants had hired the junk for thirty taels to Chung Ching, irrespective of the amount of cargo, it was reasonable to suppose that the Lowder, who would not be benefited by the excess of cargo, must have objected to his vessel being so deeply laden as to jeopardise her; it was my award, therefore, that the merchants should pay the extra freight. This decision was at once acted on, and a portion of our cargo transhipped to another junk, much to my relief.

Next morning we continued our voyage in the junk, which, lightened by three inches, was now perfectly safe, and on the third day from Swi-foo arrived at Chung Ching, and Philip and I were soon established in our old quarters.

My old friend Fan, the Christian merchant, soon put in an appearance from his shop close by, and embraced me with great emotion, while he confidentially informed me that when I left Chung Ching before he had looked upon me as dead, and prayed to the Virgin for me. Then from the depths of a capacious pocket which hung by his side, he produced with much care (handling it as though it were some rare and precious article of vertu) a cake of brown Windsor soap; this he gave to me, with an air which unmistakably said, "There; what do you think of that?" Thanking the good fellow for his thoughtfulness, I retired to have a good wash, a luxury which

I had not indulged in since leaving Ta-tsian-loo, where my last piece of soap had mysteriously disappeared.

Next day Father Deschamps, the Bishop's secretary, came to see me, and I learned from him that the expedition which had left Bhamo for Tali-foo, under Major Sladen, had returned from Momien, the state of the country rendering it unadvisable to proceed to the Mahomedan capital. Had I but known, when in the Yamun at Weisee, that Major Sladen and his party were within 120 miles of me, I should have managed in some way to communicate with that officer, and very probably have effected a junction with him. From what I further learned from the father with reference to the French expedition, which eventually reached Yunnan-foo, I found reason to congratulate myself on the fact that the Tze-fan chief had not allowed me to proceed to Tali-foo, where I should undoubtedly have lost my life. It appeared that, owing to some unexplained cause of disunion which arose amongst the officers of the French expedition, Lieut. Garnier, the second in command, had left his commanding officer at the city of Yunnan-foo, and proceeded to Tali-foo, where he would have been arrested by the Mahomedan authorities but for the timely warning conveyed to him by some French missionaries, who further assisted him to escape; but for this, he would have been put to death as a spy. The chief of the expedition, probably unaware that he was talking to an ally of the Mahomedan Emperor, had, unknown to Lieut. Garnier, proposed to the Imperial viceroy at Yunnan-foo, to send some guns and French soldiers to Yunnan for the purpose of crushing the Mahomedans. The news of this proposal had at once been sent to the Emperor, Dow-win-sheow, and Lieut. Garnier was doomed, but for the timely help of the missionaries. He, ignorant of the cause of the Mahomedan hostility, escaped from Tali-foo, and has since, I regret to say, reported very unfavourably of the Mahomedans. The Mahomedan merchant whom I saw in Weisee-foo had also told me this story, but I then attached very little importance to it, fancying that it was probably a *canard;* but it now served to explain what had puzzled me, namely, that although resident for several weeks within a few days' march of Tali-foo, I had heard no mention of the presence of the French party in that city.

After Father Deschamps' departure, a Chinese General, who occupied the room next to mine, sent one of his soldiers to say that he wished to look at my rifle and revolver. I felt little inclined to be civil to one of the class that had caused me so much trouble, so replied that he could come and see the foreign weapons, or I would bring them, as I was not in the habit of trusting them out of my sight. The soldier soon returned with a polite invitation for me to bring the guns, and I paid the General a visit. I was fully prepared to experience the wonted politeness of a Chinese gentleman, but General Tiu surpassed in courtesy and polish of manner any Chinese of my acquaintance. He was below the middle height, and his very fair complexion gave him the appearance of being delicate; his faultless attire, small neat pigtail, and long finger nails, betrayed the Chinese swell; but the exceeding gentleness of his manner and voice at once inspired me with a great liking for him. Under this pleasing exterior, however, lurked the pride of the Tartar, which he had overcome so far as to admit a Yang-jen to his presence. As it was not unknown to me that he was detained at the hotel, "waiting for a remittance" to pay his bill, which his extravagance had swelled to a large total, I was thus enabled to detect the disposition of the Mantchoo, differing essentially from that of the true Chinese, for when he asked if I would sell my rifle, I requested his acceptance of it as a gift, but the proud blood flushed his face, as he declined it, saying, "I will keep the gun, and my officers shall send you whatever price you choose to ask." Determined not to be outdone, I replied, haughtily, that I did not wish to sell the gun, and would only part with it, if he chose to accept it. This completely disconcerted the General, so much so that he accused me of being a proud man, and with exquisite delicacy explained that his unfortunate position debarred him from offering me a suitable present in return for the gun; under such circumstances he could not receive it. We became great friends, and the more so, that General Tin possessed in the highest degree that charm of manner which has always made the society of a Chinese gentleman to me most pleasurable; indeed I must own that for true politeness, the Chinese of all ranks can compete with any nation, and bear away the palm.

The difficulty of hiring a boat detained us for some days in Chung Ching. At last, however, the Lowder of a small passenger junk agreed to take us to Sha-s" for 35,000 chen; and, on October 31st, I embarked, having been escorted to the waterside by my old friend Fan, and a party of soldiers sent by General Tin, as a compliment, in return for the rifle, which I had sent to him by Philip, just before leaving the hotel.

About twelve miles below Chung Ching, our Lowder ran past a customs gunboat without bringing up; this disrespect on his part was sharply followed by a shot from the gunboat, which came unpleasantly near the junk, and caused the Lowder to bring up instanter, and wait for the boat full of officials, which was at once sent aboard us. The Lowder was bundled neck and crop into the boat, and several men took our vessel in charge. The whole affair occurred so suddenly, that I had scarcely time to produce the vice-regal passport, before we were prisoners; however, when I did hand it to our captors, matters soon changed, and we were liberated with many apologies; but as the chief official had thought fit to spit at me, and call me a foreign dog, when he came on board, I told him that I should take him on to Qui-foo, and pretending to carry out this threat, towed his boat about five miles down stream, well knowing that he would have the pleasure of sitting in his boat for the rest of that day. On the fourth day from Chung Ching, we reached Qui-foo, where the authorities, as on my upward voyage, proved very troublesome at first, but speedily recognising Tang Ta-jen, hastened to pass our junk. Just after entering Fung-si-yang or Wind Box Gorge, we came into collision with a large heavily laden junk, and our vessel was nearly capsized, and considerably damaged. From Chung Ching our passage seemed very tedious; the days, as we approached nearer our journey's end, became insufferably long. I had no books or anything to amuse myself with; I could not walk as on the upward journey, for we were carried along by the current of the river at an average rate of five miles an hour; there was nothing for it, therefore, but to eat, drink, and sleep, and by way of pastime, play Chinese chess, a game which occupied Philip and myself for hours together. Among the Chinese, chess is considered a royal game; but as played by them it differs much from that in vogue amongst ourselves. The pieces, which exceed ours in number, are termed emperors, emperor's guard, elephants, guns, horses, and soldiers. The move of the horse corresponds to our knight, that of the gun to our castle, and the elephant to our queen. Their board is divided into squares by lines, but the pieces instead of being played on the squares, are moved on the lines to the points of intersection. The game requires great study to play well, and is quite as scientific in its manœuvres as the European game. Philip narrated a story of one of the ancient kings, with reference to chess which is probably known to some of my readers, and shows the antiquity of the game amongst the Chinese. In ancient times, when the Empire of China was divided into eight independent kingdoms, the King of the two San-sies, viz., the provinces of Shan-si and Shen-si, staked his kingdom on a game of chess with a neighbouring King, and lost. The Chinese themselves say that the game was introduced from the west, *i.e.* from India, which seems to be confirmed by the fact of one of the pieces being called "cheang," an elephant; it is undoubtedly of very ancient date amongst them, and justly esteemed as a scientific amusement. From the time of leaving Qui-foo until we arrived at Sha-s^u, four days after, I was prostrated by fever, so much so, that when changing our junk for a lake boat which lay at the lower end of the town, I was carried in a chair. This attracted the attention of a crowd of bystanders, who, recognising a foreigner, commenced yelling out Yang Kwai-ts^u, and other terms of abuse, followed, as the coolies moved off, by a volley of stones, one of which came through the window at the back, and struck me on the head; fortunately the crowd were satisfied with this show of hostility towards the foreign devil, and we reached our new boat in safety. The baggage, which was transported on a curious double-handled and double-manned wheelbarrow, common in Hoo-peh, arrived soon after; and without further trouble we got under way, and by sundown had placed several miles between us and Sha-s^u. We brought up alongside a boat laden with immense quantities of crabs for Chung Ching. These crabs, taken in the lakes in spring and autumn, are sent to Sz-chuan, where they are considered a great delicacy. The boats in which they are carried are fitted up with tiers of basins, holding about a pint and a half of water each, and every crab has a separate basin, which is carefully refilled every day with fresh water, and the crabs are fed on raw

DOUBLE-HANDLED WHEELBARROW.

minced meat; cared for in this manner, they make the voyage of forty or fifty days to Sz-chuan, during which not more than one in a hundred die. In the lake country these crabs are bought for about three chen each, while in Chung Ching they are sold for as much as three taels each. Besides crabs, there were a number of a species of small water tortoises, which the Chinese call hairy tortoises. These curious little animals were about two inches long, and covered on the back with a long confervoid growth, resembling green hair.

The tortoise being a sacred emblem in China, the Chinese make pets of the hairy tortoise, which they keep in basins of water during the summer months, and bury in sand during the winter. A small lake, in the province of Kiang-see, is famous for these so-called hairy tortoises, and many persons earn a livelihood by the sale of these curious little pets. The day after leaving Sha-s", I was enabled to get up and take

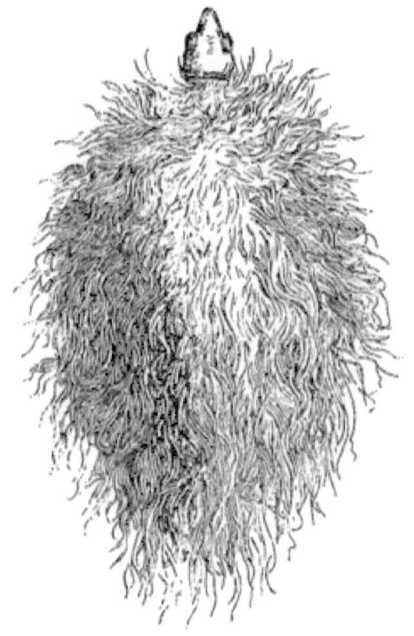

HAIRY TORTOISE.

the fresh air on the deck of our boat; we were already in the lakes, which were unusually full of water, and on every lake, busy fleets of small boats were at work, procuring loads of weeds which grow during the summer. The crews employed long double rakes, working like a pair of tongs, for gathering the weeds, which are used in the surrounding country for manure.

We were now approaching the end of our long journey,

and the prospect of its conclusion was to both Philip and myself a source of pleasure, not, however, unalloyed by mutual feelings of regret that our arrival at Hankow would separate us, who, for more than ten months, had shared hardships and dangers in which his brave fidelity and loving respect had gained for him my unceasing regard and gratitude; for there were many times when, but for the kind and gentle influence of Philip, my lot would have been much harder to bear.

On the fifth day after leaving Sha-s^u, we cleared the lakes, and re-entered the Yang-ts^u at Kin-kow, when, unfurling our sails to a rattling fair breeze, by 10 P.M. on the 11th of November, 1869, we made fast to one of the wharves at Hankow, and I was received with open arms by my friends, Messrs. Drysdale and Ringer. Oh, that evening's warm bath, supper, and English bed! One must travel as a Chinaman to feel the appreciative enjoyment of these common European luxuries.

After a few days' rest at Han-kow, during which the residents vied with each other in showing me the kindest hospitality, I bade good-bye to Philip, who promised to join me at Shanghai, in a month, for the purpose of accompanying me in a contemplated attempt to reach Bathang from Assam; and I started for Shanghai, whither the news of my imprisonment at Weisee-foo had preceded me through the French missionaries.

As we steamed past the city of Yang-chow, in the province of Ngan-hoei, we saw the British fleet, which had been sent up to demand satisfaction for an outrage committed on some Protestant missionaries, who had been beaten and otherwise maltreated. The sight of a British fleet on the Yang-ts^u for such a purpose, was curious indeed, and must, I have no doubt, have done much towards convincing the people of Yang-chow of the force of Protestantism, if not of its pacific nature. For myself, I remembered the patient French missionaries, whose only resource had been flight into mountain fastnesses, and then recalled the rebuke given by the Master to the disciple for drawing his sword against the high priest's servant; and it seemed hard to reconcile the presence of a fleet at Yang-chow for such a purpose with the doctrines professed by His servants. Probably, however, times have changed since Paul preached Christ crucified, and suffered martyrdom; and it may now be found more expedient to proclaim the Gospel from the cannon's mouth, and summon gunboats to exact reparation for our modern martyrs. At Shanghai I was warmly welcomed by many staunch friends, whose kindness soon made me forget all the difficulties and dangers which had for so many months rendered my life full of anxiety, and did much towards strengthening the determination to undertake the journey from India for the purpose of reaching Bathang, and by this means prove the practicability of sending our Assam tea to a market in Thibet.

In less than a month Philip rejoined me at Shanghai, and we set out once more for Bathang, this time *viâ* Calcutta and the Bramapootra River. Perhaps at a future date I may submit to the public a narrative of this journey: at present it will suffice to say that, after reaching the head-waters of the Bramapootra, and successfully passing through the savage and treacherous Mishmee tribes to the north of Assam, we reached a point on the frontiers of Thibet not more than a hundred and twenty miles from Bathang, where we were stopped by order of the Thibetan Governor of Zy-yul, and compelled, after suffering much from hunger and jungle fever, to return to Calcutta; not, however, relinquishing the hope of some day successfully finding this missing link in our geographical and commercial knowledge of the route from Assam to Thibet.

APPENDIX.

APPENDIX No. I.

THE only money in the proper sense of the term minted in China is the circular coin, with square central aperture for stringing, made of a mixture of copper and tin, and sometimes of iron, called chen, varying in value in every province, and indeed in almost every district. The tael, as described, is merely an ingot of silver. Most writers instead of chen employ the word "cash," a term unknown to the Chinese, except in "pigeon-English," and derived from the Portuguese "Caxa" = "caisse," whence our commercial terms, "cash," "cashier," &c. This word seems to have been used as an equivalent to "tsien," or money, by the early traders of Macao, to whom Du Halde also attributes the term "tael," for Leeang, and "Maz" = "mace," and "candareen" (?). The subjoined table may be of use to some of my readers :—

1000 {Chen or Cash} = 1 {Leeang or Tael.} average value 6s. 8d.

TRADE DIVISIONS BY WEIGHT.

10 {Chen or Cash} = 1 {Fun or Candareen.}

10 {Fun or Candareen} = 1 {Che-en or Mace.}

10 {Che-en or Mace} = 1 {Leeang or Tael.}

APPENDIX No. II.

The following legend, common amongst the Chinese, concerning the introduction of Buddhism into China, is given just as related by a Chinaman :—

The Empire under the reign of Ming-te, of the Shan dynasty, was distracted by rebellions, and the sages and great men from all parts of the Empire were summoned to meet the Emperor in council, to devise means to deliver the country from its distress. Council after council was held, and plan after plan proposed, but all failed to alleviate the public calamities, and Ming-te, in despair, refused to take food or to be comforted, until at last the inmates of his palace began to predict the untimely death of the Emperor. In this crisis the Emperor fell into a deep sleep, and saw in a dream a venerable figure with a flowing white beard, who bade him be of good cheer. Having thus comforted Ming-te, his visitant pointed to the west, and told him that the sage who alone could deliver China was to be found in that direction, and bade the Emperor send at once in search of him. Having uttered these vague directions, the apparition vanished. The Emperor, awaking, roused his household, and related his wonderful vision; a council was forthwith called, and two of the greatest sages of the Empire at once set out westwards in search of the great one by whose wisdom the blessings of peace should be restored to the Empire.

After the lapse of two years, during which the state of the Empire became worse, the two sages returned without tidings of the great one. The Emperor, enraged at the disappointment, partly consoled himself by ordering the instant execution of the unsuccessful wise men, but he then relapsed into his state of despondency, and, as before, the vision appeared to him, pointing still to the west, and having briefly ordered him again to send in search of the great one, disappeared.

This second vision threw the great men and sages about the Court into mortal terror, and nearly all fled, in fear of being sent in search of the great one, lest, proving unsuccessful, they should meet the fate of their two brethren. Ming-te, thus abandoned, was about to commit suicide, when two princes, Omee and To-foo, presented themselves before him, volunteering to go in search of the great one.

When the news of Omee and To-foo's intended journey became

known, the courtiers and sages again flocked to the palace, and the princes, loaded with honours, set out on their search, while the governors and rulers who had been summoned to the Emperor's council were sent back to their posts to carry on the wars against the rebels. A year passed, and nothing was heard of Omee and To-foo. Ming-te then, fearing for the safety of his messengers, issued orders that all the governors, officers, and soldiers of his Empire should commence a three months' prayer for the safety of the princes, and, calling on the names of Omee and To-foo, pray day and night without ceasing. On the promulgation of this edict, a general representation was made to the Emperor that if the rulers thus devoted themselves to prayer, and neglected the affairs of government, the Empire would speedily be lost beyond redemption. In this strait Ming-te hit on an expedient by which a constant prayer could be offered up throughout his Empire, without interfering with the proper government. He ordered that all malefactors should be taken from the prisons of every town, and made to pray without ceasing in houses to be erected for the purpose. These orders were carried out, but the prisoners soon escaped, and the prayer-houses were nearly all deserted. When this state of affairs was represented to Ming-te, he ordered that the prisoners should have their heads shaved, so that they might be known, and by way of a further check on their escape, commanded that a large bell should be hung up in every prayer-house, which should be sounded day and night without ceasing, while the prisoners were continually to repeat the names of Omee and To-foo, so that when the bell ceased sounding the people of the towns might know that the prisoners had escaped, and search for them, a search which generally proved successful, as the shaved heads betrayed the escaped convicts. Thus matters went on for another year, when, to the joy of the Emperor and his Court, the princes Omee and To-foo returned, and reported to Ming-te that they had found the sage in a country far to the west, sitting alone on a mountain, with his hands folded in front of him, and to all seeming dead, or at least insensible to all outward things; they were therefore unable to bring him with them, or even learn his name. They had taken a faithful life-size likeness of the seemingly dead sage, which they now displayed to the enraptured gaze of Ming-te, who at once gave orders that a figure of the sage should be set up in every prayer-house throughout his empire, before which the whole nation should on a particular day prostrate itself. He further ordered that the temples containing the sacred figure should be maintained at the public expense, and to insure their being kept in order, he issued a proclamation that all criminals who should shave their heads, and devote the rest of their life to the worship of the sage and the princes, Omee and To-foo, should be pardoned.

This popular legend curiously enough has distorted the invocation to Buddha, Omito Fo, which the Buddhist priests, whenever met with in the streets, may be heard muttering, into the names of the two princes, and it also connects itself with the fact that to this day Buddhist priests are generally held in the greatest contempt by the Chinese, and not allowed to enter their houses, as their ranks are recruited by criminals who, to escape the punishment of their crimes, take refuge in the temples, when the moment their heads are shaved in sign of their adoption of the sacerdotal career—they are safe from justice. The image described in the legend is the universal type of the figure of Buddha in Chinese temples.

APPENDIX No. III.

RUPEES pass current throughout Thibet, and as far East as Loo-diu-chow on the Ta-tow river at an exchange of three mace two candareens to the rupee. They are very commonly worn as ornaments by Thibetans and half-breeds. Those stamped with the image of the Queen as Empress of India are of more value than the old Georgian rupees, which are difficult to exchange except at a loss of several candareens per rupee. In Eastern Thibet the people say that the figure of the Queen represents the Grand Lama, and the value of the coin is thus enhanced.

The Thibetan government at Lhássa make a considerable revenue by importing rupees from Nepaul, which they melt down with thirty to thirty-five per cent. of copper as alloy; thus making what is known as Thibetan sycee, and with which they pay a great portion of the expenses of administration. This sycee, which is easily known by its colour, will not pass current beyond Ta-tsian-loo; and even there it is exchanged with difficulty at a discount of forty-five per cent., so that travellers in Thibet should always refuse it whenever offered, as the Thibetans will always try to give it in exchange, weight for weight, for rupees or China sycee.

APPENDIX No. IV.

The Khata, or scarf of felicity, has been thoroughly described by Huc, who fully does justice to the singular importance and significance attached to the use of it in all parts of Thibet. It is a silken scarf, of a delicate light blue shade, about eighteen inches long and six in width, fringed at the ends. These scarves are manufactured in Sz-chuan and Shan-si, and exported thence packed in white powder resembling chalk, and the Khata should always be covered with this powder. No present can be given, no favour asked, or compliment interchanged, without a Khata, which seems in the Thibetan mind to be equivalent to a polite verbal formula, and is utterly useless for any purpose of ornament. The Lamas especially accumulate Khatas, and I have seen in the vicinity of a Lamasery built in a glen, ropes stretched across the valley, from which hundreds of Khatas dangled.

The only explanation I could ever obtain of the use of the Khata, was that it was Thibetan custom.

An almost unlimited supply of these scarves is as necessary for a traveller in Thibet, as a stock of polite phrases to a visitant of European countries.

APPENDIX No. V.

MEMORANDUM ADDRESSED TO MR. T. T. COOPER BY AN OLD RESIDENT IN WESTERN CHINA.

After speaking so much about the present, and most likely future, state of Western China, Thibet, and the surrounding countries, allow me to pen a few considerations, not unworthy, perhaps, of your attention.

Let us suppose as certain at the beginning of this little memorandum some principles or facts which I briefly relate here :—

    1st.—You're travelling in Western China, in order to open communication between her and India, an object of paramount importance for many hundreds of millions of human beings.

2nd.—'Tis evident as daylight that poor China is falling down from every quarter; 'tis utterly impossible that she can by herself rise up, and live the life of a happy and free people.

3rd.—American United States do never exert a great influence in Central Asia.

4th.—France is not a fit power to rule over so many millions of men; her genius, her past history, her interests, show to every one and to herself that she can only be a great continental power in Europe.

5th.—The Russian yoke is the most oppressive and tyrannical one. We can see at this hour in the world if Russia could ever one day take the poor old China as a part of her immense empire, it would be the physical and moral death of this populous country.

6th.—The same ought to be said about the so sadly depressed, but very numerous, tribes, of Thibet, Khook-hoo-noor, and Mongolia.

Consequently, the only power on earth sufficiently rich and strong enough to rely together China, Thibet, and India, is England, undoubtedly; her enormous funds, her skill, perseverance, and experience in Colonial questions, her rules generally just and energetic, enable her to do the great work, to which you're so generously engaged and many—wished a long time ago. Be so kind then to listen with calmness from beginning to the end of this manuscript, to the well-grounded opinion of one who has spent the half of his lifetime in the very countries he undertakes to speak about: his opinion is not a private and personal one; many wise and good gentlemen before him expressed the same ideas in this same country.

To obtain the purpose in view, four points, places, or towns must receive an English factory; I mean Lassa, Bathang, Taly, Chung-ching. I beg leave to give some development to the aforesaid scheme.

As far as Chung-ching is concerned, remember that Szchuen is the greatest and richest province of China. The opulent town of Chung-ching is the key, the centre, the basis of all trade in Western China, except, perhaps, Yunnan, but the provinces of Szchuen, Kwei-chew, Chen-si, the eighteen principalities as they say of Eastern

Thibet, and Thibet itself, directly or indirectly, more or less are dependent on Chung-ching's trade. The public fortune of Western China, I can speak so, the funds of Government, the pay of the Chinese Army on the frontiers, are deposited and regulated in Chung-ching; the roads by footing or by navy are easy and numerous; the richest merchants of the west doubtless are in Chung-ching; the country around is fertile, pleasant, and wealthy; coal and water abound; salt is cheap; rice, corn, fruits, vegetables grow here in immense quantities; fishing is commodious and large; the population is generally more polite and pacific than in Canton or Shanghai. Chung-ching has fluvial communications with nearly all the great cities of Szchuen, Kwei-chew, and Chen-si. By Chung-ching you can entertain daily relations with Ludzow, Swifoo (Sow-chow-foo), and Kiating, and, above all, with Chen-tu, by small steamboats. Remember principally that the communications with Hankow and Shanghai are most likely practicable by steam navigation, as you know very well. Many Chinamen believe that Englishmen will speedily establish a factory in Chung-ching, and they are greatly interested in doing so; for otherwise they will not have a store-house for their goods if the communications are freely open one day between China and India across Yunnan or Thibet.

A little remark more. Don't forget that the Chinese are essentially conspirators. The Tibetians likewise. The great Chinese and Tibetian merchants are exceedingly jealous of English wealth; therefore an European factory cannot safely be established at Chung-ching, in Bathang, or Lassa, without a guard sufficiently strong for protection against native mob violence. 'Tis not required in Taly for many reasons.

2

We have named Lassa as a commercial point of great importance, and such it is undoubtedly. Moreover, what a precious spot for scientific observations. Lassa, as its name indicates, is the "spirit's land," the holy city for many millions of men, the blessed land for numerous peoples, tribes, and countries, a Jerusalem for the Jews, or Moskow for the Russians. 'Tis doubtless the more attractive point of all higher or Central Asia. What is Mecca for a Mahomedan, the same is Lassa for a Tibetian. There are in Thibet many tribes politically independent from Lassa, but not a single one religiously, and few commercially, if there are some at all. I call your attention on a fact which the Europeans seem not to be aware of; it cannot be omitted here. You believe probably, Sir, I myself believed, some years ago, that all countries known under the name of Thibet are belonging to the so-called Tibetian Government of Lassa. That is a great error, and sometimes perhaps a dangerous one. As far as I can understand till now, Thibet contains twenty-seven different tribes, or districts, or provinces. Many acknowledge the temporal King of Lassa, many do not so. I quote their names here, but, remark, according to the rules of French pronunciation and orthography, for I find not in English the correspondent sounds to the Tibetian spelling and words. A glance upon the following list suffices to perceive clearly the respective state of every Tibetian province:—

Submitted to Lassa, 17.	Independents, 10.
Dza-yu (*Upper*).	Dza-yu (*Lower*)
Sang-dzong.	Sang-ngai.
Khio-dzong.	Thera-ya.
Guie-teun.	Tchiang-dow.
Kiong-kare-naro.	Pa-chen.
Kia-re-pein-bar.	
Che-pang-do.	The fine and vast countries called Pomi have five great divisions independent of Lassa:
Slo-dzong.	
Kom-bow-rong.	
Pong-da.	Hio-ara depa.
Tchra y	Ni-lo depa.
Dzo-gong.	Pomi .. Ka-ta depa.
Tsaa-rong.	Ka-ten depa.
Ngo-dzong.	Pa-ha depa.
Kong-djio.	
Mar-kham a.	The best manufacture of rifles, swords, spears, is in Pomi, as well as the best soldiers.
One forgotten.	

Another remark more if you please. Some Chinamen and many Tibetians say that the four large countries (larger, perhaps, than England), *Tchang-mo-go-loo*, *Me-aa-a-hiong*, and *A-on-se-ta* are dependent on Lassa. They are making a mistake. These countries depend only on their respective chieftains, the most audacious of Mongolian desert. Even with a Tibetian or Chinese passport a traveller can never engage himself in these vast plains. If he does unhappily, he will soon at the remotest part of the desert see a storm of red sand rising up and running down upon him; 'tis of course the Mongolian cavalry coming post haste, as they say, to spoil and kill the unfortunate traveller.

As every one knows, Lassa is a centre where you see hastening innumerable tribes of Mongols and Tartars, but only twice a year. There are three great Lamaseries; one, according to the rules, shelters 7,700 Lamas; another, 5,500; the third, 3,300. The half of these Lama priests are Mongols or Tartars, all dressed in yellow colour, the sign of orthodoxy; many other Lamas dressed in red gowns, the schism; they don't acknowledge the supremacy of the Grand Lama. Therefore by Lassa you find yourself in communication with the interminable steppes of Central Asia. The pilgrims of Lassa are more numerous in our days than in past ages. Amongst all the peoples trading here the Nepaulese occupy the more conspicuous position. Goldsmiths they are for the greater part; ten or fifteen years since the East India Company's rupee was admitted everywhere in Thibet, and is the only coin received in Lassa. The political power of the Grand Lama supported so warmly by China two hundred years and more ago, is now daily declining, as China itself declines, but the lay power is increasing, and becomes more and more enterprising.

The relations of Lassa with India are very much improved these last few years. The ancient influence of Chinese Embassy at Lassa stands up still by a remnant of her old splendour, and by the prestige of the Grand Lama; but before the Red Lamas and common lay people the very name of Chinese is a sneer. Two ways were, about 172 years before, open between China and Lassa,—one by Si-lin, another by Tai-tsian-loo; the former is impracticable at this moment, and probably for ever; the rebellion of Mahomedans in Kan-su and the perpetual incursions of the Mongolian plunderers close that door for many generations. The way by Tai-tsian-loo is, or can be said, open to free trade, presently less, shortly more so, but this way seems also nearly abandoned by the merchants; the Chinese articles are brought into Lassa by Ambassadors and Mandarins. The Chinese trade at Lassa is not only dying, but dead. Nearly all European merchandises are found at Lassa coming from Ladack, Cashmere, Khatmandoo, and

Bhootan. Tibetians like very much European articles, but, above all, the Mongols and Tartars. Don't believe that Lassa is a very cold spot, as many do. The country is hot enough; the snow falls down rarely and very few at once. The plain of Lassa is large, pleasant enough, moderately growing corn, potatoes, vegetables; in the surrounding mountains many Tibetian highlanders, feed beefs, sheep, milch-cows, and good horses from Mongolia. There is not earth ground, only sand, notwithstanding plenty of water. During many months, in the afternoon you will not find a single Lassa man at home; all are going away, men, women, and children, even the dogs, to bathe in a pretty little river running at a little distance from the town. The storms of wind at Lassa are dreadful, as in Mongolia. For that reason the houses are very low, and for another reason you will never conjecture. It appears, or at least all Chinese and Thibetian travellers are speaking so, that the dead bodies rise again sometimes and proceed directly to their former dwelling; but unable to curb their backbones, the door being low, they fall down, are buried again, and appear no more. Be it as it may, be certain that witch-craft forms the principal study amongst the Thibetians and magical operations the essence of present Lamanism. Lassa is in the neighbourhood of, and finds itself in easy relations with the immense countries which comprise Central Asia properly speaking. The way from Khatmandoo to Lassa is a good one, through a fine country very fit for a Railway, say some travellers. Thibet has at Lassa 1000 soldiers, and Chinamen only 480. The Nepaulese (secretly) have 300.

3.

The third place fit for an European factory is Bathang, not perhaps the little town as you saw it. I mean any point, whatever it may be, in the neighbourhood of Bathang, or Kyan Kha if you prefer it. I take indifferently the one for the other. Kyan Kha, in Chinese, Markhame or Garto in Tibetian, is, as Bathang, a small town on the frontier of Eastern Thibet: it belongs not directly to the government of Lassa; Bathang belongs to Szchuen. We call Garto a great Tibetian village in which the Chinese garrison: about the beginning of the XVIIth century remained during a long time the Tibetian authorities living always in Markhame, the actual Kyan Kha. Eventually, for some political reasons, the Chinese garrison, 130 soldiers strong (at least on the paper), went itself to abide in Markhame. The Tibetian Governor of Kyan Kha has the title of Ti-give; he rules over 13 depas. This poor Colonel did never number more than 130 men in his regiment. The Chinese Commander with his 130 soldiers has under him two little officers, some civilian literati as attendants for the public correspondence, and one or two Chinese servants, all being exceedingly poor and always penniless in so cold a country as Kyan Kha. The sky of Bathang is hot enough generally, good, and wealthy. Bathang and Kyan Kha are in a position very advantageous for large commercial relations : by Bathang or Kyan Kha you can easily communicate with Assam, Burmah, Taly, Yuin-lin-ton-fou, Szchuen, Lassa, Pomi, and the gold mountains known under the Chinese name of Kin-tchouan. You're near the two great rivers of Kin-cha-kiang and Lan-tsan-kiang. Between Bathang and Kyan Kha, in a country named Sagun, there is a great deal of plumb and saltpetre; unhappily the Sagun (Saug-ngai) tribe is a very savage one. Amongst Saigun's men you will never find an honest and pacific citizen : they are and must be all robbers and plunderers. By the Bridge of Cords at Zam-ba-trow-ka, you have a passage for the fine country of Dzogong, and can rejoin here the road from Taly to Lassa. Many mountains contain mines of calcareous slate, and not very far from these slate mines, you will see almost evident signs of coaly repository. At Lychow, a small Tibetian village, there are many mines of coal negligently worked by some Chinese or Tibetian people. In the country of Larong there is a rich mine, *not* of iron as many falsely say, but really of natural steel. Thibetian workmen in the vast provinces of Pomi, principally employ that steel to forge their best rifles, swords, and spears, of so great a value everywhere. The ground is generally clay : in other hands than Thibetians, these large hills shall produce the most valuable treasures : their kind of stratification announces the presence of many precious sediments. At the date of the first war between Nepal and Thibet, about 1791 or 1792, Chinamen had open a mine of silver very abundant at one time, but since abandoned by the prohibitions and intrigues of some powerful Lamas. Lately a Chinese Company attempted to open a mine of silver. Firstly, they found many heavy parcels of silver, next with copper ; but the Mandarin's cupidity and the Lama's jealousy soon broke off the Company, and the work is now totally abandoned. In a narrow little gorge near Che-pan-kion, there is a great quantity of mineral mercury. Not very far from the same place there are numerous mines of gold, the best gold known in all Chinese possessions. These countries, I need not say, abound in pasture lands upon and amidst the hills. Therefore, if an English factory was established in Bathang or Kyan Kha you shall easily find here comfortable food, meat, butter, milk, yaks, sheep, &c. Some days from Bathang and Kyan Kha towards the south are many salt mines. This salt (two kinds, red and white) is highly valued by Tibetian people, brought everywhere into Thibet till Lassa, and furthermore in Szchuen and Yunnan. The agriculture is flourishing enough, at least more than elsewhere in Eastern Thibet. Fruits are abundant, though of an inferior quality, but should not the Tibetians be so idle and lazy a people, their ground would undoubtedly produce many good fruits and vegetables. From the salt mines a day's journey following the east bank of the Lan-tsan-kiang, we have a rich mine of sulphur belonging to the small town of Atenze, behind a little mine of saltpetre, and behind more, many mines of gold, silver, copper, iron, mercury, and other salt mines also. The Lan-tsan-kiang is one of the richest rivers of the world. Bathang, on the east bank of the Kin-cha-kiang, is continually in relations with Atenze and before the Mahomedan rebellion by Atenze with Li-kiang-foo. Hochin and Taly-foo merchants and travellers in the last months of the year are daily going to Bathang from La-pon, from To-tin, from Mon-ti-niara; in this last place there are three mines of gold. The ground near Kyau Kha and Bathang is covered with nitre. All these countries, savage, so abrupt, so dreadful at the first view, offer really many advantages and resources. As a point of communication, Bathang or Kyan Kha are happily situated in the centre, of which Lassa, Burmah, Assam, Taly, Chung-ching, Chentu, and Kin-tchouan form the large and vast circumference. Without a factory in Bathang, Sudya, Taly, Chung-ching, and Lassa are not bound together. The Chinese people live willingly in Bathang, but they dislike Kyan Kha very much. Should I have any authority in a matter of trade, I would warmly support an European establishment in Bathang.

4.

At length I arrive to the more easy and more useful English factory which ought to be established in Western China; I mean Taly. I am more vexed than yourself, Sir, that you could not reach a place of such paramount importance. Judge by this short and incomplete description.

Taly is a comparatively small town; in and outside Taly we numbered approximately 35,000 souls 600 years since; however, it exerts the greatest influence on all surrounding countries. Some 60 or 80 years before Taly was exceedingly rich; but now alas! under the accursed Mahomedan yoke, what a misery, what a heap of ruins! Many say, however, that Taly is improving by degrees this last few years. Her lake, about 45 miles long and 12 to 15 wide, is a splendid one, perfectly fit for steam navigation. The plain on the west bank of the lake contained some years ago 253 villages from 50 to 600 families each one, the middle term being 325 families by village, every family numbering five persons; the total amount of population was therefore of 401,125 souls in the sole plain of Taly; fine sky, good harvest, excellent fishes, tree fruits, and vegetables of every description; superior pig-meat (coming from Lau Kong, such as you never heard spoken of before); the best water perhaps in the world, water rolling down from the top of an enormous mountain amidst some vast caverns of marble: good and numerous horses; strong little mules for weight to Bhamo; kind and gay population. You will find here all the elements of a very agreeable settlement for Englishmen. All around Taly there are nine great plains, as fine as great, and a little more so. I give their names as follows:—Ten-tchouan, Lan Kong, (I recommend very much this last to your attention for her sulphuric hot waters,) Kien-tchouan, Lykiang, Hochin Kiang-ouy, Ngieon-tsin, Yunan-hien, and, above all, Yuin-tchong, eight days' journey at the south of Taly between Taly and Ten-yue-tchow. Yuin-tchong is a very fine country, a beautiful one indeed, but not so good for your purpose as Taly, not so good as Taly, I repeat it; pray, Sir, remember that I speak so for many reasons too long to be detailed here; some of them shall appear evident by the following observations:—

Being in Taly you're by the fact itself in easy and frequent intercourse with innumerable peoples, tribes, and countries. Chinese, Thibetians, Ly-sou, Moso, Lama Jen, Lou-tse, Sy-fan, Lo-lo, Miao-tsa, Tchong-kia-tse, Pau-y, Ching-pany or Laocians, Pong-toug, Lo-hay, Ta-ye-jen, Ta-lay-ka-y-tse, Ou-mow, Ta-mow-ka, Ou-gai, A-ka, Pon-mong, above all with the great family of Min-kia, &c., &c. If you build a factory in Yuin-tchong, many of these tribes will never, or very rarely, appear in your store-houses for fear of malignant fevers and small-pox, viz., the Moso, Ly-sou, Lou-tse, Lama Jin, principally the Thibetians, always trembling at the very name of small-pox. But all will gladly meet you in Taly. I must say that these little tribes appear to decline by degrees: they are not very rich, but they like Taly; they go there more joyfully than elsewhere, for Taly is their holy city. Thibetians say that the burial-ground of their forefathers stands in Taly, and, in fact, we see till now many tombstones with Thibetian inscriptions. Before the unhappy and long Mahomedan rebellion, the trade of Taly was great and extensive with Burmah, Laos, Canton, Kong-tcheon, Szchuen, and Thibet. In all these countries you will find mines of coal, gold, (silver in Yunnan-hien), stones for earthen-ware, musk, horns of deer, pearls, diamonds (in Ten-yue-tchou), amber, plumb, iron, and above all copper of every kind, red, yellow, and white in immense quantities. This last article consti-tutes the fundamental wealth of Yunnan. At the very hour the Mahomedan storm arose twelve years ago; there were in Yunnan 132 mines of copper. Government knowing only 37. What a profit for the Mandarins! At this hour all mines are abandoned, except, perhaps, one or two—one of silver, the other of tin. The fine and vast careers of white marble in Taly are abandoned also. What a calamity for a great province as Yunnan undoubtedly is!

From Taly to Bhamo asked you, Sir, from Tally to Kwei-tchao and Szchuen a railway, is it possible? I believe that, such is my opinion, at least for many places, but I am too much alien to that kind of industry to ascertain anything in this way. What I know perfectly is that Taly and nearly all surrounding countries above-named are very wealthy, open to many tribes in all directions, an excellent settlement for any military station, infantry and cavalry, without any powerful or dangerous neighbour, and without any fear of being cut off from India. The people are generally of good and peaceful character (a little stubborn, perhaps). If made free from the detested yoke of the Mahomedans, they will, doubtless, become very grateful to the Englishmen, and more devoted to them than to Chinamen, unable heretofore to protect them as they say oftentimes.

Frenchmen wish and hope to rely Yunnan with Saigon. The idea is right indeed, but the wish shall never be accomplished for a man acquainted with these countries; it is clear and certain that somewhat easy relations between Yunnan and Cochin China are almost impracticable. Chinamen will never traverse the unwholesome forests of Laos to go to Saigon with the prospective of a very perilous return. The natural way from China to India is, undoubtedly by Bhamo, a way followed by many merchants centuries ago. The trade of Taly and Yuin-tchong with Amarapoora has been flourishing in old days; it can easily become the same and largely greater under the flag of England. Many Chinamen say that 40 or 50 years before Burmese merchants went to Taly every year in the second moon to purchase the Chinese articles at the renowned fair of the third moon. I believe that, but during 15 years I never saw a single Burmese in Taly, nay more, nor a single Laocian.

Let me conclude this little memorandum by some reflections more valuable perhaps than the memorandum itself. England wants large issues for the various products of her wonderful manufactures. We propose here four undertakings worthy of the English commercial energy; these four undertakings can be realized, there is not a doubt about it, but perhaps not without time, struggles, and difficulties. As far as the difficulties, the greatest one you shall find in Lassa; the second in Chung-ching. For Bathang or Kyan Kka and Taly principally I do not perceive any serious obstacle. Chinese trade in Chung-ching being a powerful one, will oppose you strongly not by violence, I hope so, but by inertia. The pride of the Lama priests in Lassa, their secret disdain for, and their hatred against, all European nations, shall cause you many troubles and delays that is inevitable. As far as the time, it is required for everything in the world. These people will not at the first moment run down from their hills to your storehouses; no, that is their genius. You're a foreigner, therefore an unknown man. Be just, kind, and generous before them, they will trust in you by degrees. The great worth, skill, and power of Englishmen in Colonial questions is to have patience and perseverance: patience is time. Besides this, their enormous capital enables them to wait a long time; that is a secret that ought to be learned by every one trading in Western China and Thibet.

The people and tribes amongst whom you wish to come at this hour are not very savage, violent, or corrupt, but so far remote from the sea-coast, severed from their birth from relations with other nations, they are not acquainted with their own indigence and misery; their taste of course is a little rough. They will not at first purchase your precious articles, though liking them very much. After a more or less long period, your trade shall become an extensive one and useful for all.

In these countries the common people have not any violent prejudice against foreigners. You shall meet some foes in your way, however; I mean the Mandarins and Literati and Mahomedans in China, the Lamas in Thibet. The Lamas, after the popular movement springing out just at this moment against them at Lassa, shall become perhaps a little less rapacious and proud. Four of the Lama Chiefs, the most powerful, have been killed by an exasperated mob. The Mahomedans are making strenuous efforts to maintain their authority in Yunnan and their influence everywhere in China. They could not yet resist against the meanest shock coming from abroad, because they have not stricken root in the hearts of the Native population oppressed so long, unmercifully plundered and trampled under foot with an unparalleled brutality. Poor people of Yunnan! They would rise up in arms to a man if they could trust in their defenders. Finally, the Mandarins and literati have lost all their fascination and prestige a long time ago. People understand at once that they are utterly unable to save the Great Chinese Empire; that is clear and evident for every one. Would the Mandarins and literati at this supreme hour sincerely look out for the prosperity and happiness of their poor people, they could not ensure the means of any efficient improvement; *alea jacta est*, the old destiny of this wonderful Empire has fallen down from their hands: the saviour for them will come from another country.*

APPENDIX No. VI.

TRANSLATION OF MEMORIAL ADDRESSED BY THE LHÁSSA AUTHORITIES TO PEKIN, TRANSLATED THROUGH THIBETAN AND MANCHEE INTO CHINESE.

AH-ROOUG-I-HSI-CHU, the Hu to Ko tu and Superintendent of the affairs of Shangshang, reports that he has received through Chin-mo-tsan the following petition from the subordinates of Cha-shi-lan-pu at the three great temples in Shangshang from all the gentry, heads of monasteries, priests, and common people.

Hsitsang † (Thibet) is the native country of Buddha, and the inhabitants of no other country, except the Ghoorkas, with whom continual trade and intercourse are kept up, are allowed to cross

---

* The name of the writer of this Memorandum is withheld at his own request.   † Or, Tse-tsang.

the borders to travel. In the 25th year of Tookuang (1846) two Englishmen suddenly made their appearance in Thibet, and were immediately sent back to the place from whence they set out by His Excellency Kie-shew [Ex-Governor of the Two Kuang and then Chinese resident at the Court of the Lama]. The coming of these persons at once offended all the tutelary deities of Thibet: year after year the people were afflicted with various sicknesses, the horses and cattle were struck with epidemics, the land was ravaged by locusts, the crops were deficient, and the country in many ways suffered injury.

We have had the honour to receive letters of instruction, informing us that Englishmen are desirous of travelling in Thibet, and asking whether or not they might do so; we would remark that Thibet is known to be a poor and barren country, that travellers who have come to it, have always exercised an evil influence over it, and have not conformed to the tenets of the Buddhist religion. The news of this probable arrival of foreigners has already thrown priests and people alike into a state of excessive alarm, and they have all prayed me to make the matter the subject of a Memorial [to your Majesty]. If your Majesty takes into your gracious consideration that Thibet has for many years only been concerned with the preservation of the religion of Buddha, and that, unlike the inner land (China), our territory is of small extent, your Majesty will feel bound to inform the English that they should not come to travel in Thibet, and also that, with reference to their request for permission to pass through it, it is not expedient that they should make it a route to travel by.

If, in spite of our opposition, they persist in coming, your servants (literally we, the small ones) can only band together all the tribes professing the same religion, and, with unanimity of purpose, do our utmost to prevent them. Until our affairs are ruined and our strength is exhausted, we dare not on any account give up the ancestral fount of Buddhism and destroy the faith which mankind has hitherto held.

[Said gentry, priests, &c.,] also declare that there is no country bearing the name of Tien-chu-kuo (a common Chinese name for India) bordering on the two Thibets; there is a country called Chia K'a'rb. If English travellers wish to pass through Chia K'a'rh, not only would their way lead through high mountains and dangerous paths, but it would be very difficult to re-open the most important roads which two years ago were either cut across or blocked up. If Englishmen wish to reach Pileng by going round Khaita [we object that] our district of Tong-ku-to has not long been at peace with Ghoorka, and we cannot on account of such a matter as granting a way through our country, again create a cause of misunderstanding between the two territories.

It is not that we do not wish to obey the letter of instructions; the real reason is, that our country and our people being poor, the common people few, and the priests numerous, it would be difficult for us to imitate the example of the inner land.*

The Pileng spoken of is England; last winter a letter was received at Shangshang from the Chief of Cho-menghsiung, stating that the Pileng people wish to open a trade with Thibet, viâ Cho-menghsiung; this has thrown the priests and people of Thibet into a state of alarm, and although I have despatched messengers to stop [the English] in a friendly manner, the excitement has not yet subsided. It is now reported that an English Doctor named Toshow (?) [Cooper] has come from Sz-chuen to travel in Thibet; priests and people have been astounded, and men's minds have been filled with alarm, a state of feeling which it is impossible to prevent. Although I have again and again addressed advice to them on the subject, they have all said that they will honour and obey the principles of Buddha even to the death.

Further, in Eastern and Western Thibet in all the monasteries together, there are considerably over 100,000 Lamas, not one of whom but is of an obstinate and determined character; and to the commands of these Lamas alone the whole population render obedience. These men are opposed to the officers or people of other countries entering their territory, and their determination is not to be broken down.

I therefore pray your Majesty to discuss the matter with the English Government, informing them that no English subject, in a public or private capacity, whether he is provided with a passport or not, need come to travel in Thibet; and you will thus not only remove the terror and suspicions of the Tong-ku-to priests and people, but will prevent Englishmen from undergoing (needless) fatigues by land and water, advantage will thus accrue to the friendly relations between the two countries [of China and Thibet] and the minds of the Thibetans will be set at rest.

---

* "Imitate the example of the inner land" in opening commercial and treaty relations with foreign countries.

To sum up; the Thibetan Lamas will to the death prevent people from visiting their country, and if the Lamas have so made up their minds, the hearts of the people will be still more excited, and though I am desirous of bringing the matter to an amicable solution, it will be impossible for me to obey [the letter of instructions].* If people are allowed to come and travel in Thibet as soon as ever they cross the borders, it will be impossible to prevent the commission of outrages against them by the people of the country.

* "Letter of instructions." The Chinese authorities in Pekin do not know from what source the letter of instructions mentioned in several places in the Memorial issued.

GEOGRAPHICAL INDEX.

	PAGE		PAGE
Atenze	297, 405	Hung-ya-chien	430
		Hankow	11, 18
Bathang	245		
		I-chang	58
		I-chang Gorge	63
Chow-see	35		
Chen-pin Lake	25		
Chung-ching	97 & Ch. III.	Jess-un-dee	288
Coolow-pai	58	Jeddo Mountains	223
Chen-tu-foo	154		
Chung	89		
Chung-chow (two of this name)	94, 167	Kwang-moo-sen	25
Chin-chi-chien	179	Kuan-kow	22
Compo	316	Kiang-see	73
		Kwei-chow	74
		Kwan-du-kow	61
Fang-kow	28	Kung-tan-ho	93
Fung-siang	82	Kia-ting-foo	434
Fung-chien	93	Kien-chow	147
Fu-chow	93	Kin-ma	166
Fei-yue-ling	178	Kin-chin-chien	166
		Kung-ze-diu	277
		Kyan-kha	283
		Kha-kha	323
Goneah	303	Kien-cho-chee	439
		Kincha-kiang	276
Hu Rapid	87		
Hu-tung	96	Lukan Gorge	67
Ho-tow	102	Lam-min-yuen	77
Hi-yau-ki	180	Lo-shih	95
Ho-kow	226	Li-min	103
Ho-chin	317	Loung-chang	141

474

INDEX.

	PAGE
Loo-din-chow	197
Lan-tsan River	302
Lu-ts^u	310
Lu-dzow	439
Liu-kiang	143
Lithang	232
Leisus	335
Main-yang	33
Miaou-ts^u	note, 352
Man-ts^u Country	205
Mitan Gorge	69
Ma-kia-shan Mountains	184
Moso Tribe	312
Mooquors	317
Nu-kwan	28
Nin-cheang-foo	143
Ngee-too	195
Nou-kiang	310
Omce-shan	434
Owha-liu-pin	195
Pah-yang	57
Pah-tung	77
Pei-cha	83
Pa-moo-tan	280
Qui-foo	33
Sz-chuan	Ch. IV.
Sheow-tza-wan	23
Shewan-sha-kow	28

	PAGE
Sha-s^u	35–52
Shi-pow-chai	88
Swi-foo	440
Show-quan	177
Sui Shan Mountains	300
Soo-pa-long	276
Shcow-wei-see	323
Sz-ze-to	335
Tung-tzce	55
Tsang-hoo Lake	34
Tung-niu	66
Tsing-tung	67
Tung-kau-tze	81
Tung-yan	85
Tali-foo	348, & Appendix
Tho-king	141
Tz^e-chow	145
Tung-nan River	169
Ta-lin-piu	180
Ta-lee	199
Tung-olo Mountains and Village	224
Tsan-ba Mountains	238
Tsung-tza	284
Tong	296
T'sali Valley and Mountain	292, 295
Tz-coo	309
Tung-lan	339
Tsung-tain	392
Ta-tow-ho River	199
Ta-tsian-loo Gorge and Town	202
Ta-so Mountain	240
Wu-shau-chieu	79
Wan-chien	53, 86
Win-chin-chien	140
Win-che-chieu	177
Wei-see	324
Wha-foo-pin	307
Yang-ts^e River and Trade	98

	PAGE		PAGE
Yung-yan-chien	86	Ya-long	227
Ya-tzow-foo	170		
Ya-ho	170		
Yang-min Mountains	176		
Yen-giu	253	Zy-yul	231
Ya-ts"	314	Zaudi Tribes	231

THE END.

BRADBURY, EVANS, AND CO., PRINTERS, WHITEFRIARS.

www.ingramcontent.com/pod-product-compliance
Lightning Source LLC
Chambersburg PA
CBHW021426300426
44114CB00010B/665